Adventure Guide™ *to*

The Sierra Nevada

WH Morrison & M Purdue

HUNTER

HUNTER PUBLISHING, INC.
130 Campus Drive, Edison NJ 08818
(732) 225 1900, (800) 255 0343, fax (732) 417 0482
hunterp@bellsouth.net

4176 Saint-Denis
Montréal, Québec
Canada H2W 2M5
(514) 843 9882; fax (514) 843 9448
info@ulysses.ca

The Boundary, Wheatley Road, Garsington
Oxford, OX44 9EJ England
01865-361122; fax 01865-361133
windsorbooks@compuserve.com

ISBN 1-55650-845-X

© 2000 Hunter Publishing. Inc.

Maps by Kim André & Lissa Dailey, © 2000 Hunter Publishing, Inc.

Cover: *Lake Ediza, with Minarets in the background, Ansel Adams Wilderness Area* (Mammoth Lakes Visitors Bureau)

For complete information about the hundreds of other travel guides offered by Hunter Publishing, visit our Web site at:
www.huntertravelguides.com

All rights reserved. No part of this book may be reproduced, transmitted or utilized in any form or by any means, electronic or mechanical, including photocopying, recording, or by any information storage and retrieval system, without permission in writing from the publisher. Brief extracts to be included in reviews or articles are permitted.

Every effort has been made to ensure that the information in this book is correct, but the publisher and authors do not assume, and hereby disclaim, liability to any party for any loss or damage caused by errors, omissions, misleading information or potential problems caused by information in this guide, even if such errors or omissions are a result of negligence, accident or any other cause.

4 3 2 1

Contents

Introduction	1
How to Use This Book	1
Safety	3
Leave No Trace in the Wilderness	3
The Land	5
Snowy Range	6
A Ridge of High Peaks	7
Flora & Fauna	7
The Sierra Foothills	8
The Sierra Forest	10
History	10
California Natives	10
Spanish California	11
American Pioneers	12
Mountain Men	13
The Fremont Explorations	13
The California Trail	14
The Donner Party	15
The Bear Flag Revolt	15
The Mother Lode	15
The Gold Rush	15
California Today	16
Sierra Nevada Today	17
The Sierra Crest	18
Getting Here & Getting Around	18
Across the Sierra Crest	19
Highway Border Crossings	19
Information	20
General Information	20
State Parks	20
National Forests	20
National Parks	20
Other Public Land	20
Fishing & Hunting	21
Transportation	21
The Eastern Sierra	23
Owens Valley	23
Adventures on Foot	23
Dome Lands Wilderness	23
Golden Trout Wilderness	24
Kennedy Meadows	24
Lone Pine	25
What to See & Do	25

Contents

Adventures on Foot	26
The Mt. Whitney Trail	26
Meysan Lake	28
Backpacking to Mt. Whitney	29
Cottonwood Lakes	31
Adventures on Water	31
Cottonwood Lakes	31
Where to Stay	32
Where to Dine	32
Independence	33
What to See & Do	33
Where to Stay	33
Big Pine	33
What to See & Do	33
Adventures on Foot	33
Onion Valley	33
North Fork Trail	34
Adventures on Water	35
Fishing Between Lone Pine & Big Pine	35
Where to Stay	35
Camping	35
Public Campgrounds – Lone Pine to Bishop	35
Private Campgrounds – Lone Pine to Bishop	37
Where to Dine	37
Bishop	37
What to See & Do	37
Adventures on Foot - Bishop to Mammoth	38
Hiking	38
Rock Climbing the Gorge	40
Adventures on Wheels - Bishop	41
Biking	41
Off-Road Driving	41
Adventures on Water	43
Best Fishing Spots	43
Where to Stay	44
Camping	44
Public Campgrounds	44
Private Campgrounds	48
Where to Dine	49
Mammoth Lakes	49
What to See & Do	49
Adventures on Snow	49
Downhill Skiing	49
Cross-Country Skiing	50
Adventures on Foot	50
Bishop & Mammoth Wilderness Packers	50
Self-Guided Trails	51
Where to Stay	52

Where to Dine	52
The Devil's Postpile	52
What to See & Do	52
June Lake/Mammoth Lakes	53
What to See & Do	53
Adventures On Foot	53
Hiking	53
Adventures on Horseback	56
Packers	56
Adventures on Wheels	56
Mountain Biking	56
Mammoth Mountain Bike Park	60
June Lake	61
Adventures on Snow	62
Snowmobiling	62
Downhill Skiing	63
Cross-Country Skiing	63
Dogsledding	63
Ice Climbing	63
Where to Stay	64
Where to Dine	64
Route 395 North	64
Mono Lake	65
What to See & Do	65
Mono Lake	65
Mono Craters	65
Adventures On Water	65
Fishing along the Eastern Slopes	65
Where to Stay	66
Camping	66
Public Campgrounds	66
Private Campgrounds	68
Bodie	69
What to See & Do	69
Bridgeport	72
What to See & Do	72
Mono County Courthouse	72
Mono County Museum	72
Adventures on Foot	72
Mono Lake to Bridgeport	72
Adventures on Wheels	74
Where to Stay	74
Eastern Sierra Outfitters	75
Lone Pine/Big Pine/Bishop	75
On Foot	75
On Horseback	75
On Wheels	75
On Water	76

Mammoth Lakes/Mono Lake/Bridgeport	76
On Foot	76
On Horseback	76
Camping & Outdoor Gear	77
On Wheels	77
On Water	77
Nevada & Lake Tahoe	**79**
Carson City	79
What to See & Do	79
Where to Stay	81
Where to Dine	81
Virginia City	82
History	82
What to See & Do	85
The Castle	86
Comstock Mine	86
Belcher Mine	86
Mark Twain	87
Where to Stay	87
Where to Dine	87
Lake Tahoe	88
Tahoe History	88
Fremont	88
After Statehood	88
Lake Tahoe Today	89
Getting Here & Getting Around	93
Local Transportation	93
Information Sources	94
What to See & Do	94
Family Activities	94
Trout Farm	95
Sleigh Rides	95
Teen Activities	95
Grover Hot Springs State Park	95
Casinos	95
Wedding Vows	97
Marriage Licenses	97
Cultural & Historical Sights	98
Lake Tahoe's Visitor Center	98
Emerald Bay	98
Tallac Historic Site	99
Ponderosa Ranch	99
Historical Society Museum	100
Nevada's First Settlement	100
Cultural Events	100
Adventures on Foot	100
Hiking Trails	100

Desolation Wilderness	101
Tahoe Rim Trail	101
Vista Trail	101
Granite Chief Wilderness	102
Mokelumne Wilderness	102
Mount Rose Wilderness	103
Other Trails	103
Rock Climbing	105
Golfing	107
Tennis	107
Adventures on Horseback	108
Adventures on Wheels	108
Mountain Biking	108
Mountain Biking in Nevada	109
Off-Highway Vehicles	110
Adventures on Water	111
Boating	112
North Lake Tahoe Cruises	112
Water Skiing, Windsurfing & Jet Skiing	112
Scuba Diving	112
Parasailing	113
Fishing	113
Rafting	113
Adventures on Snow	114
Skiing	114
Alpine Meadows Ski Area	114
Boreal Ski Area	114
Camp Richardson	114
Clair Tappan Lodge	115
Diamond Peak Ski Resort	115
Donner Ski Ranch	115
Granlibakken at Lake Tahoe	115
Heavenly Ski Resort	115
Hope Valley Cross-Country Center	116
Kirkwood	116
Lakeview Cross Country Skiing	116
Northstar-At-Tahoe	117
Mount Rose	117
Plumas Eureka Ski Bowl	117
Royal Gorge Cross Country Resort	117
Sierra At Tahoe Ski Resort	118
Ski Homewood	118
Soda Springs	118
Spooner Lake	118
Sugar Bowl	118
Squaw Valley USA	118

Contents

Tahoe Donner	119
Dogsledding	119
Backcountry Adventures	120
Snowmobiling	120
Where to Stay	121
South Lake Tahoe	121
Campgrounds in the Tahoe Basin	122
Public Campgrounds	122
Private Campgrounds	123
Where to Dine	124
South Lake Tahoe	124
Stateline	125
Lake Tahoe Outfitters	125
General Outfitters	125
On Horseback	126
On Wheels	126
On Water	127
In the Air	128
On Snow	128
Leaving Tahoe	129
Reno	129
Getting Here & Getting Around	130
Airlines	130
Rental Cars	130
Other Ground Transportation	131
What to See & Do	131
Where to Stay in Reno	132
Where to Dine in Reno	133
The Western Sierra	**135**
Gold Country North	135
Climate	136
Grass Valley	136
What to See & Do	137
Lola Montez House	137
Where to Stay in Grass Valley	137
Where to Dine in Grass Valley	138
Auburn	138
Where to Stay in Auburn	138
Where to Dine in Auburn	139
Coloma	139
Where to Stay in Coloma	140
Tahoe to Placerville	141
Placerville	142
Where to Stay in Placerville	142
Where to Dine in Placerville	142
Folsom	143
Sacramento	144
Getting Here & Getting Around	144

Airlines	144
Ground Transportation	144
History	144
American Trappers	145
"Old Sacramento"	145
Sacramento Today	146
Railroad Museum	148
Towe Ford Museum	148
Old Sacramento Walking Tour	148
Other Attractions	148
Gold Country North Adventures	149
Adventures on Foot	149
Adventures on Wheels	150
Bicycling	150
Off-Road Driving	151
Adventures on Water	152
The American River	152
North Fork	153
Middle Fork	154
South Fork	154
Safety	157
Adventures on Snow	158
Gold Country North Outfitters	158
General Outfitters	158
On Horseback	159
On Wheels	159
On Water	160
Where to Stay in Sacramento	161
Where to Dine in Sacramento	162
Gold Country South	162
The Golden Chain	163
Amador	163
Where to Stay & Dine in Amador	164
Central Eureka Mine	164
Angels Camp	165
What to See & Do	165
Where to Stay in Angels Camp	165
Jumping Frog Jubilee	165
Other Things to do in Calaveras County	165
Mokelumne Hill	166
West Point	166
San Andreas	166
Murphys	167
Where to Stay in Murphys	167
Bear Valley	167
Where to Stay in Bear Valley	167
Gold Country South Adventures	169

Adventures on Foot	169
Hiking	169
The John Muir Trail	171
The Pacific Crest Trail	173
When to Go	174
Rules & Regulations	175
Trail Restrictions	175
Wilderness Permits	175
Campsite Restrictions	176
Trail Mishaps	176
Other Precautions	177
Rock Climbing	179
Spelunking	180
California Caverns	180
Mercer Caverns	181
Adventures on Horseback	181
Adventures on Wheels	182
Mountain Biking	182
Eldorado National Forest	182
Stanislaus National Forest	182
Four-Wheel Driving	183
Adventures on Water	184
Merced River	185
Other Rivers for Whitewater Rafting	185
Adventures on Snow	186
Routes Home or to the Parks	187
Mariposa	187
Where to Stay in Mariposa	187
Oakhurst	188
Gold Country South Outfitters	188
General Outfitters	188
On Horseback	189
On Wheels	189
On Water	190
Yosemite National Park	**190**
Western Routes to the Park	190
Sacramento to Yosemite	190
Los Angeles to Yosemite	190
The Tioga Road – The Eastern Approach	191
History	191
The Great Sierra Wagon Road	191
Upgrading of the Tioga Road	192
The Tioga Road Today	193
History of the Park	193
Yosemite's Formative Years	193
Valley Saved for Posterity	194
A Common Danger	194

Muir Follows the Dictates of His Heart	194
First Visit	195
Yosemite Today	196
What to See & Do in Yosemite Valley	197
Glacier Point	197
Half Dome	197
Mirror Lake	198
Sunnyside Ranch	198
Mount Watkins	198
Shuttle Buses & Park Services	199
Valley Bus Tours	201
Hunting	201
Fishing	201
Activities for Children	201
Park Animals	201
A Helping Hand For Yosemite	202
Adventures In Yosemite	202
Adventures on Foot	202
Hiking	202
Glacier Point	203
Valley Floor Trails	204
Yosemite Falls	204
Mirror Lake	205
Vernal & Nevada Falls	205
Half Dome	206
South of the Valley	206
North of Yosemite Valley	207
Rock Climbing	209
Adventures on Wheels	210
Adventures on Snow	211
Where to Stay in Yosemite Valley	211
Camping in Yosemite Valley	213
Tioga Road Campgrounds	214
Tioga Pass Campgrounds	214
Other Campsites Near Tioga Road	215
Group Camps	215
Reservations	215
What to See & Do Outside Yosemite Valley	215
Grand Canyon of the Tuolumne	216
Tuolumne River Rafting	216
Camping in Stanislaus National Forest	218
Merced River Hiking	218
Yosemite Valley North to Tuolumne River	219
Hetch Hetchy Reservoir	219
Yosemite's Big Trees	219
Mariposa Grove	219
Wawona Tree	219

Yosemite to Mariposa Bus Tours	219
Mariposa Grove Museum	220
Tuolumne Grove	220
Tuolumne Meadows	220
Where to Stay Outside Yosemite Valley	220
Campgrounds Outside Yosemite Valley	221
More Distant Accommodations & Dining	222
Where to Stay	222
Visalia	222
Oakhurst	223
Where to Dine	223
Visalia	223
Oakhurst	223
Yosemite Information Sources	224
South of Yosemite	224
Sierra National Forest	224
Nelder Grove	225
Trails into the Sierra National Forest	225
Reserving Campsites in the Sierra NF	226
Kings Canyon & Sequoia	226
Hiking Trails	228
Visitor Centers	228
Generals Highway	228
Grant Grove	229
The General Grant Tree	229
Converse Basin	229
Getting Here & Getting Around	229
Airlines, Bus & Rail Service	229
Driving Conditions	231
Trailers	231
Vehicle Lengths	231
Steep Grades	231
Winter Driving	231
Other Hazards	231
Ticks	232
Cougars	232
Weather	232
Moro Rock – Crescent Meadow Road	233
Adventures on Foot	233
Redwood Canyon	235
Crystal Cave	235
Adventures on Water	236
Hume Lake	236
Campgrounds in Sequoia & Kings Canyon	236
Campground Regulations	237
Sequoia Campgrounds	237
Park Information Sources	239

Fresno	239
What to See & Do in Fresno	239
Adventures on Foot	240
Adventures on Wheels	241
Adventures on Water	242
Kings River	242
Mammoth Pool Reservoir	243
Tule River	243
Adventures on Snow	245
Where to Stay in Fresno	245
Where to Dine in Fresno	247
Bakersfield	247
What to See & Do	247
Where to Stay in Bakersfield	248
Where to Dine in Bakersfield	248
Sequoia National Forest	250
South of Yosemite Outfitters	251
General Outfitters	251
On Water	252
On Wheels	252
Appendices	253
Appendix A	253
Fishing Regulations	253
Appendix B	254
Special Passes	254
Index	255

Maps

Eastern Sierra	22
Pacific Crest Trail	39
Reno-Tahoe	78
Lake Tahoe	90
Western Sierra	135
Routes to the Mother Lode Country	143
Sacramento	147
Old Sacramento	149
Old Mines Along Highway 49	163
Bear Valley Approaches	168
Routes to Yosemite	190
Yosemite	200
Kings Canyon/Sequoia	230
Tule River	244
Bakersfield	249

Acknowledgements

I'd like to express my appreciation to the Ahwannee Whitewater Association, the California Trade and Commerce Agency, the Calaveras County Visitors Authority, the US Forest Service of the Department of Agriculture, the National Park Service, US Department of Interior, and the California State Library. Each of them went out of their way to be helpful.

My young friend Breezy Dawn Rice used her expertise to take over the task of putting my text on a computer. As always, she's a joy to work with.

Wilbur H. Morrison

My sincere thanks to go out to my colleagues in the Outdoor Writers Association of California, whose collective professionalism is surpassed only by the pleasure of their camaraderie; to the folks at California Map & Travel Center in Santa Monica, Calif., whose support for travel authors is unwavering; and to my publisher and editor Michael Hunter and his staff for their guidance and patience.

Matt Purdue

Accommodations Price Scale	
$	Up to $50 per day
$$	$50 to $100
$$$	$100 to $175
$$$$	More than $175

Introduction

The Sierra Nevada exceeds in size the entire Alps region of Europe. It is a land that mingles past and present in a colorful mixture of modern life with tantalizing glimpses of the last half of the 19th century. Each year about five million people visit the area. It recalls the West when it was wild and unruly, and often the only official justice was meted out by the hangman's rope. Life was difficult in California back then, but it was never dull. The strong survived and the weak fell by the wayside.

How to Use This Book

There are many access points for the Sierra Nevada. Each year, millions of travelers approach the mountains from the south, from Southern California and Nevada. Millions more come in from the west, via the San Francisco Bay Area. Still more enter the range from the east, via Reno, Nevada. For the sake of clarity, we have to start this book somewhere and have chosen to follow a linear path from the south. No bias is intended; we simply chose Southern California as a logical starting point.

If you read the book front to back, you'll follow a path from the southern end of the Sierra Nevada range, up the eastern side of the mountains on US 395 through the dry western edge of the Great Basin, then stray briefly into the Reno area of Nevada. From Reno you'll explore Lake Tahoe, then sweep down the western slopes toward Sacramento, California's capital city. Next you'll head south-southeast along the western side of the Sierra, through the region known as Gold Country, then on to some of the most spectacular jewels in the National Park System – Yosemite, Sequoia and Kings Canyon. From there the adventure continues south to the southern tip of the Sierra Nevada, near the book's starting point.

Of course we don't assume that you'll explore the region in this order. The table of contents and the index are set up to make it easy for you to find the adventures you are looking for, no matter what your point of origin and final destination may be.

The book is divided into major geographic sections to reflect the areas that share common characteristics and are each easily accessible as individual regions:

- The Eastern Sierra
- Nevada & Lake Tahoe
- The Western Sierra, encompassing Gold Country
- Yosemite National Park
- South of Yosemite

2 How to Use This Book

Each geographic section is subdivided into various parts. First you'll read about the locality's history and get basic traveler's information, such as contact numbers and addresses for tourism bureaus, plus airline and rental car information for the main gateway cities. Then you'll explore the cities, towns and attractions – museums, parks, reservoirs – mainly accessible from your vehicle. Since any adventurer sometimes welcomes a warm bed and a hot meal, local descriptions also include selected lodging and dining spots that have been chosen based on quality, uniqueness and trusted recommendations.

The adventures sections bring you detailed advice on how to explore the region on foot, on horseback, on water, on wheels, and on snow, assuming you are willing to invest at least a little sweat equity.

Adventures on Foot

From easy strolls on paved, often handicapped-accessible pathways to multi-day backpacking excursions in the wilderness, adventures on foot will get your boots moving on the Sierra's slopes. Besides walking and hiking, this section also features rock climbing and other human-powered activities.

Adventures on Horseback

There are many opportunities to see the Sierra Nevada from the saddle in much the same way the first Europeans did in the late 18th century. This section provides directions to trails as well as contacts for packers.

Adventures on Wheels

Both people-powered vehicles – namely road and mountain bikes – and those powered by the infernal combustion engine are popular on the trails of the Sierra Nevada. This section highlights the best routes and off-highway vehicle areas. Keep in mind that vehicles of all kinds are prohibited in federal wilderness area and other sensitive spots. It is important to respect all signs and restrictions; riding in the Sierra is a privilege, not a right, and land managers take violations very seriously.

Adventures on Water

Swimming, boating, rafting, canoeing. With hundreds of miles of rivers and streams plus thousands of lakes and reservoirs, including Lake Tahoe, the Sierra is a great place to step off dry land.

Adventures on Snow

Some parts of the Sierra receive up to 400 inches a year of the white stuff, making this a winter playground for millions of visitors. Here you'll find info on skiing – both downhill and cross-country – and other cold-weather activities.

Continuing this adventuresome theme, you'll read about camping opportunities, where you can lay your head under the Sierra stars. Both public and private campgrounds are included, from primitive walk-in sites where you'll have to pack even your water to RV parks with full hook-ups and cable TV links.

Finally, each regional section concludes with a list of outfitters, highlighting the experts in each area who can equip you with gear, advice and expertise to help you get the most out of your adventure. Retail establishments and guide services of all types fill these listings.

Fishing and hunting are exceptional in the Sierra Nevada, but licenses are required and regulations fill a book of their own. See *Appendix A* for fishing requirements. *Information Sources* on page 20 includes the addresses of organizations that can be most helpful in planning your trip. Information about special passes for the elderly and the disabled are included in *Appendix B*.

Safety

Although this is a year-round vacation land, severe winters can be dangerous because of deep snow packs at higher elevations. Plan your trip well, covering all contingencies, and you'll enjoy an experience that is unique. Much of this country is still primitive and unoccupied. You will endanger life and limb if you foolishly disregard normal precautions.

Leave No Trace in the Wilderness

Following the "Leave No Trace" ethic is simply a way of life in the Sierras. Although the massive granite peaks of the range make this region seem indestructible, the country is actually a place of fragile beauty. From the oak-dotted foothills to the rushing streams, the verdant forests to the lonely glacial lakes, human impact and abuse leave a lasting impression on the land.

Adhering to the Leave No Trace guidelines ensures that what few pristine areas remain in the Sierras will be there when you come back next season, and makes even the most highly impacted locales more enjoyable for everyone. For more information on the Leave No Trace ethic, call ☎ 800-332-4100. The following tips are taken directly from Leave No Trace literature.

Plan Ahead & Prepare

- Know the regulations and special concerns for the area you will visit.
- Visit the backcountry in small groups.
- Avoid popular areas during periods of high use.
- Choose equipment and clothing in subdued colors.
- Repackage food in to reusable containers.
- Camp and travel on durable surfaces.

On the Trail

- Stay on designated trails.
- Walk single file in the middle of the path.
- Do not shortcut switchbacks.
- When traveling cross-country, choose the most durable surfaces available: rock, gravel, dry grasses or snow.
- Use a map and compass to eliminate the need for rock cairns, tree scars and ribbons.
- Step to the downhill side of the trail and talk softly when encountering pack stock.

At Camp

- Choose an established, legal site that will not be damaged by your stay.
- Restrict activities to the area where vegetation is compacted or absent.
- Keep pollutants out of water sources by camping at least 200 feet (70 adult steps) from lakes and streams.

Pack It In, Pack It Out

- Pack everything that you bring into wild country back out with you.
- Protect wildlife and your food by storing rations securely.
- Clean up all spilled foods.
- Properly dispose of what you can't pack out.
- Deposit human waste in catholes dug six to eight inches deep at least 200 feet from water, camp or trails. Cover and disguise the cathole when finished.
- Use toilet paper or wipes sparingly. Pack them out.

- To wash yourself or dishes, carry water 200 feet from lakes or streams, and use small amounts of biodegradable soap. Scatter strained dishwater.
- Inspect your campsite for trash and evidence of your stay. Pack out all trash, both yours and others'.

Leave What You Find

- Treat our natural heritage with respect. Leave plants, rocks and historical artifacts as you find them.
- Good campsites are found, not made. Altering a site should not be necessary.
- Let nature's sounds prevail. Keep loud voices and noises to a minimum.
- Control pets at all times. Remove dog feces.
- Do not build structures or furniture or dig ditches.

Minimize Use & Impact of Fires

- Campfires can cause lasting impacts on the backcountry. Always carry a lightweight stove for cooking. Enjoy a candle lantern instead of a fire.
- Where fires are permitted, use established fire rings, fire pans or mound fires. Don't scar large rocks or overhangs.
- Gather sticks no larger than an adult's wrist.
- Do not snap branches off live, dead or downed trees.
- Put out campfires completely.
- Remove all unburned trash from fire ring and scatter the cool ashes over a large area well away from camp.

The Land

The North American plate is thought to have overridden part of the Pacific Ocean floor, crumpling what are now the Sierra Nevada and Coast Ranges. Landmarks such as Mount Baker in Washington, Lassen Peak in California and Crater Lake in Oregon still hint of the volcanic fury lying restlessly beneath the earth. The Sierra Nevada forms a great barrier like a granite wall that towers skyward, culminating in jagged peaks against a deep blue sky. Owens Valley, a long, deep depression, is hemmed in by steep walls rising 7,000 feet above the valley floor on the west and 10,000 feet on the east. Some 150 million years ago compressive forces within the earth wrinkled the older sedimentary layers into giant folds. Much later, volcanoes spewed lava, ash and cinders over the land. At about the same time, huge mountain blocks were uplifted along fractures in the earth's crust and tilted, while basins in the Owens Valley sank.

The great granite cliffs, domes and spires of the Sierra Nevada consist of lava that congealed slowly underground 100 million years ago and was miles thick. This was followed by uplift and erosion in the same chamber where the flows built Mesozoic volcanoes during the period of the dinosaurs, marine and flying reptiles and evergreen trees. Mists and time shroud the majestic links to earth's dim past on the western slopes of the Sierra Nevada, where giant sequoias and their coastal cousins survive in mild climates like those thousands of years ago in the northern hemisphere. The Pacific Coast has continuous mountain chains, including the Sierra Nevada and the Cascades in Oregon and Washington. These mountains offer barriers to weather systems. They do not prevent the flow of moist marine winds, but the winds are forced to rise over and around through gaps in the mountains.

A barrier against the rain-bearing Pacific winds, the Sierra Nevada gradually transformed the climate of the interior, creating vast deserts and treeless grasslands.

During an earthquake in 1872, as much as 20 feet was added to the difference in height between the bottom of Owens Valley and the crest of the Sierra Nevada. The fault scarp is still visible. Moisture-laden rains dump 10 times more precipitation on the mountains' western slope than in the Owens Valley. California's Mt. Whitney, at 14,494 feet, is the highest peak in the 430-mile-long Sierra Nevada.

Snowy Range

John Muir, a naturalist and explorer, first came to Yosemite in 1868, calling it "the grandest of all the special temples of nature I was ever permitted to enter." Muir saw this mirage-like ribbon of mountains from the western side of the range. He said the rugged mountains were "gloriously colored and so luminous that they seemed not clothed in light but wholly composed of it like the wall of some celestial city."

In 1776, Pedro Font, a Spanish priest, named the snow-belted mountain chain the Sierra Nevada, or "Snowy Range." Muir called it the "range of light." He said as he "trudged through the foothills, mountain winds and delicious crystal water cooled my chronic fevers. We are now in the mountains and they are in us, kindling enthusiasm, making every nerve quiver, filling every pore and cell." As he climbed higher on forest-lined trails, suddenly a deep valley yawned before him. He was spellbound by what later became known as Yosemite Valley, its beauty and spiritual glow. "The whole landscape showed design," he said, "like man's noblest sculptures. Canyons became mountain streets full of life and light. The river speaks with a thousand songful voices. An immense hall or temple is lighted from above. Here nature has gathered her choicest treasures." He later described "how ineffably, spiritually fine is the morning glow on the mountain tops. Perhaps the Sierra should not have been named the Snowy Range but the Range of Light." Muir returned often to this enchanting wilderness.

A Ridge of High Peaks

Between Mount Whitney and Lake Tahoe is the true Sierra Nevada, a land of granite, glacial ice and alpine lakes. At elevations of 6,000-9,000 feet along the eastern slope are forests of pine and fir, while along the western slope are forests of giant sequoias, wild-flowered meadows and steep V-shaped river canyons.

North of Los Angeles, the Coast Ranges and the Sierra Nevada join to form the transverse ranges that include the Tehachapi, San Gabriel and San Bernardino mountains.

Walt Whitman wrote eloquently about the Sierra Nevada:

> *Ever the dim beginning,*
> *Ever the growth,*
> *the rounding of the circle. . . .*
> *Strata of mountains,*
> *Soil, rocks, giant trees,*
> *Far-born, far-dying,*
> *Living long.*

Flora & Fauna

A discussion of the incredibly varied species of plants and animals found in and around the Sierra Nevada would – and indeed does – fill many volumes. The flora and fauna in Sierra country is as diverse as the terrain. A traveler flying low over the Sierra from west to east would note a topography that stretches from the oak-dotted grasslands of the western foothills up through the thick belt of coniferous evergreen trees so closely associated with our popular notion of "forest." Continuing up the western escarpment, the traveler would next encounter the windswept alpine region extending above treeline to the crest of the mountains. Descending the steep eastern slopes, the belt of coniferous trees is again present in abundance, followed by the sagebrush-dominated scrubland and chapparal of the lower eastern side.

Some of the plants and animals are found in most or all of these biotic communities, but as a general rule each one is unique in the types of life it supports. You don't have to study botany or biology to enjoy a relaxing and inspiring adventure in the Sierra. But you owe it to yourself to become familiar with the amazing variety of plants and animals in this landscape. With just a bit of study and understanding, it's easy to see why gorgeous, soul-stirring places like the Sierra Nevada – and the teeming life here – are worth preserving and protecting for future generations of wildflower seekers and wildlife watchers.

Following is a brief discussion of the plants and animals found in the four communities mentioned above.

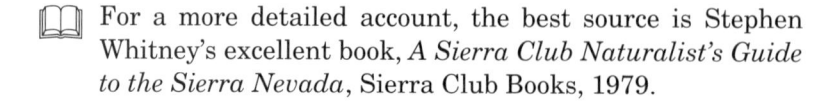

> For a more detailed account, the best source is Stephen Whitney's excellent book, *A Sierra Club Naturalist's Guide to the Sierra Nevada*, Sierra Club Books, 1979.

The Sierra Foothills

The foothills extend from the edges of California's great Central Valley at about 500 feet above sea level all the way up the beginning of the coniferous treeline as high as 5,000 feet. The foothills are characterized by hot, dry summers followed by a short wet season that generally lasts from November through April, although most rain falls from December through February. The plants and animals here have adapted to this relatively dry climate.

THE GRASSLANDS: The lower foothills are covered with wild grasses. Whereas two centuries ago much of the Central Valley and lower Sierra foothills were dominated by native California grasses such as purple needlegrass and foothill bluegrass, almost all of the native species have been replaced by grasses native to the Mediterranean. A large part of this invasion is due to the spread of livestock brought into California in large numbers by Mexicans and the Spanish in the 18th and 19th centuries. Today the most common grasses are wild oats, red broom, foxtail fescue and soft chess. Springtime sees the annual concert of color put on by the grasses and the native wildflowers of the foothills. The rich green of the grasses is interspersed by explosions of color moroe vivid than anything that's ever come from a painter's brush. Indeed, visitors come from all over the world to witness fields of baby blue-eye, purple owl's clover, goldfields, prettyface, paintbrush, lupine, evening snow, milkweed and, of course, the state flower, the California golden poppy.

> *Note that in California it is illegal to pick the golden poppy or any flowers on public land.*

The animals native to the grasslands are generally small and quick, all the better to survive on a relatively sparse diet and avoid predation by larger grassland intruders who cruise the foothills looking for food. If you're looking for wildlife, you'll have to look closely to spot amphibious species such as the Western spadefoot and Western toad. Reptiles include the Southern alligator lizard, common kingsnake, garter snake, gopher snake and a creature commonly confused with the gopher snake, the Western rattlesnake. Common birds include the burrowing owl, mourning dove and Western meadowlark, while the mammals tend toward the compact, notably the California ground squirrel, San Joaquin Valley pocket mouse, Western harvest mouse, and numerous moles, shrews and gophers.

Many larger creatures use the grasslands to hunt and might be spotted there while they're visiting. In the air these include the turkey vulture, red-tailed hawk, golden eagle, American kestrel, great horned owl, Western bluebird and red-winged blackbird. Visiting mammals include the black-tailed jackrabbit, gray fox, coyote, bobcat, mule deer and several types of bats.

THE FOOTHILLS: The foothills are also dotted with woody trees that form a subcommunity of plants and animals, perfect places to grab a shady nap on a hot summer day. The most common trees at these lower altitudes are the blue oak, canyon live oak, interior live oak, valley oak and digger pine. Acorns from the oaks were a staple of the diet of the Native Americans who once flourished here. Many of the shrubs common to the Mediterranean-like chapparal are also found here, notably gooseberry, toyon, poison oak, buckbrush, manzanita and coyote brush. As in the grasslands, wildflowers abound in springtime, with tower mustard, Chinese caps, larkspurs, miner's lettuce, Chinese houses, lupines, mariposa tulips and irises leading the riot of color. Animal life is increasingly varied. Commonly sighted creatures include many of those found in the foothill grasslands, as well as salamanders and newts, California quail (the state bird), woodpeckers, scrub jays, towhees and finches. Mammals that roam the wooded foothills include raccoons, skunks, ringtails and even the rare mountain lion.

In the riparian areas of the foothills, where water plays a larger role in shaping the ecosystem, common trees include varieties of cottonwood and willow plus white alder, California laurel and western sycamore. Buttercups, western dog violet, stream orchid and watercress are a few of the resident wildflowers. Red-legged frogs and ringneck snakes are among the land-dwellers found along the streams and creeks of the foothills, not to mention birds such as the wood duck, screech owl, belted kingfisher, dipper and song sparrow.

Near the other extreme, the dry, heat-resistant chapparal of the foothills, a plant community which depends on fire rather than water for much of its reproductive success, boasts scrub oak, leather oak, chamise, deerweed, bush monkeyflowers and toyon, among others. Reptiles, including the Western whiptail and striped racer, are common, while birds, like Anna's hummingbird and the wrentit, and mammals, such as the California pocket mouse and dusky-footed wood rat, tend to be small and well hidden.

The Sierra Forest

The thick belt of forest that dominates the Sierra, ranging from as low as 2,000 feet above sea level all the way up to the subalipine region at 11,000 feet, is the largest and most diverse of the biotic communities. Not surprisingly, this is where most humans also spend their time, and it's the area that provides the best chance to spot wildlife and enjoy a walk among the verdant flora.

In the mixed coniferous zone, ponderosa pine, Jeffrey pine, sugar pine, Douglas fir and white fir are common on the drier slopes of the Western Sierra, with quaking aspen and black cottonwood found along streams. This is also home to the world-renowned giant sequoia (*Sequoiadendron Giganteum*), commonly thought to be the largest living thing on the planet. Sequoia and Kings Canyon national parks are home to the largest of these behemoths. The eastern slopes of the Sierra are less diverse; Jeffrey pine and white fir dominate the more arid landscape. From the bottom up, animals such as the Pacific tree frog, rubber boa, California mountain king snake, gray squirrel, northern flying squirrel, long-tailed weasel and black bear are common, along with many of the foothills creatures. Birds like the sharp-shinned hawk, Cooper's hawk, Steller's jay and mountain chickadee fill the skies.

History

California Natives

The land we now call California was once home to a greater diversity of Native Americans than any other region on this continent. In the middle of the 18th century, before the first invasion of the Spanish into Alta California, it is estimated that at least 300,000 natives, perhaps as many as a million, lived in 60 different linguistic groups across the land. They made war and peace with each other, developed complex cosmologies and lifeways, learned to use indigenous plants for making everything from waterproof baskets to fish poison, created beautiful works of art and established complex trading networks that spread throughout the region.

From the time the Spanish first colonized Alta California in 1769 through 1832, a span of just 63 years, the native population plummeted to an estimated 100,000. Long before the well-recorded conflicts between whites and Native Americans living on the plains, the genocidal war against the California natives was in its final stages. Disease took a tremendously heavy toll and "heathen Indians" who escaped from the missions were tracked like animals. When the mission era ended in 1848 and foreigners surged into California in search of gold, native peoples were simply pests to be exterminated. While smallpox, cholera and other diseases wiped out entire villages, federal troops, local lawmen, vigilantes, bounty hunters and average citizens killed, kidnapped, raped, enslaved and subjugated thousands of California Indians.

California's indigenous population, including those groups that populated the Sierra Nevada, has never fully recovered. The southern Sierra was home to such groups as the Kawaiisu, Panamint and Koso Shoshone and Tubatulabat. The rugged eastern Sierra supported Owens Valley Paiute, Eastern Mono, Northern Paiute/Bannock and Washo, centered around Lake Tahoe. On the western slopes lived groups such as the Foothill Yokuts, Monache, Sierra Miwok and Nisenan.

Today, many of California's natives are eagerly rediscovering their heritage. While in Sierra Nevada country you'll have the chance to see evidence not only of their colorful past, such as the stunning pictographs on the Tule River Reservation, but also of a native renaissance, such as that occurring in Bishop, which boasts the impressive Paiute-Shoshone Cultural Center and a new casino, the Paiute Palace. Of course the Paiute have entered the 21st century. You can check all this out on their site Web site: www.paiute.com.

Spanish California

Sebastian Vizcaino reaffirmed Spain's title to California in 1602. During his explorations he named many coastal features. It wasn't until 1768 that King Charles, fearing possible encroachments by other countries, ordered the colonization of California.

The following year Gaspar de Portola's lieutenants discovered San Francisco Bay. Presidios, or military forts, were built in San Diego, Santa Barbara, Monterey and San Francisco, but the headquarters of the military government was established at Monterey. Growth was small and Spanish California remained a remote, ill-supplied outpost of European civilization.

In 1822, when Mexico won its independence from Spain, California swore allegiance to Mexico, but remained self-governing.

In 1842 there was a minor gold rush north of Los Angeles, but California's economy under Mexican rule was dominated by cattle raising – mostly for hides – by the ranchos. This began to change when Americans started to arrive in growing numbers.

American Pioneers

A group led by Captain Joseph Walker explored the Sierra Nevada in 1833. In the process, they learned that there was no easy passage from the desert to the Pacific Ocean because of a maze of valleys. Walker's clerk, Ze-

*"An Old-Time Mountain Man with his Ponies." Frederic Remington
Clarence P. Hornung Collection*

nas Leonard, spoke with disgust when he said, "There are everlasting snows on the summits and no practicable place for crossing."

In 1834, a brigade of trappers under Walker, "apprehensive of perishing for water," watched in horror as their dogs died of thirst with "piteous and lamentable" howls. The brigade became lost. Their need for water became so acute that when one of their cattle or horses died the men would immediately "catch the blood and greedily swallow it down." Later, when their horses smelled a stream ahead, they were saved.

Mountain Men

Jed Smith and Joe Walker were leaders among hundreds of mountain men. They were a legendary company of hunters, trappers and explorers that included Kit Carson, Jim Bridger, Étienne Provost, Joe Meek, Thomas Fitzpatrick, David Jackson and Andrew Henry. When Smith tried to walk overland to California, his group found South Pass in 1824. He was the first to mark a direct route across the Nevada desert, developing what became the California emigrant trail. During his travels he discovered Yosemite and traced the Walker Pass/Owens Valley route. Walker later led wagon trains, and surveyed routes for transcontinental railroads. He guided one of Fremont's surveys, and prospected into his 60s.

In two decades of trading – 1820-1840 – mountain men scouted much of the West, finding the best paths and passes from the Rockies to California.

The Fremont Explorations

Explorer John C. Fremont crossed the Sierra Nevada in mid-January 1845, at a spot near Pyramid Lake. Despite low provisions and orders from Washington to return east, he reconnoitered the Sierra Nevada and nearby areas for a year. He described his experiences later, saying, "This vast country is filled with rivers and lakes which have no communication with the sea." He said the land was "a huge depression with interior drainage," which he called the "great basin." He found that the mountains, covered with snow, made passage torturous. Horses and mules slipped off ice canyon walls. Indian guides deserted them. Men died and the living ate their starving horses and dogs. They were beset by frostbite and snow blindness.

On February 6, Fremont and a scouting party climbed on snowshoes to the top of a broad promontory south of Lake Tahoe. He said later, "far below us, dominated by the distance, was a large snowless valley, bounded on the west by a low range of mountains at a distance of one hundred miles." Scout Kit Carson recognized them with delight "as the mountains bordering the coast." This was the Sacramento Valley. The band, wan and sick from their ordeal, reached Sutter's Fort. Captain John Augustus Sutter

General John C. Fremont. Photo by Matthew Brady.

had come to California in 1839 and received a large land grant from Mexico along the Sacramento River. Of the 104 mules and horses in Fremont's band, only 33 remained. One man had wandered off in a crazed fit of cold and hunger but was later rescued. Fortunately for Fremont's party the winter had been mild.

The California Trail

Sutter's Fort – site of Sacramento today – was located on 50,000 acres and illustrated the promise of California. The backbreaking toil of hauling wagons of immigrants across some 70 miles of the Sierra Nevada was haunted by their fear of early snows. In the dozen years starting in 1846 more than 165,000 pioneers made the crossing to escape economic depression gripping the East.

The Donner Party

Members of the ill-fated Donner Party in 1846-1847 struggled toward a pass in the Sierra Nevada in a desperate attempt to escape winter's entrapment. Dissension and fatigue forced them to turn back to their camp. They had taken a northerly course along the Truckee River high in the central Sierra. There began a nightmare that ended in robbery, murder, starvation and cannibalism. Of the 87 who took a new route south of the Great Salt Lake, five died in the desert and 35 in the Sierra snows. Only 47 arrived at Sutter's Fort.

The Bear Flag Revolt

During the 1840s, many Americans were suspicious of the US government's territorial intentions, but in California other Americans were discontented under Mexican rule. In 1846, a small group of Californians organized "The Bear Flag Revolt." Fremont dropped his scientific tag and became head of the militant group that aided in the takeover of California. Twenty-three days after it began, Commodore John Sloat, reacting to news that Mexico and the United States were at war, raised the American flag at Monterey. There was little military action, and hostilities later ceased with the signing of the Treaty of Guadaloupe Hidalgo on February 2, 1848. California had now become part of the United States.

The Mother Lode

A month earlier, one of Sutter's foremen, James Marshall, had been inspecting a millrace when he spotted a few shiny flakes among the pebbles. News of the event leaked out and Marshall's discovery sparked one of history's biggest, most frenzied migrations – the California Gold Rush. Crews abandoned their ships in San Francisco and farmers left their land. New settlements sprang up, prices soared and speculations ballooned, fed by the thousands who poured across the continent by land or by sea to their El Dorado. Violence was common; often the only official justice was the hangman's rope. Some newcomers were well educated, and often new towns had opera houses and their own "society." Mexican miners called it the "Mother Lode" country, "La Veta Madre."

The gold was in a rich vein, primarily on the western slopes of the Sierra Nevada. Prospectors were lured to the West from all parts of the world by extravagant claims that gold littered the hillsides. Incredibly, in a few places this was true. A 195-pound nugget was found near Carson Hill.

The Gold Rush

Almost 550 mining towns were built during the first hectic years of the Gold Rush. Only about half remain today. The others withered and died

Miners of Forty-nine. NY Public Library.

like the hopes of most miners. A few of these cities, such as Sonora, Placerville and Grass Valley, have grown and prospered through agriculture, lumbering and the lure of millions of tourists to this magnificent country. State Route 49 runs the length of the Mother Lode country. Many of the weather-worn buildings of the Gold Rush period survive to enchant each new generation. There are historical parks along the route, ghost towns and empty mines to remind you of the old days.

Although the richest gold-bearing quartz was only a mile wide and 150 miles long, the Mother Lode extends about 245 miles, from Mariposa to Sierra City. Trails worn by gold miners are now major highways, such as I-80 and US 50, making travel easy along east-west routes.

The gold played out in the late 1850s and the state went through several boom and bust cycles. The completion of the transcontinental railroads and large-scale agricultural developments created an economy with more permanence than gold mining.

California Today

After the Gold Rush, California's growth was first sparked by the automobile and the state's almost ideal climate. People came by the millions seeking a better way of life, and most of them found it. Huge cities, such as Los Angeles and San Francisco, grew at a phenomenal rate as farmers left the Midwest, blacks left the segregated South, and Asians and Latin Americans hurried to the promised land. Despite a long recession, California has become a diverse society in which no single industry is dominant. It is the center for film and television production; the entertainment industry employs more than 200,000 men and women. Although aircraft and spacecraft industries are but a shadow of their former greatness, they are both important to California's economy. Tourism is a huge business, providing jobs for 681,000 Californians and producing $54 billion in income for the state.

Agriculture has always been a staple California product. This is the nation's leading agricultural state due to its mild climate and productive soil. Half of the fruits, nuts and vegetables grown in the nation come from California's farms. Its vineyards, more than 800 of them, produce a high percentage of the wine bottled in America; much of it is premium quality.

Sierra Nevada Today

Fortunately for the Sierra Nevada, it has not known the spectacular growth of other regions, although it has been suffering from over-usage in recent years. One-fifth of Sierra land has experienced a decline in native land animals. Two-thirds of its streams are degraded and almost 90% of the oldest and largest trees no longer exist in national forests. There are urgent plans under consideration to create a system of forest reserves, by adopting a "slow-growth" strategy that will limit development of "flammable wild lands." Under consideration is a proposal to scale back by 40% the amount of land now available for new construction. At the present rate of growth nearly half of the remaining open land will be consumed by human settlement. The area's growth over the next 50 years is estimated at anywhere from 650,000 to two million new people. This would have a serious impact on the Sierra environment. It has also been recommended that limitations be put on sulfur emissions from oil refineries and chemical plants in the San Francisco area and in the San Joaquin Valley. Agricultural burning would be eliminated during summer months in Sierra communities as well.

Some of the fastest-growing local communities have been faulted for not monitoring the effects of growth on the environment. Chiefly responsible are conversion and fragmentation of wildlife habitats, introduction of non-native plants and animals, and the damage caused to watersheds by construction, operation and contamination by overtaxed sewer systems. If given a chance, nature has a remarkable capability of restoring itself to health, but it needs cooperation from people. The Sierra Nevada is rich in plant and animal diversity, with more than 3,500 native species of plants and 400 species of mammals, birds, reptiles and amphibians.

The Sierra Crest

With the ridge of high peaks of the Sierra Nevada mountains forming its backbone, the high country is a superb setting for outdoor recreation. Natural attractions range from emerald-hued Lake Tahoe to the sparkling Mammoth Lakes and majestic Mount Whitney. This region has three of the nation's most beautiful national parks – Yosemite, Kings Canyon and Sequoia. There are other places equally magnificent, including Devils Postpile National Monument, Mono Lake National Recreation Area and a number of wilderness areas and smaller state parks. There are virtually unlimited opportunities for year-round sports – many on public lands. There's downhill and cross-country skiing at dozens of winter resorts and, in the summer months, boating on numerous lakes. Fishing is superb on wild and scenic rivers while more energetic vacationers can pack in to the backcountry.

The Sierra Nevada remains one of the earth's most fascinating regions. It will provide boundless enjoyment for those who appreciate its beauty and grandeur, and respect its fragility.

Getting Here & Getting Around

From southwestern California, the most direct route to the Sierra Nevada is north out of the Los Angeles area on I-5. After leaving the San Fernando Valley, you'll probably want to choose which side of the Sierra to visit first: the western slopes (rolling, oak-dotted foothills; Yosemite Village; Kings Canyon and Sequoia national parks; gold country; whitewater rafting) or the eastern side (Inyo National Forest; Mt. Whitney, the tallest point in the Lower 48; Mammoth Lakes; Devil's Postpile; Mono Lake).

If you're headed **for the west side**, continue north on I-5 over Tejon Pass and the Grapevine to CA 99. Note that Tejon Pass, elevation 4,144 feet, is commonly closed or bottled up by snow, so allow plenty of driving time during inclement weather. Proceed due north on CA 99 toward the gateway cities of Bakersfield, Fresno, Merced, Modesto, Stockton and, eventually, Sacramento.

To access the east side of the Sierra, follow the signs for CA 14 north through Lancaster, Palmdale and Mojave. At Inyokern, a tiny town in Indian Wells Valley, CA 14 becomes US 395 and continues north through the small burgs of Lone Pine, Independence, Bishop, Mammoth Lakes, Lee Vining and Bridgeport before crossing into Nevada. US 395 eventually leads to Nevada's capital, Carson City.

From southeastern California and Arizona, get thee to Barstow in the middle of the Mojave Desert. From Barstow follow lonely CA 58 west for 30 miles to US 395 north to reach the eastern Sierra, or continue west through Mojave, over Tehachapi Pass (4,065 feet) and into Bakersfield to reach CA 99 and the western Sierra.

From Las Vegas, you can take I-15 south to Barstow and follow the above directions, or drive north from Vegas on US 95, slide west through Death Valley National Park (site of Badwater, lowest point in the US) and pick up US 395 near Lone Pine (just 30 miles from the highest point in the US outside Alaska).

From the San Francisco Bay Area, most folks simply take I-80 east all the way to the northern end of Lake Tahoe, or if they're headed for South Lake Tahoe, leave I-80 at Sacramento and drive US 50 east through the heart of gold country. At Placerville in the Sierra foothills, US 50 intersects with CA 49, named in a stroke of tourist industry genius to commemorate the discovery of gold here in 1848. CA 49 rolls south through Gold Country all the way to Yosemite National Park. From Sacramento, drivers can also pick up CA 99 for a quick run to the central and southern Sierra.

Across the Sierra Crest

Thankfully, the Sierra Nevada has never been the road builder's best friend. If you don't count the CA 178/CA 190 connection, which runs around and across the extreme southern tip of the mountain range in Kern County, there are only six highways over the Sierra crest between southern California and Lake Tahoe. Three of those roadways are closed in winter, which in the unpredictable high country can begin as early as September and last into June in extreme cases.

To go from west to east or vice-versa year-round in Sierra country, you can use Interstate 80 north of Lake Tahoe, US 50 south of Lake Tahoe in El Dorado County, or nearby CA 88. But keep in mind that even these roads are subject to closure during severe weather. The three seasonal highways, in order from north to south, are CA 4 between Stockton and US 395 at the Nevada border; CA 108 between Sonora and US 395 near Bridgeport; and the famous Tioga Pass Road, which runs through Yosemite's high country between CA 120 and the town of Lee Vining.

> The **California Department of Transportation** maintains a toll-free number for statewide road conditions, ☎ 800-427-7623.

Highway Border Crossings

California is a world leader in the production of agricultural products and livestock, and the state does its utmost to protect these interests. Near every highway border crossing, the **California Department of Food and**

Agriculture operates inspection stations charged with regulating the entry of produce, plants and wild animals. Don't be surprised if you are stopped and asked if you are carrying any fruits or vegetables, especially if you have out-of-state license plates. These people are not the Thought Police or the vanguard of some vast government conspiracy, but simply hard-working state employees trying to keep alien pests out of local fields. Your cooperation is helpful. If you have any questions about what you can and can't bring into California, call ☎ 916-654-0312. Note that dogs older than four months must be accompanied by a current rabies certificate.

Information

If you're looking for an information source that you don't see listed in this guide, try contacting any of the following for details.

General Information

California Division of Tourism, PO Box 1499, Sacramento, CA 95812, ☎ 800-462-2543.

State Parks

California State Park System, Department of Parks and Recreation, PO Box 942896, Sacramento, CA 94296, ☎ 916-653-6995. For stste park camping reservations, contact **Destinet**, 9450 Carroll Park Drive, San Diego, CA 92120, ☎ 800-444-7275.

National Forests

US Forest Service, 630 Sansome Street, Room 807, San Francisco, CA 94111, ☎ 800-365-2267.

National Parks

National Park Service, Fort Mason, Building 201, San Francisco, CA 94123, ☎ 415-556-0560.

Other Public Land

Bureau of Land Management, 2135 Butano Drive, Sacramento, CA 95825. ☎ 916-978-4610.

US Bureau of Land Management, 2800 Cottage Way, Sacramento, CA 95825. ☎ 916-978-4400.

US Bureau of Reclamation, 2800 Cottage Way, Sacramento, CA 95822. ☎ 916-978-4919.

Fishing & Hunting

Department of Fish & Game, 1416 9th Street, Sacramento, CA 95814, ☎ 916-653-7664. For fishing and hunting licenses, ☎ 916-227-2244.

Transportation

California Department of Transportation, Public Information, 1120 N Street, Sacramento, CA 95814. For road conditions, ☎ 800-427-7623.

The Eastern Sierra Nevada

1. Donner Summit
2. Donner Memorial State Park
3. Squaw Valley
4. Sugar Pine Pt. State Park
5. Emerald Bay State Park
6. Desolation Wild Area
7. DL Bliss State Park
8. Mokelumne Wilderness
9. Grover Hot Springs State Park
10. Emigrant Wilderness
11. Hetch Hetchy Reservoir
12. Hoover Wilderness
13. Bodie State Hist. Park
14. Ansel Adams Wilderness
15. Half Dome
16. Yosemite Falls
17. Devils Postpile Nat'l Monument
18. Kaiser Wilderness
19. Dinkey Lakes Wilderness
20. Golden Trout Wilderness
21. South Sierra Wilderness
22. Dome Lands Wilderness
23. John Muir Wilderness

© 2000 HUNTER PUBLISHING, INC.

The Eastern Sierra

The eastern slopes of the Sierra Nevada provide magnificent views of the Sierra Crest and a myriad of recreational opportunities, such as the best skiing in California on the alpine meadows of Mammoth and June Mountains, and Bodie (a preserved ghost town). Mono Lake features geological wonders and hundreds of other lakes and streams are renowned for their fishing.

(%) Days of Sunshine	Max-Min Temperature
Winter 74%	44°-16°
Spring 77%	60°-32°
Summer 80%	79°-45°
Fall 79%	51°-35°

Owens Valley

Owens Valley, at 4,000 feet, is a high-plains landscape replete with glorious fall colors, gorgeous spring wildflowers, and year-round fishing in the Owens River. The Pleasant Valley Reservoir area (☎ 619-878-2411) features hang gliding, biking and equestrian activities for outdoor adventurists. From Owens Valley you can access the southeastern corner of the Sierra. This land of dry, blazing summers and frozen, damp winters is best visited in spring and fall.

Adventures on Foot
Dome Lands Wilderness

Dome Lands Wilderness, the Sierra Nevada's southernmost federally designated wilderness, is situated northwest of the Owens Valley. Its uncrowded spaces are a welcome respite for backpackers used to fighting for wilderness permits on the busier trails of the central and northern Sierra. The most convenient access to Dome Lands from US 395 is via County J41 (Nine Mile Canyon Road) between Pearsonville and Little Lake. From US 395, follow County J41 north 11 miles to the Bureau of Land Management Ranger Station and turn left onto a rough, unpaved road. Proceed seven miles, passing Chimney Creek campground, to the wilderness boundary. From here you can pick up trails to see for yourself the region's namesake granite spires, pinnacles, outcrops and domes, formed by a process called exfoliation, in which slabs of granite peel away like onion skin over millions of years.

Pick up the **Rockhouse Basin Trail** and hike near the Kern River, the perfect place to wet a line or take an afternoon dip, especially during the oven-like summer months. You might stay with the Kern or take one of the side trails up and out of the V-shaped Kern River Canyon to add some aerobic exercise to your trek. Try **Manter Creek Trail** to the summit of White Dome (elevation 7,555 feet), six miles from the trailhead, and enjoy the views down the canyon. For a 23-mile loop, opt for **Dome Lands Trail**, which runs lateral to Tibbetts Creek to **Woodpecker Trail**, turn south, and escape to Manter Meadow. From here pick up Manter Creek Trail and follow it back to **Rockhouse Basin Trail**, where you pick up the trail back to your vehicle. For more information on Dome Lands Wilderness, including details on permits, contact the **Sequoia National Forest Cannell Meadow Ranger District**, ☎ 619-376-3781.

Golden Trout Wilderness

Golden Trout Wilderness and the area adjacent to it are also prime hiking and backpacking spots that are usually devoid of crowds, except during busy summer weekends. Situated just north of Dome Lands, Golden Trout Wilderness is named for the state fish, which is endemic to this region of the southern Sierra. A great springboard into the backcountry is at **Troy Meadows**. From US 395 on the east side of the Sierra, take County J41 (Nine Mile Canyon Road) north for 31 miles. J41 becomes Sherman Pass Road on the way to Troy Meadows, which has a campground. From the campground you can take **Smith Meadow Trail** (which becomes **Black Rock Trail**) to **Jordan Hot Springs Trail** headed west. This path leads to the site of the abandoned resort that was once operated near the springs, about 5½ miles from the trailhead. You can extend the hike to an overnighter by continuing on Jordan Hot Springs Trail, turning south at **Lion Trail**, then right on **Hells Hole Trail**. Along the way, Ninemile Creek plunges over a series of waterfalls. The trail ends at Hell's Hole, 11½ miles from the start.

For more information on Golden Trout Wilderness, contact the **Sequoia National Forest Cannell Meadow Ranger District**, ☎ 619-376-3781, or **Inyo National Forest Mount Whitney Ranger District**, ☎ 619-876-6200.

Kennedy Meadows

From County J41 you can also access Kennedy Meadows, located between the BLM Ranger Station and the Sherman Pass Road turnoff. Kennedy Meadows is a popular hiking and horseback riding staging area and a stop on the Pacific Crest Trail. It is also the access point for the **South Sierra Wilderness**, 63,000 acres of meadows, tree-lined ridges, rolling hills and craggy, peaks hiding 30 miles of hiking and equestrian trails. From here you can hike north 63 miles to **Mt. Whitney**, the highest point in the Lower 48 states and the southern terminus of the John Muir Trail. You can also head south 50 miles to Walker Pass.

Lone Pine

Highway 395 traverses the primary region from Bridgeport to Olancha through the eastern side of the Sierra Nevada. Lone Pine, the first important stop on 395, is 193 miles from San Bernardino. Together with Bishop and Mammoth Lakes, it is the primary outfitting area.

Backpacking can be enjoyed in many of these areas. The John Muir Trail, extending from the summit of Mt. Whitney to Yosemite National Park, is the best-known backcountry trail.

What to See & Do

Lone Pine is the closest community to **Mt. Whitney**. To reach the mountain, take the Whitney Portal Road west for about 10 miles, and you'll be within 11 miles of the summit. A trail takes you to the top at 14,494 feet – the highest peak in the contiguous United States. **Alabama Hills**, a few miles northwest of Lone Pine, is noted for the films that have been made there. The area is a mass of weather-beaten rocks bordering the highway. A **film festival** is held here on Columbus Day weekend in October to celebrate the region's more than 70 years of filmmaking. There's a parade, visits to film locations, an arts and crafts fair, a movie memorabilia show, a pit barbecue and western dancing.

In mid-May there's a 100-mile **Death Valley-to-Mt.-Whitney bike race**. It starts at Stovepipe Wells in Nevada and ends at Whitney Portal. Bikers spend the night in Lone Pine.

Also in May, on Mother's Day, there's a **26-mile marathon** from Lone Pine across the foot of the Sierras below Mt. Whitney. The return walk is through the Alabama Hills. ☎ 760-876-4444 for information.

There's a **pack train** that leaves Lone Pine on the Whitney Portal Road leading to Shepherds Sawmill and Taboose passes. In addition, there are short trips to Kings Canyon and Sequoia. Write **Whitney Pack Trains**, PO Box 248, Bishop, CA 93515, or ☎ 760-935-4493 in summer or 872-8331 in the off-season.

Adventures on Foot
The Mt. Whitney Trail

The Mt. Whitney Trail is easily the most beaten path in the Sierra, maybe even the most popular trail in the country. If you are craving a solitary backcountry experience, look elsewhere. The path to the highest point in the Lower 48 attracts Lycra-clad tourists from around the world, who jump at the opportunity to drive a well-paved road all the way up to the trailhead at 8,361 feet, then bag the peak at 14,494. As many as 300 people a day knock boots on this famous 11-mile path. The crazies are actually intent on completing the round trip in a 24-hour period. Some make it, many don't.

There are other pristine trails in the vicinity of Mt. Whitney where you won't have to jockey for position while you eat lunch beside a gurgling brook, nor wait in line for a seat in a solar latrine. But if you must check off Whitney from your life list, there are hoops to jump through and serious precautions to take.

When three local fishermen, Charley Begole, Johnny Lucas and Al Johnson, became the first to summit Whitney in August, 1873, they could have had no idea that 125 years later folks would be forced to book a spot on the trail half a year in advance. Between May 22 and October 15, the US Forest Service requires both day and overnight hikers to obtain a wilderness permit for the Mt. Whitney Trail, which can be reserved up to six months before the day of departure. Do not waste a minute, as quotas for Fridays, Saturdays and holidays in June, July, August and September fill up very quickly. Call the **Inyo National Forest Wilderness Reservation Service** at ☎ 888-374-3773 or 760-938-1136, or fax them at 760-938-1137. The phone lines are open 8 AM to 4:30 PM Pacific time, Monday through Friday, but are closed between October 30 and November 22.

Between October 16 and May 23, only overnight hikers need a permit, which can be issued at the Forest Service station in Lone Pine, 640 South Main Street, 93545. At press time overnight permits were $3 each plus $1 per person. Day hike permits were $2 per person.

Acclimating to high altitude is required before the hike, and the most convenient place to do it is at **Whitney Portal campground**, set at 8,000 feet and just a quarter-mile from the trailhead. Reserve your campsite as soon as you book your permit by calling ☎ 800-280-2067.

> *Once you've mastered the logistics, the hike might seem easy by comparison. But just because this trail is extremely popular, it's not to be taken lightly. One of the keys to safe hiking in the High Sierra is acclimatization, giving your body ample time and fuel to adjust to*

high altitudes. Because of the dramatic elevation gain on the Mt. Whitney Trail, spend as much time as possible at altitude prior to beginning your hike and hydrate, hydrate, hydrate. Do not expect to drive up from Lone Pine and begin hiking without getting sick.

The trailhead is 14 miles west of Lone Pine via Whitney Portal Road. Adjacent to the trailhead is the **Mt. Whitney Store**, a small T-shirt shop and snack stand, and the last place to inquire about trail conditions. If you plan on completing the hike in one day, give yourself at least 14 hours, longer if the trail is not completely clear of snow and ice.

The hike begins by climbing gently, switchbacking through stands of bone-dry sagebrush and sinewy pinyon pine. After crossing Carillon Creek, the path splashes through the North Fork of Lone Pine Creek .8 mile from the start, offering stunning over-the-shoulder views of sunrise over the White Mountains through the V-shaped canyon mouth.

Two more miles of moderate climbing through a thickening forest of willow and lodgepole pine lead to a perky waterfall formed by Lone Pine Creek. Just around a corner the cutoff to Lone Pine Lake – a cerulean pond just off the main path – leads down to the left. Mt. Whitney Trail continues westward, the forest thinning to reveal jaw-dropping views of the vertical granite walls so characteristic of the eastern Sierra. The path levels out at Bighorn Meadow and soon reaches **Outpost Camp** (3.6 miles from the trailhead, 10,360 feet above sea level), an often crowded overnight spot with a solar latrine. This is one of two areas on the trail open to camping. Fires are prohibited.

From Outpost Camp, Mt. Whitney Trail climbs aggressively toward **Mirror Lake** (4.3 miles, 10,640 feet), resting in a large cirque below the towering ramparts of Thor Peak. You lose sight of Whitney's summit here, but the view of Mirror Lake from the trail as you climb the southern wall of the cirque is literally breathtaking. For many flatlanders, this is where the thin air becomes all too apparent, as you zig-zag between boulders on the now treeless trail. This is also where your acclimatization and hydration pay off.

If you are a native flat-lander, be prepared for the symptoms of altitude sickness – nausea, dizziness, headache, fatigue and disorientation are most common – and heed them well. If you or one of your group becomes ill, descend immediately.

Soon the footpath skirts the unimaginatively named **Trailside Meadow** at 5.3 miles (don't be fooled by the five-mile marker stenciled on a nearby boulder). This is a good resting spot, but be careful not to tread on the fragile high-country flowers and grasses. Another mile of climbing in this gorgeously austere world brings you to **Trail Camp** (12,039 feet), a popular stopping point for campers. A pond here is the last reliable watering hole, so fill up your water bottles. Be sure to use the solar latrine unless you plan on packing out your waste later.

Beyond Trail Camp lie the infamous 96 (or 98 or 100, depending on who's counting) switchbacks that take you up 1,738 feet of elevation in just over two miles to **Trail Crest** (13,777 feet). It might seem obvious that the exposed switchbacks comprise the toughest part of the trek, but many hikers report that the final push to the summit beyond Trail Crest is actually more punishing because the peak seems so tantalizingly close. Beyond Trail Crest, the path actually descends briefly to a junction with the John Muir Trail (9.0 miles, 13,480 feet), then begins an ascent of another 1,015 feet over two miles to the summit. The final segment of the trail requires some boulder-hopping and careful footwork, often difficult when your brain is screaming for oxygen.

On a clear day, the views from the peak stretch 100 miles in a 360° alpine nirvana. The High Sierras roll on to the north, with the Great Western Divide visible in the northwest. The Kaweah Peaks lay to the west, and to the east are the 11,000-foot Inyo Mountains, looking like lumps of brown sugar far below. Whitney's little sister, Mt. Langley (14,027 feet), is due south about five miles.

A stone hut standing on Whitney's summit was built in 1909 by the Smithsonian. Camping is allowed on the summit, and while it's a rush to snooze in America's penthouse for about the price of a McDonald's Happy Meal, be prepared for wicked weather, and have plenty of water.

> Unless you are properly outfitted for a night on the exposed granite, it is important to be off the summit before the Sierra's infamous afternoon thunderheads roll up, and in plenty of time to get down before nightfall. Unless, that is, you are familiar with hiking down rocky trails by moonlight.

For more information, contact the **Inyo National Forest Mt. Whitney Ranger Station** in Lone Pine, ☎ 760-876-6200.

Meysan Lake

Within a pine cone's throw of Whitney Portal is a trail that sees just a tiny percentage of the hordes that crowd the Mt. Whitney Trail. Yet the trek to Meysan Lake is every bit as beautiful and perhaps even more strenuous. The trail leaves the east side of Whitney Portal campground and climbs four miles to Meysan Lake, gaining a thigh-thumping 3,900 feet along the way. At 3.3 miles you'll come upon **Grass Lake**, having gained more than 3,400 feet. The final push to Meysan Lake includes a bit of off-trail scrambling to reach the lake, set in a glacial cirque surrounded by the Sierra. Above are the granite guardians – from north to south, Mt. Irvine, Mt. Mallory and Mt. LeConte – all topping out above 13,000 feet.

Backpacking to Mt. Whitney

If the idea of stomping up the Mt. Whitney Trail alongside hundreds of hikers is about as appetizing as crowding onto the 7:30 train on a Monday morning, consider reaching the summit via one of the backcountry routes. One of the best options is a multi-day, 42-mile backpacking trek through some of the grandest high country in the Sierra.

The hike begins on Inyo National Forest land outside of Lone Pine, California, and rolls through the southern portion of the John Muir Wilderness. You'll set boots on portions of both the Pacific Crest Trail and John Muir Trail. A wilderness permit is required for all overnight stays. During the quota period of the last Friday in June through September 15, permits can be reserved by calling ☎ 888-374-3773 or 760-938-1136, or by faxing 760-938-1137. The phone lines are open 8 AM to 4:30 PM, Monday through Friday, and permits cost $3 plus $1 per person. While this is one of the more popular trails in the area, especially on weekends, the daily quota of 60 people per day keeps waffle-stomper gridlock to a minimum.

The trailhead for Cottonwood Lakes and the exit point at Whitney Portal are more than 30 miles apart, so arrange a car shuttle before lighting out. To reach the trailhead from Lone Pine, drive three miles west on Whitney Portal Road to Horseshoe Meadow Road and turn left. Continue about 20 miles up this precipitous two-lane to the signed parking area for **Cottonwood Lakes Trail** leading to New Army Pass. The hike begins at 10,090 feet, so expect a headache if you haven't acclimated properly.

The trail begins on a flat, dusty footpath in a forest of pines, heading west and then north along Cottonwood Creek. Cross and recross the creek several times before entering the John Muir Wilderness boundary and beginning a steady climb. The trail gains 400 feet in elevation and turns west just before reaching Cottonwood Basin. Continue west through the alpine meadows (avoiding side trails heading north) and skirt **Cottonwood Lakes #1 and #2**, which in 1998 were opened to catch-and-release fishing for the first time in 32 years.

The trail continues west past **Long Lake** (5½ miles, 11,135 feet) and **High Lake** toward the imposing, gray granite walls that ring this basin and begins a thigh-burning climb to New Army Pass. High above timberline, this moonscape is not the place to be caught during an infamous Sierra thunderstorm. From the pass at 11,475 feet, the trail descends to the northwest, entering Sequoia National Park and heading down into the Rock Creek drainage.

Turn right on the trail toward Soldier Lakes and continue through heavenly meadow country, keeping an eye out for The Major General commanding the horizon to the northeast. At a creek 2.8 miles from New Army Pass, turn left and head west again, then descend to cross Rock Creek (14½ miles, 9,525 feet). The path continues to lose altitude until hitting a junction with a trail heading south to Siberian Pass. Continue straight ahead on what is now the **Pacific Crest Trail**, through more meadows, and switchback up a ridge to find the Guyot Creek crossing and, beyond that, Guyout Flat, in the shadow of-you guessed it – Mount Guyot.

The trail continues north and descends again to idyllic **Upper Crabtree Meadow** (21.3 miles, 10,320 feet). On a clear day, you'll be able to see Mt. Whitney's spire beckoning on the eastern horizon. Hike on this flat portion northeast from the meadow to a junction with the John Muir Trail and bear right, then continue east past the Crabtree Ranger Station. Begin ascending in earnest, following Whitney Creek past tiny **Timberline Lake** toward larger **Guitar Lake** (the resemblance to a guitar is quite uncanny when viewing the lake from the east), nestled right up against the backside of the towering eastern Sierras.

Here's hoping that granite and thin air are to your liking, because that's all there is from here to Trail Crest, a killer of a climb that tops out at 13,590 feet, 27½ miles from the Cottonwood Lakes trailhead you departed days ago. The lookout from Trail Crest is staggering, offering views all the way across the Owens Valley to the White Mountains on the eastern skyline. Your lungs will be crying for oxygen, but take some delight in the tortured faces of the beleaguered hikers coming from the east side who are trying to summit Mt. Whitney in a single day. From here the well-worn trail heads north toward Whitney, passing Mt. Muir and Keeler Needle on its two-mile course to the peak at 14,494 feet.

Begin the journey home by heading back to Trail Crest and turning left, then descending the nearly 100 switchbacks to **Trail Camp**, 4.7 miles from the peak. Although a very popular spot, this might be a good place to rest up for the night. That's **Consultation Lake** below to the right. Two miles beyond Trail Camp is exquisite little **Mirror Lake** (no camping allowed), and half a mile farther is **Outpost Camp**, with its solar latrine. From here Mt. Whitney Trail continues 3.8 miles to your exit point at Whitney Portal.

For more information, contact the **Inyo National Forest Mt. Whitney Ranger Station** in Lone Pine, ☎ 760-876-6200.

Cottonwood Lakes

If the biggest, boldest, most beautiful trout in the Sierra Nevada are what you cotton for, Cottonwood Lakes is the place. Set in their namesake basin high in the southern Sierra outside of Lone Pine, the Cottonwood Lakes are a quintet of glistening sapphires – unimaginatively named Cottonwood 1 through 5 – that are some of the best-kept secrets in California.

Actually, Cottonwood 5 has been known for years to those hale and hearty anglers who could manage the strenuous seven-mile hike to an elevation of 11,000 feet. The real story now is Cottonwood Lakes 1, 2, 3, and 4, which are closer to the trailhead and open to fishing for the first time in more than 30 years.

The three-mile hike to Cottonwood 1 begins on a wide, level trail that meanders through stands of ponderosa pine and soon enters the John Muir Wilderness. The first half of the journey winds through a shallow valley overshadowed by the granite massif rising to the north. As the trail climbs gradually, it crosses Cottonwood Creek and skirts the edges of several meadows, their lush green carpets dotted with wildflowers just begging to be napped upon. But don't stop now: Voracious mosquitoes are on the prowl on the cooler, moister sections of the trail, making some kind of repellent a necessity.

Cottonwood 1 is at 11,008 feet, only 968 feet above the trailhead, but the high altitude plus the fact that almost all the climbing is done on the second half of the hike make for a rather strenuous approach. The path switchbacks time and again through the forest, then climbs almost straight up a series of stone steps before finally levelling out at the signed Cottonwood Basin. This is the perfect place to rest and revel in the awesome panorama of the Eastern Sierra, with its sharp, gray, granite backbone scraping the impossibly blue sky.

For more information, contact the **Inyo National Forest Mt. Whitney Ranger Station** in Lone Pine, ☎ 760-876-6200.

Adventures on Water
Cottonwood Lakes

LBJ was in the White House the last time some lucky fisherman wet a line in the lower portion of Cottonwood Basin. In 1918, the California Department of Fish and Game began using the Cottonwood Lakes as breeding ponds for golden trout, the official state fish. Things went swimmingly until 1966, when the DFG made all but the least-accessible lake, Cottonwood 5, off-limits to protect the breeding stock.

But over the past 30 years, rainbow trout have infiltrated the ponds and the DFG has been charged by California's Wild Trout program with opening at least one lake and 25 miles of stream each year. These two factors prompted the department to reopen Cottonwood 1 through 4 in 1998.

For the angler, of course, this means a somewhat shorter hike to find golden trout that are hungry and fearless. The Cottonwood Lakes trailhead is located 24 miles from the town of Lone Pine at a lung-clenching 10,040 feet.

The five lakes are spread out around the basin and can all be visited in a single long day if you get an early start. Try a fly rod or ultra-light spincast rig loaded with four-pound test. Only artificial lures with barbless hooks are allowed in the lakes; no live bait or Powerbait. Try the smallest dry flies in your tackle box. Catch-and-release rules apply at all the lakes except Cottonwood 5.

Where to Stay

Alabama Hills Inn is 1½ miles south on 395 at 1920 S. Main Street, 93545. Rates for one or two people and one bed are $48, and $58 for two beds. Pets are allowed for a $5 fee. ☎ 760-876-8700.

Best Western's Frontier Motel is a half-mile south on 395 at 1008 Main Street, 93545. $-$$. ☎ 760-876-5571.

The **Dow Villa Motel**, winner of three diamonds from the Auto Club, is in the center of town at 310 South Main Street and is much nicer inside than it looks outside. All 42 rooms have a refrigerator, coffee maker, premium cable TV and direct-dial phones with data ports. $$. ☎ 800-824-9317; www.sierranet.net/web/motel/dowvilla.

The **National 9 Trails Motel** is one-third of a mile south of Lone Pine at 633 South Main Street. There are 17 rooms opening onto the parking lot. $$. ☎ 760-876-4650.

The **Portal Motel**, located at 425 South Main Street, offers 17 rooms and that's about it. $-$$. ☎ 760-876-5930.

Where to Dine

Merry Go Round Dinner House is on 395 at 212 S. Main St. American dinners range from $11 to $20 and are served from 5-10 PM. ☎ 760-876-4115.

Seasons is on 395 at 206 S. Main St. Open from 11:30-2 and 5-9, it serves traditional and continental food. ☎ 760-876-8926.

Independence

What to See & Do

Independence is the next community driving north on Highway 395. Of minor importance to travelers, **Camp Independence** was established in 1862 to protect Owens Valley settlers from Indian attacks. The **commander's house** is a stately wood-frame Victorian-style structure that was rebuilt at its present location in 1889 after the camp was abandoned in 1877. It is open from Memorial Day to Labor Day, Saturday and Sunday from noon until 4 PM. The **Eastern California Museum** on Grant Street has displays that include an exhibit of the Manzanar World War II Japanese-American camp. Paiute and Shoshone artifacts are on display along with early mining and farm equipment. The museum is open daily from 10-4, and closed on Tuesdays and major holidays.

Where to Stay

Ray's Den, at 405 North Edwards Street, is the one and only place to hibernate. There are eight rooms. $-$$. ☎ 760-878-2122.

Big Pine

What to See & Do

Big Pine, with a population of 1,500, is next on Highway 395 as it continues north. It is the center for mountain recreation and the starting point for trips to the alpine area where a forest of bristle cone pines has grown for centuries. Some of these gnarled trees are more than 4,000 years old – far older than the redwoods.

Adventures on Foot
Onion Valley

West of Independence, up the eastern wall of the Sierra, is one of California's highest trailheads that can be reached by passenger car. From Independence take Onion Valley Road west as it winds up and up from US 395. Pass Independence Creek, Lower Grays Meadow and Upper Grays Meadow campgrounds on the way to a dead-end at Onion Valley trailhead, 13½ miles from town. The elevation here is a dizzying 9,100 feet. There are a number of great hiking and horseback riding trails that depart from here into the John Muir Wilderness and Kings Canyon National Park, which lies just over the Sierra crest.

> Keep in mind that special bear-proofing regulations might apply in the Onion Valley area as a result of an invasion of habituated bears. Check with Inyo National Forest Rangers in Bishop, ☎ 760-873-2500 for more information.

From the Onion Valley Trailhead, there's a 1.4-mile trail to **Robinson Lake** that gains 1,380 on the way to the water's edge. Look for the trailhead on the south side of the parking area. On the north side of the parking lot you'll find the trail to **Golden Trout Lake**. Start by climbing 1½ miles to a trail junction. Bear left and proceed .6 mile to tiny Golden Trout Lake, directly under Kearsarge Peak. With nary a tree or bush in sight, Golden Trout Lake is a favorite for those who like to nap on exposed rock.

Serious hikers will head due west, and straight up Onion Valley to Kearsarge Pass, elevation 11,823 feet. The trail passes near Gilbert Lake, Flower Lake, Heart Lake (named for its romantic shape) and Big Pothole Lake (named for its unromantic shape) on the way up to the pass. In just 3½ miles the path gains 3,000 feet, making it one of the toughest, and shortest, routes to the Sierra crest, which keeps this trail buzzing with hikers all summer long.

From Kearsarge Pass, it's another three miles west to the **John Muir Trail**. You can follow the JMT south for less than two miles to Bubbs Creek, where you cross into Kings Canyon National Park. From here a well-used trail heads west, parallel to the creek, all the way to Road's End at the bottom of Kings Canyon, a total of 20½ miles from the Onion Valley Trailhead.

North Fork Trail

North of Independence along US 395, Glacier Lodge Road heads west out of Big Pine into the Sierra. From the trailhead, 10 miles up the canyon at the end of the road, you can hike to the largest glacier in the Sierra, **Palisade Glacier**. The walk is nine miles one way. Light out on North Fork Trail, beginning at 7,800 feet, and pass First Falls and Second Falls. Paralleling the north fork of Big Pine Creek, the trail reaches a fork at 4.4 miles after gaining 2,300 feet. Bear left and pass First, Second and Third lakes, climbing gradually for another 1.6 miles to another junction. Look to the south for a view of the glacier, then turn left and head for it. Climb steeply to **Sam Mack Meadow** and reach the icy toes of the glacier after a final cross-country scramble, nine miles from the start. Unless you equipped for and experienced in ice climbing, stay off the glacier. Retrace your steps back to the trailhead. You can return via Fourth and Black lakes to complete a partial loop hike by staying left at the next intersection, 1.7 miles down the trail, then turning right at the next junction. Hike down canyon to reach the north fork of Big Pine Creek one the way back to the parking area.

Adventures on Water
Fishing Between Lone Pine & Big Pine

You'll find the best fishing in this area at the following locations. A wilderness permit is necessary if you remain overnight. In all but one instance these fishing spots are in remote areas. **Big Pine Lakes** include eight Lakes. Lake Eight has golden trout while the others have brook, brown and rainbow trout; **Black Lake** has brook trout; **Cottonwood**'s 13 lakes have golden trout in lakes One through Five. The others are open from July to October 5 for trout fishing, but with a five fish catch limit, and you can only use barbless, artificial lures. **Diaz Lake** can be reached by car. It is three miles south of Lone Pine on 395. You can fish for bass, bluegill, catfish and rainbow trout. Swimming and water skiing are permitted at Diaz Lake. **Golden Trout Lakes** are at elevations of 11,000-12,000 feet. Brook and golden trout can be caught at these four lakes. **Heart, Flower and Gilbert Lakes** have brook, brown and rainbow trout. Hidden Lake has only golden trout. **Kearsage Lakes** have rainbow trout. **Lone Pine Lake** has only golden trout. **Long Lake** has brook, brown and rainbow trout. **Sam Mack Lake** is at 12,000 feet and has brook trout. **Treasure Lakes** is a series of nine lakes at 12,000 feet with golden trout. **Willow Lake** has brook and rainbow trout.

Where to Stay

The **Big Pine Motel** is on US 395 at 370 Main Street. $ throughout the year. Pets are permitted. ☎ 760-938-2282.

The **Starlight Motel** is on 395 at 511 South Main Street. $. ☎ 760-938-2011.

Camping
Public Campgrounds – Lone Pine to Bishop

There are many fine public campgrounds between Lone Pine and Big Pine, which is 44 miles farther north. Pets are permitted in all of them. **Baker Creek** is at an elevation of 4,000 feet and located one mile northwest of Big Pine, off US 395 on Baker Creek Road. It is open all year for $5 a night. There are 70 tent or RV sites, limited to 35-foot RVs. Each has chemical toilets, piped water, tables, barbecues and fire rings. There are places to fish nearby. **Big Pine Creek** is 10 miles southwest of Big Pine off Glacier Lodge Road, at an elevation of 7,700 feet. It has chemical toilets, piped water, tables, barbecues and fire rings. The site is accessible to those in wheelchairs. There are 12 tent sites and another 18 tent or RV sites, with a 45-foot RV limit. It is open from May to October for $8 per night, but reservations are required. ☎ 800-280-2267. **Big Pine Triangle** is half a mile north at the junction of 395 and State Route 168, at an elevation of 4,000 feet. There are 40 tent or RV sites, with a 40-foot RV limit. It is open all year and provides swimming, fishing and a playground. It is wheelchair accessible. **Goodale Creek** is 14 miles northwest of Independence on 395, at 4,100 feet. It is open March through October, and there is no fee. ☎ 760-872-4881.

Gray's Meadow is at 6,000 feet, five miles west of Independence on Onion Valley Road. There are 52 tent or RV sites, with a 45-foot RV limit. It is open March through mid-October by reservation, with a $7 fee. ☎ 800-280-2267. **Independence Creek** is a half-mile west of Independence on Onion Valley Road, at an elevation of 3,800 feet. It has 25 tent or RV sites, with a 31-foot RV limit. It is accessible to wheelchairs and is open all year for a $5 fee. ☎ 760-878-2411. **Lone Pine Campground** is at 6,000 feet, and seven miles west of town off Whitney Portal Road. It has 43 tent or RV sites, with a 45-foot RV limit. It is open all year by reservation, but there's no water in winter. The fee is $7. ☎ 800-280-2267. **Oak Creek** is 4½ miles north of Independence, off US 395. There are 43 tent or RV sites, with a 45-foot RV limit. It is open from mid-April until mid-October, with a $6 fee. ☎ 760-873-2400. **Onion Valley** is 14 miles west of Independence on Onion Valley Road at an elevation of 9,200 feet. It has 29 tent sites and is open June through mid-September by reservation. ☎ 800-280-2267. **Portagee Joe**, at an elevation of 3,900 feet, is one mile southwest of Lone Pine off Whitney Portal Road, with 15 tent or RV sites. It is open all year, with a $6 fee. ☎ 760-876-5656. **Sage Flat** is eight miles southwest of Big Pine on Glacier Lodge Road, at an elevation of 7,400 feet. Its 28 tent or RV sites, with a 45-foot limit, are $8. It is open from April to November. ☎ 760-878-2400. **Tinnemaha** is seven miles south of Big Pine on 395, at 4,000 feet. Its 55 tent or RV sites are $5, and it is open all year. ☎ 760-878-2411. **Turtle Creek** is six miles southwest of Lone Pine off Horseshoe Meadows Road, at an elevation of 5,120 feet. It is open March through October, and there's no fee. ☎ 760-872-4881. **Upper Sage Flat** is at 7,600 feet and 8½ miles southwest of Big Pine, on Glacier Lodge Road. It has 21 tent or RV sites, with a 45-foot RV limit. It is accessible by wheelchairs, and is open May to October by reservations, with an $8 fee. ☎ 800-280-2267. **Whitney Portal** is at 8,000 feet, and 13 miles west of Lone Pine on Glacier Lodge

Road. Its 21 tent or RV sites, with a 44-foot RV limit, are priced at $10. It is open from mid-May to mid-October by reservation. ☎ 800-280-2267. The **Whitney Group Camp** is at an elevation of 8,100 feet. It is 13 miles west of Lone Pine on Whitney Portal Road and is open from mid-May to mid-October by reservation. ☎ 800-280-2267. The fee is $25.

Private Campgrounds - Lone Pine to Bishop

There are quite a number of privately owned campgrounds, and the three best are listed below. **Boulder Creek RV Park** is four miles south of Lone Pine, at 2550 Highway 395. At an elevation of 3,700 feet, it has 29 RV sites and another 29 with electricity. It has the usual facilities but also includes a place to purchase groceries and propane. With a pool, playground and cable television, it is open all year by reservation at $22 for two people and an additional dollar for each person beyond two. Write in care of PO Box 870, Lone Pine CA 93514. ☎ 760-876-4243. The **Foothill Mobile Home Park** is four miles south of Lone Pine on 395, at an elevation of 3,700 feet. It has 12 RV sites, six of which have electricity and is open all year at a fee of $12 for four people and $2 for each extra person. Write to PO Box 762, Lone Pine, 93545. ☎ 760-876-4120. **Fort Independence Campground** is 2½ miles north of Independence on 395. At an elevation of 3,900 feet, it has 10 tent and 38 RV sites; 40 of the sites have electricity and water. It is open all year at $15 per RV site, and $8 for tent space. Write PO Box 67, Independence, 93526. ☎ 760-878-2910.

Where to Dine

Rosie's Steak and Spaghetti Restaurant has meals for $11-20. It is located on 395 at 100 N. Main St. It is open from 5:30 PM to 10 PM, but closed on major holidays. It serves American food and is smoke-free. It would be wise to obtain reservations on weekends. ☎ 760-938-2254.

Bishop

What to See & Do

Bishop is near the northern end of the Owens Valley, about 15 miles from Big Pine. This community of 3,700 people is located between the state's two highest mountain ranges. It is the center of a large recreational and resort area. **Bishop Creek Canyon** is west of the town on Bishop Creek Highway (State Route 168) and within **Inyo National Forest.** It is lined by striking 1,000-foot granite cliffs. The creek flows through the canyon, dropping 400 feet per mile for 14 miles, creating a wild tumble of sparkling water. Such is the force of the flow that it has been harnessed to produce electricity in a series of dams. In the fall, the surrounding aspen groves in the canyon give the area a spectacular beauty. Several interesting events are held, including the **Blake Jones Early Opening Sierra Trout Derby** in early March, Memorial Day weekend's **Mule Days** and the **Tri-County Fair/Wild West weekend** over Labor Day. For details, ☎ 760-873-8905.

Adventures on Foot - Bishop to Mammoth
Hiking

West of the town of Bishop, high on the eastern wall of the Sierra Nevada, there are a number of fantastic trails that lead into the mountains. From Bishop, take CA 168 into **Bishop Creek Canyon**. The stunning canyon is lined with 1,000-foot-high granite cliffs that explode with autumn colors in the fall. The creek, although dammed in spots to produce electricity, tumbles down 400 feet per mile for 14 miles.

Continue 17 miles to the turnoff to North Lake on the right and follow the spur road to the trailhead, near the Bishop Pack Outfitters station. For a rather strenuous 5.2-mile round-trip that gains 1,600 feet on the way up, take the **Lamarck Lakes Trail** southwest through a forest of dreamy aspen and across two footbridges as it heads into the high country. Pass the spur trail to Grass Lake at .7 mile and continue up through a series of steep switchbacks to 10,200 feet, where the trail becomes a boulder-bordered path pointed toward the Sierra crest. You'll reach **Lower Lamarck Lake** at two miles, then **Upper Lamarck Lake** after crossing about half a mile later.

The **Paiute Pass Trail** (30E01), which leads due west from the road's end, stretches all the way up and over the Sierra crest, climbing 2,300 feet in 4.4 miles. Along the way you can dip your toes in the chilly waters of **Loch Leven** and **Piute** (sic) **Lake**. You can turn this day hike into a multiday backpack by continuing west over the pass into Humphrey's Basin and the John Muir Wilderness. This is also the border between the Inyo National Forest on the east and the Sierra National Forest on the west. Hike on what is now called **Piute Canyon Trail** near a dozen small lakes including **Upper and Lower Golden Trout**, **Tomahawk** and **Knob**. About 6½ miles west of Paiute Pass the trail reaches a junction at Hutchinson Meadow. From here you can travel southwest toward the Glacier Divide and an intersection with the **John Muir Trail/Pacific Crest Trail** five miles distant, or north on the **French Canyon Trail** 4½ miles to Pine Creek Pass. From the pass you can head west, deeper into the wilderness

The Pacific Crest Trail

The Eastern Sierra

toward Lake Thomas A. Edison, north into the popular Little Lakes Valley and Pioneer Basin, or east to a trailhead and road end at Pine Creek Road.

It's easy to begin a hike in **Little Lakes Valley**, as well, by taking US 395 to the town of Tom's Place and heading southwest on Rock Creek Road all the way to the trailhead near Rock Creek Lake. From here it's only about 4½ miles south to the heart of Little Lakes Valley, a slice of heaven on earth. Here emerald meadows and sapphire waters combine to dazzle the senses, all set in a forest nook topped by the 13,000-feet-plus peaks of Bear Creek Spire, Mt. Abbot and Mt. Mills. If this land doesn't make you forget your troubles, nothing will.

You can also head north into the Sierra over Mono Pass (12,000 feet) into the John Muir Wilderness and Pioneer Basin. At the six-mile mark you'll hit a junction with the **Mono Creek Trail**, which leads west and deep into the backcountry. **Golden Lake** is just a mile to the west, and the **Pioneer Basin Trail** leads 2½ miles into the basin.

Rock Climbing the Gorge

If you're cruising US 395 and hanker for a mind-blowing rock climbing experience, ask anyone you see wearing Lycra and climbing shoes to point the way to the Gorge. This slit carved by the Owens River offers an eight-mile stretch of world-class climbing that attracts rock jocks from across the globe. If the usually friendly locals aren't willing to divulge any secrets, just take US 395 north from Bishop about 14 miles to Gorge Road and turn right. Proceed east for half a mile, then turn left. Continue north for three miles to the first parking area.

If the area is crowded, you can continue north for another 1½ miles to a dirt road. Follow the power lines toward the Gorge, where you'll find a steep scramble to the bottom. Finally, you can opt for the north parking area by driving another 1½ miles.

Most of the routes in the area are well anchored and rated 5.10 to 5.12. Verticals and slight overhangs are the dominant features. The volcanic tuff can be murder on your ropes, so locals in the know suggest using a rope bag and taking at least 180 feet of line.

> To get the most out of the gorge, consult Martin Lewis's excellent book, ***Owens River Gorge Climbs***, now in its eighth edition. The guide is available in local sports shops or direct from the author by writing to Martin Lewis Publishing, PO Box 3952, Mammoth Lakes, CA 93546.

Adventures on Wheels - Bishop

Biking

While mountain bikes are prohibited from trails in the federally protected wilderness areas in the Sierra west of Bishop, that shouldn't stop you from powering out on a ride in the flatlands near town. Much of the landscape is as unique as it is unforgettable.

North of Bishop, drive seven miles on US 395 to the turnoff for **Pleasant Valley Road** and head north. After parking, unload the bikes and head northeast toward the Owens River, which is dammed here to form Pleasant Valley Reservoir. While much of the Owens Valley is dry and seemingly inhospitable to life, the river is a moving oasis for lush, green plants, tall trees, shrubs and wildlife of many shapes and sizes. The dirt road here passes through such a verdant environment. You'll first ride through a meadow and across Mill Creek before heading down in to the riparian lowlands. Continue past Pleasant Valley campground, across the **Owens River** and along the reservoir. Before long the water narrows to a river again, and aspen, cottonwood and willow trees line the cool banks. The road eventually leads to a power plant, about 5½ miles from the beginning of the ride. From here retrace your tire tracks back to your vehicle.

For a look at the other extreme of Owens Valley, arid, out-of-this-world volcanic terrain that speaks of the region's violent past, pick up unpaved **Chalk Bluffs Road** just past the Pleasant Valley campground and turn left. This road leads into the **Volcanic Tableland**, a vast expanse of sagebrush and pink tuff. The road curves north and approaches a set of power lines. You'll soon turn right and follow the power lines across the Tableland and, 7½ miles from the start, turn right on **Casa Diablo Road** (4S04) and head back toward the Owens River. Nine miles later you'll reach a five-way junction. Turn right and ride alongside the river for five miles, through a gap between two boulders and past Pleasant Valley campground to reach the road you came in on.

Off-Road Driving

If you've got an off-highway vehicle, or even a rugged sport-utility vehicle, check out two dazzling drives near Bishop. The **White Mountains Loop** (okay, this isn't the Sierra Nevada, but close enough) begins just east of Bishop off US 6. Take Silver Canyon Road east. The unpaved, twisting and steep road runs about 11 miles into the White Mountains and is not for the faint of heart. At the top of Silver Canyon Road, where the road ends at a T intersection, you'll be near the **Ancient Bristlecone Pine Forest**, home to the trees that are some of the oldest living things on Earth. You can take the **Ancient Bristlecone Pine National Scenic Byway** (4S01) north toward the White Mountain Natural Area and all the way toward White Mountain Research Station at 11,650 feet. You can also turn south on 4S01 for a short drive to paved White Mountain Road, which leads back to CA 168 and, eventually, to Big Pine. Allow a whole day for this trek if you visit the end of 4S01. The total distance is about 50 miles.

Another excellent excursion begins on the south side of Bishop and travels 55 miles out and back. Take **Underwood Lane** toward the southwest corner of town. Where the street curves right at a power station, turn right onto a sandy road. Stay left at a fork four miles from the start and follow **Fireroad 7S10** another eight miles on Inyo National Forest land to another fork. Turn left and proceed toward **Coyote Flat**, crossing a creek. Look to the southwest for views of Palisade Glacier. The road bears right at the foot of Sugarloaf Peak and ends near a campground on Baker Creek near the John Muir Wilderness Boundary.

Choosing a Mountain Guide

Finding the right mountain guide can not only make the difference between having a pleasant or miserable holiday, but also between coming back safely or on a stretcher. Here are a few suggestions for seeking out a guide.

- **AMGA Certification:** Ask if your prospective guide is certified by the American Mountain Guide Association. Professionals are not only experienced climbers and skiers but also teachers and safety experts. The AMGA provides the only national training and testing procedures for mountain guides. These standards comprise the only internationally recognized system for qualifying guides in the US. AMGA certified guides are qualified on the basis of exacting standards.
- **Local Knowledge**: Is the guide service actually based locally? It's best to hire someone with the local expertise that only a guide from the area will have, rather than a big-city outfit that trucks in guides for the high season.
- **Experience**: Are they familiar with the route or trip on which you are asking them to accompany your group?
- **Group Size**: Most services have maximum client-to-guide ratios. Group sizes can vary from one guide service to another, so find out if you will be with a group of 12 or four, or in between.
- **Permit and Insurance**: All outfitters should have government-issued permits to operate on public lands. Don't be too shy to ask about insurance coverage, and read any releases or waivers carefully before signing them.

Adventures on Water
Best Fishing Spots
Between Bishop & Mammoth Lakes

The following are the best fishing grounds along the eastern slopes of the Sierra Nevada. Trout are in all streams and lakes and those that have other types of fish will be so noted.

Barney Lake, at 10,000 feet, has brook and rainbow trout. **Big McGee Lake**, at 10,557 feet, has brook and rainbow trout. **Blue Lake**, at 10,200 feet, has brook and rainbow trout. **Convict Lake**, at 7,580 feet, has brook, rainbow and brown trout. It is accessible by automobile and is 13 miles northwest of Toms Place, off 395, on Convict Lake Road. **Crowley Lake**, at 6,781 feet, has brook, brown, rainbow, and cutthroat trout and Sacramento perch. It can be reached by car four miles north of Toms Place, off 395. **Davis Lake** is at an elevation of 9,800 feet, and has brook, brown and rainbow trout. **Dingleberry Lake** is at an altitude of 10,650 feet, and has brook trout. **Fish Slough Pine** has bass and catfish, and is located six miles north of Bishop, at an elevation of 4,300 feet.

Fourth Recess Lake is at 9,704 feet and has brook and rainbow trout. **French Canyon** is at 11,000 feet, with 20 lakes two to six acres in size. It has golden trout. **Garnet Lake**, at 9,704 feet, has brook and rainbow trout. **George Lake** is at 10,700 feet, with brook and rainbow trout. **Green Lake**, at 11,050 feet, has rainbow trout. The **Hilton Creek Lakes**, 10 in all, range in altitude from 9,800 feet to 11,360 feet. They have brook, brown, golden and rainbow trout. **Horseshoe Lake** can be reached by car six miles west of Mammoth Lakes, off State Route 203, at an elevation of 8,800 feet. It has brook and rainbow trout. Swimming is permitted. **Humphreys Basin** is composed of 20 lakes at 11,000 feet, with brook and golden trout. **Lake Genevieve**, at 9,910 feet, has only brook trout. **Lake George**, at 8,800 feet, can be reached by car. It is six miles west of Mammoth Lakes, off State Route 203. It has brook and rainbow trout. **Lake Mamie**, at 8,800 feet, can be reached by car, 5½ miles west of Mammoth Lakes, off State Route 203. It has brook, brown, and rainbow trout. **Lake Mary** is five miles west of Mammoth Lakes, off State Route 203. It is at an altitude of 8,931 feet. There are brook, rainbow, and brown trout.

Lake Sabrina can be reached by car or shuttle bus, 17 miles southwest of Bishop, on State Route 168. It has brown, brook and rainbow trout. **Lake Valentine** is at 9,900 feet. It has only brook trout. **Lake Virginia** is at 10,319 feet, with golden trout. The **Larmarck Lakes** are at 10,300-11,000 feet. The two lakes have brook and rainbow trout. **Little Lakes Valley**, at 9,700 feet, has 29 lakes with brook, brown, golden and rainbow trout. The **Marie Louise Lakes** are at 10,550 feet, with brook trout.

North Lake, at 9,700 feet, can be reached by car. It is 20 miles southwest of Bishop, off State Route 168. It has brook and rainbow trout. **Pine Lake** is at 9,862 feet, with brook and rainbow trout. **Pleasant Valley Reservoir**, at 4,200 feet, has brown and rainbow trout. **Purple Lake**, at 9,862 feet has brook and rainbow trout. **Rock Creek Lake,** at 9,682 feet, has brook, brown and rainbow trout. It can be reached by car by driving eight miles southwest of Toms Place, on Rock Creek Road. **Sotcher Lake** is at 7,650 feet, with brown and rainbow trout. It can be reached by car or shuttle bus. It is 11 miles west of Mammoth Lakes, on State Route 203. **South Lake**, at 9,750 feet, has brook, crown and rainbow trout. It is 22 miles southwest of Bishop, off State Route 168. The **Tamarack Lakes**, at 11,660 feet, have golden trout. **Twin Lakes**, at 8,480, feet has brook, brown, and rainbow trout. It is four miles west of Mammoth Lakes, off State Route 203.

> *Fishing regulations are outlined in Appendix A. Please note that wilderness permits are required for overnight use.*

Where to Stay

There are two **Best Western** motels in Bishop, each equally good:

The **Creekside Inn** is a half mile north of US 395, at 725 N. Main Street. It is open from May 16 to September 30. $$-$$$. It permits only small pets. There's a nearby restaurant. ☎ 760-872-3044.

The **Holiday Spa Lodge**, 1025 North Main Street. $$. ☎ 760-873-3543. **Bishop Days Inn**, $$, does not permit pets. It is located west of 395, at the corner of Home Avenue at 724 W. Line Street, 93514. ☎ 760-872-1095. **Bishop Inn** is a half of a mile north of 395, at 805 N. Main Street, 93514. Pets are permitted. $$. ☎ 760-873-4284. The **Chalfant Bed and Breakfast House**, an early American-style house built in 1898, is just west of 395, at 213 Academy Street, 93514. $$-$$$. ☎ 760-872-1790. There's an apartment for two to four people priced at $90-120.

Camping

Public Campgrounds - Bishop to Mammoth

Highway 395 swings to the west. In this area there are a great many public campgrounds. Unless noted, they all have chemical toilets, piped water, tables, barbecues and fire rings, and they accept pets. We present them here in alphabetical order.

Agnews Meadows is 9½ miles northwest of the towen of Mammoth Lakes off State Route 203 – Minaret Summit Road – at an elevation of 8,400 feet. It has 22 tent or RV sites, with a 55-foot RV limit. It is open mid-June through late October, with an $8 nightly fee. ☎ 760-873-2400. **Agnews Meadows Group Camp** is nearby. RVs are not permitted. It is open from mid-June through early October by reservation. Fees are $20-35. ☎ 800-280-2267. The **Aspen Group Camp** is at 8,100 feet, three miles southwest of Toms Place on Rock Creek Road. It is open from mid-May to mid-October by reservation. The fee is $40. ☎ 800-280-2267.

Big Meadow, at an elevation of 8,600 feet, is four miles south of Toms Place on Rock Creek Road. There are five tent or RV sites, with a 45-foot RV limit. It is open from July to September for a $10 nightly fee. ☎ 760-873-2400. **Big Springs** is 10 miles north of Mammoth Lakes, at an elevation of 7,300 feet. There are 24 tent or RV sites, with a 45-foot RV limit. It is open from late May to mid-October, and there are no fees. ☎ 760-873-2400. **Big Trees** is at an elevation of 7,500 feet and 12½ miles southwest of Bishop on State Route 168. There are nine tent or RV sites, with a 45-foot RV limit. It is open from July to September with an $8 fee. ☎ 760-873-2400.

Bishop Park, at an elevation of 7,500 feet, is 14½ miles southwest of Bishop on State Route 168. There are six tent sites and 16 tent or RV sites, with a 45-foot RV limit, at $8. The camp is wheelchair accessible and is open from May through October. ☎ 760-873-2400. **Bishop Park Group Camp**, at 7,500 feet, is 14½ miles southwest of Bishop on State Route 168. It is open from May through mid-October by reservation. The fee is $40. ☎ 800-280-2267. **Camp High Sierra**, at 8,499 feet, is two miles southwest of Mammoth Lakes, on State Route 203. There are 12 RV and 30 tent or RV sites, with a 30-foot RV limit. It is wheelchair accessible and open June through September for fees ranging of $10-15. Some primitive cabins can be reserved at $20-25. ☎ 760-934-2368.

Coldwater is 4½ miles southwest of Mammoth Lakes on Lake Mary Road, at an elevation of 8,900 feet. There are 77 tent or RV sites, with a 45-foot RV limit. It is open from mid-June through late September for a $11 fee. ☎ 760-873-2400. **Convict Lake**, at 7,600 feet, is 10½ miles southwest of Mammoth Lakes off Highway 395. It has 88 tent or RV sites, and a 50-foot RV limit. It is open in late April through October at $10 a site. ☎ 760-873-2400. **Crowley Lake** is six miles northwest of Toms Place off 395, with 47 tent or RV sites at $6. ☎ 760-872-4881. It is open March through May . **Dead Man** is four miles southwest of Crestview, off 395, at 7,800 feet. It has 30 tent or RV sites, with a 45-foot RV limit. It is open June to mid-October and there's no fee. ☎ 760-872-2400.

Devil's Postpile National Monument is 13½ miles west of Mammoth Lakes on State Route 203 at 7,560 feet. It has 21 tent or RV sites. It is open from June to mid-October with an $8 fee. ☎ 760-934-2289. East Fork is at

9,000 feet and five miles south of Toms Place, on Rock Creek Road. It has 53 tent and 80 tent or RV sites, with a 45-foot RV limit. It is open late May through October and has a $10 fee. ☎ 760-873-2400. **Forks** is 13 miles southwest of Bishop on State Route 168, at 7,800 feet, with eight tent or RV sites, with a 45-foot RV limit. It is open from May to mid-September for a $8 fee. **Four Jeffrey** is 13½ miles southwest of Bishop on State Route 168, at 7,800 feet. It has 53 tent-only and 80 tent or RV sites, with a 45-foot RV limit. It is open from late April through October for an $8 fee. ☎ 760-873-2400.

French Camp, at an elevation of 7,500 feet, is a quarter of a mile south of Toms Place, on Rock Creed Road. It has six tent sites and 80 tent or RV sites, with a 45-foot RV limit. It is open April through October for a fee of $10. ☎ 760-873-2400. **Glass Creek** is at 7,600 feet, and a quarter of a mile west of Crestview, off 395. There are 50 tent or RV sites, with a 45-foot RV limit. ☎ 760-873-2400. **Hartley Springs** is three miles north of Crestview off 395 at 8,400 feet. It has 20 tent or RV sites, with a 45-foot RV limit, and charges no fee. It is open June to mid-September. ☎ 760-873-2400. **Holiday,** at 7,500 feet, is half a mile southeast of Toms Place, off 395. There are 35 tent or RV sites, with a 45-foot RV limit, and a fee of $10. This is an overflow campground that is opened as needed. ☎ 760-873-2400. The **Horseshoe Lake Group Camp** is at 8,950 feet, seven miles southwest of Mammoth Lakes, off Lake Mary Road. Its six sites have limited RV access. It is open from mid-June to mid-September by reservation, at a fee of $20 to $25. ☎ 800-280-2267.

The **Horton Creek Recreation Site,** at 4,900 feet, is 13 miles northwest of Bishop, on 395. It has 52 tent sites or RV sites. It charges no fee. ☎ 760-872-4881. **Intak**e is at 7,500 feet, three miles south of Toms Place, on Rock Creek Road. It has 14 tent and 16 tent or RV sites, with a 45-foot RV limit. It is open July to September with a $10 fee. ☎ 760-873-2400. **Iris Meadows** is three miles south of Toms Place, off Lake Mary Road, at 9000 feet. It charges $10 for 16 tent or RV sites, with a 20-foot RV limit. ☎ 760-873-2400. **Lake George**, at an elevation of 9,000 feet, is five miles southwest of Mammoth Lakes, off Lake Mary Road. It is open from mid-June to mid-September with an $11 fee. ☎ 760-873-2400. **Lake Mary**, at 8,900 feet, is four miles southwest of Mammoth Lakes, off 395, on McGee Creek Road. It has 28 tent or RV sites, with a 45-foot RV limit. It is open from late April to mid-September for an $11 fee. ☎ 760-873-2400.

McGee Creek is 10 miles west of Mammoth Lakes, off State Route 203, with 28 tent or RV sites, with a 45-foot RV limit, for an $8 fee. It is open late April through October by reservation. ☎ 800-280-2267. **Minaret Falls** is four miles southwest of Mammoth Lakes, off State Route 203, on Minaret Summit Road. The camp is at 7,400 feet and sites must be reserved at a fee of $8. It is open from mid-June to late October. ☎ 760-873-2400. **Mono**

Creek is at 7,400 feet, four miles southwest of Lake Thomas A. Edison. Its 14 tent or RV sites, with a 16-foot RV limit, are priced at $10. It is open from June through September by reservation. ☎ 760-487-5155. **New Shady Rest,** at 7,800 feet, is half a mile east of Mammoth Lakes, off State Route 203. There are 51 tent or RV sites, with a 55-foot RV limit. It is open from mid-June to early September at $9 a site. There is no fee throughout the winter for tent-only, walk-in camping. ☎ 760-873-2400.

Palisade is five miles south of Toms Place, on Rock Creek Road, at an elevation of 8,600 feet. There are only two tent and three tent or RV sites, with a 45-foot RV limit. It is open from July to September for $10 a site. ☎ 760-873-2400. **Pine City**, at 8,900 feet, is four miles southwest of Mammoth Lakes off Lake Mary Road. It has 10 tent or RV sites, with a 50-foot RV limit. It is open from mid-June until mid-September, for an $11 site fee. ☎ 760-873-2400. **Pine Glen Group Camp**, at the eastern edge of Mammoth Lakes, is three miles west of 395, at 7,760 feet. It is wheelchair accessible and is open from late May to late September by reservation at $20-35 a night. ☎ 800-280-2267. **Pine Grove**, at 9,300 feet, is 6½ miles south of Toms Place, on Rock Creek Road, with five tent and six tent or RV sites, and a 25-foot RV limit. It is open from late May to October, with sites at $8. ☎ 760-873-2400. **Pleasant Valley** is seven miles northwest of Bishop, at 4,200 feet off 395. It is open all year for a $6 fee. ☎ 760-878-2411.

Pumice Flat is at 7,700 feet and 11½ miles west of Mammoth Lakes off State Route 203–Minaret Summit Road. It has 17 tent or RV sites, with a 55-foot RV limit. It is open from mid-June through mid-September for a nightly fee of $8. ☎ 760-873-2400. **Pumice Flat Group Camp** is 11 miles west of Mammoth Lakes, off State Route 203–Minaret Summit Road, at 7,700 feet. It has four sites. It is open from late January to mid-September by reservation, and a fee of $20-45. ☎ 800-280-2267. **Red's Meadow** is at 7,600 feet and 14 miles southwest of Mammoth Lakes, off State Route 203 (Minaret Summit Road). It has 56 tent or RV sites, with a 55-foot RV limit. $8 fee. ☎ 760-874-2400.

Rock Creek Lake is at 9,699 feet and eight miles south of Toms Place, off Rock Creek Road. It has 10 tent sites and is open from May through November for an $8 fee. ☎ 760-873-2400. **Rock Creek Lake Group Camp** is at 9,600 feet and eight miles south of Toms Place, on Rock Creek Road, with 10 tent sites at $40. It is open from mid-June through mid-October by reservation. ☎ 800-280-2267. **Sabrina** is at 9,000 feet and 16½ miles southwest of Bishop, on State Route 168. It has 20 RV and 18 tent or RV sites, with a 45-foot RV limit. It is open from May to September at $8 a night. ☎ 760-873-2400. **Sherwin Creek** is three miles southeast of Mammoth Lakes, off State Route 203, on Sherwin Creek Road, at 7,600 feet. It has 87 tent or RV sites, with a 50-foot RV limit. It is open from late April to mid-September by reservation. $10 fee. ☎ 800-280-2267.

Soda Springs is at 7,700 feet and 11 miles west of Mammoth Lakes, off State Route 203–Minaret Summit Road. It has 29 tent or RV sites, with a 45-foot RV limit. It is open from mid-June to late October for $7. ☎ 760-873-2400. **Tuff** is at 7,000 feet and a half mile northwest of Toms Place, on 395. There are 34 tent or RV sites, with a 45-foot RV limit. It is open from mid-April to mid-October by reservation for $8 a night. ☎ 800-280-2267. **Twin Lakes**, at an elevation of more that 8,700 feet, is three miles southwest of Mammoth Lakes, via Lake Mary Road. The 21 tent or RV sites are open from late May through October for $11 a night. ☎ 760-873-2400. **Upper Pine Grove** is at 9,300 feet and 6½ miles south of Toms Place, on Rock Creek Road, with eight tent or RV sites, with a 45-foot RV limit. It is open from July to October, with sites for $10. ☎ 760-873-2400. **Vermilion** is at Lake Thomas A. Edison, with 11 tent and 20 tent or RV sites, and a 16-foot RV limit. It's at an elevation of 7,700 feet, and open from June through October for a $10 nightly fee. ☎ 760-487-5155. **Willows** is at 9,000 feet and 18 miles southwest of Bishop, off State Route 168. It has seven tent or RV sites, with a 45-foot RV limit. The fee is $8 and it is open from May to October. ☎ 760-873-2400.

Private Campgrounds – Bishop to Mammoth Lakes

These camps have all the amenities of the public camps but with many added services such as grocery stores, swimming facilities and nearby fishing. The best of them are listed below.

Brown's Owens River Campground, at 6,800 feet and 14 miles southwest of Mammoth Lakes, is off 395, on Bentron Crossing Road. It has 75 tent or RV sites, and is open from May through September by reservation with fees of $10 for four people and $1 for each additional person. Write 219 Wye Road, Bishop, CA 93514. ☎ 760-872-0216. **Brown's Town Campground**, at 4,200 feet, is 1.25 miles south of Bishop, on 395, with 150 tent or RV sites – 44 have electricity and water. It is open from March through November by reservation and a fee of $22 for up to six people. There's an extra person charge of $1 to $2. Write Route 1. Bishop, CA 93514. ☎ 760-873-8522. **Creekside RV Park** is two miles north of Bishop, at 2275 Sierra Highway, at 4,300 feet. It has 49 tent or RV sites. Forty-two have electricity and water, and 30 have flush toilets. Propane is available here. Pets are acceptable, but there's a fee of $1. It is open from May through mid-October by reservationn. Fee is $18 for two people, and $1 to $2 for each extra person. Write Box 30, South Lake Road, Bishop, CA 93514. ☎ 760-873-4483.

The **Highlands RV Park** is at 4,200 feet and two miles north of Bishop, at 2275 N. Sierra Highway. It has 102 RV sites; all are electrified. It is open all year by reservation at $18 for two, and $1 for each extra person. Propane is available here. Write 2275 N. Sierra Highway, Bishop, CA 93514.

☎ 760-873-7612. **Mammoth Mountain RV Park** is a quarter-mile east of Bishop, on State Route 203, with 134 RV sites, and eight tent or RV sites without electricity in the summer. It is open all year by reservation for $25 for two people and $4 for each extra person. Write PO Box 288 Mammoth Lakes, CA 93546. ☎ 760-934-3822.

Where to Dine

The **Brass Bell** is on 395 at 635 Main St. It is open from 11-2 and 5-9, serving American food priced at $11-20. ☎ 760-872-1200. The **Fire-House Grill**, on 395 2206 N. Sierra Highway, serves American food and is open from 4:30-10 PM. ☎ 760-873-4888. The **Whiskey Creek Homestyle Fare Restaurant** is a third of a mile north of 395, at 524 N. Main St., and is open from 7 AM to 9 PM, May 31 to October 1. ☎ 760-873-7174.

Mammoth Lakes

What to See & Do

After leaving Bishop, the sights become more interesting and exciting, especially when you reach Mammoth Lakes, 35 miles from Bishop. En route you'll pass **Lake Crowley**, long known as a marvelous recreation and fishing area. ☎ 800-845-7922.

Mammoth Lakes, with a population of 4,800, is at an altitude of 7,860 feet. It is one of California's most popular all-season resorts. It provides access to recreational facilities and points of interest in the **Inyo National Forest**, which contains 6,100 miles of hiking trails. The recreation area encompasses 200,00 acres, including portions of the Pacific Crest Trail, the John Muir Trail and the Devil's Postpile. For details, ☎ 760-924-5500.

Adventures on Snow
Downhill Skiing

Ranked among the best downhill skiing and snowboarding destinations in America, **Mammoth Mountain** attracts all types of winter recreationists from Olympic-level athletes to first-time skiers. Mammoth Mountain rises to 11,053 feet and is home to 3,500 acres of skiable terrain. The resort offers 28 lifts, 150 trails and a vertical drop of 3,100 feet. Terrain is rated 30% beginner, 40% intermediate and 30% advanced. The longest run in a luxurious three miles. Boasting an average annual snowfall of a whopping 353 inches, Mammoth Mountain is known for its winter powder and its warm-weather skiing. The resort claims one of the longest ski seasons in the country, regularly running into June and the 4th of July holiday. In 1995 Mammoth was open for skiing into August.

The ski school offers private, group and family lessons, along with a variety of special programs, including children's ski school, senior ski camps and advanced ski clinics. Custom ski camps, snowboard lessons and video analysis are also offered. Lessons are available at the Main Lodge and at Warming Hut 11.

In December, the mountain's Night of Lights enlivens the area with lights, sounds and colors. Ski races are scheduled throughout the winter, and spring brings sundeck festivities and Easter egg hunts in the snow.

The ski area is open daily, 8:30 AM to 4 PM. All-day lift tickets for the 1999-2000 season were priced at $52 for adults, $39 for teens 13-18 and $26 for kids 7-12 or seniors 65 and over. For more information, ☎ 760-934-0745. For more on Mammoth Mountain snow activities, see page 62-63.

Cross-Country Skiing

The **Sierra Meadows Ranch Ski Touring Center** is on Sherwin Creek Road at Mammoth Lakes. The address is PO Box 4058, Mammoth Lakes, CA 93546. ☎ 760-934-6161. Equipment rentals are available and there's a ski school. It is open Thanksgiving and Christmas holidays and weekends.

The **Tamarack/Rossignol Cross-Country Ski Center** is 2½ miles west of Mammoth Lakes, on Lake Mary Road. It has rentals, a ski school, about 25 miles of trails, a day lodge and cabins. The lodge is open all year; the trails are groomed from mid-November through April 15, subject to snow conditions. Write PO Box 69, Mammoth Lakes, CA 93548. ☎ 760-934-2442.

Adventures on Foot
Bishop & Mammoth Wilderness Packers

There are a number of outfitters that will pack you in to wilderness areas. **Agnew Meadows Pack Outfitters** is eight miles northwest of Mammoth Lakes, on State Route 203. Write PO Box 395, Mammoth Lakes. CA 93545. ☎ 760-934-2345 or 800-292-7758. You can leave from here for the Ansel Adams Wilderness, the Pacific Crest Trail, Yosemite National Park and Shadow and Thousand Island Lakes. The **Bishop Pack Outfitters** is located 18 miles southwest of Bishop, at North Lake. Destinations include the John Muir Wilderness, Inyo and Sierra National Forests and Kings Canyon National Park. Write to Route 1, 247 Cataract Road, Bishop, CA 93514. ☎ 760-873-4785 in summer. **Mammoth Lakes Pack Outfit** is on

Lake Mary Road, between Twin Lakes and Lake Mary. It is set up for day trips, horseback vacations that include fishing and hunting, and horse drives twice a year in the John Muir Wilderness. Write PO Box 61, Mammoth Lakes, CA 93546. ☎ 760-934-2434, fax 760-934-3975.

McGee Creek Pack Station is nine miles north of Toms Place, on McGee Creek Canyon Road. It covers the John Muir and Ansel Adams Wildernesses and Yosemite National Park. Write Box 162, Mammoth Lakes, CA 93546. In summer, ☎ 760-935-4324, 760-878-2207 in the off-season. **Pine Creek Outfitters and Pack Station** is 20 miles northwest of Bishop, on Pine Creek Road. They cover the John Muir Wilderness, Inyo and Sierra National Forests and Kings Canyon National Park. Write PO Box 968, Bishop, CA 93515. ☎ 760-387-2797. **Rainbow Pack Station** is 15 miles southwest of Bishop, on State Route 168 (Line Street.) It covers Bishop Basin, John Muir Wilderness, Sequoia and Kings Canyon. Write PO Box 1791, Bishop, CA 93515. ☎ 800-443-2848. **Red's Meadow Pack Outfit** is 13 miles southwest of Mammoth Lakes, at the end of State Route 203. It covers Yosemite and John Muir and Ansel Adams Wildernesses. Write PO Box 395, Mammoth Lakes, CA 93546. ☎ 760-934-2345 in summer and 873-8331 in the off-season.

Rock Creek Pack Station is 10 miles southwest of Toms Place, at the end of Rock Creek Road. It will take you to the John Muir and Ansel Adams Wildernesses and Yosemite, Kings Canyon and Sequoia National Parks. ☎ 760-935-4493 or 760-972-8331. **Sierra Meadows Equestrian Center** is in Mammoth Lakes, on Sherwin Creek Road. It covers Inyo National Forest. There's a restaurant, barbecues, summer hayrides and winter sleigh riding, day trips and horse boarding. Write PO Box 4058, Mammoth Lakes, CA 93546. ☎ 760-934-6161.

Self-Guided Trails

Self-guided trails in the Mammoth area will take you to four alpine lakes with magnificent views of the mountains, covered with lodgepole and Jeffrey pine forests and unusual geological formations. Contact the US Forest Service, ☎ 760-924-5500, for more information and see below, pages 54-56.

This whole area is ideal for fishing, boating, snowmobiling, cross-country skiing and hiking. Interpretative programs by naturalists are available. The Visitor Center's Ranger Station is open daily from 6 AM to 5 PM, July 1 to mid-September. The fee is $8, but half that for children from age five through 13. ☎ 760-934-2571 for gondola and ski information. For weather information and conditions, ☎ 760-934-6611.

Where to Stay

Mammoth Lakes Travel Lodge (☎ 6209 Minaret Road, Mammoth Lakes, CA 93546) is 1.3 miles west of town on State Route 203, and then north on Minaret Road. Rates are $60-80. There's a restaurant nearby. No pets. ☎ 760-934-8007, or toll-free 800-934-8576. **Mammoth Mountain Inn** is on State Route 203, five miles west of town, adjacent to the Mammoth Mountain Ski Area. This is a popular resort with rooms at $80-165 There's a dining room and coffee shop open from 6 AM to 10 PM, with prices of $8-24. ☎ 760-934-2581. **Quality Inn** is a third of a mile west on State Route 203, PO Box 3507,. Mammoth Lakes, CA 93546. Its rates start at $69 and top out at $109. No pets. There's a restaurant nearby. ☎ 760-934-5114. The **Shilo Inn** is on State Route 203, just east of Old Mammoth Road, PO Box 2179, Mammoth Lakes, CA 93546. Rates are $109-145. No pets. Restaurant nearby. ☎ 760-934-8881.

Where to Dine

The **Chart House** is one block south of State Route 203 and is open 11:30-10, with dinners up to $10. They specialize in steak and seafood. ☎ 760-934-4526. The **Matterhorn Restaurant** is at Alpenhof Lodge and is open from 7-10 AM and from 5:30-10 PM. It features continental food. ☎ 760-934-1369. **Nevada's** has American food priced at $21-30 and is located almost one mile west on State Route 203, at Minaret Road and Main St. ☎ 760-934-4466. **Ocean Harvest Restaurant** is two blocks south of State Route 203, on Old Mammoth Road, serving seafood from 5:50 PM for approximately $20. ☎ 760-934-8539. The **Restaurant at Convict Lake** is four miles south of State Route 203, and two miles west of 395 at Convict Lake turnoff. It serves American food between 11-3 and from 5:30-9:30 PM. ☎ 760-934-3803. Reservations are suggested. **Slocum's Italian and American Grill** is on State Route 203, two blocks west of Old Mammoth Road. Italian dinners are served from 5:30-10 PM, at a price of $11-20. ☎ 760-934-7647.

The Devil's Postpile

What to See & Do

The **Devil's Postpile National Monument** is near Mammoth Lakes and surrounded by Inyo National Forest. It lies at 7,600 feet, with a sheer wall of symmetrical basalt columns more than 60 feet high. They are the centerpiece of this 800-acre monument. This is a remnant of a basalt flow that was worn smooth on top by glacial action. You can walk to the top, where the surface resembles a tile inlay.

Rainbow Falls, two miles by trail from the Postpile, drops the Middle Fork of the San Joaquin River about 100 feet into a deep pool. It is about a half-mile from Red's Meadow. You can stand on a raised landing after descending a steep stairway. At midday the sun shines on the mist, creating all the colors of the rainbow. You can fish here, but hunting is not permitted.

The Postpile can be reached by State Route 203, off Highway 395, heading west. You'll end up at the Mammoth Visitor's Center in the Mammoth Mountain Ski Area's parking lot. There, take a shuttle bus to the Postpile Ranger Station. A half-mile trail leads to the Postpile. Private vehicles are not allowed beyond Minaret Summit, just beyond the ski area's parking lot, during the day, without a campground permit. From early July to Labor Day rangers conduct interpretative walks and campfire programs. Pets are permitted, but they must be on a leash. The monument opens in mid-June and closes October 31. The ranger station is open daily from 8-5, July 1 to Labor Day. The shuttle costs $6, children $5 for the round-trip. Campsites are $8 a night. For further details, ☎ 760-934-2289.

June Lake/Mammoth Lakes

What to See & Do

June Mountain, at June Lake, on State Route 158, has excellent facilities for skiing, with good rental shops. There's a ski school, dining places, a day lodge, warming huts and child care. It is open daily from December to April with a tram, two high-speed quad chairs and five double chairs. Thirty-five percent of the runs are for novices, 45% for intermediate skiers, and 20% for advanced skiers. The longest run is 2½ miles long, with a 2,590 foot vertical drop. The daily adult ticket is $35 for all lifts, $25 for ages 13-18, and $18 for ages seven-12. A season pass costing $1,200 can also be used at Mammoth Mountain. If you purchase it before September 30 each year the price drops to $850. Write PO Box 146, June Lake, CA 93529. ☎ 760-648-7733.

Adventures On Foot
Hiking

With such close proximity to first-class lodging, fine dining and all the accoutrements of Mammoth Lakes, trails in the Mammoth area attract thousands of hikers a year from all over the world. While many of the trails are well traveled, don't take them lightly. Be prepared for changing weather conditions and acclimate, acclimate, acclimate. Know the signs of altitude sickness (headache, nausea, loss of appetite, disorientation) and if you or anyone in your party becomes ill, descend immediately. For more information on hiking in Mammoth and to obtain maps and permits, contact the **Inyo National Forest Mammoth Ranger District**, ☎ 760-934-2505.

One of the most grueling, and perhaps most rewarding, hikes in the Eastern Sierra is found just south of Mammoth Lakes near **Convict Lake**. This strenuous treak covers 15½ miles round-trip and gains 3,000 feet on the way in, but provides access to no fewer than eight high country lakes. While the fisherman crowd little crystal-clear Convict Lake, which is surrounded by soaring granite peaks, and rub elbows in the 88-site campground, you can get above and beyond all the hustle and bustle if you're willing to sweat profusely on the way up. From the intersection of US 395 and CA 203 near Mammoth Lakes, drive 4½ miles south on US 395 to Convict Lake Road and head west. Drive two miles to the end of the road and take a short road leading off to the right when you reach the lake.

Begin at the signed Convict Lake trailhead (elevation 7,600 feet) and hike along the lake's north shore. Soon you'll enter a steep-walled canyon and find yourself walking alongside **Convict Creek**. The trail crosses the creek, which can be extremely hazardous if the water is high. From here it's up and up to an enchanted land of dazzling lakes. The trail actually leads into the John Muir Wilderness and ends at **Dorothy Lake** (elevation 10,340 feet), which hides brook trout and rainbow trout, and her smaller sisters. From Dorothy, a trail heads north toward **Lake Genevieve** (elevation 9,910 feet) and her smaller sisters. Plan on spending at least one night in the high country.

Another standout hike outside of the crush of hikers that sometimes descend on the Mammoth Lakes area is the 11.2-mile round-trip trek to **Valentine Lake**. To reach the trailhead, take US 395 south from CA 203 about two miles and go west on Sherwin Creek Road. Continue 2½ miles to a spur road on the left, which you follow to the trailhead at 7,600 feet above sea level. The hike, which gains 2,100 feet on the way up, is all business from the start, climbing swiftly via a set of tough switchbacks to 8,500 feet. From here the trail parallels **Sherwin Creek**, climbing vertically through two more sets of switchbacks toward Valentine Lake, a little beauty set in a grand bowl surrounded on three sides by the walls of the Sierra.

Closer to town, try the often-overlooked **Upper Crater Meadow** hike, which totals 7.8 miles. To reach the trailhead from downtown Mammoth Lakes, follow Lake Mary Road until it dead ends at **Horseshoe Lake**. The lake is a decent choice for trout fishing and, with its wide beach, even swimming – but don't dawdle here. Find the trailhead on the west side of the lake at 8,900 feet above sea level and head due west. Go straight at each junction, headed into Mammoth Pass. Soon you'll glimpse tiny **McCloud Lake** through the trees just before the trail slowly curves around to the south, climbing steeply. At 2.2 miles the trail forks. Take the left fork toward Upper Crater Meadow, a dreamy spot perfect for lunch that you'll reach at the 3.8-mile mark. Here you'll find a trail junction. Head north on the **Pacific Crest Trail**, noting the Red Cones ahead of you to the northwest, for half a mile to another junction. Bear right, begin a rather steep descent, then take a right at the next fork. At 5.6 miles from the trailhead, you'll reach an intersection with the trail that returns to Horseshoe Lake. Turn left and retrace your steps.

Not too far away is an amazing, and strenuous, 10.2-mile out-and-back hike to lonely **Deer Lakes**. To reach the trailhead at Lake George, take Lake Mary Road of Mammoth Lakes. At Lake Mary, turn south and follow the signs for Lake George. The trailhead, at 9,200 feet above sea level, is located in the northeast corner of the lake near the campground. You ascend quickly, gaining 500 feet in half a mile to an intersection. Head left and begin a series of switchbacks that soon take you to an elevation of 10,200 feet. The trail continues southwest, then due south after ascending to the Mammoth Crest. Hike along the crest for about 2½ miles, at elevations approaching a head-clearing 11,500 feet, before dropping off the west side of the crest toward the three pocket-sized Deer Lakes. Surrounded by boulders, stunted trees and the dark gray Mammoth Crest, the Deer Lakes are a little slice of Eden, with rainbow trout to boot.

Off the southwest end of Lake Mary, past Coldwater Campground, is the parking lot for the **Duck Pass Trail**, providing access to a number of alpine lakes, the Mammoth Crest and some magificent backpacking. A strenuous 8.8-mile out-and-back dayhike up to the crest skirts six lakes on the way up to the trail's namesake, **Duck Lake**. From the sometimes crowded parking lot at elevation 9,200 feet, light out to the southeast through a pine forest. After a mile you'll pass spectacular **Arrowhead Lake** on the left. Next comes **Skelton Lake**, **Red Lake** and **Barney Lake**. At this point you've hiked 2.8 miles and gained 1,300 feet, just in time to begin the switchbacks up the nearly vertical wall of Duck Pass to Mammoth Crest. This is picture-postcard high country, with Duck Lake and Pika Lake visible to the south. The trail leaves Duck Lake behind at 4.4 miles, just over 2,000 feet above the trailhead. From here it's another .8 miles to the junction with the **John Muir Trail**, which leads west to Reds Meadow and south to Purple Lake. You can complete a serious loop hike by heading west about nine miles to a junction with the trail heading back to Horseshoe Lake, bearing right, then left at the next intersection. After reaching Horseshoe Lake, 16 miles from the Duck Pass Trailhead, turn right, skirting the east end of Horseshoe Lake, and head two miles to the Lake George trailhead. Walk through the campground, pick up another trail on the northern tip of Lake George that leads to Lake Barrett. From Lake Barrett, head northeast and exit at Lake Mary. Then walk up the road through Coldwater Campground to the Duck Pass trailhead to complete a 20-mile loop.

If you take the Devil's Postpile shuttle bus up CA 203 through Mammoth Lakes, you'll first pass the Minaret Summit turnoff. Beyond the turnoff the highway shoots north for about two miles to a spur road leading to **Agnew Meadow** and its trailhead. After a short walk to the meadow, it's possible to hike to at least a dozen lakes in a single, long day. Take a trail heading west-southwest across a small creek and alongside the fenced meadow for one mile to a junction. Continue north on the wide and dusty **River Trail** to **Olaine Lake** (2.2 miles from the trailhead). Half a mile later bear left toward **Shadow Lake** and cross the Middle Fork San Juaquin River on a footbridge. At 3.8 miles the trail reaches Shadow Lake and curves around the northern and eastern edges of the lake. The trail eventually heads southwest across Shadow Creek, then turns south and switchbacks painfully through the 9,000-foot plateau on the way to **Rosalie Lake** (5.7 miles from the trailhead), **Gladys Lake** (6.2 miles) and **Emily Lake** (10.1 miles).

Adventures on Horseback
Packers

The **Frontier Pack Station** is four miles west of June Lake at Silver Lake, on State Route 158. Trips are taken to Yosemite, Rush Creek drainage and Ansel Adams Wilderness. Write Box 18, Star Route 3, June Lake, CA 93529. ☎ 760-648-7701 in summer or 760-873-7971 in winter. **Virginia Lakes Pack Outfit** is 19 miles southwest of Bridgeport, on Virginia Lakes Road. In summer, write Route 1, Box 1070, Bridgeport, CA 93517. In the off-season, write 4300 Cox Road, Fallon, NV 89406. ☎ 760-867-2591.

Adventures on Wheels
Mountain Biking

Like a Moab of the West, Mammoth has become a haven for mavens of the fat-tire variety. In the winter, the Mammoth area accumulates more snow than any other ski locale in the Sierra. In the warmer months, mountain bikers from across the West pedal into town to sample the dozens of trails, invigorating alpine air, dazzling views and tourist-friendly community.

There are enough miles of trails to keep a skilled mountain biker busy for weeks or months. US Forest Service Fire Roads criss-cross the mountains and foothills, offering gut-busting climbs and teeth-chattering descents. One trail even climbs to 10,000 feet above sea level, making it one of the highest rides in the Sierra. But even novices and less-experienced riders can find room to move in and around Mammoth. If you aren't inclined to tackle the local inclines, the flatlands around town – some on paved roads – and the geothermal areas south of Mammoth, which contain the most obvious evidence of the area's still-smokin' volcanic vibe, offer easy and moderate terrain, along with all-day loop rides.

Then there's the crown jewel of the Sierra's MTB kingdom, especially for those seeking a more, well, prepackaged adventure. **Mammoth Mountain Bike Park** (MMBP) is the summer incarnation of the expansive winter ski and snowboard destination. It provides miles of single-track and all the snazzy amenities you'd expect at a world-class ski resort. See pages 60-61 for more information.

> *While in the Mammoth area, take necessary precautions against altitude sickness. Even at the base of Mammoth Mountain, the elevation is 8,800 feet, enough to send your head spinning if you are not acclimated. Aspirin and plenty of water are necessary remedies, but the only thing that really works is time. Give yourself a few easy days, perhaps even three or more, for your body to adjust before cranking up the trail.*

For more information on recreation and other activities in the region, contact **Mammoth Lakes Visitors Bureau**, PO Box 48, Mammoth Lakes, CA 93546, ☎ 760-934-2712.

At the east end of the town of Mammoth Lakes, **Shady Rest Park** offers enticing rides on partially paved trails through a forest setting. Not only is the park suited for children or novices, beginning and intermediate MTBers looking for a quick ride might use it as a launching point for more adventure rides.

To reach the park from US 395, take CA 203 west past the US Forest Service Ranger Station and turn north on Sawmill Cutoff Road. After 100 yards you'll spot a sign for the paved **Town Bike Trail**, which you can pick up here for a 0.8-mile ride to the park. You can also opt to keep driving into the park and pick up Town Bike Trail near the parking area. For an easy two-mile loop that will at least get your tires dusty, head east from the parking area past four water tanks and hang a left onto an unpaved single track. This is the start of a counter-clockwise circuit around the park. Continue north along the border of the park, then take a left when the trail meets Fireroad 3S27 that runs off to the north. Follow the power lines around the park and turn left again at Fireroad 3S08, which runs south back toward Sawmill Cutoff Road. From there turn left toward the water tanks to complete the loop.

For a more challenging yet still easy four-mile loop, continue east past the water tanks, instead of turning north, and out into the sagebrush country on **Sawmill Road** (3S25). At the 1.4-mile mark, turn left and ride north for a few minutes and follow a single track on the left under a set of power lines. At 2.8 miles you'll reach the edge of **Shady Rest Park** and a three-way junction. Turn right and follow the directions for the rest of the Shady Park loop to complete the ride, or turn left and pedal toward the water tanks to shorten the trek.

Up for something a little more strenuous? Try **Knolls Loop**, an 11-mile ride with a 500-foot elevation gain and a trip down Cardiac Hill. Ride to the northwest corner of Shady Rest Park to the signed Knolls Loop trailhead. Follow the signs marked with blue diamonds along a single track (which eventually becomes Fireroad 3S08) for a few minutes before turning left and then left again – always following the blue diamonds. You'll be on Fireroad 3S35 heading southwest, following the road as it curves and climbs. As the road reaches a hilltop, stay to the right and descend into a swale, then ascend a serious grade toward a junction. Stay right again and when you hit a five-way intersection, again go right, heading north and then east. About 1½ miles later, you descend to an intersection with Fireroad 3S08, which you can follow south back to the trailhead. For the full ride, continue straight (east). At the next junction, turn right, pedal for 300 feet and turn left. At the next intersection, turn left and head for the top of Obsidian Knoll. Now turn right and descend Cardiac Hill, following the trail as it turns sharply to the right and meets a road. Stay right and continue heading west back toward Shady Rest Park and end of the loop.

Just west of the US Forest Service Ranger Station, drive south on Old Mammoth Road for about one mile to Mammoth Creek Park. The park is a staging area for a great 8½-mile loop ride that is basically flat and friendly. From the parking lot take the paved bike trail through a tunnel under Old Mammoth Road onto 3S09. You'll soon be riding alongside **Mammoth Creek**. Turn right at a small dirt trail and cross the creek on a wooden bridge. Continue to the second road on the left and turn, then drop back down toward the creek. Halfway through the ride you'll spot a single track on the left. Follow that, crossing the creek again and then paralleling it. At the next junction with 3S09, bear left and continue along the creek. The road climbs and curves and passes the small dirt trail you took on the way in. Continue straight on 3S09 through the tunnel and back to the parking lot.

On the west end of Mammoth Lakes, an area called **North Village** is a good launching point for a few forested rides. For a five-mile, high-altitude trek along **San Juaquin Ridge** that is best left to advanced riders, drive up CA 203 to **Minaret Summit**, turn right at the overlook and park. From the small, unpaved parking lot (elevation 9,200 feet) take an old Jeep road toward the left and climb though a forest of juniper. Soon you'll angle to the right up a grueling section and across a tree-studded bowl. On the far side of the bowl, the trail again becomes steep and ascends to the top of San Juaquin Ridge. The views from here, elevation 10,700 feet, are enough to take your breath away if the altitude hasn't done it already. Return the way you came.

Another attractive ride heads downhill from Minaret Vista Overlook. From here the **Mountain View Trail**, a 5.6-miler that loses 900 feet as it descends to Earthquake Fault Picnic Area near CA 203. From Minaret Summit parking area head down a Jeep road and down a shallow ravine. You'll switchback twice before hitting a single track that climbs and drops before descending a steep slope to a Jeep road, 1.4 miles from the summit. Turn left at the next Jeep road, then take the next right and, quickly, the next left onto another stretch of single track. This portion winds across two bridges before running into another Jeep road, 3.6 miles from the summit. Turn right and continue on a well-graded dirt road to a single track that slides down to the left. Follow this trail as it turns into a narrow road, hang a right at the next junction onto another road, then take a left at the next intersection. This Jeep road will wind around to the right and end at the picnic area parking lot.

For a close-up look at Mammoth's volcanic past, try a 10-mile loop ride around the **Inyo Craters**. With only 500 feet of elevation gain and loss, this ride is rated moderate. It can be somewhat hazardous due to two creek crossings. To reach the trailhead from North Village, take CA 203 north and west about one mile to **Mammoth Scenic Loop Drive** (3S23). Turn right and continue about 2½ miles to the unpaved **Inyo Craters access road** (3S30). Turn left and drive one mile to the trailhead. The craters are a quarter-mile hike away. Said to be some of the youngest volcanic features in the Mammoth region, the craters were formed about 500 years ago when hot gasses erupted on the surface. Today small lakes can be found in the bottom of the craters.

After viewing these strange geologic features, mount up and ride out of the parking area, taking the first road on the right. Follow the small brown signs through a forest of lodgepole pine. After cresting a knoll, you'll be riding in through the sagebrush steppe of **Pumice Flat**. Make a long descent toward Deadman Creek and cross carefully, especially on those rare days when the creek is running swiftly. Continue on this Jeep road across the creek, over a small hill, then down to another creek crossing near a footbridge. Turn right at the next two intersections and follow the the gravel path alongside **Deadman Creek**. Soon you'll enter a small canyon lined with black obsidian, then descend past two campgrounds. Look for the signed junction with 2S29 and turn onto this Jeep road that cuts south-southwest through a forest of Jeffrey pine. Continue on this path, following the brown signs, back to the parking lot.

If the Inyo Craters whet your appetite for more geologic fun, you'll love pedaling through the geothermal region near **Hot Creek**. There is an excellent 21-mile loop ride with just 300 feet of elevation change. Along the way you'll see the boiling hot springs, fumaroles and periodic geysers near the **Hot Springs Geologic Site**. Begin by driving east from Mammoth Lakes on CA 203 to where it ends at a junction just under the US 395 overpass, not far from the Casa Diablo geothermal plant and the old Mono County sheriff's substation.

Now saddle up and take paved **Sheriff's Substation Road** (3S05) northwest over a small hill to the end of the blacktop. Here the road turns right and after a few minutes turns sharply right. Stay on 3S05, past the junctions with 3S13 and 3S59. Near the five-mile mark bear to the left and descend into Little Antelope Valley. The road bends to the right as it traverses the valley. Just before climbing out of the valley take a left on 3S06. Just past a chalk mine, almost eight miles from the trailhead, take a right and shoot down a narrow canyon. Hang a left and proceed to the source of Little Hot Creek and its dozens of hot springs. At the 11½-mile mark, this jeep road terminates at 2S07. Turn right, pass the intersection with 3S05, cross a bridge and crest a small hill to find another intersection. Go right, climb another hill and take the next right fork onto 3S45, **Hot Creek Fish Hatchery Road**. Head toward the airport and pass Hot Creek Ranch, where you'll find pavement leading off to the right. Continue to the right past the California Department of Fish and Game trout hatchery and Mammoth Pool to the end of 3S45 near an old school. Proceed across the road to a jeep road leading across an old lava flow. This road leads two miles to a paved road, where you turn north to rejoin Sheriff's Substation Road (3S05) and head back to your car.

> *A note on the hot springs: As tempting as it might be to take a dip, swimming and bathing are highly discouraged due to the danger of scalding and the high concentration of chemicals in the water. Respect all fenced-off areas and avoid riding near the edges of any thermal areas to protect the delicate soils and plantlife.*

Mammoth Mountain Bike Park

Unlike anything in the Sierra, Mammoth Mountain Bike Park combines all the comforts of a posh, Tyrolean ski resort with the chain-grease, scabbed-over vibe of hard-core fat-tire fanatics. Riders of all abilities and classes have begun flocking to Mammoth in recent years to ride the 70-plus miles of single track. Mammoth was the first ski mountain to take bikers to the top in a gondola, and certainly the popularity of big-time mountain bike racing here has increased the mountain's stock among riders. The sport's inaugural Kamikaze downhill competition was held here in 1985 and today the Mammoth Mountain Bike Race is the largest event of its kind in North America.

If you don't have an array of corporate race sponsors painted on your helmet and want to take in the entire mountain at your own pace, carefully check the park's calendar of events before you go. You don't necessarily want your trip to coincide with a major race weekend, when the trails that are open can be bustling.

You can ride the gondola (with or without a bike) to the summit at 11,053 feet or the chair lifts to other parts of the mountain and take your own sweet time coming down. The park offers covered water stops across the slopes, and a grill, café and bar are open at the mountain's base. The **Mammoth Mountain Bike Center** features mountain bike rentals, complete maintenance and repair, accessories, riding apparel, beverages and snacks. The rental fleet comprises new Schwinn S.30's equipped with full Rock Shox suspension. Be sure to ask about the park's free orientation rides and skill clinics. A shuttle bus leaves downtown Mammoth Lakes every half-hour, allowing riders to coast all the way back into town at the end of the day.

As of press time, pricing was as follows.

- One-day (9AM to 6PM) unlimited access to the shuttle, chair lifts and trail system: $23 for adults $12 for kids 12 and under.
- Two-day unlimited access: $39 and $20.
- Bike rentals run $35 for eight hours, $25 for four hours or $15 per hour. Mandatory helmets are included.

For more information, ☎ 888-4-MAMMOTH or visit www.mammoth-mtn.com.

June Lake

A close runner-up to Mammoth in the race for the hearts and minds of mountain bikers, June Lake has some stupendous trails that are often overlooked by the enthusiasts at June's big sister to the south. The June Lake area offers smooth dirt roads, crystal-blue lakes and alpine air that riders crave.

The tour de force is a 21-mile loop ride that links the basin's four lakes – June, Gull, Silver and Grant – like a string of pearls. The ride begins in **Gull Lake Park**, north of the of June Lake Village on Granite Avenue. From the park, take the winter access road and follow a set of power lines east. You'll find a Jeep road where the winter access road traverses a basin of volcanic pumice. Take the Jeep road across a meadow, over a small hill, down into another basin and over another hill. Head straight downhill to another set of power lines, where you hang a left and begin a long descent. At the bottom, turn left on a gravel road. After crossing a dam and heading down to the right, turn left, cross a bridge and descend again on a dirt road.

This road soon ends at CA 158. Turn left onto the blacktop and skirt the west side of **Grant Lake**, headed south. Continue around the lake to a parking area and enter **Reversed Creek Canyon**. After leaving the canyon ride through a meadow and around the west side of **Silver Lake**, where you can rest up at the marina. From here the ride becomes steep, climbing out of the canyon through a forest dotted with granite outcrops. After reaching June Mountain Ski Area, cross the road and pick up the winter access road, where you turn left and return to Gull Lake Park.

If you don't have time for a 21-miler, try the 9.3-mile **Hartley Springs Loop**. The ride begins on the west side of US 395 half a mile south of CA 158 at a signed trailhead. The ride heads out to Hartley Springs on Fire Road 2S10 and descends into a forest of red fir trees. The return path follows Fire Road 2S48 and cuts through Hartley Springs campground.

Adventures on Snow
Snowmobiling

If for some reason you long to crank up a noisy, greasy, exhaust-spewing machine in the middle of a peaceful, snow-blanketed landscape, then Mammoth is the place. The area has dozens of snowmobile trails and outfitters that offer rentals and guided rides. Most of the trails are located east of US 395, north of CA 203, and directly north of the town of Mammoth Lakes adjacent to Mammoth Scenic Loop Road. Be sure to respect all posted signs and ride with care. And be aware that snowmobile rentals aren't cheap, running at least $30 an hour for a single rider and $60 an hour for double rides. Most outfitters have age restrictions and require a valid driver's license for each rider.

One of the oldest and most respected operations is **DJ's Snowmobile Adventures**, located about 10 minutes north of Mammoth Lakes. From the intersection of US 395 and CA 203, drive three miles north to Smokey Bear Flat, where DJ's boasts of having machines "on the snow and ready to go" without the hassle of towing to a staging area. From here you can ride toward Lookout Mountain, elevation 8,352. For information and reservations, ☎ 760-935-4480 or www.mammothsnowmobiling.com.

Mammoth Snowmobile Adven-Tours operates in the Inyo Craters and San Juaquin Ridge areas north of Mammoth Lakes. The outfitter offers the standard rentals, guided tours, moonlight rides and a ticket office conveniently located in the middle of town in Sierra Center Mall. For information and reservations, ☎ 800 279 3226.

Downhill Skiing

See pages 49-50.

Cross-Country Skiing

Although Mammoth Mountain and its world-class downhill resort dominate the region, Nordic skiers are not left out by any means. Located just a few minutes from the town of Mammoth Lakes, **Tamarack Lodge Resort and Cross Country Ski Center** is of the most popular cross-country ski areas in California. Tamarack offers well-maintained tracks and skating lanes on over 25 miles of trails. Situated in a forested bowl, Tamarack's trails pass through thick stands of evergreens and around picturesque Lake Mary, hidden in the shadow of the High Sierra. Elevations range above 8,000 feet, offering varied terrain for skiers of all skill levels. The fully stocked ski center is home to the friendly staff and a full range of ski lessons and rentals. To reach the main lodge, head up Lake Mary Road 2.3 miles from downtown Mammoth Lakes. For more information, ☎ 800-237-6879 or visit www.tamaracklodge.com. Overnight accommodations are also available in the alpine-style hotel. Rates for a room with private bath run between $75 and $155 during the winter and $85 to $130 during the summer.

Dogsledding

To round out the smorgasboard of winter fun available in the Mammoth Lakes area, why not try a ride on a dogsled? The rigs at **Sled Dog Adventures** are pulled by pure-bred Siberian huskies and malamutes. Based at the western terminus of CA 203 near the Mammoth Mountain Ski Area, Sled Dog Adventures offers rides to Minaret Vista, including an unforgettable *Minaret Wintermoon Dinner Ride*. For about $70 per person you get a glass of champagne under a romantic winter moon or Sierra sunset and a 45-minute ride followed by dinner at the Mammoth Mountain Inn's Mountainside Grill or Yodler Restaurant. For current rates and more information, ☎ 760-934-6270.

Ice Climbing

If you've skied the double-black diamonds, snowmobiled until your lower body is numb and caught a whiff of what it's like to drive a dogsled, your winter sports experience still isn't complete. Try ice climbing to top it off. About an hour north of the town of Mammoth Lakes are some of the most popular ice climbing walls in the West. It's the perfect place to try this extreme sport for the first time, or simply watch the experts tackle the frozen verticality. Climbing season generally runs from November through March, but conditions can vary widely.

Head north on US 395 toward the town of Lee Vining. Just before the city limits, turn west on CA 120 toward Yosemite. This route over the Sierra crest is closed in winter, but no worries. In three miles you'll reach a locked gate. If the gate is open, conditions are probably too warm for ice climbing; come back next year. Otherwise, turn left onto Poole Road and drive north two miles to the end of the road near a power plant. Park and walk north into the canyon for about 20 minutes to the main wall. If conditions are right, there can be as many as 20 routes established in the canyon, offering multi-pitch and mixed ice climbing. Many of the routes have bolt anchors.

Check with the locals about ice and weather conditions before heading out. For help in finding a local guide who can show you the ropes, contact **Wilson's Eastside Sports**, 224 North Main Street, Bishop, 93514, ☎ 760-873-7520, or send email to store@eastsidesports.com.

Where to Stay

June Lake Motel and Cabins is three miles west of 395, on State Route 158, south of the junction at the June Lake Loop turnoff. Star Route 3, Box 14B, June Lake, CA 93529. Pets are charged $5 The rates vary with the season and days of the week. $$. ☎ 800-648-6835. **Whispering Pines Chalets and Motel** is 5½ miles west of 395, on State Route 158, by way of the June Lake Loop turnoff. Write Star Route 3, Box 14B, June Lake, CA 93529. Rates vary according to the season and days of the week. $$-$$$. Pets are not allowed. These are motel units with kitchens, housekeeping cabins and A-frame chalets. ☎ 760-648-7762, or, from California only, ☎ 800-648-7762.

Where to Dine

Carson Peak Inn, ☎ 760-648-7575. Nightly 5-10 PM, two miles west of town on CA 158. Beautiful country setting, with hearty American fare such as steak, ribs, seafood. Entrées are $11-20.

Route 395 North

The route north on 395 takes you through lush countryside where stock raising is prevalent, with beautiful mountainous terrain, particularly on the west side of the highway. This is rugged country with snow-fed mountain lakes. There's still some gold and silver mining, but it isn't of much consequence.

Mono Lake

What to See & Do
Mono Lake

Mono Lake is 12 miles north of June Lake. It is east of 395 and Lee Vining. Formed more that 700,000 years ago, this is one of the oldest lakes in North America. Waterbirds flock here by the millions because it's a vital food source for them. The mineral level in the lake is so high that only algae, brine shrimp and the pupae of the ephydra fly can tolerate its briny waters. In 1941, Los Angeles tapped area streams as a water source. Without normal replenishment, the lake's level has dropped about 40 feet, exposing formations of calcium carbonate. You can learn more about the lake's geology and its wildlife at the Mono Lake Committee's Information Center and Bookstore on 395, north of Lee Vining. It is open Friday through Sunday 9-4, and in summer daily from 8 AM to 5 PM. ☎ 760-647-6572. A self-guided tour of the lake at 6 PM along the shoreline is recommended. The center and trail are wheelchair accessible.

Rental kayaks are available from Caldera Kayaks. Reach them at their Lake Crowley office, ☎ 760-935-4942.

Mono Craters

The Mono Craters, south of the lake, are a group of volcanic cones that became active only 600 years ago. Panum Crater, three miles east of 395, originally was a crater a quarter-mile wide, but later eruptions reduced its size. Today there are towers or spines 20-50 feet high. A path leads from the end of the dirt road off State Route 120 to the crater. In summer, there are guided tours. ☎ 760-647-3044 or 760-647-3000.

Adventures On Water
Fishing along the Eastern Slopes

See *Appendix A* for licenses and regulations. If you remain overnight in a wilderness area you must have a permit. The following places are recommended for fishing, but almost all lakes, ponds, streams and rivers are stocked. **Bridgeport Reservoir**, at 6,455 feet, has brown and rainbow trout. Swimming is permitted, along with water skiing. It can be reached by car, two miles north of Bridgeport on State Route 182. **Ellery Lakes**, at 9,538 feet, has brook, brown, cutthroat and rainbow trout. You can drive to it; it's six miles west of Lee Vining Road, on State Route 120. **Grant Lake**, at 7,135 feet, has brown and rainbow trout. It is accessible by car, five miles south of Lee Vining, on State Route 158. **Gulf Lake**, at 9,100 feet, has brook, brown and rainbow trout. You can reach it via State Route 158, a mile southwest of June Lake. **June Lake** is at 7,616 feet, and permits swimming in addition to fishing for brown, brook and rainbow trout. You can drive there – it's two miles southwest of 395, on State Route 158. **Lower Twin Lake** is at 7,081 feet, with brown and rainbow trout. By car, drive four miles west of Mono City, off 395. **Saddlebag Lake** is at 10,087 feet, and reachable by car. Drive 10 miles west of Lee Vining on State Route 120. It has brook, cutthroat and rainbow trout. **Silver Lake**, at 7,212 feet, has brook, brown and rainbow trout. It is four miles west of June Lake on State Route 158. **Summit Lake** is at 10,240 feet, and has brook and rainbow trout. **Tioga Lake**, at 9,651 feet, can be reached by car. It is eight miles west of Lee Vining on State Route 120. It has brook and rainbow trout. **Trumbull Lake**, at 9,200 feet, has brook, rainbow, and brown trout. By car it is seven miles west of Conway Summit, off 395. **Upper Twin Lakes**, at 7,092 feet has brown, kokanee and rainbow trout. Swimming and water skiing are permitted. It is 12 miles southwest of Bridgeport by car. The **Virginia Lakes**, at 9,450 feet to 9,770 feet, have brook, brown and rainbow trout. They are seven miles west of Conway Summit, off 395.

Where to Stay

Best Western Lake View Lodge is on 395. Its rates vary according to the season, $-$$. No pets are allowed. There's a restaurant nearby. ☎ 760-647-6543. **Murphy's Motel** is on Highway 395. $-$$. Only small pets are allowed, for a $5 fee. ☎ 760-647-6316.

Camping

Public Campgrounds – June Lake to Bridgeport

These campgrounds have either pit or chemical toilets, stream water or piped water, and allow pets. Some of the more expensive camps have flush toilets, tables, barbecues and fire rings.

Aspen Grove is 5½ miles west of Lee Vining, off State Route 120, at 8,000 feet. There are 55 tent or RV sites. It is open from April through October, with a $5 fee. ☎ 760-934-6876. **Big Bend** is 6½ miles west of Lee Vining, off State Route 120, at 7,800 feet. It has 17 tent or RV sites, with a 16-foot RV limit. It charges $8, and is open mid-May through October. ☎ 760-873-2400. **Buckeye**, at 7,000 feet, is 13½ miles west of Bridgeport, off 395 and Twin Lakes Road. It has nine tent and 65 tent and RV sites, with a 30-foot RV limit. It is open from late May to October by reservation, with a $7 fee. ☎ 775-331-6444. **Buckeye Group**

Camp is at 7,000 feet, 13½ miles west of Bridgeport, off 395 and Twin Lakes Road. It is open from May to October by reservation, at $30 a night. ☎ 775-331-6444.

Ellery Lake, at 9,500 feet, is nine miles west of Lee Vining, on State Route 20, with 12 tent or RV sites and a 20-foot RV limit. The fee is $8 and it is open from June to early October. ☎ 760-873-2400. **Green Creek** is at 7,500 feet and 13 miles southwest of Bridgeport, off 395, on Green Lakes Road. It has four tent and seven tent or RV sites, with a 22-foot RV limit. It is open late May to October, for a $7 fee. ☎ 775-331-6444. **Gull Lake** is one mile southwest of June Lake, on State Route 158, at 7,500 feet. It has 10 tent or RV sites, with a 45-foot RV limit. It charges $8, and is open from late April through November. ☎ 760-873-2400. **Honeymoon Flat** is at 7,000 feet and eight miles southwest of Bridgeport on Twin Lakes Road. It has six tent-only and 41 tent and RV sites, with a 22-foot RV limit. It is open May to late October by reservation, for a $7 fee. ☎ 800-280-2267.

Junction is 10 miles southwest of Lee Vining on State Route 120, at an elevation of 9,600 feet. It is open from June to mid-October and charges no fee. **June Lake** is on the northeast shore of the lake on State Route 158, at 7,600 feet. It has 22 tent or RV sites, with a 45-foot RV limit. It is open from late April through November by reservation and a $10 fee. ☎ 800-280-2267. **Lower Lee Vining**, at an elevation of 7,000 feet, is three miles west of Lee Vining, on State Route 120. It has 60 tent or RV sites, and is open from May through October, for a $5 fee. ☎ 760-934-6876.

Lower Twin Lake, at 7,000 feet, is 11 miles southwest of Bridgeport, on Twin Lakes Road. It has five tent and nine tent or RV sites, with a 22-foot RV limit. It is open from May to October by reservation and an $8 fee. ☎ 800-280-2267. **Lundy**, 10 miles northwest of Lee Vining, off 395 on Lundy Lake Road, has 51 tent or RV sites, at an elevation of 8,000 feet. It is open May through October for a $5 fee. ☎ 760-934-6876. **Ohl Ridge** is at 7,600 feet and 1½ miles north of June Lake, off State Route 158. It has 148 tent or RV sites, with a 55-foot RV limit. Open from late April to November by reservation and payment of a $10 fee. ☎ 800-280-2267. **Paha** is 10 miles southwest of Bridgeport, at 7,000 feet, on Twin Lakes Road. It has 12 tent and 10 tent or RV sites, with a 22-foot RV limit. It is open from May to October by reservation and a $8 fee. ☎ 800-280-2267. **Reversed Creek** is a mile southwest of June Lake, off State Route 158, at 7,600 feet. There are 17 RV sites, with a 45-foot RV limit. It is open from mid-May to mid-October with a $10 fee. ☎ 760-873-2400. **Robinson Creek** is at 7,000 feet and 10 miles southwest of Bridgeport, on Twin Lakes Road. It is open from May through October by reservation and an $8 fee. ☎ 800-280-2267.

Saddlebag Lake is at 10,000 feet, 12 miles west of Lee Vining, off State Route 120 on Saddlebag Road. It has 20 tent or RV sites, with a 16-foot RV limit, but trailers are not recommended. It is open from June to early October with an $8 fee. ☎ 760-873-2400. **Sawmill**, at 7,000 feet, is 11 miles southwest of Bridgeport on Twin Lakes Road. It has two tent and six tent or RV sites for $7 each. It is open from May through October. ☎ 760-331-6414. **Silver Lake** is four miles west of June Lake on State Route 158, at 7,200 feet. It has 65 tent or RV sites, with a 45-foot RV limit. The fee is $10, and it is open from late April through November. ☎ 760-873-2400. **Tioga Lake** is at an elevation of 9,700 feet, 19½ miles southwest of Lee Vining, on State Route 120. There are 12 tent sites priced at $8, and the camp is open from June to early October. No trailers are permitted. ☎ 760-873-2400. **Trumbull Lake** is 20 miles south of Bridgeport, at 9,500 feet, off 395, on Virginia Lakes Road. It has 36 tent or RV sites, with a 35-foot RV limit. It is open from June through mid-October by reservation, with a $10 fee. ☎ 800-280-2267. **Upper Lee Vining** is at 7,000 feet, four miles west of Lee Vining, off State Route 120. It has 33 tent or RV sites, and is wheelchair accessible, for a fee of $5. It is open from May through October. ☎ 760-934-6876.

Private Campgrounds

In general, privately owned campgrounds offer more services than those that are state or federally owned. The extra amenities usually include hookups for electricity, water and sewage. In addition, most have showers, cable TV, disposal stations and laundries. I've listed the three camps that I consider are best for all-around excellence.

Paradise Shores Trailer Park is at 6,500 feet, 2½ miles north of Bridgeport, on State Route 182. It has eight tent and 36 RV sites with electrical and water hookups, and 25 with sewage hookups. It is open from mid-April through October by reservation. The fee is $12 for two people and $3 for each extra person. Write PO Box 602, Bridgeport, CA 93517. ☎ 760-932-7735. **Pine Cliff Resort** is 2½ miles north of June Lake, off State Route 158, on Ohl Ridge Road, at 7,800 feet. It has 60 tent and 178 RV sites with electricity and water hookups. It is open from May through October by reservation. The fee is $14 for two, and $2 for each extra person. It is open from May through October by reservation. Write PO Box 38, June Lake, CA 93526. ☎ 760-648-7558. **Willow Springs Trailer Park** is at 6,000 feet, five miles south of Bridgeport, on US 395. It has 30 RV sites with electricity, water and sewage hookups. It is open from May through October by reservation. The fee is $20 for two and $2 for each extra person. Write PO Box 1040, Highway 395, Bridgeport, CA 93517. ☎ 760-932-7725.

Bodie

What to See & Do

Bodie State Park, a must-see, is off the main 395 highway traveling north, 20 miles southeast of Bridgeport. To visit this fabulous ghost town, take CA 270 to the Dogtown site. Please note the last three miles are unpaved, and it is often inaccessible in winter.

Once a community of 10,000 people, Bodie had a reputation as one of the most lawless gold-mining camps in the 19th century. The town was named after William Bodey, who was one of the first to discover gold there in 1859. William Bodey never benefited from his findings because he died in a blizzard three months after striking gold. The spelling of Bodey was changed to Bodie by the citizenry for easier comprehension. It was a rich digging here, with almost $100 million in ore removed from the ground.

Lottie Johl.

Mine Supervisor Theodore Hoover's residence in Bodie. His brother, Herbert, later became President of the United States. Courtesy of Gary Gawer.

Bodie History

In 1878, the *Bodie Standard News* wrote as truthfully about the place as anyone ever has.

"Had an angel come to earth and said there are many millions of dollars to be had for the digging, but there are penalties attached, would men have accepted the gift?

'Go, take the treasure,' he would have said, ' but listen to the terms. You will go where desolation has from time immemorial held its peace. Your eyes will look out in the morning upon the desert, and only on the desert. Your children will grow up where they will never hear a bird sing, never see a green field or the blessings at noon of the shade of a great tree.

'Once a week you will bring from the depths a broken body that was an hour before a strong man.

'Your natures will grow metallic in thought. Your dreams will be money only.

'You will see so few blessed and so many suffer that your heart will grow callused, and thousands of you will doubt any good in man, all mercy in God.'"

Lottie Johl's former home in Bodie. Courtesy of Gary Gawer.

Bodie's 65 saloons were notorious in their heyday. A preacher called the town "a sea of sin, lashed by the tempests of lust and passion." Sex was for sale in elegant bagnios and poor cribs with such notorious women as Beautiful Doll, Madame Moustache and Rosa May. Gold nuggets were often given as tips, but only after the ladies' services were paid for in silver and gold coins.

The *Bodie Standard* wrote of this violent era, "There is some irresistible power that impels us to cut and shoot each other to pieces." Bodie had its share of bad men, such as Washoe Pete, Tom Adams and Rough-and-Tumble Jack, who achieved legendary fame in the West for their meanness. In nearby Aurora, an 11-year-old girl, whose family was moving to Bodie, wrote in her diary, "Good-bye God. I'm going to Bodie."

The last three miles of the road has a washboard surface, but in spring and summer the old town is delightful. In winter, don't even try to reach it. There could be 10-20 foot snow drifts, with temperatures 20 to 30° below zero.

Lottie Johl

Lottie, a beautiful prostitute, and Bodie's town butcher Eli Johl fell in love. They got married, much to the horror of the townspeople. He built here a five-room house, but the good people of Bodie shunned her. At a masquerade ball, she was selected as the loveliest lady. When she was unmasked, people recoiled in shock to learn her identity and her title was taken from her. Soon after, a doctor prescribed medicine for a mild illness. It proved to be poison and Lottie died. Eli built a beautiful memorial to her and those who came to sneer went away in tears.

Today there are 170 deep-grained, russet and gold buildings, 5% of the original structures, in a state of arrested decay. They will never be restored, but steps have been taken to assure they won't deteriorate. The original builders used whatever materials were available. Some metal sidings are patterned Victorian sheet iron and flattened tin cans.

It is the best all-around ghost town in the West. Its longevity has been assured because not many people go there.

The little jail is still there, of course, empty. Murderers once filled its cells. It is reported there was at least a murder a day until June of 1881. *Bodie Daily Press* reported, "Bodie has become a quiet summer resort; no one killed here for a week."

The small Methodist Church is well preserved but off-limits to visitors. Vandals stole many of the interior ornaments, including an oilcloth imprinted with the Ten Commandments.

There are no tourist facilities in Bodie. The museum is open daily from 9-7 on Memorial Day weekend through Labor Day, and 9-4 the rest of the year. Day use is $5 per car, and a dollar less for senior citizens. There's a $1 fee for pets, and they must be on a leash. ☎ 760-647-6445

Bridgeport

What to See & Do

Bridgeport is 28 miles north of Lee Vining, on 395. A **Jamboree** is held the last weekend of June. This is a professional rodeo with everything from barrel racing to bull riding. A four-day event, it features a Harley Davidson Rally, drag races, motorcycle rodeos, seminars, music and dancing.

A **Fourth of July celebration** is held at Bridgeport on a weekend with a parade, barbecue, dances, contests and fireworks. Bridgeport also holds a **Mountain Man Rendezvous** in mid-October. This three-day holiday includes knife-throwing contests, black powder shooting competitions, barbecues and music. Western wear is indicated, so get yourself an outfit and take part.

Mono County Courthouse

The Mono County Courthouse was built in Aurora in 1880: it's the second-oldest courthouse in the state. It was erected after the county seat was moved from Aurora to Bridgeport when it was learned that the first courthouse was in Nevada. It is open to the public during normal business hours.

Mono County Museum

The Mono County Museum occupies an old school house built in 1880. It contains photos, documents and other memorabilia about the county's heritage. School was conducted here until 1954, when the building was slated for destruction. Wiser heads prevailed and it became a museum. It is open Memorial Day weekend through September from 10 AM to 5 PM.

Adventures on Foot
Mono Lake to Bridgeport

There are several High Sierra trailheads west of Mono Lake. From US 395 drive just north of the lake and turn west on Lundy Canyon Road (2N01). Head up-canyon nearly all the way to Lundy Lake and look for the trailhead on the east end of the lake. The **Lakes Canyon Trail** is great for a rather strenuous day hike up to clear, blue **Oneida Lake**. The trail heads west along the south shore of Lundy Lake. This is open, rocky country where a few pines offer what little shade there is. The trail turns south, offering views of private Lundy Lake resort before turning up Lake Canyon and beginning a stiff climb alongside the South Fork of Mill Creek. The trail becomes green and lush and the pines more prominent as the trail ascends 1,800 feet in the first 3.2 miles before passing **Crystal Lake** and entering the Inyo National Forest's **Hoover Wilderness**. Keep an eye out for signs of a long-abandoned mining operation. Stay out of any and all mining tunnels you might find. The trail passes the windy shore of **Oneida Lake** at 9,600 feet and peters out 4.8 miles from the trailhead. Return the way you came.

To access the upper reaches of Lundy Canyon and explore the glory of a lake-dotted wonderland, continue driving on an unpaved road along the north shore of Lundy Lake past Lundy Lake Resort to the **Lundy Canyon trailhead**. The trail climbs steadily through a lush riparian area fed by Mill Creek and its many tributaries. Waterfalls along the canyon walls, multiple stream crossings and an abandoned cabin keep things interesting before you hit a junction at **Lake Helen**, 2.3 miles and a blistering 1,900 feet above the trailhead. Turn left and climb a talus slope along the headwall of the canyon, then traverse Lundy Pass. On the other side of the pass, you'll climb gradually past **Hummingbird Lake** to another junction four miles from the trailhead. Continue straight or turn left and follow one of two trails around **Saddlebag Lake** to the resort on the other side. Or turn right to reach the Steelhead Lake Trail.

Steelhead Lake Trail heads northwest about a mile before reaching a junction. Bear left to reach a basin bounded by Cascade Lake and Steelhead Lake, where the trail dead ends after a mile. Bear right to complete a loop that leads you back to **Lake Helen**, the **Lundy Canyon Trail** and the path back to the trailhead. Look for a spur leading heading left up toward Hess Mine on the shores of Steelhead Lake.

If you feel the need to get away from anything and everything, try a multiday backpack out of the **Twin Lakes trailhead** west of Bridgeport. The trail here provide access to the high country of Hoover Wilderness and Yosemite National Park. From Bridgeport, take Twin Lakes road west about 13 miles to Mono Village at the west end of Upper Twin Lake. Head west and south, climbing and climbing along Robinson Creek to a trail junction, 6.2 miles from and 2,400 feet above the trailhead. To reach the Yosemite Park boundary, head west and proceed 1½ miles to **Peeler Lake**. Continue west another two miles to a three-way junction at bucolic **Kerrick Meadow**. From here you can head south into the tourist-free northern reaches of Yosemite. Kerrick Canyon is nine miles away. You can also walk north out of the park and back into the Hoover Wilderness, where you can wander for days without passing the same pine twice.

Adventures on Wheels

Just south of Bridgeport, find a relatively smooth dirt road that makes for a great bike road or quick excursion in your four-wheel drive. About 4½ miles south of Bridgeport on US 395, head south on Fire Road 142. The road leads south for a mile to a junction with Fire Road 144, where you turn west. Know you'll be traveling through the sagebrush-covered **Lower Summers Meadow**. About 6½ miles later, the road becomes rough and challenging as it begins to climb toward **Upper Summers Meadow**. Continue as long as it's safe and return the way you came.

North of Bridgeport, you can take the back way to the historic town of **Bodie** rather than fighting the tourists on the paved road. From Bridgeport, head north on CA 182 alongside **Bridgeport Reservoir** four miles to fire road 046. Turn east and proceed about eight miles to a junction with fire road 169, near Bodie's Upper Town. You can turn north to visit Lower Town. Continue south on Fire Road 169 for about 14 miles to CA 168, which leads 13 miles west to Bridgeport to complete your loop.

Where to Stay

Best Western's Ruby Inn is in the center of town on 395, at 333 Main Street, 93517. It accepts only small pets. From May 1 to September 30 the rates are $65-95, and from February to March 31, and October 1 through January 31, the rates are $55-90. There's one two-bedroom unit. ☎ 760-932-7241. The **Cain House**, in the center of town, is a historic bed and breakfast place. It allows no pets. It's on 395, at 333 Main Street, 93517, with a restaurant nearby. ☎ 760-932-7040. $90-140. The **Walker River Lodge** is on 395, at 1 Main Street, 93517. It permits pets. From May 1 to October 31 the rates are $65-120 for one or two persons. From February 1 through March 13, and November 1 through December the rates start at $50 and go up to $80. ☎ 760-932-7383.

Eastern Sierra Outfitters

Lone Pine/Big Pine/Bishop
On Foot
The following shops sell sporting goods and/or outdoor gear.

■ **Big Pine**
Big Pine Station Sporting Goods, 430 South Main Street, ☎ 760-938-2311.
Roy's Guns & Tackle, 320 North Main Street, ☎ 760-938-2380.

■ **Bishop**
Allen Outdoor Products, 200 South Main Street, ☎ 760-873-5903.
Bishop Sports, 125 North Main Street, ☎ 760-872-1943.
Buttermilk Mountain Works, 2333 North Sierra Highway, ☎ 760-872-1946.
Mac's Sporting Goods, 425 North Main Street, ☎ 760-872-9201.
Wilson's Eastside Sports, 224 North Main Street, ☎ 760-873-7520.

■ **Lone Pine**
Gardner's True Value, 104 South Main Street, ☎ 760-876-4208.
Lone Pine Sporting Goods, 220 South Main Street, ☎ 760-876-5365.
Slater's Sporting Goods, 130 South Main Street, ☎ 760-876-5020.

On Horseback
The following outfitters offer backcountry horsepacking or riding instruction.

■ **Bishop**
Bishop Pack Outfitters, 247 Cataract Road, ☎ 760-873-4785.
Mill Pond Equestrian Center, 590 Rocking K Road, ☎ 760-873-6037.
Onion Valley Pack Station, Pine Creek Road, ☎ 760-387-2797.
Pine Creek Pack Trains, Pine Creek Road, ☎ 760-935-4493.

On Wheels
■ **Bishop**
Bikes of Bishop, 651 North Main Street, ☎ 760-8732-3829.
Brian's Bicycles, 192 East Pine Street, ☎ 760-873-7911.

On Water

The following businesses provide fishing guide services and/or tackle.

■ Big Pine

Big Pine Station Sporting Goods, 430 South Main Street, ☎ 760-938-2311.

Roy's Guns & Tackle, 320 North Main Street, ☎ 760-938-2380.

■ Bishop

Allen Outdoor Products, 200 South Main Street, ☎ 760-873-5903.

Bishop Sports, 125 North Main Street, ☎ 760-872-1943.

Buttermilk Mountain Works, 2333 North Sierra Highway, ☎ 760-872-1946.

Mac's Sporting Goods, 425 North Main Street, ☎ 760-872-9201.

Wilson's Eastside Sports, 224 North Main Street, ☎ 760-873-7520.

■ Lone Pine

Gardner's True Value, 104 South Main Street, ☎ 760-876-4208.

Lone Pine Sporting Goods, 220 South Main Street, ☎ 760-876-5365.

Slater's Sporting Goods, 130 South Main Street, ☎ 760-876-5020.

Mammoth Lakes/Mono Lake/Bridgeport

On Foot

The following outfitters offer hiking and horsepacking instruction and/or services.

■ Bridgeport

Ken's Alpine Shop, 258 Main Street, ☎ 760-932-7707.

■ Mammoth Lakes

Mammoth Adventure Connection, 1 Minaret Road, ☎ 760-934-0606.

Mammoth Mountaineering School, 3325 Main Street, ☎ ☎ 760-934-8700.

Rick's Sport Center, 3241 Main Street, ☎ 760-934-3416.

On Horseback

The following outfitters offer backcountry horsepacking or riding instruction.

■ Mammoth Lakes

Convict Lake Resort, RR 1, Box 204, ☎ 760-934-3800.

Mammoth Lakes Pack Outfitters, Lake Mary Road, ☎ 760-934-2434.
McGee Creek Pack Station, RR 1, Box 162, ☎ 760-935-4324.
Red's Meadow Pack Station, PO Box 395, ☎ 760-934-2345.

Camping & Outdoor Gear

The following shops sell camping equipment and/or outdoor gear.

■ Mammoth Lakes

Footloose Ski & Sports, 6175 Minaret Road, ☎ 760-934-2400.
Goody Box, 89 Laurel Mountain Road, ☎ 760-934-9215.
Kittredge Sports, 3218 Main Street, ☎ 760-934-7566.
Mammoth Ace Hardware, 126 Old Mammoth Road, ☎ 760-924-3849.
Mammoth Sporting Goods, 1 Sierra Centre Mall, ☎ 760-934-3239.
Rick's Sport Center, 3241 Main Street, ☎ 760-934-3416.

■ June Lake

Summit Safari, 4627 Route 158, 93529, ☎ 760-648-1129

On Wheels

■ Mammoth Lakes

Brian's Bicycles, 3059 Chateau Road, ☎ 760-924-8566.
Footloose Ski & Sports, 6175 Minaret Road, ☎ 760-934-2400.
High Sierra Cycle Center, 123 Commerce Drive, ☎ 760-924-3723.
Mammoth Mountain Bike Center, 1 Minaret Road, ☎ 760-924-0706.
Mammoth Sporting Goods, 1 Sierra Centre Mall, ☎ 760-934-3239.
Sandy's Ski & Sports, Main Street, ☎ 760-934-7518.
Storm Riders, 6180 Minaret Road, ☎ 760-934-5831.

On Water

The following businesses provide fishing guide services and/or tackle.

■ June Lake

Summit Safari, 4627 Route 158, 93529, ☎ 760-648-1129

■ Mammoth Lakes

Trout Fitter, CA 203 at Old Mammoth Road, ☎ 760-934-3676.
Trout Fly, 26 Old Mammoth Road, ☎ 760-934-2517.
Tube Tenders, PO Box 3455, ☎ 760-934-6922.

Reno-Tahoe Territory

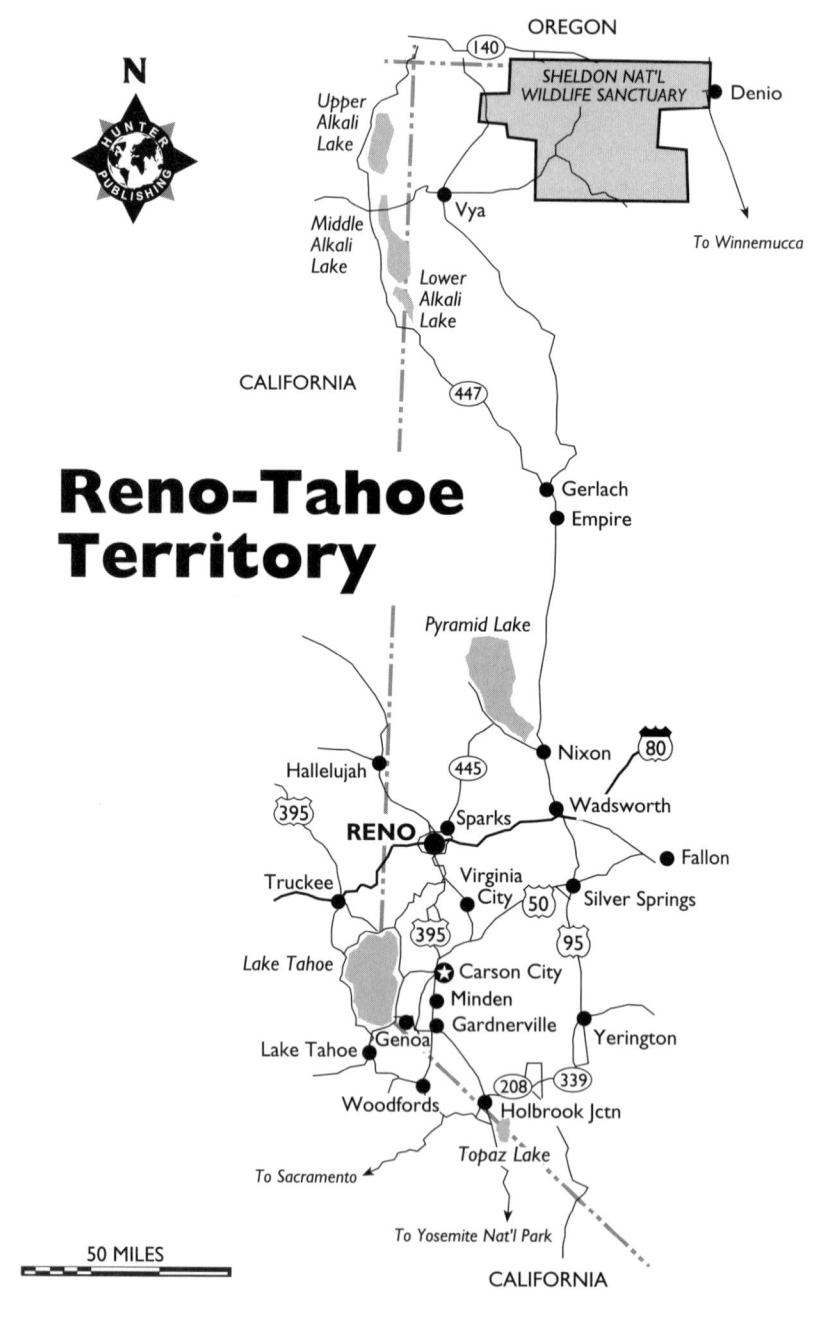

Nevada & Lake Tahoe

Carson City

US Highway 395 now takes you northwest for about 75 miles, where it merges with US 50 three miles south of Carson City. Two blocks north of the State Museum and a block north of Washington Street at East Williams Street, 50 diverges from 395 and continues east to Virginia City or west to South Lake Tahoe.

What to See & Do

Carson City is Nevada's state capital. The city was named after the famous scout, Kit Carson, who explored much of this area. The city's Chamber of Commerce, at 1900 Carson Street, has a free **self-guided tour map** that illustrates and describes the city's historic sites. It hosts a **Kit Carson Trail Walk** that costs $3 – but children 12 and under can participate for free. A **guided tour** of 15 historic homes is conducted each Saturday during the summer. A different home is highlighted each week, with a narrator in period dress discussing the house's past. The **Nevada State Museum** is considered one of the 10 best regional museums in the West. Several other notable museums are located in Carson City.

Kit Carson. NY Public Library.

Unlike most Western capitals, Carson City has managed to retain a good portion of its 1864 romanticism, as well as the hospitality that attracted waves of homesteaders. The most stunning examples of the city's 19th-century glory is found in the architecture.

The **Capitol Building & Museum**, 101 North Carson Street, ☎ 702-687-5030, comprise the second-oldest capitol structure in the West. Built in 1871 of native stone quarried from the State Prison and lined with Alaskan marble, the Capitol is open daily. It's so open, in fact, that visitors can stroll through the old legislative halls (great photo ops in front of the lectern) and Supreme Court chambers, and often poke a head through the open doors of the governor's and lieutenant governor's offices. The Supreme Court chambers are a favorite stop for law students dreaming big.

The legislature and Supreme Court currently meet in the audacious neo-classical buildings across the grassy plaza from the Capitol.

Just east of the Capitol, the **Nevada State Library & Archives**, 100 Stewart Street, ☎ 702-687-5160, are housed in a structure that was built in 1992 to incorporate the old State Printing Building, which was opened in 1886. The library contains the original state constitution, an unmatched collection of historical records and a variety of changing exhibits. Open Monday through Friday, excepting state holidays, year-round.

The **Northern Nevada Children's Museum**, 813 North Carson Street, ☎ 702-884-2226, has plenty of hands-on exhibits to keep little fingers busy. Admission is $4 for adults, $2 for kids. The nearby **Brewery Arts Center**, 448 West King Street, ☎ 702-883-1976, is the original 1864 site of the West's first microbrewery, the Carson City Brewing Company. The building now houses a live theater, pottery studio and the Nevada Artists Association Gallery. The **Roberts House Museum**, 1207 North Carson Street, ☎ 702-887-2174, built in 1859 and moved to Carson City in 1873 on a railroad flat car, marks the height of Victorian Gothic architecture. The museum is filled with period furniture. Admission is $2.

On the suburban south side of Carson City, train buffs the world over flock to the **Nevada State Railroad Museum**, 2180 South Carson Street, ☎ 702-687-6953. Locomotives and train cars from the halcyon days of the Virginia & Truckee (1869-1950) – which became the most lucrative short line in the world running treasure from Virgina City to Carson City to Reno – have been painstakingly restored. The gem is an 1888 steam locomotive. Visitors can ride daily during summer months. Admission is $2.50, train rides are extra. Nearby is the **US Forest Service Carson Ranger District office**, 1536 South Carson Street, ☎ 702-826-2766. The staff can provide trail maps, books and permits for the surrounding area, including the Carson Range of the Sierra Nevada and Tahoe. The office is closed Sundays.

The **Stewart Indian Museum**, 5366 Snyder Avenue, ☎ 702-882-1808, is on the quiet campus of the former Stewart Indian Boarding School, opened in December 1890 as the Clear Creek Indian Training School. The native stone buildings are listed on the National Register of Historic Places. The school's initial mission was to "assimilate" native children into white society and strip them of their heritage. The goal later became to highlight Native American history. Before the school closed in 1980, 3,000 students had walked its halls. Today a small but wonderful museum and gift shop struggle to survive in one corner of the campus. As of presstime, budget constraints were forcing the museum to return all of its native-made pieces to the tribes from which they were borrowed and focus solely on school history. The campus hosts an incredible pow wow and arts and crafts festival in June.

For more information on adventures in Carson City, contact or visit the **Carson City Convention and Visitors' Bureau**, 1900 South Carson Street, Carson City, NV, 89701, ☎ 702-687-7410.

Where to Stay

The **Best Western Trailside Inn** is half a mile north on 395 at 1300 North Carson Street, 89701. According to the season, rates range from $39-46 to $55-65 for one person and $45-51 to $59-69 for two people. No pets. ☎ 775-883-7300. **Days Inn** charges from $40-76 for one person, $40-70 for two persons. Family-type units are available. ☎ 775-883-3343. Coffee shop nearby. It is on 395 on the north end of the city, at 3103 N. Carson Street, 89701. Small pets only. The **Hardman House Motor Inn** is the best lodging place in Carson City. It is on 395, just south of US 50, at 917 North Carson Street, 89701. Single rooms rent for $35-55. Double rooms, with one bed are $40-60. No pets. ☎ 775-882-7744. **Hotel Orleans** is 1.3 miles south, on US 50 and 395, at 2731 South Carson Street, 89701. Single rooms are $32-38 to $37-41 and $43-52, depending on the season. Coffee shop nearby. Small pets only. ☎ 775-882-2007.

Where to Dine

A favorite local breakfast and lunch stop is the **Cracker Box**, 402 East William Street, ☎ 702-882-4556. Those counting cholesterol are advised to stay away, but for a hearty plate of bacon and eggs or a juicy burger, this is the place.

Located in the 19th-century home of a state Supreme Court justice and dressed in Barbary Coast décor, **Adele's**, 1112 North Carson Street, ☎ 702-882-3353, is known as one of the city's upper-crust establishments. Open for lunch and dinner Monday through Saturday, specialties of this high-end house include seafood and roast duck. There is also an extensive wine list. Note that Adele's is closed the week between Christmas and New Year's.

Two blocks away, **Silvana's**, 1301 North Carson Street, ☎ 702-883-5100, is open for dinner only Tuesday through Saturday. Boasting a large Italian menu, Silvana's specializes in pasta, seafood and steak.

The **Carson Nugget Steak House**, 507 North Carson Street, ☎ 702-882-1626, is known for protein-powered Western cuisine. The Carson Nugget also offers the ubiquitous all-you-can-eat buffet and a 24-hour coffee shop.

South of the city center and south of the border, **El Charro Avitia**, 4389 South Carson Street, ☎ 702-883-6261, is open for lunch and dinner on weekdays, dinner only on weekends. El Charro is known for miles around for its fresh and filling Mexican fare.

Heidi's Family Restaurant is at the junction of US 50 East and 395, at 1020 North Carson St. It is open 6:30 AM to 2 PM, with meals costing up to $10. ☎ 775-297-1464.

Virginia City

To reach Virginia City, which has been restored to its former boomtown appearance, once the domain of Bret Harte and Mark Twain, take US 50 East about seven miles to its intersection with scenic State Route 341, then travel north for about 10 miles to Virginia City.

History

By 1859, thousands of miners still sought gold in western areas where the metal could be retrieved from streams or hillsides. But the gold was playing out in most places and miners were desperate to find new sources. Instead of working on their own or with partners, they worked in the mines, which offered a meager living. Meanwhile, thousands had given up the hunt and headed back east. Then news of a fabulous new silver strike spread across the Sierra Nevada. A man called Comstock had supposedly struck a rich silver vein in an arid range just across the California border in Nevada. The news was greeted with skepticism. Most had heard such stories before. But this time the rumors proved true, and many California mining towns were deserted as miners headed for what would become Virginia City.

Miners had found gold in a ravine leading down from Mt. Davidson 10 years earlier. The pickings were slim, so most miners headed across the mountains to California. Mormon farmers had already established the territory's first community of Genoa, to the southwest. Some of them later abandoned their farms and founded the little towns of Dayton and Johntown. The Carson River, near the base of the Sierra Nevada, had been a popular resting place for miners to spend a few days before starting the arduous journey across the mountains. A few tried their luck in the river but only found traces of gold in their pans. Practically all of the miners continued their journey to California.

Two Mormons, John Orr and Nick Kelly, remained behind in the spring of 1850. On a hunch they followed a small stream, a tributary of the Carson, to the far side of the mountains. About the time they were ready to give up in discouragement their earnings rose to $5 a day. Others, hearing of their success, joined them, and by 1853, there were 100 or so surface diggers in a place now known as Gold Canyon. The gold diminished soon after, and those mining it were down to an average of $2 a day. Five years later, most miners departed for Mono Lake after word got out of a gold strike there. The others explored farther up the canyon and achieved moderate success. With all of the area staked out, a few miners moved to the shoulder of Sun Mountain, to the headwaters of a small stream called Six Mile Creek.

This area was not rich in gold, but a town was founded, called Gold Hill. By fall of 1858, miners were collecting between $500-1,000 daily. The region attracted an increasing number of miners from other areas. J. F. Stone, a veteran of the California quartz mines, arrived in 1859. Miners had long complained about a troublesome blue sand that clogged their rockers and which they discarded. Stone was intrigued by the blue sand, suspecting it might contain silver. He sent a sample to an assayer in Nevada City, across the mountains. The assayer made a routine check, and his findings were so astonishing that he thought he had made a mistake. So he made a second test and the result was the same. That worthless "blue stuff" was rich in silver, a quarter gold, and worth about $4,700 a ton.

Stone confided in Judge James Walsh, a friend and mill owner in Grass Valley. That night Stone, Walsh and the assayer mounted mules and rode across the mountains to Six Mile Canyon. When they saw the tons of blue stuff tossed aside by miners in their search for gold, they knew they had found a major strike.

It is not quite clear who first discovered the original strike, although the presence of silver had long been known. California placer miners Allen and Rosea Gosch had found silver in Gold Canyon in 1857, but they didn't appreciate the importance of their discovery.

Two other prospectors, Peter O'Reilly and Patrick McLaughlin, deserve credit, as does James "Old Virginny" Fennimore, who was first to work a claim in Six Mile Canyon. Virginia City is named after him.

Today the strike is known as the Comstock Lode, after a picturesque character by the name of Henry P. Comstock. Supposedly, he rode up the canyon in 1859 on a borrowed pony with his "long legs dragging in the sagebrush." He met O'Reilly and McLaughlin while they were digging a spring to increase the water supply to their holdings. After they panned some soil, Comstock noticed gold. He arbitrarily ordered them off "his" claim. He said he had located the spring on his property earlier and that he and his partner "Manny" Penrod had been working the claim. This was dubious, but O'Reilly and McLaughlin agreed to take the two men as partners. After the four of them dug a trench up the hill from the spring they found a six-inch-wide vein that netted them "hundreds of dollars a year in gold."

> *The Nevada City paper, the* Journal *expressed the doubts of many miners when it was reported July 2, 1859, that "Of course the discoverers of this vein may*

> *have struck a good thing, but the odds were about 10 to one that instead of opening up their quartz vein they intend to open up a provision store."* They were wrong, as they soon learned.

The prospectors who discovered this rich lode, like many before them, benefited little. McLaughlin sold his share for $3,500. Penrod got $8,500 and Comstock sold out for only $11,500. Even these amounts were soon squandered in riotous living, while the property alone soon reached a market value of $80 million. In the next 20 years Virginia City and Gold Hill poured forth silver as well as gold worth approximately $300 million.

The territory became known as Washoe. It sent much of its ore to San Francisco. An important financial and banking system was set up as shares of the Comstock traded at ever-higher prices. The silver mined at Virginia City was mainly responsible for the growth of San Francisco. The mine became a huge enterprise, marking the first time the West had seen such an industrial expansion. It became the pattern for the future. President Lincoln, aware of Washoe's importance during the Civil War, hurriedly made Nevada a state.

Virginia City is in a huge, arid sink, with north-south mountain chains. The old camps are near the lower slopes of the mountain. Even today eastern California, Nevada and western Utah are thinly populated. Mark Twain, who worked for a newspaper back in the city's heyday, described

Virginia City, Nevada Territory, in the 1870s.

The Gould and Curry Mill, Virginia City, in the 1870s.

the region aptly: "No flowers grow here, and no green thing gladdens the eye. The birds that fly over the land carry their provisions with them." There's a grain of truth in his remarks.

J. Ross Browne wrote back then, "perhaps there is not another spot upon the face of the globe that presents a scene so weird and desolate in its natural aspect, yet so replete with busy life, so animate in its natural aspect, yet so replete with busy life, so animate with human interest . . . saloons are glittering with gaudy bars and fancy glasses and many-colored liquors, and thirsty men are swilling the burning poison; bill stickers are sticking up bills of auctions, theaters and new saloons. . . . A strange city truly, abounding in strange exhibitions and startling combinations of the human passions."

What to See & Do

Today's Virginia City is a busy tourist town, and mining is no longer a principal activity. The highwaymen of old are long gone, replaced by one-armed bandits in practically every building to lure small and large coins into their voracious interiors. The great old homes are now museums. For a price, you can see them. The mines that produced such wealth can be visited and you can see where "a wondrous battle raged, in which the combatants were man and earth."

You can visit Virginia City from spring to fall. Weekends are crowded, but few people stay overnight and no accommodations are recommended. If you come early, you'll appreciate more fully one of the West's most intriguing places, seeing it much as its residents did during the waning years of the 19th century. It is a spectacular look at the past, and it has many restored buildings large and small. Spend at least a day.

There are variety shows at the former **Miners' Union Hall**, where ancient melodramas and "red-hot mamas" entertain you. There's nothing in these old-fashioned performances that would upset families with children. It's pretty tame stuff compared to what children are exposed to on television today.

The Castle

Be sure to visit The Castle, the city's most authentic mansion. It is much the same as it was during boom times. It has a 175-year-old Czechoslovakian crystal chandelier, hand-blocked wallpaper from France and Comstock silver door knobs.

Comstock Mine

The technology used on the Comstock's "square-set-timbering" was a major advance in mining. It used mortise-and-tenon joints to lock the timber ends together. The timbers formed an endless series of hollow cribs 4 x 6 feet square. This honeycomb construction reinforced large underground activities far better than single timbers. The strength of structure was increased by filling the vertical columns with waste rock. This square-set timbering permitted engineers to reach great depths. This was a problem because the heat at these extreme levels was so intense that workers could spend only a short time there before they had to return to levels closer to the top to cool off. The air in this desert country was ideal but, after mining started, atmospheric pollution in Virginia City became a problem (today, however, there is no pollution).

In addition to heat and pollution, the old mines had serious problems with flooding and ore transport out of the depths of the Comstock mines. In 1865, Adolf Sutro proposed digging a horizontal tunnel from the Carson Valley, four miles away. It was completed at great expense in 1878, despite enormous complications. Unfortunately for those who invested in the tunnel, the ore had played out. Backers never recouped their investment. Sutro, however, sold his shares and made a lot of money.

Belcher Mine

The Belcher Mine was the most famous of the area digs. It produced more than $26 million worth of silver and gold between 1862 and 1916. Its stock rose from $1.50 a share in 1870 to $1,525 19 months later.

Mark Twain

Samuel Clemens came west with his brother in 1861. He later wrote a book called *Roughing It*. It's an amusing book about his journey and his impressions of Virginia City. He had been an unlucky prospector in the Esmeralda District. His true fame began when he sent Virginia City's *Territorial Enterprise* his sketches, which he signed "Josh."

He was hired at $25 a week and stayed with the paper for two years. He began signing his columns "Mark Twain." Those that survive indicate the greatness of his talent as a writer. Much of what we know about those early days was saved for later generations by such writers.

Where to Stay

Three 19th-century landmarks compete for guests here. The quite rustic **Gold Hill Hotel**, 1540 Main Street, ☎ 702-847-0111, $$-$$$, was established in 1859 and is the oldest operating hotel in Nevada. There are 13 rooms, 11 with private bath. The **Chollar Mansion**, 565 South D Street, ☎ 702-847-9777, $$-$$$, was built in 1861 and is on the National Register of Historic Places. It has four rooms, two with private bath. The **Crooked House**, 8 South F Street, ☎ 702-847-0521, $50-100, was built in the late 1800s. Its four rooms were recently refurbished.

Where to Dine

Burgers, steak sandwiches, fries and consummate American diner food are the rule of the day in Virginia City. Most of the eateries are packed along the main drag, C Street. The **Julia C. Bulette Saloon**, ☎ 702-847-9384, and the **Bonanza**, ☎ 702-847-0655, offer patio seating with views of the surrounding hills to go with the burgers and fries. Both are open for breakfast, lunch and dinner. The **Brass Rail**, ☎ 702-847-0304, serves great sandwiches. Open 10AM to 5PM.

A step up is the **Red Garter**, ☎ 702-847-0665, which not only serves blackened catfish and prime rib, but also terrific breakfasts. On B Street near Piper's Opera House, **Comstock Dinner House**, ☎ 702-847-9610, serves beef and seafood in a building constructed in 1872. The **Crown Point Restaurant** on Main Street, ☎ 702-847-0111, adjacent to the 1859 Gold Hill Hotel, serves fine French cuisine.

Lake Tahoe

Lake Tahoe, one of the true gems of the Sierra Nevada, is only an hour and a quarter drive from Virginia City, 45 miles away. Take Highway 50 back to Carson City and proceed on to Lake Tahoe. It is a marvelously scenic route that is most enjoyable.

Tahoe History

The Washoe Indians, who were hunters, gatherers and fishermen, probably discovered the lake. They lived in the Tahoe basin for thousands of years. The lake was a critical source of food as well as a sacred site.

The Washoe Indians called the lake "big water." According to them, Lake Tahoe was created when an evil spirit pursued an innocent Indian. The Great Spirit, according to the legend, tried to help the Indian by giving him a branch of leaves. Each leaf was supposed to produce a body of water that the evil spirit would have to circumvent. During the chase, the frightened Indian dropped the whole branch and thus created Lake Tahoe.

The Indians, who established summer camps along the lake, belonged to three different tribes. They gathered each year on what they called the *DaOwAga*, or "the edge of the lake." White settlers mispronounced the first two syllables and the region became known as Tahoe. It was not until 1945 that Tahoe became the lake's official name. It had been known variously as Bonpland – after a French botanist – Mountain Lake, and Bigler Lake – after California's third governor.

Fremont

There may have been earlier white visitors to the lake, but John C. Fremont is the first to record his visit. He camped near a river that flows from the mountains. Washoe Indians drew a map showing him the stream came from a mountain lake, three or four days travel away. Fremont led his party south to what is now known as the Carson River, and then turned west into the mountains. On February 14, 1845, approaching a pass, Fremont noted, "We had a beautiful view of a mountain lake at our feet, so entirely surrounded by mountains that we could not discover an outlet."

After Statehood

When California became the 31st state on September 9, 1850, a boundary was established that placed about two-thirds of the lake within the state and the remaining third in Nevada.

Martin Smith, a Pennsylvanian, built Lake Tahoe's first log cabin on the upper part of the lake in 1851. He grew food and provided housing for the few travelers who visited the lake. Three years later, Asa Hawley, anticipating construction of a wagon road to Tahoe, settled nearby and opened a trading post. It took four years for the wagon road to be built. In June of 1857, the first stagecoach crossed Johnson Pass to the southern end of the lake, at the west fork of the Carson River. One year later the road was in full use.

The lake was so remote that it didn't begin appearing on California's maps until 1859, when miners discovered the rich Comstock Lode's silver deposits in Virginia City.

There were few trees around Virginia City, so lumberjacks started to cut timber around Lake Tahoe. In the following years the amount of timber cut was equal to what would be used in the construction of homes for 200,000 people. Tahoe's forests would have been totally denuded except for the decline of activity at the mines.

Rich visitors arrived in Tahoe and built beautiful homes; the waters of the lake were tapped for drinking water.

Summer houses were built in quantity by 1906. A Reno developer offered 75-foot lakefront tract lots for $200-300 each. Two San Francisco realtors bought 44,000 acres of former timberland and divided it into sites for summer villas "suitable for millionaires and others."

Roads were paved during the 1920s and 1930s, and Lake Tahoe was no longer accessible just to the rich. In the 1950s, roads in winter were plowed, permitting year-round residence.

It was not until 1968 that the Tahoe Regional Planning Agency was formed by California and Nevada to oversee development of the basin to keep it environmentally sound.

By 1941, the *Tahoe Tattler* reported that "Lake Tahoe's Number 2 industry was night life." It claimed that 3,000 people flocked to bars, casinos and dance halls each weekend. Beer was the most popular drink, at 25¢ a glass. South Shore gaming took hold in 1944 when California's Harvey Gross opened the tiny Wheel Saloon in a log cabin. Its dramatic rise in popular favor increased, and by 1963 Harveys had 11 stories. By the late 1990s it was twice that high. Hotels, casinos and ski resorts draw millions of people today, but the high mountain wilderness and the area's spectacular beauty are the principal attractions.

Lake Tahoe Today

South Lake Tahoe is at the southern end of the Tahoe basin, six miles north of the intersection of highways 50 and 89. Its remarkable blueness, over an area 22 miles in length and 12 miles in width, makes it a spectacular sight. The lake's average depth is 989 feet, although its deepest point is 1,645 feet. Tahoe is the third-deepest lake in North America, holding

Lake Tahoe Area

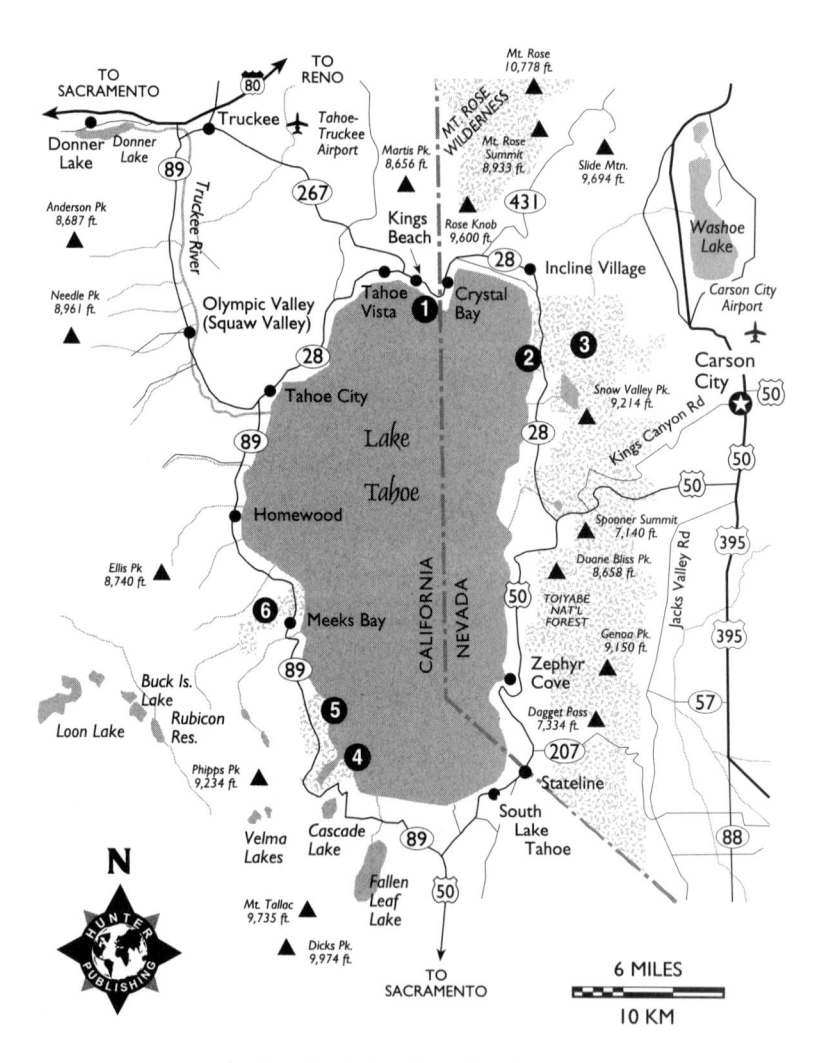

1. Kings Beach State Recreation Area
2. Sand Harbor Beach State Recreation Area
3. Lake Tahoe Nevada State Park
4. Emerald Bay State Park
5. D.L. Bliss State Park
6. Sugar Pine Point State Park

© 2000 HUNTER PUBLISHING, INC.

enough water to cover the state of California to a depth of 14 inches. In summer, the first 12 inches of the lake reaches a temperature of 69° F, while the depths below 700 feet remain constant at 39°.

Often called "the lake in the sky," Tahoe is in a valley between the main Sierra Nevada and an eastern offshoot, the Carson Range, with an altitude of 10,000 feet.

Clearing the Air on Tahoe's Water

Since Europeans and Anglos first began writing down their impressions of Lake Tahoe more than 150 years ago, they have made note of the marvelous clarity of the water in North America's largest alpine lake. To describe the water as crystal clear was an understatement. But in the last three decades, conservationists, residents and visitors alike have noticed that something is definitely amiss in the deep waters of Tahoe. In a dramatically telling – if not dogmatically scientific – example of the problems facing the lake, a 10-inch white dinner plate could be seen at a depth of 105 feet in 1968. Twenty-nine years later, a 10-inch white dinner plate could be seen only at 70 feet.

Beset by sediment runoff, urban pollution and increased growth of water plants, the fabled clarity of Lake Tahoe is becoming a thing of the past. The crisis has, however, galvanized support for the environment in and around the Tahoe Basin all the way up to the highest levels of government. In the summer of 1997, President Bill Clinton and Vice President Al Gore focused their attention, and the nation's spotlight, on Lake Tahoe and led the campaign to finalize a plan for restoring the purity of the lake. Millions of dollars are being pumped into the Basin to fund programs of all shapes and sizes. Into the next millenium, major changes are afoot here, including such initiatives as:

- Upgrading paved roads around the lake to improve erosion control and wastewater management.
- Obliterating old logging roads to return the land to its natural state and reduce sediment runoff that clouds the lake and increases algae growth. Miles of roads were cut in the 19th and early 20th centuries to provide lumber for the mines of the Comstock in Nevada. Now these obsolete tracks will be eliminated at the rate of 29 miles per year.
- Restoring streams and wetlands to filter out contaminants and improve water quality.
- Clearing brush and dead wood from US Forest Service lands over the next five years.

- Reducing excess fuel on US Forest Service land using prescribed burns and other methods. About 1,000 acres per year will be burned to help return Tahoe's forests to their natural state.
- Improving transportation by coordinating various transit systems on the south shore, adding a new beach shuttle service on the east shore along NV 28 and constructing a transit center on the north shore, among other things.
- The plans for Lake Tahoe also take into account cultural issues. The Washoe Tribe, descendents of the native culture that lived on this land before the coming of the whites, have finally garnered some attention. The tribe and the US Forest Service are working on establishing a Washoe Cultural Center at the lake. The plan also calls for granting the Washoe access to the water's edge for the first time in more than a century. Ironically, the people whose word for water's edge – *DaOwAga* – was translated to "Tahoe" have had no recognized claim on the lakeshore since the 1800s.

For more information on the effort to restore the lake, contact the **League to Save Lake Tahoe,** ☎ *916-541-5388. Join up and get the true local status symbol, a nifty "Keep Tahoe Blue" sticker.*

Lake Tahoe Facts

- The largest alpine lake in North America, Lake Tahoe is 22 miles long, 15 miles wide and covers 105,000 surface acres. The lake surface is 6,225 feet above sea level.
- Lake Tahoe is 1,645 feet deep and contains 39 trillion gallons of water.
- The Truckee River is the only outlet. It flows into Pyramid Lake in western Nevada. Sixty-three tributaries drain into Lake Tahoe.
- Five million people live within a four-hour drive of Lake Tahoe. An estimated 3½ million people visit the lake each year.
- In 1996, national forests in the Tahoe Basin generated $1,112,800 in recreation revenue and $139,000 in timber revenue for the federal government.
- Every 24 hours the lake level drops one-tenth of an inch due to the evaporation of 1.4 million gallons of water. The evaporating water would fill the daily water needs of 3½ million people.

The Lake Tahoe Basin Management Unit was formed in 1973 to manage public land on three national forests: Eldorado, Tahoe and Toiyabe. Seventy-seven percent of the Basin's land is in national forests, 16% in private hands and 7% on state land.

Getting Here & Getting Around

Seven highways connect the lake with major cities in California and Nevada. Amtrak offers rail service into Reno and Truckee (on the lake's north shore) and the area is served by air. The **Lake Tahoe Airport** lies just south of town. **Trans World Express** has direct daily flights to the lake from many cities, including Los Angeles and San Francisco. Airport shuttles, rental cars, limousines and taxis are available to take you from the airport to your accommodations. For flight schedules, ☎ 800-221-2000.

The **Reno-Tahoe International Airport**, about 60 miles northeast of Lake Tahoe, is served by 13 national airlines, with more than 100 flights daily. The scenic drive to and from the lake winds through the Sierra Nevada mountains and around picturesque Zephyr Cove. You can drive yourself in a rental car or board a luxurious Tahoe Casino Express motor coach shuttle. For details, ☎ 800-446-6128 or 775-785-2424. For flight information, ☎ 800-AT-TAHOE.

Local Transportation

Casinos along the lake's south shore in Nevada operate complimentary shuttles. Other free shuttles will take you to the ***Tahoe Queen*** and the ***M.S. Dixie II*** sightseeing boats. The *Tahoe Queen* has a 2½-hour trip from South Lake Tahoe to Emerald Bay on a paddlewheeler. It departs from Ski Run Marina at the foot of Ski Run Boulevard daily at 11, 1:30 and 3:55, from early June to early October, and at noon the rest of the year. There's a daily dinner cruise at 7 PM, June through October, and at 6:30 PM the rest of the year. Boarding and fare are $10; $9 for ages two-11. Dinner is extra and should be skipped. The food is not worth the price.

In winter there's a shuttle to get you to and from area resorts. For information about shuttles, ask your concierge or the front desk at your lodging.

For visitors, the **"Nifty 50" trolleys** are an interesting new option. These open trolleys run from June through Labor Day ferrying passengers from Harveys to Kiva Beach on one route, and from the Heavenly Aerial Tram to Zephyr Cove on another. Drivers provide interpretative information in a running narration about sites along each one-hour route. The fare, which is good all day, is $2 for either route or $3 for both.

Information Sources

For more information about Lake Tahoe, contact the following agencies:

Alpine County Chamber of Commerce, PO Box 265, Markleeville, CA 96120, ☎ 530-621-2475.

El Dorado County Chamber of Commerce, 542 Main Street, Placerville, CA 95667, ☎ 800-457-6279.

Lake Tahoe Visitors Authority, PO Box 16299, South Lake Tahoe, CA 96151. ☎ 800-AT-TAHOE.

Placer County Visitors Information Center, 13460 Lincoln Way, #A, Auburn, CA 95603. ☎ 530-887-2111 or 800-427-6463.

Tahoe North Visitors and Convention Bureau, 950 North Lake Boulevard Suite 3, PO Box 5578, Tahoe City, CA 96145. ☎ 800-824-6348.

What to See & Do

Try to see Tahoe from the air. It's the only way to truly appreciate the lake's astonishing beauty. If you don't want to fly, take a mile-long ride on the **Heavenly Aerial Tram** at Heavenly Ski Resort, where the view is spectacular. The price is $10.50 for adults, $6 for children under 12. In summer make reservations at ☎ 530-541-7544, or 541-1330 in winter. The tram will take you to 2,000 feet over Gunbarrel Ski Run. At the summit you can either sit down, relax over a meal, drink at the **Monument Peak Restaurant**, or hike from the summit trailhead on the Tahoe Vista Trail.

There are charter flights by **Oasis Aviation**, ☎ 530-541-2110, or by **Alpine Lake Aviation**, ☎ 530-541-4080, that fly year-round. For the more adventurous, take a 90-minute **hot air balloon ride.** ☎ 530-542-5944 or 800-872-9294.

Most visitors to Lake Tahoe go there to have fun in one of nature's wonderlands. Rand McNally lists it as number one for "Outdoor Fun in the USA."

Family Activities

There are dozens of reasons why families love Lake Tahoe. There are many activities specifically tailored to the interests of children. **Tahoe Amusement Park**, ☎ 530-541-1300, has rides and carnival-style games. **Fantasy Kingdom Miniature Golf**, ☎ 530-544-3833, has 20 holes obstructed by giant dragons, castles, whales and sharks. **Magic Carpet Miniature Golf**, ☎ 530-541-3787, is also lots of fun.

Trout Farm

Try your luck at the **Tahoe Trout Farm**, ☎ 530-541-1491, where admission, bait and tackle are free. No license is required and no limit is set. You pay only for what you catch.

Sleigh Rides

An old-fashioned sport is alive and well in Lake Tahoe. Local stables provide hay and sleigh rides.

Teen Activities

Teens can pick and choose from a long list of activities from June through August, including **summer camps**. For the latter you must register. ☎ 530-542-6055. There are **teenage dances** in the summer months each Wednesday. **Open gym nights** are available on Mondays and Thursdays and **archery** on Saturdays, hosted by the Parks and Recreation Department.

Grover Hot Springs State Park

If you head southwest on Highway 89, four miles from Markleeville on Hot Springs Road, Grover Hot Springs State Park is a superb place for hiking, fishing, cross-country skiing, or a dip in the hot spring-fed pool that holds up to 75 people. For reservations, ☎ 800-444-PARK. The best times to go are between May 7 and September 4.

Casinos

Lake Tahoe is best known for its world-class hotel-casinos that provide excitement in Nevada's nightlife. **Caesar's, Harrah's, Harveys and Horizon** share the Stateline area with a number of smaller places, such as **Bill's Casino** and **Lakeside Inn** and **Casino**.

In addition to traditional table games such as blackjack and poker, roulette, craps, slot machines, keno and baccarat, most places operate race and sports books. Gaming here draws visitors from all over the world.

The state of Nevada legalized gambling in 1869, banned it in 1910, then legalized it again in 1931. The **Cal-Neva Lodge**, a former prohibition speakeasy, is the oldest casino on the lake. It is on the north shore.

Harvey Gross, a Sacramento butcher, bought property on the south shore, along the state line on US 50, from the Galilee Episcopal Church. In a small log building, he opened the Wagon Wheel Saloon, a single room with a "six-stool" counter. There were three slot machines, two blackjack tables and a gasoline pump. At the time it was the only year-round pump on the south shore. His wife used her own kitchen to cook the food. By 1963 the Grosses were serving 5,000 meals every 24 hours, but they were no longer cooked by Mrs. Gross. At the time, his place had more slot machines than any casino in the world. That year Gross constructed the first high-rise building on the south shore. His 11-story casino-hotel extended far above the tops of the surrounding trees. **Harveys** today is a 22-story, 740-room hotel casino. It is one of four huge complexes in Stateline.

These casinos are basically operated for adults. **Harrah's** recently opened a **"Family Fun Center."** All casinos have video arcades for children.

These huge places are only in business to get you to gamble. Never forget that. Adult entertainment ranges from cabaret performances and revues to top musicians, singers and headline comedians. They furnish good gaming and great entertainment.

- **Caesar's**, ☎ 775-588-3515, opened in 1979. It boasts a unique atmosphere, with Roman tubs and imported marble in the rooms, togas on the waiters, with dancing until 4 AM at Nero's 2000. This is an elegant, spacious casino with liberal slot machines and high jackpots.
- **Harrah's**, ☎ 775-588-6611, has been popular since 1955. It offer gaming and entertainment.
- **Harveys**, ☎ 775-588-2411, is the largest casino at Lake Tahoe and its friendly atmosphere has endeared it to visitors. It has more slot machines than any other casino in the area, and huge progressive jackpots on mechanical and electronic slot machines. Revues and show bands provide entertainment nightly in the Emerald Theatre.
- The **Lake Tahoe Horizon Casino Resort**, ☎ 775-588-6211, operates more than 800 slot machines and video poker machines, plus other types of gambling. Three venues offer distinct entertainment options, from large-screen television and dancing to cabaret-style shows, superstar entertainment and special events.
- The **Lakeside Inn and Casino**, ☎ 775-588-7777, is a smaller, more intimate version of a full-service casino resort. The service is high quality and the food is more affordable than at the larger casinos.

If you gamble at Lake Tahoe, or any other place, use common sense. Decide in advance what you can afford to lose, and quit when you're ahead or at the figure you've established for yourself. Be sure you understand the rules of the game you want to play. If not, all casinos will offer you free lessons. Craps is the only game that provides true excitement. You can purchase a craps computer game and try out strategies until you find one you like. Craps is the only casino game in which cheering is commonplace. Blackjack requires skill to be reasonably successful in the decision-making process. Don't count on luck in this game. The smart player has a good chance to beat the house.

Wedding Vows

There's an old Washoe Indian saying that "those who come to the Lake in the Sky are blessed." There must be some truth in the legend because thousands of couples each year follow that rule and exchange their wedding vows here.

Tahoe is a perfect setting for a wedding because of its idyllic beauty, the ease of obtaining wedding licenses, and abundant coordinators and chapels. Many vacationers, with no previous thought of getting married, are so charmed by the surroundings that they get married here. Such weddings can be spur-of-the-moment inexpensive unions at small chapels, or full-scale weddings with hundreds of guests in the most breathtaking background imaginable.

A bride and groom can tie the knot on the lake's shore, at the splendid historic estate of Valhalla, on a 52-foot yacht or paddlewheeler, in a luxurious casino or in any of the South Shore's 27 chapels.

> For a free copy of the *Lake Tahoe Wedding and Honeymoon Planner*, ☎ 800-AT-TAHOE.

Marriage Licenses

Three different marriage licenses are honored at Lake Tahoe. California has two types: a public license and a "confidential" one. The state no longer requires blood tests for either license, but both parties must be 18 years old, have identification and, for the public license, proof of any dissolution within the last 90 days. The public license, which can be purchased in any county in California, requires a signature by at least one witness. The confidential license is not completely confidential. Without a court order, a third party can obtain confirmation of the marriage but none of the details, including the date of the marriage. By contrast, for a fee, any third party can obtain a copy of a public license. A public license costs $50 in El Dorado County. Costs vary throughout the state. A confidential license costs $45. A public license can be obtained at county clerk and recorder offices throughout the state. The El Dorado County Recorder Clerk has an office at the lake at 3368 Lake Tahoe Boulevard, #108, South Lake Tahoe, CA 96150, or you can ☎ 530-621-5490. A confidential license can be obtained from county or recorder clerks' offices, or through an authorized notary. Most Tahoe chapels have authorized notaries on call.

You can obtain a Nevada marriage license without a blood test or a waiting period. Both parties must be 18 and present a driver's license from any state, a certified birth certificate, a passport, or military identification. A license is good anywhere in the state up to one year from the date of purchase. The license costs $42 in Douglas County and Carson City. This cost is $7 higher than Nevada's standard $35 fee. It includes a marriage certificate, which is sent to the parties about a week after the wedding.

A Nevada marriage license is available from the **Douglas County Clerk's** satellite office at 175 US 50, Stateline, NV 89449. The **Carson City Marriage Bureau** is at 111 North Curry Street, Carson City, NV 89703. ☎ 775-782-9015. The satellite office is open evenings and weekends. On weekdays calls are forwarded to the Minden office.

Cultural & Historical Sights

Tahoe's classic blue skies, deep blue lake, snow-capped mountains, alpine forests and the area's wide variety of cultural and historical sights are among the great pleasures of the world.

Lake Tahoe's Visitor Center

For guidance, the best place to start is the US Forest Service's Lake Tahoe Visitor's Center on Highway 89 between Pope and Kiva beaches. It is open from Memorial Day through late October. There you can procure free maps, brochures, wilderness permits and watch interpretative programs. ☎ 530-573-2674. If you like to take short walks or longer hikes, several trails begin at the center. You should take time to see the lake as a whole by driving around it – a distance of 72 miles. Your trip will be enhanced if you purchase a copy of a two-hour audio cassette for $9.95. It includes a map, and the tape will guide you from one notable spot to the next with tales and legends about the lake. It will also discuss the lake's colorful characters and the best points of interest. The tape is available at the **South Lake Tahoe Chamber of Commerce**, ☎ 530-541-5255, or the **Douglas Visitor's Center Chamber of Commerce**, ☎ 775-588-5746.

If you have a large party, call **Destination Lake Tahoe**, ☎ 775-588-5746, and **Lake Tahoe Tours**, ☎ 530-544-8687, which specialize in business organizations and leisure group tours. They will plan your trips and provide chartered buses, mini-vans or limousines.

Emerald Bay

If your time is limited, you must visit **Emerald Bay State Park**. It's a tiny bay at the southwest corner of the lake, with the lake's only island, Fannette. Hike down the trail to the shore at the head of the bay. There you'll find the **Vikingsholm**. It is accessible only by boat or on foot. In 1928, Mrs. Laura J. Knight, a wealthy widow from Chicago, purchased this isolated spot and instructed Lennart Palme, a Swedish architect, to design a home resembling a Norse fortress of about AD 800. The architect's task was formidable because he had orders not to disturb even one of the lot's magnificent trees. The Vikingsholm was completed in September

1929. It is considered the finest example of Scandinavian architecture in the Western Hemisphere. The methods and materials used in its construction, including the granite boulders in the fountains and walls, are those of ancient Scandinavia. Turrets, towers, intricate carvings, even hand-hewn timbers were used to create the fortress. The sod roof, with its living grass, is like those sometimes used in Scandinavia to feed livestock in winter. Mrs. Knight tried to get many of the furnishings from Scandinavia, but the Norwegian and Swedish governments refused to export them. She had them copied in every detail when the real items were declared historically significant and not permitted to leave those countries. Each particle of wood was copied in fine detail down to measurements, coloration and aging of the wood.

Vikingsholm is open for guided tours. The price is $2 for adults and $1 for children, daily from June 17 through Labor Day. On weekends it is open only through the end of September. From the shore of the castle you can see a small stone house on Fannette Island where Mrs. Knight and her friends occasionally took tea in the afternoon. For further information, ☎ 530-525-7372.

Tallac Historic Site

The 74-acre Tallac Historic Site, ☎ 530-542-4166, is the former 100-year-old Tallac Resort, on the west shore near the Visitor Center. In its heyday, the resort included two large hotels, a casino, and numerous annexes and out-buildings. The **"Lucky Legacy" tour** ($2.50 per person) can only be taken if you call ahead and request the tour. It allows you to see the 19th-century gaming world of former resort owner Elias J. "Lucky" Baldwin. The site is also home to three estates erected as a summer retreat by wealthy Californians – the **Pope** and **McConagle mansions,** and **Valhalla. "Tea with the Tevises"** is a free tour with tea in the arboretum of the Pope estate's grounds. Tours start at 3 PM Mondays during July and August.

Valhalla has been converted into a community events center. The McConagle mansion is now the **Educational-Cultural Center and Tallac Museum.** It contains exhibits of the Baldwin family, the hotel's proprietors and the casinos. The **Washoe Indian Cultural Foundation** features artifacts, historic photographs, basket-weaving demonstrations and slide presentations.

Ponderosa Ranch

On the eastern side of the lake is Ponderosa Ranch, on State Route 28 at Incline Village, Nevada. This western theme park is the original Cartwright Ranch House where the television series *Bonanza* was filmed. There's a saloon, museum, *kiddylane*, playground, petting farm and a mystery mine. It's worth seeing, and you should plan to spend at least two hours there. It is open daily from 9:30-5, May through October. Admission is $7.50, but $2 less for ages five-11. Breakfast hayrides are available at 8-9:30 AM Memorial Day weekend to Labor Day. Admission is $9.50, $2 less for ages five-11 and $2 for children two-four. Ranch admission is included in the price of the meal.

Historical Society Museum

Throughout the summer at the Tallac Historic Site, the **Valhalla Festival of Arts and Music** showcases jazz, bluegrass, rock, mariachi and classical music. The **Valhalla Renaissance Festival** is held in June. The following month the **Native American Fine Art Festival** is held, and the **Great Gatsby Festival** is in August. For information, ☎ 530-541-4975.

Nevada's First Settlement

Fifteen miles east of the lake on Highway 206 you'll find historic **Genoa**, Nevada's first settlement. It was once a Mormon trading post, founded in 1851. Today the city has 10 buildings on the National Register of Historic Places. A replica of the original post has been turned into a museum. There's also a golf course at Genoa Lake. ☎ 775-782-4951.

Cultural Events

During July and August "**Shakespeare at Bar Harbor**" attracts large crowds, as does the annual **Lake Tahoe Summer Music Festival.** Four music and dance concerts are offered each year by the prestigious **Tahoe Arts Project.** The **Tahoe Community Orchestra** and the **Tahoe Community Choir** perform each winter and spring.

Exhibits are held in more than a dozen galleries, and college and community theatrical productions, headline acts and cabaret entertainment at the casinos contribute to an outstanding arts calendar.

The **Lake Tahoe Historical Society Museum**, 3058 US 50, has the area's most comprehensive collections of early photographs, pioneer implements, and Washoe Indian basketry. It also has a fine model of the historic *SS Tahoe* and the basin's oldest building. For information, ☎ 530-541-5458.

Adventures on Foot

Hiking Trails

The perimeter of Lake Tahoe spans thousands of square miles of forest land, much of it open for hiking, backpacking and camping.

The US Forest Service's **Lake Tahoe Visitors Center**, at 870 Emerald Bay Road, South Lake Tahoe, ☎ 530-573-2674, is a great source of hiking maps and pertinent information about a full selection of trails that start here. On the southwest side of the lake, **D.L. Bliss and Emerald Bay State Parks** occupy almost 2,000 acres in California's Sierra Nevada. Bliss is named for the pioneering lumberman, railroad owner and banker whose family donated 744 acres to the California State Park system in 1929. The main part of Emerald Bay was sold to the state for half its appraised value by Placerville lumberman Harvey West in 1969. The two parks cover some six miles of magnificent shoreline. If you don't have time to spend for a long hike, stop at the crest of **Eagle Falls** on Highway 89. The view from here is awe inspiring. Within the parks are a variety of plant life, including ponderosa and Jeffrey pines, white and red fir, Sierra juniper and black cottonwood. Wildflowers make carpets of color in season with columbine, leopard lily, lupine, bleeding heart and yellow monkeyflower. Brush areas are covered with ceonothus, current and gooseberry vines. The parks have 288 family campsites – each with a private table, cupboard and stove. Some sites at D.L. Bliss can accommodate trailers up to 15 feet. Emerald Bay will take trailers up to 18 feet and motor homes up to 21 feet. Campsites at either park can be reserved in summer by calling Destinet, ☎ 800-444-7275, or writing to 9450 Carrol Park Drive, San Diego, CA 92121.

There are also 20 primitive campsites accessible by boat.

Desolation Wilderness

Desolation Wilderness is far off the beaten track – and there are few creature comforts, Subalpine forests and granite trails abound in this southwestern part of the Tahoe Basin. The scenery is magnificent and there are few rules, although open campfires are forbidden. You can reach the area only on horseback or on foot and camping permits are required. For information, ☎ 530-573-2600.

Tahoe Rim Trail

The great Tahoe Rim Trail, a 150-mile hiking and equestrian trail, follows the ridge around the lake's basin. It is now in its final stages of completion. It passes through six counties in two states and this trail incorporates a portion of the peaceful adjacent valleys. It gives you a chance to retrace the paths of Indians and pioneers. It is moderately difficult, with a 10% grade and elevations ranging from 6,000 to 9,400 feet. You can camp only at designated sites.

Vista Trail

Tahoe Vista Trail starts at the top of Heavenly Ski Resort's aerial tram – 8,250 feet up – and traverses a mile of ridgeline above southeastern Lake Tahoe. The view on clear days reaches 30 miles. You can make the hike with or without a guide trained by the US Forest Service. **Guided hikes** are free and take about 90 minutes. They are offered twice a day through the fall. Your guide will give you a natural history lesson en route. The trail rises 1,000 feet, so it is moderately strenuous. The views of Monument Peak and the Nevada Desert are worth the effort. They are most spectacular in late summer when sunsets turn the sky bright pink and orange. No reservations are necessary but a tram ticket is required at a cost of $10.50 for adults, and $6 for ages six and under. A free trail guide with information about 10 signed stops en route is available at the trailhead's kiosk, below the Monument Peak Restaurant. Trail hours are 10-7.

Granite Chief Wilderness

This 25,000-acre wilderness area doesn't receive nearly the foot traffic that Desolation does, so it makes for a perfect escape from the crowds. Granite Chief is accessed from the west shore of Lake Tahoe by driving west on Blackwood Canyon Road south of Tahoe City to Barker Pass. The pavement ends here, but you can continue on a dirt road 2.3 miles to the **Powderhorn trailhead**. Walk four miles down the trail to the **Hellhole Trail**, which leads deep into the undiscovered backcountry. Hellhole Reservoir is a difficult nine-mile hike away. For more information and to obtain a wilderness permit, contact the US Forest Service in Truckee, ☎ 530-587-3558.

If you don't want to drive all the way to the end of the road, you can stop at Barker Pass and take a hike on the **Pacific Crest Trail** five miles to Twin Peaks. You'll head north along a ridge, savoring the views of the lake basin on one side and the wilderness area on the other. A spur trail leads to the top of Twin Peaks.

On the other side of Barker Pass, you can access **Ellis Peak Trail** and take an easy five-mile round-trip walk to and from the peak. You first switchback up to a ridge, then hike through meadows exploding with wildflowers. At an intersection with a dirt road, turn right, walk 100 yards to another path and head east. Ellis Peak is a short hike away. If you return to the first fork and walk the other way, you'll soon reach Ellis Lake. Return the way you came.

Mokelumne Wilderness

At 106,000 acres, the Mokelumne is the region's largest wilderness area. The bulk of the land is south of the Lake Tahoe basin between CA 89 and CA 4. This is a rugged, challenging region where you can celebrate your independence on Fourth of July Peak, climb the Elephant's Back to 9,500 feet or bag the peak of Round Top, the highest point in the wilderness at 10,381 feet. This is a glacier-scoured land of dozens of small lakes and streams where the trails seem to go on forever. For more information and to obtain a wilderness permit, contact the **US Forest Service Eldorado Information Center** in Camino, ☎ 530-644-6048.

Hikers can walk the historic **Mormon-Emigrant Trail** near Mokelumne Wilderness. Head south of Lake Tahoe to CA 88 and the Carson Summit. Trailheads are located at nearby Caples Lake, Kirkwood Ski Area and Silver Lake. The trail was originally blazed from west to east in the late 1840s by a group of Mormons who were sent to California to fight in the Mexican-American War. They arrived too late to join the fighting and on their return to Utah traced a new path across the Sierra Nevada that emigrants would use by the thousands.

Mount Rose Wilderness

Located entirely in Nevada in the steep, forested high country northeast of Lake Tahoe, the 28,000-acre wilderness is a favorite escape for hikers in Reno and the Carson Valley. This relatively dry region is dominated by the Carson Range, the local name for the Sierra Nevada, and sees far fewer visitors than the other wilderness areas. There are seven trailheads, the most popular one off NV 431 near Mt. Rose Summit. No wilderness permits are required, but overnight visitors should obtain a campfire permit. For more information, contact the **US Forest Service in Carson City**, ☎ 775-882-2766.

The trail to **Mt. Rose** is a difficult, six-mile round-trip that will leave you huffing, but the views from atop the windswept peak will certainly revive you. The trailhead can be found on NV 431 one mile south of the Mt. Rose Summit (a highway designation not to be confused with the actual summit of Mt. Rose). The path gains almost 2,000 feet in three miles to the zenith at 10,776, but that doesn't deter the scores of hikers who tread this trail every day.

Other Trails

Not from Mt. Rose, 6½ miles north of Incline Village just off NV 431, you can pick up the **Ophir Creek Trail** that drops steeply six miles down the eastern face of the Carson Range to **Davis Creek County Park**. Keep in mind this is a 3,300-foot elevation change, so only hike down as far as you want to walk up. The trail wanders along a Jeep road (open to mountain bikes) through wildflower-strewn Tahoe Meadows, crests a rise that offers views of the Washoe Valley below and begins to drop toward the valley floor. The hot, dusty trail continues past three small ponds before reaching the park at the bottom.

Known as the area's most strenuous day-hike, the trek to **Mt. Tallac**, in the southwestern corner of the Tahoe basin, is only for those in good physical condition. The 10-mile round-trip climbs from 6,480 feet to 9,735 feet and back again. The trailhead is on a dirt road directly across from Baldwin Beach, about 10 minutes north of South Lake Tahoe via CA 89. Along the trail you'll pass **Cathedral Lake**, just before making a serious ascent toward the peak. The panorama from the summit will take your breath away if the hike up to alpine country hasn't already.

Not far from Mt. Tallac, you can sweat it out on another strenuous trail into **Desolation Valley** and a fantastic basin filled with crystalline lakes. From Camp Richardson on CA 89, head south on Fallen Leaf Road to the **Glen Alpine trailhead** on the southwest shore of the lake. If you choose to hike all the way to Lake Aloha and back, you'll cover 11.6 miles and a 1,500-foot elevation change. The trail climbs steadily past Lily Lake, then through a trail junction. Turn north to access Cathedral and Falling Leaf Lake, or south to visit Angora Lakes. Grass Lake and the heart of Desolation Wilderness is straight ahead, followed by a series of switchbacks and rock stairs up to a ridge. Suzie Lake and Heather Lake, framed by dramatic granite walls, are on the other side of the ridge. Past Heather Lake, the trail turns south, intersects the Pacific Crest Trail and ends at **Lake Aloha**. In reality, the lake is a series of pools and small granite islands. Retrace your steps to return to you car.

How about a hike that requires a water taxi to reach the trailhead? To reach this beauty, the **Echo Lakes Trail** that runs at least five miles round-trip to **Upper Echo Lake**, drive south on US 50 from South Lake Tahoe to Echo Summit and turn on Johnson Pass Road. Stay left and drive to the parking lot at **Lower Echo Lake**. Here you'll catch a water taxi, which runs between 10AM and 6PM during summer and costs $11, across Lower Echo Lake through a narrow channel to Upper Echo Lake. From the dock take the **Pacific Crest Trail** 3.4 miles to **Lake Aloha**. The first trail segment hugs a granite wall and climbs past spur trails leading to Tamarack Lake and Lake of the Woods. Just past the spurs to Lucille Lake and Margery Lake, take a left at a junction to reach Lake Aloha.

Further south of the Lake Tahoe basin, trails heading away from Wrights Lake lead into the southern portion of Desolation Wilderness. To reach the trailhead, take US 50 south and west through the hamlet of Strawberry to Wrights Lake Road heading north. Climb the narrow road to a junction and turn right, then proceed to the lake, bearing right at the next fork to access the trailhead on the eastern edge of the water. The **Twin Lakes Trail** climbs gently through open forest, then ascends to a granite-covered wonderland. You'll reach a junction at 1.4 miles. Take a left to reach Twin Lakes and right to access Grouse Lake. The path to Twin Lakes crosses huge granite slabs and you'll have to keep an eye out for cairns marking the way. Experience using a map and compass are highly suggested to find your way to the end of the trail at **Island Lake**, 3.2 miles from the trailhead. If you take the route to Grouse Lake, you'll climb steeply through open forest to **Grouse Lake**, then continue on to **Hemlock Lake**, surrounded by granite boulders, where the trail ends, 2½ miles from the start.

Rock Climbing

Although the season can be relatively short – at higher elevations heavy snow can block access to climbing routes from October to June or July – the Tahoe area is a magnet for climbers of all levels. Not only is it a great place to learn the art of sport climbing, but Tahoe also attracts world-class athletes who come to test their skills on the granite crags, outcrops, boulders and walls found at nearly every compass point in the region. It would take an encyclopedia to describe all the climbs in the Tahoe basin, so what follows is a buffet of climbs in various locales of different lengths, on varying terrain and requiring the gamut of skill sets.

Sport-Climbing Ratings

This book refers to the sport-climbing ratings used commonly in North America, known as the Yosemite Decimal System. The ratings are a subjective measurement of the technical difficulty of the most challenging part of a climb, although the rating is usually increased if the climb is a very long one.

The first digit of each rating signifies the class of the climb according to the following scale:

- Class 1 - Easy hiking.
- Class 2 - Hiking with some altitude gain and loss
- Class 3 - Boulder hopping, occasionally using hands
- Class 4 - Climbing, using the hands, but without the need for a belay (scrambling)
- Class 5 - Technical climbing with a belay (free climbing)
- Class 6 - Aided climbing

The number following the class indicates the difficulty of the climb, ranging from .0 to .14 (and sometimes beyond). For Class 5 routes, the most popular among serious rock climbers, the lower numbers (.0 to .6) indicate that two handholds and two footholds are available for every move.

There are fewer sure holds as the numbers increase, until all holds disappear at .10. Beyond that, climbers enter the realm of myth, legend, and braggadocio – usually over pints of ale.

Ratings are generally applied by the first climber to make a particular ascent or move, then amended by subsequent climbers. By their nature, these ratings are meant only as guidelines, not hard-and-fast rules. As with all outdoor activities, use common sense before you get into trouble, taking into account personal experience, climbing partners, and the weather when determining the safest course of action.

Northwest of Lake Tahoe, the **Donner Summit area** boasts plenty of five-star routes on a mixture of boulders and crags. From Soda Springs, drive east on Old Highway 40 to Donner Pass Road. From the summit, you come across **Goldilocks Wall** (elevation 7,042 feet), **School Rock** and **Grouse Slab**, a short walk north on the Pacific Crest Trail. The biggest crag north of Old Highway 40 is **Black Wall**. The top of **Donner Peak** offers excellent bouldering on granite. Near Donner Summit, climbers can scramble up crags and in cracks in the **Truckee River Basalt Area**. Head south from Truckee on CA 89 and look for the crags on the east side of the road. You'll have to wade across the river to reach the approach slope. Big Chief is a few miles south of Truckee.

In the Tahoe Basin, you can enjoy a day of bouldering on the north shore at **Brockway Summit** near a residential area. From the California-Nevada border on the north shore, drive west on CA 28 to Speedboat Avenue and park at the end of the road. Look for the boulders along both sides of the road. On the west shore, visit **The Amphitheater** for a day of sport climbing on the basalt crags. Head four miles north of Tahoe City on CA 89. The climbing area is on the east-facing hillside across from the entrance to Alpine Meadows. **As You Like It** and **Poor Man's Pump** are two popular expert routes. The nearby basalt columns of **Twin Crags** are another favorite area one mile west of Tahoe City above the north side of CA 89 near the Twin Crag summer home tract.

On the south shore, the neighborhood of **D.L. Bliss State Park** supports an active climbing community. Find plenty of fine bouldering near Balanced Rock, about one mile north of the park entrance. Another good boulder field is half a mile south of the park entrance. Near Emerald Bay, nifty crag and crack climbing can be found on **Eagle Lake Buttress**, where climbers come to tackle routes like **A Line**, **Orange Sunshine** and **Monkey Business**. To reach the buttress, park at the Eagle Creek Canyon trailhead and hike to **Eagle Lake**. Follow the drainage west of the lake to the crest of a ridge, then hike .25 mile north to the base of the buttress. If you don't have time for the hike to Eagle Lake, try **Smoke Rock** or **Mayhem Cove**. At the Eagle Creek Canyon trailhead, you can spot Smoke Rock through the trees from the parking area. Smoke Rock boasts routes rated up to 5.11. You can reach Mayhem Cove by following a faint trail from the top of Smoke Rock.

Challenging bouldering and crag climbing can be round on the south face of **West Twin Peaks** on the rocks of **Pie Shop**. The rough-faced crags and boulders are in South Lake Tahoe. Drive one mile beyond the airport, then turn on Sawmill Road and park at the end. You'll spot the boulders on the hill above. To reach Pie Shop, hike northwest toward the eastern summit of Twin Peaks, then turn bear left into a gully toward Pie Shop on the western summit of Twin Peaks. There are dozens of classic routes here for experienced climbers, including **Humble Pie** (rated 7), **True Grip** (10b), **Natural High** (11c) and **Double Dragon** (12d).

South of the Lake Tahoe Basin off CA 88, intermediate and expert climbers can explore a world of granite crag and face climbing at **Kirkwood Lake**. From Kirkwood Lake campground, just north of the village of Kirkwood, hike west on a trail from the campground loop road to access the two developed crags.

On the Nevada side of Lake Tahoe, some excellent crag climbing and bouldering can be found within sight of the water. **Incline Rock** is 3½ miles north of Incline Village, with parking on the left just south of the vista point. The 75-foot-high granite face is 100 yards uphill. Overhangs present experts with 5.11a and 5.12a opportunities. In Incline Village above Diamond Peak Ski Area on Tyrol Drive, **Lycra Eliminator** offers more overhangs and five aided routes. Farther south, at the junction of US 50 and NV 28, **Spooner Crag** is found on a side road heading west just west of the intersection. The crag is 75 yards uphill offering sport crag climbing on 50 feet of face. There are 10 routes including **Jello Wars** (5.11a). The famous **Cave Rock** also has 80 feet of face and difficult overhangs above and below US 50. There are more than 20 routes, all 5.11c and heavier, including **Asylum** (5.11d) and **Slayer** (5.14a).

Golfing

Golfers will find Tahoe a perfect spot, enhanced by its setting. Birdies are more enjoyable and bogeys somehow are more acceptable in the shadow of Tahoe's majestic peaks. There are five public golf courses. **Bijoy Municipal**, ☎ 530-555-3500, has nine holes, 2,015 yards with a 33 par; **Edgewood Tahoe**, ☎ 775-588-3566, is the site of the Isuzu Celebrity Golf Championship, with 18 holes, 7,563 yards, a par of 72, and a driving range; **Glenbrook**, ☎ 775-749-5201, has nine holes, but two sets of tees for an 18-hole total of 5,566 yards, a par of 71, and a driving range; and **Lake Tahoe Golf Course**, ☎ 530-577-2121, has 18 holes, 4,070 yards, a 66 par and a driving range.

Tennis

Kirkwood, Ceasar's and **Harveys** have private tennis facilities and charge fees for court time. Public courts are found at Kirkwood, South Tahoe High School, South Tahoe Middle School and Zephyr Cove/Whittel High School. In some cases, reservations are required.

Adventures on Horseback

For those who enjoy riding, horses can be rented and pack trips arranged at stables. The best stables are at **Soren's Resort, Zephyr Cove, Camp Richardson's Corral, Kirkwood** and **Sunset Ranch**.

You can give your pack trip a unique twist by bringing along a llama or two to do the hauling. Some stables rent llamas that will dutifully tote your food and equipment while you enjoy the ride on horseback.

If you want to ride into **Desolation Wilderness**, with its 80 lakes and numerous streams, you must have a permit. Day riders can obtain the permit from the self-service stations at the trailheads. Riders planning to spend the night must go to the Forest Reserve Service Office or the Visitor's Center to obtain a permit.

Adventures on Wheels
Mountain Biking

Biking is a favorite pastime for tourists, and you can rent mountain bikes or any other kind, even those built for two. Motorcycles, mopeds and scooters are also for rent. Try the backcountry roads and areas designated for off-highway vehicles.

The **Pope-Baldwin Bike Path**, which runs parallel to Highway 89, is a popular paved, nearly flat 3.4-mile trail. It passes through Camp Richardson and offers several scenic sidetrips to Pope and Baldwin beaches, the Tallac Historic Site, the US Forest Service's Lake Tahoe Visitors Center and Fallen Leaf Lake. The **South Lake Tahoe Bike Path** starts at US 50 near El Dorado Beach and Picnic Area. This paved path crosses Trout Creek and the Upper Truckee Marsh to Lake Tahoe. It also connects with other hiking trails and lanes throughout the Lake Tahoe region and into Nevada.

> *The Forest Service provides a list of 10 mountain biking trails varying in length from one to 18 miles. Detailed maps are available for $3. Contact them at 870 Emerald Bay Road, Suite 1, South Lake Tahoe, CA 96150; ☎ 530-573-2600.*

One of the most challenging of these trails is called **"Mr. Toad's Wild Ride."** It is located near Pioneer Trail and Oneida Street on the south shore. The trail is recommended only for the experienced biker because it drops from 9,000 feet to 6,800 feet in three miles.

Not too long ago, ski resort operators figured out that their revenue streams don't have to melt away when the snow does as long as they cater to the mountain biking crowd. The resorts charge riders to use the chairlifts and offer complete rental and repair facilities. Both **Northstar-at-Tahoe** and Squaw Valley open their "slopes" in the summer to bikers. Northstar, off CA 267 northwest of the Lake Tahoe basin, boasts more than 100 miles of trails and more than enough rugged real estate to satisfy even the most advanced mountain biker. Unlike US Forest Service terrain, Northstar's trails are marked and mapped, and if you've got legs like heavy-duty pistons, you can ride for free all day. Northstar charges nothing for admission, but does charge to use the chair lifts. Some of the best riding is off the Echo and Lookout lifts to Route 507. From here you can ride to Watson Lake along the **Fiberboard Freeway** (route 100), the north shore's popular off-road trail. You can complete a nine-mile loop from the lake by taking the route 100 to Sawmill Flat, where you pick up **Big Springs Trail** back to Northstar Village. You can extend the loop ride to a stiff 25 miles by continuing along route 115, an extension of the Fiberboard Freeway, about 7½ miles from Mount Watson all the way to Tahoe City. For more information, contact Northstar-at-Tahoe, ☎ 530-562-1010.

Advanced rides will love **Squaw Valley Bike Park**, off CA 89 northwest of the lake. After purchasing a trail pass, you can take the lift up to an elevation of 8,200 feet and test your mettle on the strenuous trails to Shirley Lake or the loop through Cornice II and Red Dog back to the base of the mountain 2,000 feet below. For more information, contact Squaw Valley USA, ☎ 800-545-4350.

Nearby at **North Tahoe Regional Park**, there are a number of trails for riders of all abilities, a bike race track, restrooms, nature trails and a playground. You can also access the Fiberboard Freeway from here. To reach the park, from Tahoe Vista on the northern end of Lake Tahoe, take National Avenue until it ends at Donner Road and turn west to Shelter Road and the park entrance. For more information, ☎ 530-546-5043.

Mountain Biking in Nevada

High above Lake Tahoe on the Nevada side of the border, one of the West's best mountain bike trails begins near the intersection of NV 28 and US 50 at **Spooner Lake**. The 10-mile round trip is classified as moderately strenuous. Begin by following the signs for North Canyon Road, which parallels **North Canyon Creek**. After about three miles and 600 feet of climbing, the trail makes a high-altitude, heart-thumping ascent past Snow Valley Peak on the right toward **Marlette Lake**. Don't stop now: The views are definitely worth the effort. Finally, at 8,100 feet, the trail descends to the lake. A left at an intersection at the bottom of the hill leads to the dam and a great picnic spot. The lake supplies water to Virginia City via a system of pipes and flumes designed and built in 1873. The ride can be extended into a 24-mile loop by continuing on the **Flume Trail**, a sometimes steep and wild ride. Ten miles from the Spooner Lake trailhead, the trail hits Tunnel Creek Road. A right turn leads to an uphill climb. Continue straight and watch for the Franktown Campground signs, then stay on the road around a tight turn. At the 12-mile mark, turn right onto **Red House Flume Trail** and parallel the metal flume pipe to a sign pointing right toward Hobart Reservoir. Follow that across the dam into an aspen grove marked by historic graffiti left by Basque sheepherders. A hard right turn leads uphill to the lake and an intersection at 14.7 miles. Turn right and follow the signs to Marlette Lake and Spooner Lake, as the trail gains another 750 feet. You get most of this back two miles later on a steep descent to Marlette Lake, where a left heads back to the trailhead at Spooner Lake.

With a car shuttle parked at Hidden Beach Trailhead on NV 28, the trail can be a one-way trip. Just continue northwest on the Red House Flume Trail from Hobart Reservoir and follow it seven miles past Twin Lakes to the highway. This route drops from 8,000 feet to 6,400 in seven miles. Note that bikers share this route with both hikers and equestrians, and must yield the right-of-way to both. At presstime, Tahoe is generally devoid of the animosity that often exists between these three user groups, and bikers are actually highly regarded here for respecting their fellow recreationists and the environment in general. Put simply, don't screw it up.

For more information, contact **Lake Tahoe Nevada State Park**, ☎ 775-831-0494.

Off-Highway Vehicles

Motorcycles, mopeds and scooters can be taken on these scenic forest routes. Off-highway vehicles – trail bikes, Jeeps, and all-terrain vehicles – are popular with local residents as well as visitors.

The **McKinney/Rubicon**, near the west shore of the lake, is a difficult, nationally-known four-wheel drive route approximately 22 miles long. Its reputation is justly deserved due to its narrow passages, rocky climbs and occasional mud holes.

Hellhole Road, contrary to its name, is short and easy. The summit of the route is a good place to have a picnic and enjoy the scenery. There are several other off-highway trails varying in distance and difficulty. Tours ranging from a half-day to three days can be arranged.

The US Forest Service, the California and Nevada State Parks and the Chamber of Commerce will provide more information on location and difficulty of the trails. The chambers will also refer you to rental shops and four-wheel tour companies. Weather conditions change quickly, so take along proper clothing and sufficient sunscreen and water.

Four-wheel drivers can also get their fix on an 11-mile, highway-to-highway ride up to **Genoa Peak** (elevation 9,150). From Tahoe Village in the southeast corner of the lake basin, take NV 207 east up Kingsbury Grade to Daggett Pass and turn north onto unpaved **Genoa Peak Road** (Fire Road 036). Bump and grind about 6½ miles to a junction with Logan House Road (Fire Road 035) going off to the west. Genoa Peak rises just to your east. If you want to bag the peak, continue straight ahead to a very rugged road on the left that leads up toward the peak. After tackling the peak – you might want to walk from here – continue north on Fire Road 035 for 3.8 miles to US 50.

A rough 22-mile loop can be found on the west shore of Tahoe near Meeks Bay. From Tahoma, take **McKinney-Rubicon Road** west up toward **McKinney Lake** (2.3 miles away) and **Lilly Lake**, where you can stop to wet a line. Just beyond Lilly is Miller Lake and a one-mile spur road leading to undiscovered **Richardson Lake**. Back on McKinney-Rubicon Road, continue west to a fork, turn right and head up toward Bear Lake and wind up to a junction with Fire Road 03. Turn right and climb toward **Barker Pass** (elevation 7,620 feet), then proceed another half-mile to the pavement, which leads seven miles to the lakeshore at **Tahoe Pines**.

On the northern end of Lake Tahoe, you can rock and roll for hours near **Brockway Summit** off CA 267. A 13-mile out-and-back trip highlighted by a visit **Watson Lake** begins 3.2 miles north of Kings Beach to **Mt. Watson Road** (Fire Road 073). The gravel is smooth going for about four miles until the road turns to rough dirt. After six miles you'll come to the turnoff on the left for Watson Lake (16N73C), which bumps along for a little more than half a mile to the lake. Return the way you came.

If you continue up CA 267 just past Mt. Watson Road, you can access an eight-mile out-and-back trip to **Martis Peak** (elevation 8,656). Take Fire Road 1802 east along Martis Creek about two miles to Fire Road 1692. Follow this logging road for another 1.3 miles to a fork and bear left, heading due north. The trail becomes rocky and rough as it curves west, then north again for the approach to the summit, marked by a lookout tower. Return the way you came.

Adventures on Water

The **beaches** are superb. Some of the best areas are on the lake's south shore. They include Baldwin, Regan, South Lake Tahoe Recreation Area, Nevada, Zephyr Cove, Emerald Bay, Kiva, Pope, Camp Richardson, Timber Cove and Round Hill Pines.

Boating

You can either swim in the incredibly blue waters or go boating – one of the best ways to enjoy the lake. The water is generally calmer and the breezes are more gentle in the morning. You can rent a boat of virtually any type – motorboat, sailboat, kayak, canoe, innertube or rowboat. If you bring your own boat the South Shore has numerous marinas and piers to launch it. The anchorages at Camp Richardson Cave Rock, Lake Side, Ski Run Tahoe Keys, Timber Cove and Zephyr Cove are equipped to handle your boat.

Although the parks in the Tahoe Basin have no launching facilities, boats can be launched from private docks six miles to the north or south. Campers can swim and fish for rainbow, brown and mackinaw trout or kokanee salmon – a landlocked form of the Pacific sockeye. These fish have all been successfully introduced into the lake. The parks are open from late May until the end of September, depending upon the weather.

North Lake Tahoe Cruises

For your trip around the lake you might consider **North Tahoe Cruises**, which leave from Round House Mall and Marina in Tahoe City off State Route 28, at 700 North Lake Boulevard. These two-hour historical trips along the northwest shore of the lake depart daily at 11 AM, and 1:30 and 3.30 PM from mid-June until mid-September. Trips from May to mid-June and mid-September through October 31 are run if weather permits.

The ship has a snack and cocktail bar. Sunset cocktail cruises depart at 6 PM. Champagne continental breakfast cruises also are offered. Reservations are recommended. The fare is $15, two dollars less for those over 60 and $5 for children from three-12. For reservations, ☎ 530-583-0141.

Water Skiing, Windsurfing & Jet Skiing

You'll find no better lake in which to water ski, windsurf, as well as **scurfing**. The latter is a combination of skiing and surfing. You ride a small surfboard pulled by a boat. Windsurfers find conditions at their best in the afternoon when winds pick up and you're carried along at a fast and exciting pace.

Combine the thrill of water skiing with the control of driving the boat and you're jet skiing. Lake Tahoe's smooth water is perfect for skimming on a ski. You'll have no problem finding a place to rent the equipment.

Scuba Diving

Do you scuba dive? Try Lake Tahoe. In summer the normal temperature of Tahoe's water is a comfortable 55-68°. The water is so clean and clear it af-

Opposite: The General Sherman Tree, 275 feet high and nearly 103 in circumference, earns the title of the world's largest living thing. (Jordan Joiner)

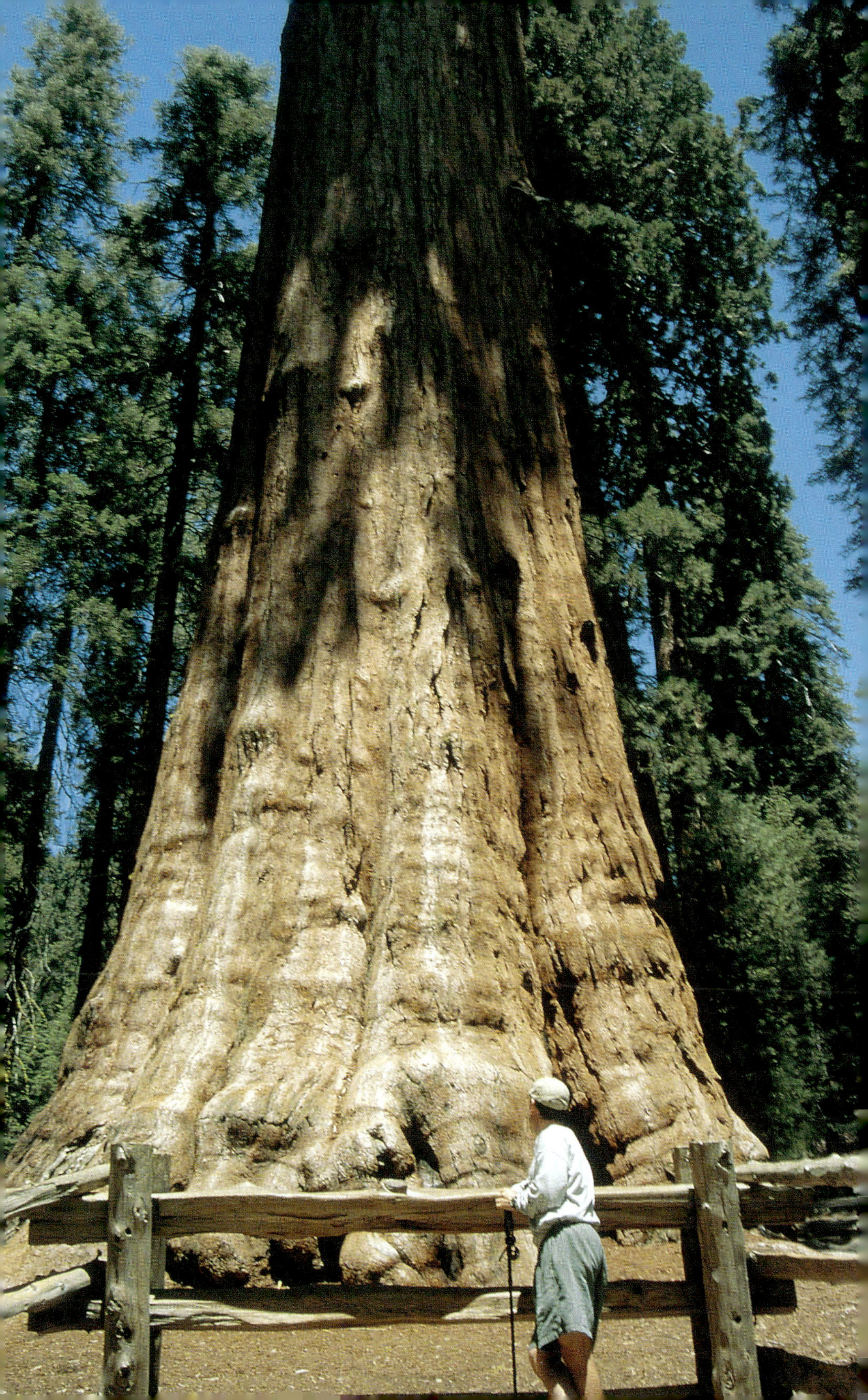

The tiny town of Lee Vining is the gateway to Mono Lake. (Jordan Joiner)

Mono Lake's tufas are pillars of calcium carbonate, or limestone, framed by seepages from underground springs. (Jordan Joiner)

Marshall Gold Discovery State Historic Park near Coloma. James Marshall started the California gold rush in 1848 at this spot on the American River. (Jordan Joiner)

Old Sacramento, a 28-acre National Historic Landmark, contains 53 structures dating back to the gold rush. Take a virtual tour at www.oldsacramento.com. (Jordan Joiner)

California Gold Country is spread throughout the Sierra Nevada foothills, which are dotted with native oak trees. (Jordan Joiner)

Llamas are often used in the Sierra Nevada by hikers who would rather let these beasts carry the camping gear. (Jordan Joiner)

The southern entrance to Sequoia National Park. (Jordan Joiner)

Tunnel Log in Sequoia National Park, a 275-foot-high giant sequoia that toppled in 1937 due to natural causes. The tunnel was cut in 1938. (Jordan Joiner)

Crescent Meadow in Sequoia National Park. Since Sierra meadows are fragile ecosystems, visitors must stay on designated trails. (Jordan Joiner)

The steep trail to the top of Sequoia National Park's Moro Rock, a huge granite outcrop, climbs more than 300 feet in a quarter-mile. (Jordan Joiner)

Grass Valley, California. (Dave Carter)

Bodie State Historic Park. (Mammoth Lakes Visitors Bureau)

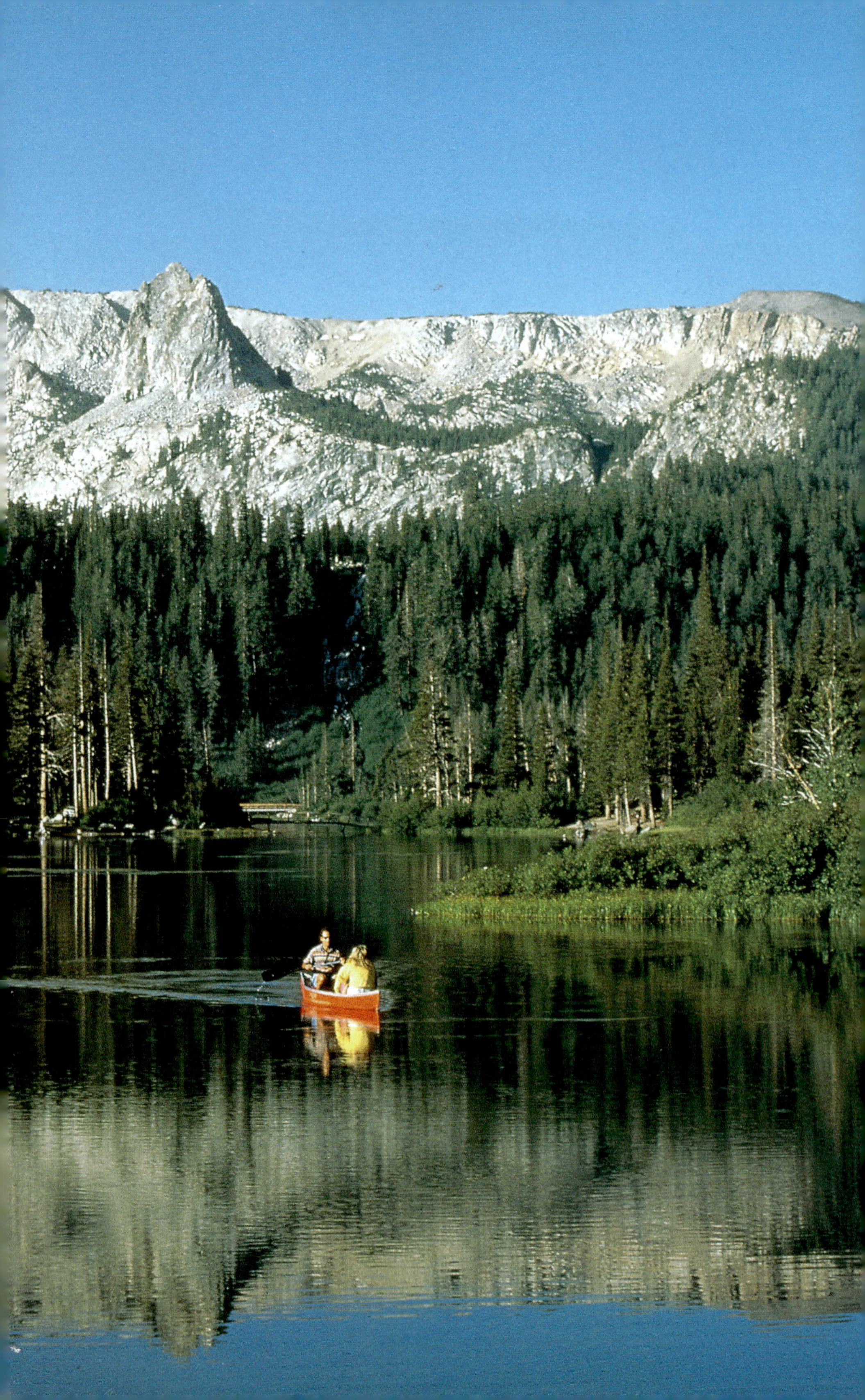

fords near flawless visibility. Twenty-five feet offshore divers can view the wonders of huge submerged boulders. There are dramatic vertical drops and schools of trout.

Parasailing

Thrillseekers should try parasailing. Secure in a parachute harness, you grip the tow rope firmly and run toward the water with a parachute trailing behind you. At the lake's edge, you become airborne. You lift high into the air and glide above the waters of the lake.

Fishing

If you're an avid fisherman, at Lake Tahoe, along with the hundreds of smaller backcountry lakes in the region, you'll think you're in fish heaven. The Forest Service recommends several spots in addition to Lake Tahoe. They include the Upper Truckee River, Echo Lakes, Fallen Leaf Lakes, and the east and west forks of the Carson River (see *Appendix A*).

Rafting

There are two quite different river rafting experiences in the vicinity of Lake Tahoe. One is tranquil, pacific and like lying on a moving, liqueous psychiatrist's couch. The other is like riding a whitewater bucking bronco.

Familes and folks seeking relaxation head by the thousands for the **Truckee River** around Tahoe City. From here the river drains slowly but surely out of the northwest corner of Lake Tahoe and meanders gently past pine trees and sandbars. This is flatwater at its flattest; in fact, during dry years there may not be enough water flowing to allow rafting at all. Keep in mind that the water gets mighty crowded during the summer and most of the river runs alongside busy CA 89, so if you're looking for a remote stretch of liquid living, try elsewhere, maybe kayaking along the north shore near the coves and beaches around Crystal Bay. For a list of rafting guides and rental shops, see page 127 under *Outfitters on Water*.

If you're in the mood for a heart-thumping, pulse-pounding ride that will not only raise the hair on the back of your neck but leave it soaking wet, head south of the Tahoe Bain for the **East Fork of the Carson River**. This is an especially good river for both intermediate rafters and wildlife watchers. Between the Class II and Class III rapids, the water flows through pine forests, steep-sided gorges and chaparral-blanketed hillsides in a remote part of the Sierra. The most often used put-in is off CA 89 just south of Markleeville at a site called Hangman's Bridge. You can float downstream 20 miles, nearly all the way to Gardnerville, Nevada. Along the way make sure you stop at **East Carson Hot Springs** and soak in the

Opposite: Twin Lakes, Mammoth Lakes Basin.
(Mammoth Lakes Visitors Bureau)

natural hot tubs. Unless you are a skilled boater and want to set up the long car shuttle between the put-in and take-out, consider making the run with a permitted rafting guide. For a list of outfitters, contact the **US Forest Service in Carson City**, ☎ 775-882-2766.

Adventures on Snow

Winter sports have made Lake Tahoe famous, particularly after the 1960 Winter Olympics were held here. It has the largest concentration of standout skiing in the world, with 15 alpine and 13 cross-country ski areas noted for their dry, light powder snow. To purchase lift tickets in advance during the ski season, ☎ 800-AT-TAHOE.

Skiing

Alpine Meadows Ski Area

Located west of Lake Tahoe just south of Squaw Valley, Alpine Meadows is more than just an overflow lot for Squaw. With a vertical drop of 1,800 feet, more than 2,000 acres of skiable terrain and enough chair lifts to handle 15,500 skiers an hour, the resort is one of the area's best-loved. The prohibition against snowboarders makes it a favorite among the purist powder hunters, who also appreciate Alpine Meadows' loose boundary policry that allows adventurous souls hiking access to a two-mile-long portion of the Sierra crest near Scott and Summit lifts. The depth of the snowpack in Alpine Bowl also gives this resort one of the longest seasons of any in the area – commonly lasting until Memorial Day. To reach the hill from I-80 east of Donner Lake, travel south on CA 89 for nine miles, then turn west on Alpine Meadows Road. The resort provides free shuttle service from the west shore of Lake Tahoe. ☎ 800-441-4423.

Boreal Ski Area

Boreal is one of four small resorts just off I-80 near the village of Norden, west of Donner Lake. For travelers from the Bay Area who would rather spend their vacations skiing than fighting gridlock around Lake Tahoe, Boreal is the largest (380 acres) choice of these four mini-mountains, which also include Soda Springs, Royal Gorge and Donner Ski Ranch. There are 75 trails lacing up and down 600 vertical feet, the longest of which is a mile long. ☎ 530-426-3666.

Camp Richardson

Ever skied on a beach? For free? At Camp Richardson Cross-Country Ski Center, you can glide right along the Tahoe waterline when the white stuff covers the shore. Located on the southern end of Lake Tahoe, Camp Richardson has nearly 20 kilometers of groomed trails, plus plenty of unmarked routes to follow, and there's no trail pass to buy. Don't miss a trip to **Fallen Leaf Lake**. The resort offers overnight lodging and meals at the Beacon Restaurant, along with Friday night ski tours with a bonfire. Camp Richardson is off CA 89 between the US 50 junction and Emerald Bay State Park. ☎ 530-541-1801.

Clair Tappan Lodge

Operated by the Sierra Club, Clair Tappan offers six miles of beginner- and intermediate-rated cross-country trails and overnight accomodations in the lodge for club members and non-members alike. Reservations are highly recommended. Located on CA 40 west of Donner Lake. Take the Soda Springs exit off I-80. ☎ 530-426-3632.

Diamond Peak Ski Resort

Set in the northeast corner of the Tahoe basin above the town of Incline Village, Nevada, Diamond Peak is often overlooked by the hordes of visitors from California. Their loss is your gain. At 655 acres, Diamond Peak is only one-eighth the size of Heavenly, but with 35 trails and an average snowfall of 250 inches, there is enough to satisfy even the most rabid downhiller. The resort also has more than 35 kilometers of cross-country trails and even rents off-trail adventure skis. The **Vista View Trail** to Knock Your Socks Off Rock is simply one of the most scenic Nordic routes in the country. Diamond Peak even caters to dogs, welcoming pooches during specified days and times. To reach the slopes from CA/NV 28 in Incline Village, go east on Country Club Drive one long block to Ski Way and turn right. ☎ 775-832-1177.

Donner Ski Ranch

At 120 acres, Donner is a cozy mountain that is perfect for first-timers wanting a quick run to the slopes or a family bonding weekend. There are 11 downhill trails, split evenly between beginner and intermediate terrain, on 600 vertical feet of mountain. The entire resort is open to snowboarders, who come for the cheapest lift tickets in the region and stay for the halfpipes. Don't miss Anniversary Week in late January, when lift ticket prices are discounted to single digits. Take the Soda Springs exit off I-80 10 miles west of Truckee. ☎ 530-426-3635.

Granlibakken at Lake Tahoe

Granlibakken is Norwegian for "hill sheltered by fir trees," but it might as well mean "charming resort perfect for neophytes." There is one poma lift serving the open slope and its two runs. There are also a few miles of cross-country routes. Snowboarding is prohibited. From Tahoe City take CA 89 half a mile south to Granlibakken. ☎ 530-583-9896.

Heavenly Ski Resort

The downhill slopes of Heavenly Ski Resort are within minutes of all lodging on the South Shore. With its approximately 4,800 acres, Heavenly is one of America's largest and most beautiful ski resorts, sprawling across the California-Nevada border. At 10,100 feet, it is at the highest altitude in the Tahoe basin. From here there are magnificent views of Lake Tahoe, the surrounding mountains and, in contrast, the Nevada desert.

Heavenly, which celebrated its 40th anniversary in 1996, is known for its well-tended slopes, wide open bowls and steep chutes. Occasionally there's an insufficient amount of natural snow, but the resort has ample snow-making capability. Twenty-four lifts and an aerial tram carry you to the peaks. If you're a top-notch skier, try the longest runs that range up to 5½ miles with an unmatched vertical drop of 3,500 feet. These are not for the inexperienced or the weak of heart. For reservations and information about special ski packages, ☎ 800-2-HEAVEN.

Hope Valley Cross-Country Center

Located at Sorenson's Resort south of the Tahoe basin, Hope Valley has a small lodge and rental shop. Of the more than 60 kilometers of marked trails, fewer than 20% of them are groomed, so be prepared for a little adventure here, but at least there's no trail pass to buy. Only one trail begins at the ski shop at Sorenson's. The rest of the trailheads are scattered east and west of the lodge along CA 88. Note that the trails are on National Forest land and are open to snowmobiles. ☎ 530-694-2203.

Kirkwood

Somewhat off the Tahoe basin's beaten path, Kirkwood tends to attract more serious skiers than the resorts surrounding the lake. There is plenty of terrain to satisfy adrenaline junkies, and with the hill stretching between 7,800 and 9,800 feet above sea level, excellent early- and late-season skiing is definitely a plus. Kirkwood boasts 65 runs, the longest of which is 2½ miles, with only 15% set aside for beginners.

Kirkwood's impressive cross-country center is perhaps the best of its kind in the West, with more than 80 kilometers of carefully groomed trails. There are three separate trail systems that you can connect with to form one large Nordic network. Telemark skis and snowshoes are also available for rent, and the cross-country center runs overnight backcountry ski tours on a regular basis. Kirkwood is 30 miles south of South Lake Tahoe via US 50, CA 89 and CA 88, just west of Carson Pass. ☎ 209-258-6000.

Lakeview Cross Country Skiing

There are 17 trails covering about 65 kilometers at this hidden spot just outside of Tahoe City. Each March, Lakeview hosts the Great Ski Race, a Nordic marathon from Tahoe City to Truckee. Expert skiers can try the **Great Ski Race Trail** anytime. For a less strenuous workout, try the **Eagleview Trail**, which has great views of the lake. The resort is just off CA 28 two miles northeast of Tahoe City. ☎ 530-583-9353.

Northstar-At-Tahoe

A truly all-inclusive destination resort, Northstar offers one of the most complete winter vacations in the West. There are eight chairlifts, two surface lifts and a six-passenger gondola serving the area's 2,000 acres and 61 runs, the longest of which is a breathtaking three miles. Northstar's terrain is divided between easier runs on the front side of Mount Pluto and more advanced trails on the back side. Ski-in, ski-out lodging is a highlight, and the ski village features dozens of dining options, a ski mall, recreation center, sleigh rides and snowmobile tours. One of the area's most crowded resorts offers free shuttle service from Tahoe Vista, Kings Beach, Incline Village and Truckee. Six miles south of Truckee off CA 267. ☎ 800-GO-NORTH.

Mount Rose

Located in the northeast corner of the Tahoe basin on the Nevada side of the border, the ski runs at Mount Rose actually cover two hills, the area's namesake and Slide Mountain. The resort's steep slopes are best suited for intermediate and advanced skiers, who revel in the fact that Mount Rose has one of the highest summits and longest seasons in the basin. More than 40 runs are squeezed into 900 acres. From Incline Village, take NV 431 to the Mount Rose turnoff. ☎ 775-849-0704.

Plumas Eureka Ski Bowl

Operated by the non-profit Plumas Ski Club under a lease from Plumas Eureka State Park, the Ski Bowl is a throwback to the first days of alpine skiing. The sport here dates back to the 1860s, when miners first rigged the ore buckets that were strung up Eureka Peak as a makeshift chairlift. There are 20 runs served by three surface lifts for beginners and intermediates. The Ski Bowl operates on weekends and holidays only. The hill is open to snowboarders, but the lifts are not. From Truckee take CA 89 north for one hour to Greagle and turn west on Johnsonville Road. Drive five miles to the state park. ☎ 530-836-2380.

Royal Gorge Cross Country Resort

If your idea of a perfect day on skis has nothing to do with double black diamonds, long lift lines and rambunctious snowboarders, try the Nordic vibe at Royal Gorge. North America's largest Nordic skiing resort boasts 83 miles of trails winding through a 9,000-acre area that receives an average of 600 inches of snow a year, making for one of the deepest bases – alpine or Nordic – in California. It's hard to decide which is more enjoyable: the views into 4,400-foot-deep Royal Gorge or the exclusive accommodations at Wilderness Lodge and Rainbow Lodge B&B. Located just three-fourths of a mile off I-80 at the Soda Springs/Norden exit. ☎ 800-500-3871.

Sierra At Tahoe Ski Resort

One of the South Shore's major downhill facilities is Sierra At Tahoe. Twelve miles west of South Lake Tahoe on US 50, the resort features 2,000 wind-protected acres of El Dorado National Forest. ☎ 530-659-7453.

Ski Homewood

A favorite of families and snowboarders, Homewood has two base areas offering separate access to a total of 57 runs and 1,300 acres of terrain, 85% of which is rated for intermediate and advanced skiers. Ferry service on the *Tahoe Queen* from South Lake Tahoe to Homewood on the west shore of the lake is available when weather permits, and a free shuttle bus runs between the lifts and the village of Homewood. The hill is just off CA 89 six miles south of Tahoe City. ☎ 530-525-2992.

Soda Springs

This is the first ski hill that drivers from the Bay Area hit heading east on I-80. Most of them pass it by, which usually means few crowds on Soda Springs' 200 acres and 16 runs. There are two lifts and 80% of the terrain is rated for beginners and intermediates. Located a mile south of I-80 via CA 40. ☎ 530-426-3669.

Spooner Lake

In sumer months, mountain bikers drool over these trails. When winter sets in, it's the skiers' turn to revel in the views from the Nevada side of Lake Tahoe. Spooner Lake offers more than 90 kilometers of machine-groomed tracks and 21 trails, including a 20-kilometer loop around Marlette Lake. Newcomers to this 8,000-acre area in and around Lake Tahoe Nevada State Park will enjoy the short loop around Spooner Lake. To reach Spooner Lake, take US 50 to the junction with NV 28 on the east side of Lake Tahoe and follow the signs for the state park. ☎ 775-887-8844.

Sugar Bowl

Another old-fashioned ski hill, Sugar Bowl's Mount Disney is named for one of the resort's first investors and early powder hounds, Walt Disney. Sugar Bowl sports 58 runs on its 1,100 acres, including the trails on Mount Judah that were just opened in 1994. Shuttle buses are available from Donner Lake and Soda Springs. The hill is just west of Donner Lake and south of I-80 on CA 40. ☎ 530-426-3847.

Squaw Valley USA

A true world-class resort, Squaw Valley was the site of the 1960 Winter Olympics and even four decades later manages to exude Olympian grandeur. Squaw is spread across six separate peaks and more than 8,000 acres in Olympic Valley off CA 89 northwest of Lake Tahoe. With a vertical drop of 2,850 feet from base to summit, a 150-passenger cable car, six-person gondola, four quad chairlifts, eight triple chairs, 15 double chairs and two surface lifts, Squaw has room for thousands of skiers of every ability level. An expert run called **Palisades** has been features in dozens of ski films, **KT-22** (so called because it takes 22 kick turns to reach the bottom) was the site of one of the most challenging Olympic downhill events ever and the moguls of the West Face attract professionals from around the globe.

Not up for the slopes? Squaw also features an Olympic-size ice skating rink, the full-service **Resort at Squaw Creek**, a snowboard park and even bungee jumping. The cross-country area consists of about 20 kilometers of groomed trails running around the golf course and resort structures. There is little to challenge the advanced skier, but it's great for beginners. Squaw Valley USA is off CA 89 12 miles south of Truckee and six miles north of Tahoe City. ☎ 916-583-6985.

Tahoe Donner

This 120-acre hill has 11 runs and a vertical descent of 600 feet, making it a fine choice for beginners coming from the Bay Area or staying in Truckee. The longest run measures one mile, snowboarders are welcome and the resort is served by two chairlifts and one surface lift. From I-80, exit on Donner Pass Road just west of Truckee and follow the signs for six miles to the slopes. ☎ 530-587-9444.

Tahoe Donner Cross-Country

Not to be confused with the undersized Tahoe Donner alpine resort, the cross-country area is one of the finest in the region. With more than 70 kilometers of machine-groomed trails, Tahoe Donner provides access to Donner Ridge at 7,800 feet above sea level. Don't miss the bucolic meadows of **Euer Valley** and the **Home Range trails**. From I-80 in Truckee, take Donner Pass Road to Northwoods Boulevard, turn left and proceed three miles to the ski area. ☎ 530-587-9484.

Dogsledding

Ever imagine yourself as Jack (or Jackie) London, mushing through the frozen Yukon behind a team of panting sled dogs? Experience it first-hand with **Husky Express**, one of the West's best-known dogsledding operations. Dotty Dennis, who runs Husky Express, has been active in dogsled racing since 1972, having competed all over North America and worked as a handler on the Iditarod Trail. Dennis offers tours by the hour (about $50 per adult and $20 per child with a $90-per-sled minimum). Those fees aren't cheap, so you might be better off taking her Musher's Course, one of the most unusual adventures in the Sierras.

The two-day course covers every aspect of outfitting and driving a team of two or three of Dennis' sled dogs. The package includes hands-on training, (human) food, lodging and instructional materials. Groups are limited to four mushers. The 1998 price was $225 per person.

In partnership with Husky Express, **Sierra Ski Touring** offers Skijoring Clinics, which combine dogsledding and cross-country skiing. Run by David Beck, a veteran of four decades on skis and author of *Ski Touring in California*, Sierra Ski Tours also hosts High Camp outings, multi-day backcountry adventures for serious Nordic enthusiasts.

For more information on Husky Express and Sierra Ski Tours, based in Hope Valley about 30 miles south of Lake Tahoe via CA 89, ☎ 800-833-MUSH or write PO Box 176, Gardnerville, NV, 89410.

Backcountry Adventures

Alpine Skills International, based in a lodge at Donner Summit on CA 40 northwest of the Tahoe basin, offers instruction and tours covering winter sports for beginners and extreme athletes alike. Learn to snowcamp on a weekend-long cross-country ski tour, or test your mettle on a three-day course that explores the backcountry between Sugar Bowl and Squaw Valley. Alpine Skills International also provides instruction in high altitude and winter mountaineering, snow climbing and ice climbing. Accommodations are available in the Donner Summit lodge. For more information, ☎ 530-426-9108 or write PO Box 8, Norden, CA 95724.

Snowmobiling

If skiing doesn't interest you, try snowmobiling. A number of rental centers provide the equipment, and you can race across beautiful terrain at 25-30 miles per hour. Guided tours covering 25 miles and lasting two or three hours can be arranged into remote wilderness areas. Solo riders must be 16 or older and have a driver's license. Children eight or younger are frequently allowed to ride with a parent.

Tahoe is clearly one of the West's most popular destinations for snowmobiling. Most of the US Forest Service lands around the basin are open to snowmobiles, as long as there is at least six inches of snow on the ground. Note that the machines are prohibited in roadless and wilderness areas. Also keep in mind that in recent years, as more people have begun to appreciate the peaceful and restorative properties of the backcountry, the thunderous noise and gasoline fumes emitted by snowmobiles have led many to wonder if these machines belong in the wilderness at all.

The **Little Truckee Summit region** near Yuba Pass, immediately north of Truckee off CA 89, is Tahoe's biggest snowmobile area. You can ride on Tahoe National Forest land past **Prosser Creek Reservoir** west of CA 89 and along **Gold Lake Road** all the way to Gold Lake. On the north shore of Tahoe, you can ride near **Brockway Summit** off CA 267. There are 13 miles of well-kept trails, with paths leading to Stumpy Meadows, Watson Lake and Mount Watson. On the Nevada side of the north shore, you can cruise around **Tahoe Meadows** off NV 431. In the shadow of Mt. Rose, Tahoe Meadows is also a popular cross-country ski area. The meadows are just over the south side of the summit on the east side of the highway. Another Nevada-side ride can be had at **Spooner Summit**. There are enough groomed trails here to enable half a day of quality snowmobiling. Find the trails near Spooner rest stop off US 50.

Blackwood Canyon Sno-Park, on the west shore of Lake Tahoe south of Tahoe City, provides miles of ungroomed and unmarked trails rolling through the canyon's forests and meadows. Riders can follow **Barker Pass Road**, which is closed in winter. The area is also heavily used by cross-country skiers. Drivers will need a California Sno-Park permit to park in the area, available for a small fee by contacting the US Forest Service, ☎ 530-573-2600.

South of Lake Tahoe, you can ride the groomed and ungroomed trails in **Hope Valley** and along **Blue Lakes Road** in the **Toiyabe National Forest**. Take CA 88 south from the lake basin to Hope Valley, go west, then turn south on Blue Lakes Road toward Hope Valley campground, where the trails begin. You can zip all the way to Ebbetts Pass on CA 4, past the Blue Lakes and Twin Lake.

Where to Stay
South Lake Tahoe

Best Western's Station House Inn is 3½ blocks from the casino center and two blocks north of US 50, via Lake Park Avenue, at 901 Park Avenue, 96150. The rates vary by season, but not much. $$-$$$. No pets. It has its own restaurant. ☎ 530-542-1101. **Best Western's Timber Cove Lodge** is on the lake 1½ miles from the casino center, and a half-mile west of Ski Run Boulevard, at 3411 Lake Tahoe Boulevard, 98150. No pets allowed. Its rates vary by the season and the day of the week. $$-$$$$. ☎ 530-541-6722. **Embassy Suites Resort** is at Casino Center, 4130 Lake Tahoe Boulevard, 96150. $$$$. There's a dining room and a host of unusual services. ☎ 530-544-5400.

Forest Inn Suites are a block southwest of US 50, adjacent to the casinos, at 1101 Park Avenue, 96150. $$$-$$$$. No pets. ☎ 530-541-6655 or 800-822-5950. The **Holiday Inn Express**, $$$, is one block southeast of town off US 50 and adjacent to the casinos, at 3300 Lake Tahoe Boulevard, 96150. No pets. ☎ 530-542-0330. **Lakeland Village** is 1½ miles west of Casino Center, on US 50, at 3535 Lake Tahoe Boulevard, 96150. No pets. Restaurant nearby. This is an apartment hotel. $$-$$$$. ☎ 530-544-1685.

The **Royal Valhalla Motorlodge** is north of Highway 50, at 4104 Lakewood Boulevard, 96157. No pets. $$-$$$. ☎ 530-544-2233. **South Tahoe Travelodge** is two blocks west of Casino Center, at 3489 Highway 50, 96156. $$-$$$. No pets. ☎ 530-544-5266.

The **Tahoe Keys Resort** can be reached by taking the exit on State Route 59 to 599 Tahoe Keys Boulevard, 96159. $$$-$$$$. They accept pets, but with a $100 deposit. ☎ 530-544-5397. The **Tahoe Seasons Resort** is 1.3 miles southeast of US 50, and a half-mile northeast, on Saddle Road and Keller, 96157. No pets. $$$-$$$$. The restaurant is open from 7 AM until noon, but is open for lunch and dinner during the ski season. ☎ 530-541-6700.

Club Tahoe is in Incline Village in North Lake Tahoe. Exit State Route 28 at Village Boulevard North, travel a third of a mile east to 914 Northwood Boulevard. This is an apartment complex. $$$-$$$$. No pets. ☎ 775-831-5750. The **Hyatt Regency Lake Resort and Casino** is a half-mile west of State Route 28 toward Lake. ☎ 775-832-1234. Take Country Club Drive for two miles to Lake Shore Country Club Drive. $$$$. There are two dining rooms and a coffee shop with food priced at $8-25.

At Stateline, **Caesar's Tahoe** is one of the best. $$$-$$$$. Four restaurants and a coffee shop are open 24 hours a day. No pets. ☎ 775-588-3515. **Harrah's Hotel and Casino** is on a par with Caesar's, and in the same area. $$$-$$$$, with almost identical services. ☎ 775-588-6611. No pets. The same can be said of **Harveys Resort Hotel**, $$$-$$$$. No pets are allowed either. ☎ 775-588-2411.

Campgrounds in the Tahoe Basin

There are 24 campgrounds and RV parks in the Tahoe Basin, and 11 more nearby. Camping is usually on a first-come, first-served basis, although individual and group reservations can be arranged. Call the Tahoe Douglas Visitor Center/Chamber of Commerce, at ☎ 530-541-5255 or the Lake Tahoe Basin Management of the US Forest Service at ☎ 530-573-2600. Ask for the "Lake of the Sky" journal. This is an outdoor guide that includes a complete campground roster.

Public Campgrounds

There are hundreds of campsites along the west shore of Lake Tahoe. They have a tendency to fill quickly during summer months, so call ahead for availability and reservation information. All of the following campgrounds have piped water unless noted.

William Kent, three miles south of Tahoe City on CA 89, has 55 tent sites and 40 spots for RVs, along with a dump station. It is open June through September and sites are $12 per night. ☎ 530-573-2600.

Lake Forest, two miles north of Tahoe City on CA 28, has 21 tent and RV sites along with a boat ramp. It is open April through October and sites are $10 per night. ☎ 530-583-5544.

Tahoe State Recreation Area, a quarter-mile north of Tahoe City, is a popular spot, with 39 tent and RV sites, a pier, playground and boat ramp. It is open only during summer months and the fees are $12-$14 per night. ☎ 530-583-3074.

Sugar Pine Point State Park, 18 miles north of South Lake Tahoe on CA 89, has a large campground for 175 tent campers or RVers. There are showers, a dump station and the campground is wheelchair accessible. It is open all year and sports two miles of lakefront property. Fees are $12-$14 per night. ☎ 530-525-7982. Nearby **Meeks Bay**, one mile south of Sugar Pine Point, has 40 sites for tents or RVs and is open May through October. The fee is $12 per night. ☎ 530-573-2600.

Kaspian, four miles south of Tahoe City on CA 89, is an exquisite little campground with 10 sites for tent campers only. It is open May through September and runs $10 per night. ☎ 530-573-2600.

Emerald Bay State Park, eight miles north of South Lake Tahoe on CA 89, is one of the most popular parks in California, so plan ahead to get one of the 100 sites for tenters or RV campers. The park also has 20 sites for boat-in campers. Camping is allowed June through September. The fees are $12-$14 per night for tents or RVs, $8 per night for boats. ☎ 530-541-3030.

D.L. Bliss State Park, 11 miles north of South Lake Tahoe, is another favorite spot, with 168 sites for tents or RVs and showers. It is located 11 miles north of South Lake Tahoe on CA 89 and the fees are $12-$14 per night. ☎ 530-525-7277.

Private Campgrounds

Sandy Beach is eight miles north of Tahoe City on CA 28. There are 50 sites with full or partial hookups for motor homes, along with showers, flush toilets and a boat ramp. It is open April through October and fees vary according to site.

Camp Richardson Resort, two miles north of South Lake Tahoe on CA 89, is a privately run, full-service campground on US Forest Service land. There are 230 sites for tents or RVs, some with electrical hookups. There are also showers, a playground, recreation hall, boat rentals and a launch ramp. Fees run $17-$22 per night. ☎ 530-541-1801.

Where to Dine
South Lake Tahoe

Evans American Gourmet Cafe serves American food. It is on State Route 89, one mile north of US 50, at 536 Emerald Bay Rd. Dinners are $30-41. ☎ 916-542-1990. **LewMarNel's** is at the Best Western Station House Inn, 991 Park Avenue. It is open from 7:30-10; 11-4; and 5:30-10. Reservations are suggested. It serves continental food priced at $11-20. The **Tahoe House** is about one mile south of Tahoe City on State Route 89, at 625 W. Lake Boulevard. It serves Swiss and California-style food for $11-20 for dinner.

Located in the South Lake Tahoe Embassy Suites Resort, **Zackary's**, 4130 Lake Tahoe Boulevard, ☎ 530-543-2140, is a local favorite that has been impressing diners of all tastes since 1991. Known for a creative-yet-comfortable menu, Zackary's features everything from wood-fired, brick-oven pizza to American and Continental specialties. The restaurant is open for lunch from 11 AM to 2 PM and for dinner from 5 PM. Reservations are suggested.

The **Cantina Bar & Grill**, 711 Emerald Bay Road, ☎ 530-544-1233, has been at the same location since 1977 and it is easy to understand why. The Cantina serves authentic, flavorful Mexican and Tex-Mex specialties, boasts more than 30 different beers and promotes a fun, laid-back atmosphere. After all, residents voted The Cantina's margaritas the best at the lake. The chicken mole, roast chicken in a rich, chocolate-cilantro sauce, is highly recommended.

Both located at 1041 Fremont Avenue, **Dory's Oar** restaurant and the **Tudor English Pub**, ☎ 530-541-6603, provide a spot to unwind and enjoy a pint and an excellent meal. The menu at Dory's includes a range of fresh fish, notably mahi mahi and wahoo, and meat specialty dishes with a European flair. The Tudor has English beers on tap and an array of hearty appetizers. Owners Keith and Jeannette Simpson, originally from Surrey, England, are said to have catered events for the Royal Family.

Featured in *The New York Times* and *Bon Appetit* magazine, **Nepheles Creative California Cuisine**, 1169 Ski Run Boulevard, ☎ 530-544-8130, has been on the scene since since 1977. Named for the Greek goddess of Epicurean delights, Nepheles has an award-winning wine list featuring California vineyards. Chef Mark Vassau is noted for his daily specials prepared with fresh fish, meats and vegetables. Nepheles even offers hot tub spas at hourly rates.

In the mood for Japanese? **Samurai Restaurant**, 2588 Highway 50, ☎ 530-542-0300, features a traditional tatami room and sushi bar and teppan grill. Dinner is served nightly beginning at 5 PM.

Serving authentic Italian fare for more than two decades, **Tep's Villa Roma**, 3450 Lake Tahoe Boulevard, ☎ 800-490-3066, offers a stunning antipasto salad bar, a great king salmon ravigoti and favorites like chicken rollatine.

Stateline

There are more than 100 restaurants on the South Shore with something for every taste and budget. The casino area serves as the cuisine center, with more than 25 top-quality restaurants. They range from 24-hour coffee shops to exquisite five-star gourmet restaurants. **Llewellyn's/Harveys** is the "tops" in dining because it is located on the hotel's 19th floor, where all tables have an unobstructed view of the lake. It also has AAA's coveted four-diamond rating. Meals are $21-30. Reservations are suggested. ☎ 775-588-2411. Dinner is served in the **Summit Room** on Harrah's 16th floor, with prices of $21-30. ☎ 775-588-2811.

> The free **South Shore Dining Guide**, distributed at hotels, motels, stores and area chambers of commerce, provides details for 25 restaurants.

Lake Tahoe Outfitters
General Outfitters

■ Olympic Valley
Adventure Specialists, 1136 Snow Crest Road, ☎ 530-581-3866.

■ Reno
Reno Mountain Sports, 155 East Moana Lane, ☎ 775-825-2855.

■ South Lake Tahoe
Camp Richardson Outdoor Sports, 1900 Jameson Beach Road, ☎ 530-542-6584.
Cutting Edge Sports, 4008 Lake Tahoe Boulevard, ☎ 530-542-4000.
Cutting Edge Sports, 1032 Emerald Bay Road, ☎ 530-542-2284.
Long Rock Adventures, PO Box 11973, ☎ 530-577-6306.
Sportsman, 256 Lake Tahoe Boulevard, ☎ 530-542-3474.

■ Tahoe City
Alpenglow Sports, 415 North Lake Boulevard, ☎ 530-583-6917.
Peak Guide Service, ☎ 530-583-8125.

■ Truckee
Sports Exchange, 10095 West River Street, ☎ 530-582-4510.

Sierra Mountaineer, Bridge Street at Jiboom Street, ☎ 530-587-2025.
Sugar Bowl Ski & Sports, 11260 Donner Pass Road, ☎ 530-587-1369.
Truckee Mountain Sports, 11400 Donner Pass Road, ☎ 530-587-3933.

On Horseback

■ Carson City
Tin Cup Adventures, 220 Wayne Road, ☎ 775-849-0570.

■ South Lake Tahoe
Camp Richardson's Corral, 4 Emerald Bay Road, ☎ 530-541-3113.
Cascade Stables, 2199 Cascade Road, ☎ 530-541-2055.
Sunset Ranch, 2101 Emerald Bay Road, ☎ 530-541-9001.

■ Truckee
Northstar Stables, 910 Northstar Drive, ☎ 530-562-1230.
Tahoe Donner Equestrian Center, 15275 Alder Creek Road, ☎ 530-587-9470.

On Wheels

■ Incline Village
Bob's Speed Shop, 1058 Tiller Drive, ☎ 775-831-2619.
Village Bicycles, 800 Tahoe Boulevard, ☎ 775-831-3537.

■ Kings Beach
Brockway Ski & Sports, 7900 North Lake Boulevard, ☎ 530-546-7437.
Tahoe Bike & Ski, 8499 North Lake Boulevard, ☎ 530-546-7437.

■ South Lake Tahoe
Anderson's Bicycle Rental, 645 Emerald Bay Road, ☎ 530-541-0500.
Blazing Saddles Bike Shop, 1219 Emerald Bay Road, ☎ 530-544-2453.
Lakeview Sports, 3131 Harrison Avenue, ☎ 530-544-0183.
Sierra Cycle Works, 3430 Lake Tahoe Boulevard, ☎ 530-541-0183.
South Shore Bike Shop, 1132 Ski Run Boulevard, ☎ 530-541-1549.
Tahoe Bike Shop, 2277 Lake Tahoe Boulevard, ☎ 530-544-8060.

■ Tahoe City
Back Country, 255 North Lake Boulevard, ☎ 530-581-5861.
Cycle Paths, 1785 West Lake Boulevard, ☎ 530-581-1171.
Olympic Bike Shop, 620 North Lake Boulevard, ☎ 530-581-2500.
TSR Mountain Bike Rental, 185 River Road, ☎ 530-583-0123.

■ Tahoe Vista
Enviro-Rents, 6873 North Lake Boulevard, ☎ 530-546-2780.

■ Truckee
Back Country, 11429 Donner Pass Road, ☎ 530-582-0909.

Paco's Truckee Bike & Ski, 11200 Donner Pass Road, ☎ 530-587-5561.

On Water

■ Carson City
Strictly Scuba, 4375 South Carson Street, ☎ 775-884-3483.

■ Kings Beach
Kings Beach Aqua Sports, ☎ 530-546-2782.

Tahoe Paddle & Oar, 8299 North Lake Boulevard, ☎ 530-581-3029.

■ Nevada City
Wolf Creek Wilderness, 300 Spring Street, ☎ 530-265-9653.

■ Reno
Reno Mountain Sports, 155 East Moana Lane, ☎ 775-825-2855.

Tropical Penguins Scuba, 180 West Peckham Lane, ☎ 775-828-3483.

■ South Lake Tahoe
Action Watersports, 3411 Lake Tahoe Boulevard, ☎ 530-544-5387.

Blue Ribbon Fishing Charters, ☎ 530-541-8801.

Don Sheetz Guide Service, ☎ 530-541-5566.

Eagle Point Sport Fishing, ☎ 530-577-6834.

George's Fishing Trips, ☎ 530-544-2353.

Kayak Tahoe, 3411 Lake Tahoe Boulevard, ☎ 530-544-2011.

Paradise Watercraft Rentals, 1900 Jameson Beach Road, ☎ 530-541-7272.

Prime Time Fishing Charters, ☎ 530-577-7420.

Rick Muller's Sport Fishing, ☎ 530-544-4358.

Ski Run Boat Company, 900 Ski Run Boulevard, ☎ 530-544-0200.

Sun Sports, 1018 Herbert Avenue, ☎ 530-541-6000.

■ Tahoe City
Hooker for Hire Sportfishing, ☎ 530-525-5654.

Kingfish Guide Service, ☎ 530-525-5360.

Lighthouse Water Sports, 950 North Lake Boulevard, ☎ 530-583-6000.

Mac-A-Tac Fishing, ☎ 530-546-2500 or 775-831-4449.

Mickey's Big Mack Fishing Charters, ☎ 800-877-1462.
Tahoe City Kayak Shop, 255 North Lake Boulevard, ☎ 530-581-4336.
Tahoe Water Adventures, 120 Grove Street, ☎ 530-583-3225.
Tahoe Whitewater Tours, PO Box 7466, ☎ 530-581-2441.
Truckee River Rafting, 205 River Road, ☎ 530-583-5606.

■ Tahoe Paradise
Bruce Hernandez Guide Service, 867 Angoria Creek Drive, ☎ 530-577-2246.
Kayak Tahoe, Richardson's Resort, PO Box 11129, ☎ 530-544-2011.
Tahoe Viking Sportfishing, ☎ 530-541-1806.

■ Truckee
Clearwater Fishing Guides, ☎ 800-354-0958.
Irie Rafting, 13600 Donner Pass Road, ☎ 530-587-1184.
Reel Magic Sportfishing, ☎ 530-587-6027.

■ Zephyr Cove
Activities Unlimited, PO Box 798, Zephyr Cove, ☎ 775-588-4722.
Don's Fishing Charters, ☎ 775-588-4916.
First Strike Sportfishing, ☎ 775-588-HOOK or 530-577-5065.
O'Malley's Fishing Charters, 1048 Myron Drive, Zephyr Cove, ☎ 775-588-4102.
Tahoe Sports Fishing, ☎ 800-696-7797 or 530-541-5448.

In the Air

■ South Lake Tahoe
Balloons Over Lake Tahoe, ☎ 530-544-7008.
Lake Tahoe Balloons, PO Box 19215, ☎ 530-544-1221.
Skydive Lake Tahoe, ☎ 530-583-4084.

■ Tahoe City
Lake Tahoe Parasailing, 700 North Lake Boulevard, ☎ 530-583-7245.

■ Truckee
Mountain High Balloons, 10867 Cheyenne Way, ☎ 530-587-6922.

On Snow

The following outfitters offer snowmobiling tours in the Tahoe area.
Eagle Ridge Snowmobile Outfitters, PO Box 4581, Incline Village, NV, 89450, ☎ 702-831-7600.

High Country Snowmobiling, PO Box 1025, Carnelian Bay, CA 96140, ☎ 916-546-0132.

High Sierra Snowmobiling, 7900 North Lake Boulevard, Kings Beach, CA 96143, ☎ 916-546-9909.

Lake Tahoe Winter Sports Center, PO Box 11436, Tahoe Paradise, CA 96155, ☎ 916-577-2940.

Mountain Lake Adventures, PO Box 9653, South Lake Tahoe, CA 96158, ☎ 916-583-9131.

Northstar-at-Tahoe, PO Box 129, Truckee, CA 96160, ☎ 916-562-1010.

Snowmobiling Unlimited, PO Box 1591, Tahoe City, CA 96145, ☎ 916-583-7192.

TC Sno Mo's, PO Box 1198, Tahoe City, CA 96145, ☎ 916-583-1516, 916-583-1516.

Zephyr Cove Snowmobile Center, PO Drawer 830, Zephyr Cove, NV 89448, ☎ 702-882-0788.

Leaving Tahoe

You have two options after leaving Lake Tahoe. You can proceed to Reno by returning to Highway 395 via State Route 50 and driving 55 miles north to "The Biggest Little City in the World." You can take a more direct route to Sacramento on State Route 50, or bypass the capital and turn south on Highway 49 through the heart of the Mother Lode Country. There are some fine schools and museums there, as there are in Tahoe, and a collection of 200 antique, classic and special interest automobiles on display.

Reno

No Sierra Nevada guidebook would be complete without the rundown on Reno. The most popular Sierra gateway city, Reno offers the closest international airport to the high country. Each year hundreds of thousands of mountain-bound adventurers move through Reno on their way to Lake Tahoe and beyond. Many of them use Reno as a base camp, traveling to the Sierra by day and returning to Reno by night, lured by the bright lights of its hotels, casinos and restaurants.

But of course there is more to Reno than cardsharps, all-you-can-eat buffets and tinkling slot machines. Visitors will find relaxing walking tours, fascinating museums and picturesque parks if they are willing to leave the glitter behind.

For more information, contact:

Greater Reno-Sparks Chamber of Commerce, 405 Marsh Avenue, ☎ 775-686-3030.

Reno/Sparks Indian Colony Tribal Council, 98 Colony Road, ☎ 775-329-2936.

Getting Here & Getting Around

Reno is situated at the junction of east-west-running I-80 and north-south-trending US 395. The Truckee River flows right through downtown. In years of heavy snowmelt, the river has flooded city streets. Just south of the city limits, NV 431 is a direct route into the Sierra and the northeastern corner of the Lake Tahoe basin. Reno-Tahoe International Airport is served by the commercial carriers listed below.

Airlines

Air 21, ☎ 775-328-6400.
Alaska Airlines, ☎ 800-235-9292.
American Airlines, ☎ 800-433-7300.
America West Airlines, ☎ 800-359-2472.
Canadian Airlines, ☎ 800-426-7000.
Delta Air Lines, ☎ 800-221-1212.
Delta Connection-Sky West, ☎ 800-453-9417.
Northwest Airlines, ☎ 800-225-2525.
Reno Air, ☎ 800-736-6247.
Southwest Airlines, ☎ 800-435-9792.
TriStar Airlines, ☎ 800-218-8777.
TWA, ☎ 800-221-2000.
United Airlines, ☎ 800-241-6522.

Rental Cars

Rental cars are available at the airport and some downtown Reno hotels.
Avis, ☎ 800-331-1212.
Budget, ☎ 800-527-0700.
Dollar, ☎ 800-800-4000.
Enterprise, ☎ 800-325-8007.
Hertz, ☎ 800-654-3131.

Lloyd's International, ☎ 800-654-7037.

National, ☎ 800-CAR-RENT.

Thrifty, ☎ 800-367-2277.

Tahoe Rent-A-Car, ☎ 530-544-4500.

Truckee Rent-A-Car, ☎ 916-587-2841.

Other Ground Transportation

Ground transportation from Reno to Tahoe is readily available if you don't want to rent a vehicle.

Reno-Tahoe Connection, ☎ 775-825-3900.

Sierra Shuttle, ☎ 530-525-9110.

Tahoe Casino Express, ☎ 800-446-6128.

What to See & Do

A good place to start exploring is the **River Walk**, on the south banks of the Truckee River between the Sierra Street and Virginia Street bridges. About a block west of the River Walk is **Wingfield Park**, actually an island that boasts the Wingfield Park Amphitheater, hosting special events in warmer months. Call the Reno/Sparks Convention and Visitors Authority, ☎ 800-FOR-RENO, for a schedule.

The Virginia Street Bridge

Take note of the Virginia Street Bridge, which has spanned the Truckee since 1905 and is near the site of the original spot of the first tourist boom in Nevada. In 1852, H.H. Jameson established a trading post here to serve pioneers on the Emigrant Trail, and in 1859 C.W. Fuller built an inn and toll bridge to service travelers headed from California to Virginia City. In 1863, Fuller sold his property to Myron Lake, who made enough money from wagon trains crossing his bridge near this site to kickstart the settlement now known as Reno.

From here, it's an easy walk to Reno's main drag, **North Virginia Street**, home to nine hotel-casinos within a six-block stretch between 1st Street and 6th Street. From a historical point of view, the most significant of them may be **Harold's Club** at 2nd and Virginia. If there is a shrine to Nevada's true cash crop, this is it. Gambling was legalized in the state in 1931, but it wasn't until Raymond Smith and his son Harold entered the picture in downtown Reno with their clean reputations and clever marketing that gaming became accepted as a mainstream diversion.

Harrah's, situated behind Harold's Club at 219 North Center Street, ☎ 775-788-3773, has been at that location since 1946. William Harrah opened the casino nine years after arriving in Reno.

Since this isn't the *Gambling Guide to the Sierra Nevada*, it's time to leave the casinos and visit the **National Bowling Stadium** and its huge geodesic bowling-ball-shaped dome, 300 North Center Street, ☎ 775-334-2600. More than 100 lanes full of pinheads can bowl here at one time. When arms get tired, the Omnimax movies shown in the dome are the main attraction.

Reno's best adventures await away from downtown. On the north side of the city, the campus of the University of Nevada, 1650 North Virginia Street, boasts three treasures. **Fleischmann Planetarium**, ☎ 775-784-4812, houses a theater and telescope. The **Nevada Historical Society**, ☎ 775-688-1190, is one of the best museums of its kind in the West. And the **Keck Minerals Museum**, ☎ 775-784-4528, is a must for rockhounds or treasure lovers.

About 10 minutes north of the university, where North Virginia Street hits North McCarran Boulevard, **Rancho San Rafael Park** is another in-town highlight. (See below under *Adventures on Foot*.) The **Wilbur D. May Museum and Arboretum**, 1502 North Washington Street, ☎ 775-785-5961, are a tribute to this Renaissance man and philanthropic heir to the May Company fortune. **Great Basin Adventure**, a nifty historical theme park, is also located here.

On the northern outskirts of the city, **Animal Ark Nature Center**, 1265 Deerlodge Road, ☎ 775-969-3111, is a well-known, non-profit haven for orphaned and injured wildlife, including black bears and kit foxes. The staff welcomes visitors daily from April through October, but call first for hours. To get there, take US 395 north to Red Rock Road, turn right, go 11.5 miles to Deerlodge Road and turn right.

On the suburban south side of Reno, the **National Automobile Museum**, 10 South Lake Street, ☎ 775-333-9300, houses one of the world's best collections, highlighted by the 1907 Thomas Flyer that won The Great Race from New York to Paris and James Dean's 1949 Mercury.

The **Reno-Sparks Convention & Visitors Authority**, 4590 South Virginia Street, ☎ 800-FOR-RENO, is housed in Reno pioneer Myron Lake's mansion dating back to the 1870s.

Where to Stay in Reno

Since C.W. Fuller first opened an inn near his Truckee River crossing in the 1859, Reno-Tahoe Territory has been attracting folks from both east and west. Today, first-class, high-rise hotel-casinos have sprouted from the banks of the Truckee.

Low-slung motels also abound in Reno, some of which look like they've been around since the 1860s. As in Las Vegas, many hotel-casinos offer midweek specials, and many of the rooms look exactly alike, giving folks all the more reason to spend time in the pits.

Among the downtown hotels, the big daddy is the **Silver Legacy**, 407 North Virginia Street, ☎ 800-687-8733, $$, with more than 1,700 rooms on 38 floors. There is a shopping arcade downstairs, as well as a gym with an instructor on-site. **Harrah's**, 210 North Center Street, ☎ 800-427-7247, $$, boasts nearly 600 rooms, a heated pool and other amenities, including a barber shop. Nearby, the **Eldorado**, 345 North Virginia Street, ☎ 800-648-5966, $$, is a 26-story giant with more than 800 rooms, convention facilities and some impressive suites. **Circus Circus**, 500 North Sierra Street, ☎ 800-723-6500, $$, has a heated pool, free airport shuttle and skier rates.

Away from downtown, the new **Peppermill**, 2707 South Virginia Street, ☎ 800-282-2444, $$$, rises from the suburbs like an iceberg. It has more than 1,000 rooms, two heated pools and a hair salon. The **Atlantis**, farther south of downtown at 3800 South Virginia Street, ☎ 800-723-6500, $$, also towers over the local strip malls with its 18 floors and 600 rooms.

Adventurers on tighter budgets might try the chain motels first, most notably the **Days Inn**, 701 East 7th Street, ☎ 775-786-4070, $$, **Motel 6**, 1901 South Virginia, ☎ 775-827-0255, $, and **Vagabond Inn**, 3131 South Virginia Street, ☎ 775-825-7134, $$. And how about the **Adventure Inn and Wedding Chapel**, 3575 South Virginia Street, ☎ 800-937-1436, $$, which features theme rooms?

Where to Dine in Reno

Food served in Reno ranges from copious amounts of fast food to generic hotel-casino fare and first-class menus. One of the finest restaurants in northern Nevada is **Pimparel's La Table Francaise**, 3065 West 4th Street, ☎ 775-323-3200. The French cuisine is made with fresh, seasonal ingredients and changes every two months. The restaurant also does its own baking. Reservations are recommended.

One of the best views in Reno can be found at **The 19th Hole**, 1200 Razorback Road, ☎ 775-825-1250. It lies on the Lakeridge Golf Course and the lights of the city are a nice appetizer to the seafood and steaks. The 19th Hole is open for lunch and dinner, Tuesday through Saturday.

Famous Murphys, 3127 South Virgina Street, ☎ 775-827-4111, is a rousing pub with good food, including a seafood and oyster bar. The dining room closes at 10 PM and the bar is open until 4 AM.

For a rustic ambiance with high-end cuisine, try the **Glory Hole**, 4201 West 4th Street, ☎ 775-786-1323, a steak and seafood joint set in an Old West saloon outfit like a silver rush mining camp. **Ichiban**, 210 North Sierra Street, ☎ 775-323-5550, serves fresh Japanese steak, seafood and sushi for lunch and dinner.

Among the hotel-casinos, the **Eldorado**, 234 North Virginia Street, ☎ 775-786-5700, and **Peppermill**, 2707 South Virginia Street, ☎ 775-826-2121, offer full-blown food courts open from morning until late in the evening. The large hotels also have 24-hour coffee shops and speciality restaurants ranging from **La Strada** at the Eldorado, ☎ 775-348-9297, one of the top Italian eateries in the country, to **Le Moulin** at the Peppermill, ☎ 775-689-7226, **Trader Dick's** at John Ascauga's Nugget, ☎ 775-356-3300, and **Empress Garden** at the Flamingo Hilton, 255 North Sierra Street, ☎ 775-785-7000.

The Western Sierra
Gold Country North

You can drive to Sacramento from Reno on I-80 through part of the gold country. **Truckee** is 12 miles west of Reno, where restored 19th-century false-front buildings house shops and restaurants. For detailed information, contact Donner Chamber of Commerce and Visitors Center,

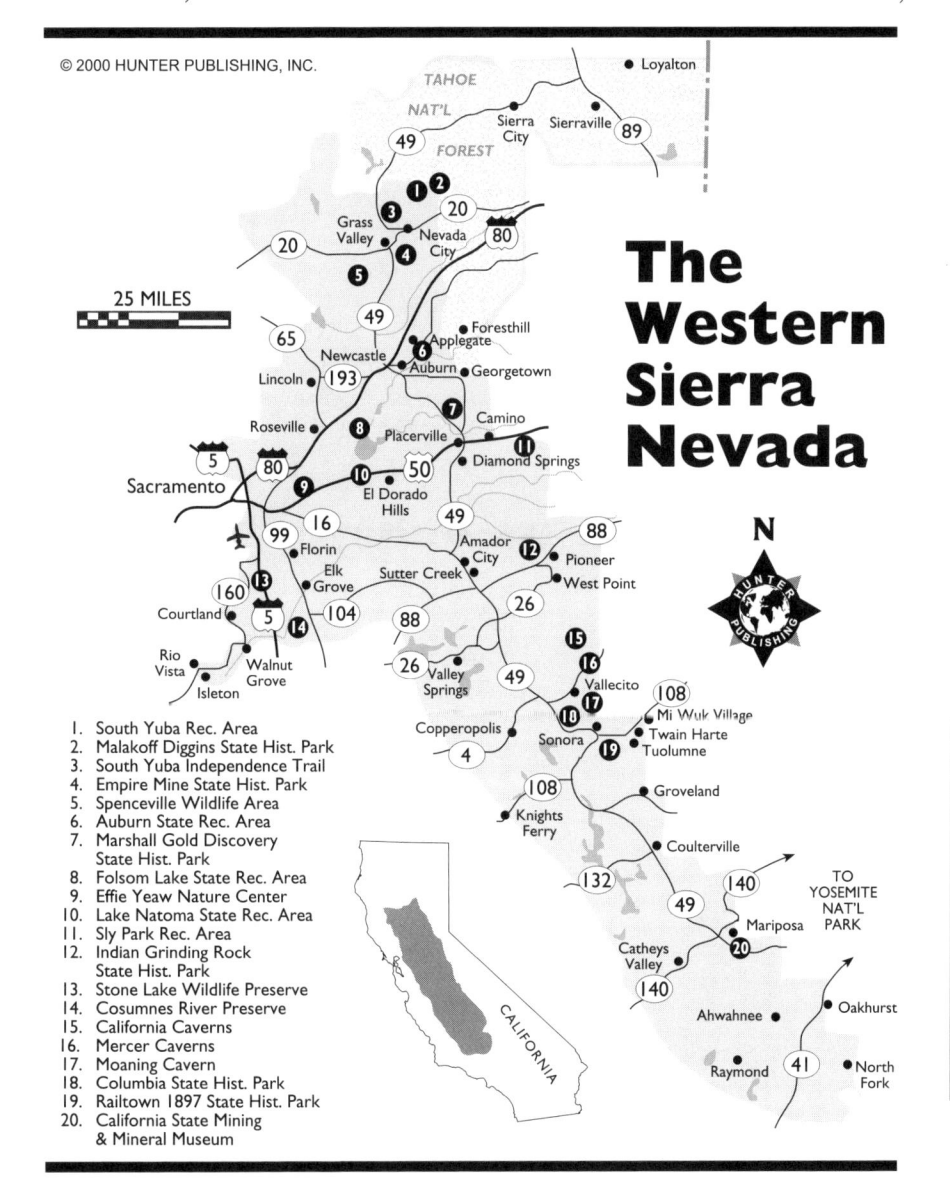

1. South Yuba Rec. Area
2. Malakoff Diggins State Hist. Park
3. South Yuba Independence Trail
4. Empire Mine State Hist. Park
5. Spenceville Wildlife Area
6. Auburn State Rec. Area
7. Marshall Gold Discovery State Hist. Park
8. Folsom Lake State Rec. Area
9. Effie Yeaw Nature Center
10. Lake Natoma State Rec. Area
11. Sly Park Rec. Area
12. Indian Grinding Rock State Hist. Park
13. Stone Lake Wildlife Preserve
14. Cosumnes River Preserve
15. California Caverns
16. Mercer Caverns
17. Moaning Cavern
18. Columbia State Hist. Park
19. Railtown 1897 State Hist. Park
20. California State Mining & Mineral Museum

PO Box 2757, Truckee, CA 96160, ☎ 800-548-8388. The **Truckee River** is popular with trout fishermen, but this is true of many other streams and lakes in other areas. I-80 will take you to the 153-acre **Donner Memorial State Park**. You cross **Donner Pass** nine miles farther on. Near Emigrant Gap, on State Route 20 West, there are interesting views of old mining camps and sweeping views of the countryside for a distance of 40 miles. **Nevada City** was built on seven steep hills and the streets were former miners' trails. Its Victorian houses and elegant mansions make the city the showcase of the Mother Lode. ☎ 916-265-2692.

(%) Days of Sunshine	Max-Min Temperature
Winter 52%	53°-39°
Spring. 81%	72°-46°
Summer 95%	91°-57°
Fall 81%	72°-49°

Climate

Most rain falls in the winter months, with an average of more than 40 inches from November through April. Temperatures are moderate the year round, with a high of 93 in July and an average temperature in the 60s in winter, with a low of 40 at night.

Grass Valley

Five miles beyond Nevada City, at the intersection of State Route 49, is Grass Valley. This was once the area's richest gold mining town. The 784-acre **Empire State Park**, the largest and richest gold mine, and the **Northstar Powerhouse Mining Museum**, are interesting attractions.

Grass Valley's modern charm obscures the fact that beneath its streets $960 million in gold was extracted by the Empire and other nearby mines. Some of the original miners' cottages and Victorian homes are now bed and breakfast establishments.

Each summer, the **"Music in the Mountains"** brings the historic halls of St. Joseph's Chapel alive with classical music.

Lola Montez. California State Library.

Grass Valley is the hub for three major state highways. It's a natural stopping point and provides access to all of Nevada County's historical and scenic attractions. If you are going to Reno, you should travel Route 49 south to a point four miles east of Auburn where it meets I-80. You can take the latter route directly to Sacramento, or stay on 49 as it continues south.

For further information, contact the **Grass Valley/Nevada County Chamber of Commerce**, 248 Mill Street, Grass Valley, CA 95945. ☎ 916-273-4667 or from California and Nevada only, ☎ 800-655-4667.

What to See & Do
Lola Montez House

The Lola Montez House (248 Mill Street, ☎ 916-273-4667) has been restored to what it was when the famous courtesan and dancer lived there in the 1850s. She had many lovers, including King Ludwig I of Bavaria. Born in Ireland in 1820, her real name was Eliza Gilbert. A woman of awesome audacity, she learned Spanish dancing. Her dark hair, blue eyes and enticing figure made her popular. Without technique, she relied upon her beauty. She led a troupe of performers across the United States in 1852, and settled briefly in the gold mining town.

"Notorious I have always been, but never famous."

With these words Lola Montez accurately described herself. One of the most sought-after courtesans of the 19th century, Montez was born in 1819 as the daughter of a Spanish beauty and a British soldier. Bedmate of kings and commoners, she came to San Francisco in 1852 and married wealthy publisher Patrick Hull. They lived for two years in Grass Valley, until her husband deserted her. Known for her "Spider Dance," her bad temper and shocking lifestyle, she spent her last two years in poverty and died at the age of 42 in a squalid boarding house in New York's "Hell's Kitchen."

Where to Stay in Grass Valley

The **Holbrooke Hotel**, 212 West Main Street, ☎ 800-933-7077, $$-$$$$, was established in 1851 and boasts the oldest bar in the state and a guest register that reads like a historical *Who's Who*. Service is friendly and sumptuous. Ulysses S. Grant, Benjamin Harrison, Grover Cleveland, James A. Garfield, Mark Twain and Bret Harte have all walked these halls. There is a fine restaurant on the premises.

Murphy's Inn, 318 Neal Street, ☎ 916-273-6873, $$$, is a cozy bed and breakfast housed in a restored 1866 home. The house was originally built for Edward Coleman, owner of the North Star mine. Rates include breakfast.

Where to Dine in Grass Valley

Try the **Dining Room** at the Holbrooke Hotel, 212 West Main Street, ☎ 800-933-7077, an elegantly casual restaurant inside the 150-year-old hotel, if you're in the mood for a memorable dining experience. Entrées run about $15 per person

Just downt the street, **Tofanelli's**, 302 West Main Street, ☎ 916-272-1468, is open for late breakfast, lunch and dinner in a more shorts-and-t-shirt atmosphere. Pasta, burgers and Mexican food are the house specialities. Try Earl's tostada with marinated tofu and brown rice ($7.25) for a real kick.

Auburn

Placer County, which borders on the north with Nevada and Sierra Counties, once included Coloma, where gold was discovered in 1848. Auburn, now the Placer County seat, has a **landmark courthouse** and serves as the hub of southern Placer County. Visitors can follow zigzag trails made by gold seekers to reach many historical and natural attractions. It is four miles west of the junction of State Route 49 and I-80, and would be worth a side trip for those heading south on 49 to Placerville.

Auburn's State Recreation Area is a 42,000-acre park with four compounds, 50 primitive campsites, fishing, rafting, gold panning, picnicking, hiking and biking.

The **Auburn Chamber of Commerce** at 1101 High Street, ☎ 916-885-5616, can supply you with information about tours of "Old Town."

Where to Stay in Auburn

The **Auburn Inn**, 1875 Auburn Ravine Road, ☎ 800-272-1444, $$-$$$, has 78 rooms and three suites in a two-story motel-style building. There is a pool and hot tub and some of the rooms are handicapped-accessible. Restaurants are nearby.

There is also the standard motel fare. Consider the **Best Western Golden Key**, 13450 Lincoln Way, ☎ 530-885-8611, $$, with 68 rooms and a heated pool, or the **Holiday Inn**, 120 Grass Valley Highway,

☎ 530-887-8787, $$-$$$, which has 96 rooms, indoor corridors and full conference faclities. The **Sleep Inn**, 1819 Auburn Ravine Road, ☎ 530-888-STAY, $$, is a great bargain. It's one of the newest places in town, with an outdoor pool and hot tub, and it serves free continental breakfast.

Where to Dine in Auburn

The **Headquarters House at Raspberry Hill**, 14500 Musso Road, ☎ 530-878-1906, is set amid the pines on the Dunipace Angus cattle ranch. Try the fresh-caught salmon and enjoy the live entertainment on weekend nights.

Coloma

By back-tracking to State Route 49, you can take this road about 18 miles to Coloma where the California Gold Rush actually began. It is now in El Dorado County. The **Marshall Gold Discovery State Historic Park** in Coloma encompasses most of the community's 300 acres. There's a replica of Sutter's Mill. Before you visit, stop at the **Gold Discovery Museum** for a detailed brochure. ☎ 916-889-6500 for information.

The Discovery of Gold

In August, 1847, James W. Marshall, an eccentric 37-year-old carpenter from New Jersey, was hired by John Sutter as foreman to build a sawmill 30 miles east of his fort at Sacramento. It was a crisp morning in January when Marshall left his men dawdling over their breakfast while he checked the depth of the millrace. His men had been digging it deeper for days, and each night Marshall released the river into it to wash out the debris. He was satisfied with the progress this morning, knowing the channel would soon be deep enough to power the mill's big saws. Noticing a glitter from a small object in the water, he stopped to retrieve it. He suspected the piece was gold because of its weight. He hurried back to camp. "Men," he said. "I believe I've found a gold mine."

A few days later, Sam Brannon, a storekeeper in San Francisco, galloped through the city's streets. "Gold from the American River," he shouted.

Some people were not impressed. Gold had been found earlier in California, so few people got excited. But the news spread like wildfire across the nation and, by fall, around the world.

A San Francisco newspaper tried to quell the excitement, saying, "The field is left half planted, the house half built, and everything neglected but the manufacture of shovels and pickaxes." Gold-seeking "Argonauts" rushed to California from all over the world. California's population increased sixteen-fold in four years, and the world's output of gold literally doubled. Towns sprang up almost over night with such names as You Bet, Lousy Ravine, Volcano, Bogus Thunder, and Git-up-and-Git. Life was rough and violent, and most miners died an early death. More substantial towns, whose buildings were made of brick and stone, survive, but only as ghost towns. Mt. Shasta and Weaverville farther north enjoyed boom times supplying lumber for the "Mother Lode" country.

Henry Bigler wrote on January 24, 1848, "This day some kind of mettle was found in the tail race that looks like gold, first discovered by James Martial [sic] the boss of the mill."

Four days after Marshall made his find, he began to appreciate his discovery. He sought out Sutter to assure secrecy, but by now the news had spread. In Sutter's office, when a clerk entered, Marshall yelled, "My God! Didn't I tell you to lock the door?" He and Sutter not only locked the door, but put a wardrobe against it.

Sutter and Marshall were not enriched by the gold. All of Sutter's men deserted him for the gold mines. Thousands of dollars worth of wheat and hides were destroyed by rot. Sutter had hoped to establish an agricultural empire, but that dream collapsed with the discovery of gold.

He now claimed supernatural powers and wandered through the gold fields – a legend in his time – but he was never able to repeat his discovery. He died penniless in 1885, obsessed with the idea that all the gold in California really belonged to him.

Where to Stay in Coloma

The **Coloma Country Inn**, 345 High Street, ☎ 530-622-2217, $$-$$$, is set in a restored 1852 farmhouse in the middle of Marshall Gold Discovery State Historic Park. There are five rooms, three with private bath, and two suites, including one with a full kitchen. A deluxe continental breakfast and afternoon tea and lemonade are served daily. Bikes are available for use by guests.

Sutter's Mill, with view of Coloma, California. Gleason's, 1852.

Tahoe to Placerville

After driving about eight more miles from Coloma, you will arrive in Placerville, at the intersection of Highways 49 and 50. You can continue south on 49 or drive to Sacramento on 50.

If you take the east-west route on Highway 50 to Placerville, take time to enjoy its many scenic and historical attractions. From an elevation of 6,229 feet at Tahoe, your route ascends for 22 miles to 7,382 feet at Echo Summit and then descends to 30 feet above sea level at Sacramento.

Before you start this trip, get your car in tip-top condition, especially the brakes, because some of the downgrades are steep. On these slopes, in addition to braking, put your car in low gear. Tire chains are a must in mountain areas during most of the year, particularly from mid-October through April. The California highway network will keep you up to date on road conditions. ☎ 415-557-3755.

Thirty miles after reaching the top of Echo Summit, you'll pass several entrances to **Desolation Wilderness**. This is a fine hiking and backpacking region, but it is open only to those with permits.

En route is **Camino**, originally a station on the Placerville-Lake Tahoe stagecoach route. Two miles to the east of Camino there's a road to **Apple Hill**, where more than 40 apple farms are open to the public during harvest time, from mid-September through December. You might try the locally made wines, fruit, nuts, vegetables, arts and crafts. There are nearly 20 Christmas tree farms in the area. Interest is high in October with a wide variety of events. In the spring, there is the **Apple Blossom Festival**, and from mid-April through May the area is delightful. There are hay rides and a trout derby. For more information, ☎ 916-644-7692.

Placerville

The next town is truly unique. Placerville (a placer is a deposit of sand and gravel with valuable minerals) is famous for its **El Dorado Historical Museum** and the **Old Hangtown Gold Bug Mine**. Its buildings were constructed from 1850-1870, and they bring the past vividly into focus. For further information, ☎ 916-985-4474.

Relics of this wild region during the days of the Gold Rush have stories to tell that will enthrall you. Most visitors dreams of finding gold today – and there's still some to be found – but instant riches have given way to touring historic sites, staying at charming bed and breakfast inns, quaint hotels, and award-winning wineries.

Sacramento, the jumping off place for the 49ers, is only another 50 miles to the west of Placerville, on Highway 50.

Where to Stay in Placerville

The **Cary House Hotel**, 300 Main Street, ☎ 530-622-4271, $$, is in the middle of old town, which is rife with antique stores and cafés. The 34-room hotel is housed in a building constructed in 1857, and each room has its own unique charm.

The **Chichester-McKee House**, 800 Spring Street, ☎ 530-626-1882, $$, offers three rooms in a home built in 1892. Stained glass and oak furnishings give the place a true Gold Country feel. A full breakfast is part of the package.

Where to Dine in Placerville

It won't be mistaken for a gourmet café, but **Smith Flat House**, 2021 Smith Flat Road, has 150 years of history behind it. The building dates back to the 1850s and has served as a Pony Express depot and dance hall. American fare fills the menu, and there's a saloon in the basement, complete with its own mine shaft. Open for lunch and dinner Tuesday through Saturday, dinner only Sunday and lunch only Monday.

Routes to the Mother Lode Country

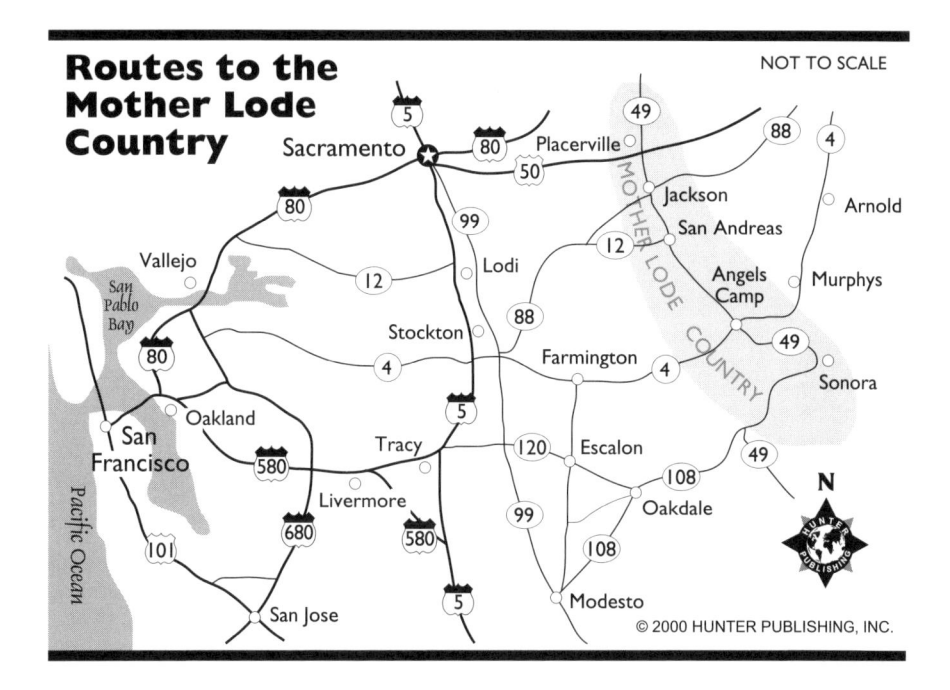

NOT TO SCALE

© 2000 HUNTER PUBLISHING, INC.

Folsom

If your plans include Sacramento, stop at Folsom en route. It is only 20 miles east of the capital.

Folsom is one of the original gold mining towns, although today it is best known for **Folsom Prison**, two miles north of town. There's a four-block section of Folsom on Sutter Street that has been restored to its 1850 appearance, including a theater offering melodramas on weekends. The highlight of this area is **Folsom Lake Recreation Area**, which, in 18,000 acres, offers a variety of activities, including rafting on the American River.

Along the **American River** there are more than 30 miles of trails for biking, hiking and horseback riding. **Folsom Lake** and **Lake Natoma** offer water sports such as rafting, kayaking, sailing, wind surfing and water skiing. There are more than 20 public and private golf courses near the two cities.

The past comes alive at the **Folsom History Museum** on Sutter Street, the site of one of the oldest Wells Fargo assay offices. The Folsom Powerhouse, which produced the first commercial application of electricity, features a breathtaking view of the American River and Rainbow Bridge.

For more detailed information on attractions and activities, write the **Folsom Chamber of Commerce**, 200 Wool Street, ☎ 916-985-2698, or the **Rancho Cordova Chamber of Commerce**, ☎ 916-361-8700.

Sacramento

Another 20 miles will take you to California's capital. Sacramento is situated at the confluence of two major rivers, the Sacramento and the American. It served as a supply and transportation center during the Gold Rush. The city and the county are rich in historic attractions.

Getting Here & Getting Around

Sacramento is only 90 miles from San Francisco, 192 miles from Yosemite, 140 miles from Reno, 53 miles from the wine country in Napa Valley and 105 miles from Lake Tahoe.

There are several easy approaches to Sacramento. Downtown can be reached from the north by taking I-5 via the "J" and "Q" Streets exits. From the south, I-5 and State Route 99 provide access by way of I-80 and the 16th Street exit. From the east or west, take business route I-80 and the 16th Street exit. In addition, US Route 50 from the east and the I-80 business route will take you downtown via the 16th Street exit.

If you wish to bypass Sacramento, take I-80, which runs northwest of the capital, to connect you with east/west corridor traffic.

Airlines

Sacramento Metropolitan Airport is served by about a dozen airlines, including:

American, ☎ 800-433-7300.

Continental, ☎ 800-525-0280.

Delta, ☎ 800-221-1212.

Northwest, ☎ 800-225-2525.

United, ☎ 800-241-6522.

Ground Transportation

Amtrak, ☎ 800-USA-RAIL, provides daily service to Sacramento. For local transportation, contact **AAA Taxi and Shuttle Service,** ☎ 916-334-5555.

History

American California began in this area, which had long been inhabited by the Nisenan Indian tribe, a branch of the Maidu. They had lived in the valley for 10,000 years before any settlers arrived from Mexico.

Lieutenant Gabriel Moraga and Spanish soldiers from Mission San Jose discovered the Sacramento and American Rivers in 1808. The Sacramento was named "Jesus Maria" and the Feather River was called the "Sacramento."

American Trappers

The first American fur trappers, led by the legendary Jedediah Smith, passed through the area in 1827-1828. Fur trappers from the Hudson's Bay Company came in the late 1820s and 1830s. Arrival of trappers proved deadly to the Indians because they brought with them smallpox, for which the Indians had no resistance. Approximately 20,000 Indians died from the disease in the Sacramento Valley during an epidemic in 1833.

"Old Sacramento"

The area now known as "Old Sacramento" was settled in 1839 by Jon Augustus Sutter, who landed on the banks of the Sacramento River. He had received a 48,000-acre land grant from Governor Alvarado of Mexico, who had jurisdiction over the area.

Sutter came to the United States from Switzerland in 1834 to escape debtor's prison after a failed business venture. He left behind a wife and four children. He landed in New York and later lived in St. Louis, Hawaii and Alaska before settling in Sacramento on August 12, 1839.

During his stay in Hawaii, he befriended King Kamehameha, who gave him eight Kanakas (Hawaiians) to accompany him on the leg of his journey to the West Coast. A Belgian, a German and an Indian completed his party.

Sutter was so impressed by the land along the river that he decided to build a settlement on higher ground about a mile from where he first landed. He called it "New Helvetia" (New Switzerland). His intention was to provide a haven for European emigrants. In what was largely uncharted territory, he envisioned a large trading post. The discovery of gold on the American River 30 miles east of his fort destroyed that dream.

California at this time was largely unpopulated. San Francisco had a population of 460 and Sacramento had 150 people. These were the area's largest communities.

Gold seekers "cradle-rocking." NY Public Library.

News of gold wasn't revealed in the nation's capital until President Polk spoke to Congress about a report he had received from Colonel Mason in San Francisco. The rush was on!

Sacramento continued to grow and the state of California was admitted to the union in 1850. Sacramento became the state's capital four years later. Many of the elaborate mansions built in the city by merchants are still in evidence.

Old Sacramento lies along the banks of the Sacramento River. It's a historic park, 28 acres in extent, that gives a fascinating glimpse of the past while catering to the needs of modern Americans. It has the greatest concentration of historic buildings in California.

Sacramento Today

Sacramento is a fascinating city and definitely worth a visit. It has fine restaurants, antique shops, art galleries and an abundance of outdoor activities. "**Old Town**" is a must, as is **Sutter's Fort**. But there are many other things to see.

The **Sacramento waterfront** changed almost overnight at the start of the Gold Rush as businesses sprang up to provide supplies for the fortune hunters who rushed to the state from all over the world. A shrewd businessman, Sam Brannan, became California's first millionaire. With thousands arriving each month, he ignored the gold and concentrated on producing the necessities of life for the incoming gold seekers.

John Sutter

Sutter, with his fort and varied business enterprises, should have become a millionaire, but his workers deserted him to join the 49ers.

Sutter's creditors hounded him for payment of outstanding debts. Although his son, John Sutter, Jr., arrived from Switzerland to help his father, there was little he could do. Help was impossible to find. He surveyed land along the Embaracadero, dividing it into lots, and auctioned them off to pay his father's creditors. Sam Brannan tried to help the young Sutter, but without success.

The elder Sutter sold all his holdings in 1849 for $40,000, but continued to lose money because he was an inept businessman.

He died in Washington, D.C., while applying for a grant from Congress to help European emigrants en route to California.

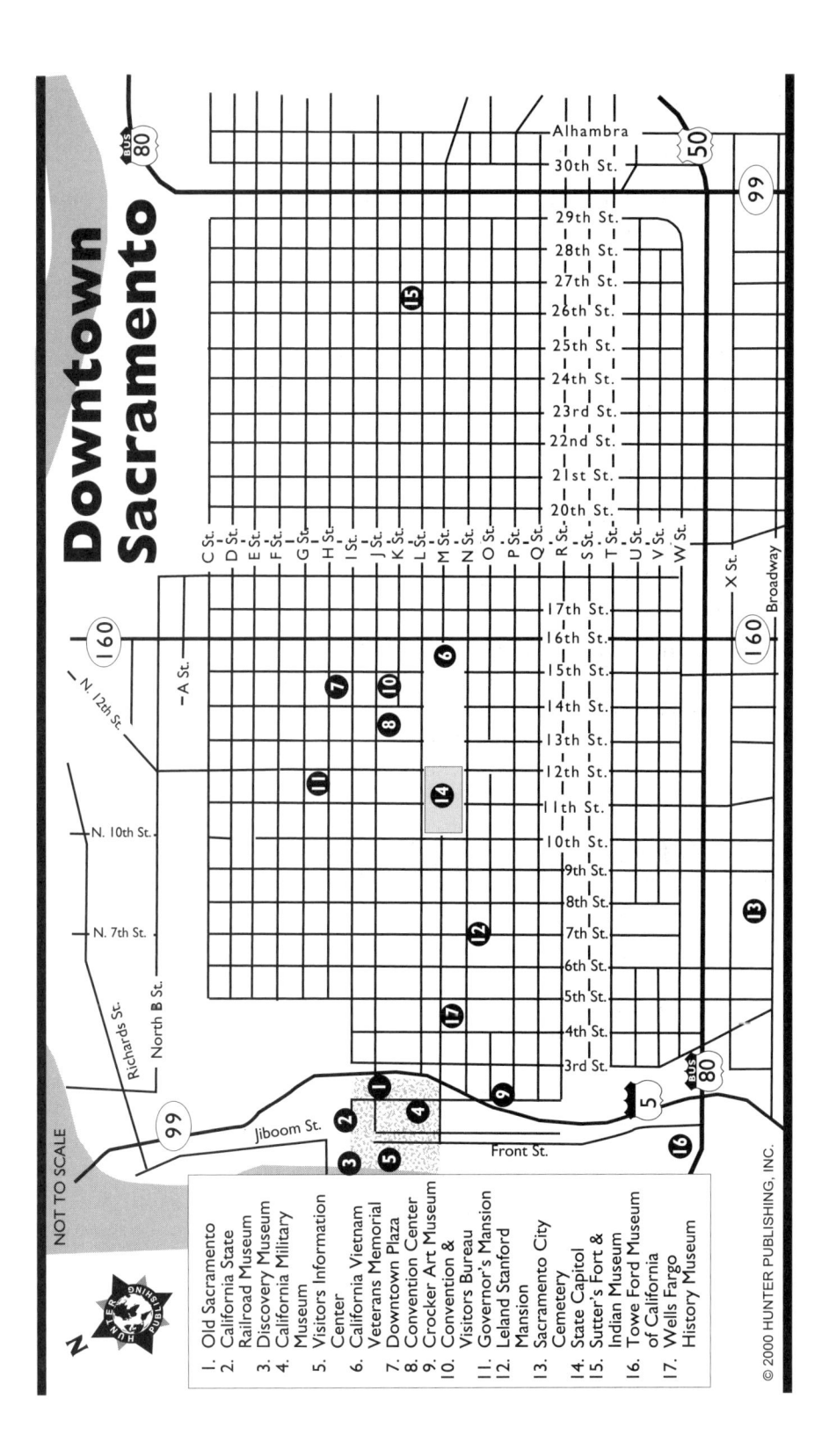

Downtown Sacramento

1. Old Sacramento
2. California State Railroad Museum
3. Discovery Museum
4. California Military Museum
5. Visitors Information Center
6. California Vietnam Veterans Memorial
7. Downtown Plaza
8. Convention Center
9. Crocker Art Museum
10. Convention & Visitors Bureau
11. Governor's Mansion
12. Leland Stanford Mansion
13. Sacramento City Cemetery
14. State Capitol
15. Sutter's Fort & Indian Museum
16. Towe Ford Museum of California
17. Wells Fargo History Museum

© 2000 HUNTER PUBLISHING, INC.

The Western Sierra

Railroad Museum

The city was the western terminus of the short-lived Pony Express and the transcontinental railroad. This area reflects the city's transportation legacy with one of the largest railroad museums in North America. The **California State Railroad Museum** displays 21 restored locomotives and cars in its 100,000 square feet of space. In 40 one-of-a-kind exhibits, railroad history is depicted from 1850 to the present. Historic equipment and exhibits on the transcontinental railroad and 19th-century rail travel are displayed in the reconstructed 1866 Central Pacific Railroad Passenger Station.

Towe Ford Museum

A mile from the railroad museum, on the edge of Old Sacramento, is another facility dedicated to transportation. The Towe Ford Museum contains the world's most complete collection of antique Ford automobiles. Every model produced by Ford between 1903 and 1953 is represented. There are more than 150 cars and trucks. Many are in excellent condition, while others have been authentically restored. The collection also includes original and restored cars from the late '50s, '60s and '70s.

Old Sacramento Walking Tour

The best way to see Old Sacramento is by walking through it. A self-guided tour can be obtained from the Visitors Information Center, 1104 Front Street. One hundred unique shops and 20 unusual restaurants await you. Each year special events draw thousands to participate in the **Jazz Jubilee, Festival de la Familia, the Pacific Rim Festival** and two collectors' fairs.

For more information, call or write Old Sacramento Management Office, ☎ 916-264-7031, or 558-3912, for information on special events.

Other Attractions

Among other interesting museums are the **California Military Museum** (1119 Second Street, ☎ 916-442-2883), the **Discovery Museum** (101 I Street, ☎ 916-264-7057) and the **Crocker Art Museum**, which has early American and European paintings (☎ 916-684-5423). Other interesting sights include the **California State Indian Museum** (2618 K Street, ☎ 916-324-0971), with its extensive tribal exhibits of California's Native Americas. The *Delta King* **river boat** provides a 44-room waterfront hotel with restaurants and theater. There are also river boat cruises, such as those on the *Mathew McKinley* and *Spirit of Sacramento*. ☎ 916-552-2933. The *River City Queen* is also a possibility. ☎ 916-921-

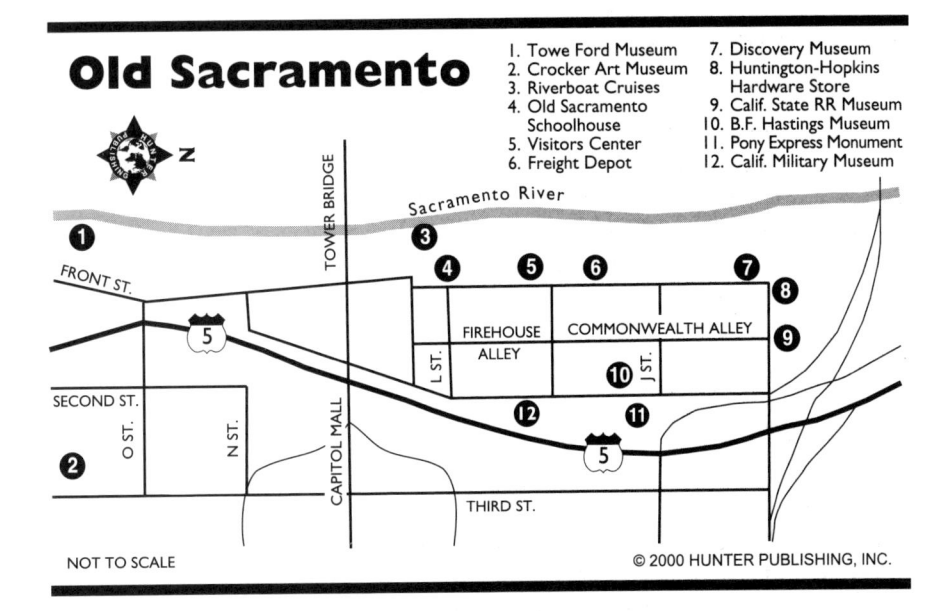

Old Sacramento

1. Towe Ford Museum
2. Crocker Art Museum
3. Riverboat Cruises
4. Old Sacramento Schoolhouse
5. Visitors Center
6. Freight Depot
7. Discovery Museum
8. Huntington-Hopkins Hardware Store
9. Calif. State RR Museum
10. B.F. Hastings Museum
11. Pony Express Monument
12. Calif. Military Museum

1111. And last, but not least, is **Sutter's Fort Museum**. This is a replica of the 1839 fort built by John Sutter. ☎ 916-445-4422.

Gold Country North Adventures

Adventures on Foot

The American River is more than just a rafter's paradise. There are plenty of trails near the river that offer amazing riparian hikes on the way from Tahoe to Sacramento not far from I-80, but far enough to make you forget the buzz of rubber on asphalt. The hikes are on Tahoe National Forest Land. For more information, contact the Nevada City ranger station, ☎ 530-265-4531.

One of the more well-traveled trails leads seven miles to **Loch Leven Lakes**. The trailhead is located near the Big Bend Visitor Center. From I-80 just east of Cisco Grove, take the Rainbow Road exit and follow the signs. From the trailhead at 5,680 feet, the path climbs to the southwest through a forest of Jeffrey and lodgepole pines. The trail crosses a set of railroad tracks and continues climbing up and over a ridge. Lower Loch Leven Lake is the next stop. A mile away is Middle Loch Leven Lake and, just beyond, Upper Loch Leven Lake. Each lake offers backcountry camping. The trail is also open to horses.

East of Auburn in the **Foresthill** area, you can hike down to and along the American River, checking out the rapids and the soaking-wet river rats while staying high and dry on the bank. Journey on a great multiday trek on the **American River Trail** from **Mumford trailhead**. Begin by driving east on Foresthill Road about 30 miles to the trailhead on the left side of the road. The initial part of the hike drops almost vertically down to the river, losing more than 2,700 feet of elevation in the first 3.25 miles. Once at the river, turn right and follow the American River Trail upstream. You'll have to cross two tributaries of the river, Tadpole Creek and New York Creek, which can be hazardous during heavy runoff, before ending the trip 10.7 miles from the trailhead. The **Bearcroft Trail** reaches the river one mile upstream from New York Creek and leads back up to Foresthill Road. This route is even steeper than the Mumford Trail, climbing 3,240 feet in 2.25 miles. If you hustle up this trail, you'll hit the road four miles from your car at Mumford trailhead.

Italian Bar Trail isn't far from the Mumford hike. Find the trailhead by driving 19 miles east of Auburn on Foresthill Road and turning left on Humbug Ridge Road. It shouldn't come as a surprise that this trail, too, loses altitude rapidly, descending 3,000 feet in 2.25 miles to the banks of the North Fork American River.

Deep within the American River wilderness, you probably won't have much company on the **Sailor Flat Trail**. Just the drive to the trailhead is a bear, covering 51 miles on Foresthill Road east of Auburn. Take a left on Sailor Flat Road and continue one mile to the trailhead. You can leave one vehicle at the Mumford or Bearcroft trailheads to make this a long one-way hike. Sailor Flat Trail begins on an old mining road, then drops steeply, plunging just over 3,000 feet in 3.25 miles to the North Fork American River. Here you can pick up the American River Trail and continue the hike.

Euchre Bar Trail marks another strenuous hike in and out of the North Fork American River Canyon. It's a complicated drive to the trailhead: Take the Alta exit from I-80 east of Auburn and turn right on Morton Street, then left on Casa Loma. Turn right at the sign for Rawhide Mine and continue .75 mile to the parking lot. Again, this path leads you on steep switchbacks down to the riverbank. then crosses a suspension bridge over the water. Continue upstream for another 7.4 miles as the trail climbs Dorer Ranch Road past abandoned mines dating back 150 years.

Adventures on Wheels
Bicycling

At the popular **Folsom Lake State Recreation**, which can be reached from Sacramento by taking I-80 or US 50 northeast from Sacramento, one of the finest paved bike paths in the country awaits. The recreation area's 32-mile bikeway links the lake with many other county parks along its route before ending in Sacramento. Beginning at Beal's Point and ending at Discovery Park in Old Sacramento, the trail goes past the southwest corner of Folsom Lake, the west shore of Lake Natoma and the American River.

There are plenty of enticing unpaved trails along the American River northeast of Sacramento, too. Begin on the **Clementine Trail**, northeast of Auburn where Foresthill Road crosses the North Fork of the American River. The path runs northeast, parallel to the North Fork, for about four miles to Lake Clementine dam. Here you can access the **Culvert Trail**, which leads three miles south to the head of the **Confluence Trail**, where the North Fork meets the Middle Fork of the American River. From the confluence it's possible to set out on a strenuous 15-mile, figure-eight loop ride that extends west-southwest toward the town of Auburn and east-northeast between the two river forks along Foresthill Divide. Part of this ride crosses the Mammoth Bar Off-Highway Vehicle Area, so be on the lookout for machines. See the USGS 7.5-minute topo maps covering Auburn and Greenwood for details.

East of Auburn, you can pick up the **Knickerbocker Trail**, a popular path where you're bound to meet fellow bikers. Take CA 49 east to the town of Cool and access the trail behind the fire station. This 9.5-mile loop can be extended an additional 10 miles by riding connecting trails. Watch out for horses.

Beginners will appreciate the three-mile **Stagecoach Trail** that runs from Russell Road in the town of Auburn to the Foresthill Road bridge.

Off-Road Driving

There are two extensive off-highway vehicle areas on the **Foresthill Divide**, accessible from Foresthill Road. Use Mammoth Bar Road to access the **Mammoth Bar OHV area** near the Middle Fork of the American River. There are picnic areas and several loop trails on these flat 1,200 acres. The area is open all year. Maps are available at the California State Parks Auburn office on CA 49, ☎ 530-885-5821. The **Sugarpine OHV area**, north of Foresthill, is huge, offering more than 65 miles of trails. The staging area is off Sugarpine Road. Maps are available at the US Forest Service office on Foresthill Road next to the middle school.

The **Michigan Bluff Trail** is open to motorcycles as well as hikers, horses and mountain bikes, so ride with care. The trailhead is off Michigan Bluff Road, northeast of the town of Foreshill on the south side of Foresthill Road. The trail drops dramatically about two miles down to Eldorado Creek. At the bottom of the drainage you can extend your journey by hiking across a footbridge and continuing upstream on the opposite side of the canyon.

Adventures on Water
The American River

Stretching its watery fingers from the High Sierra into the canyons and foothills northeast of Sacramento, the American River is one of the best-loved riparian escapes in California. The American flows in three forks – North, Middle and South – as it drops from the Crystal Range into Folsom Lake. The South Fork is by far the most popular of the three. More than 100,000 people descend on the South Fork every year, making it the most visited piece of whitewater in the state. Folks are attracted to the peaceful backcountry setting and the diversity of plant and animal life, as well as the adrenalin rush of running the rapids. The North and Middle Forks, meanwhile, are wild, untamed and, for all but experienced rafters, potentially dangerous.

> *Respect for the river is vital on any stretch of water. Even seemingly mundane rapids can cause problems for unprepared boaters and the most placid stretches of river can hide underwater obstacles and hazardous currents that will surprise an unwary adventurer. So proceed with caution and, if it's your first time on the American, consider traveling with a licensed and experienced guide. For a partial list, see* Outfitters on Water, *page 160.*

If you plan on a multiday trip, note that overnighters must obtain a River Camping Permit at the Auburn State Recreation Area on CA 49, one mile south of the town of Auburn. The permit is required for many locations on the North Fork and Middle Fork. Riverside campers are also subject to a nightly fee, as are vehicles parked at campgrounds overnight.

For more information on the mighty American, contact the **California State Parks American River District Headquarters** in Folsom, 7806 Folsom-Auburn Road, ☎ 916-988-0205.

Mariah Wilderness Expeditions

This outfitter would be notable enough as the only woman-owned whitewater rafting company in California. But that's not the only thing that sets Mariah apart. Since 1982, the company has served more than 72,000 guests and has been honored for safety and service. Guiding on the American, Merced, Tuolumne and Kings rivers, Mariah offers dozens of trips – from half-day floats to seven-day adventures – designed for all abilities. From corporate team building to wine and rafting trips and storytelling family excursions, there's something for every family member.

Guests stay at the company's private riverside campground on the South Fork of the American River. For more information, ☎ 800-462-7424, PO Box 70248, Point Richmond, CA 94807; www.mariahwe.com.

North Fork

One of the most popular segments runs from Iowa Hill Bridge to Ponderosa Bridge, a 9.5-mile jaunt that offers rapids of the Class IV and Class V variety. The run is usually made in a single day. River rats from far and wide come to challenge the likes of Chamberlin Falls, Staircase Rapids and Bogus Thunder. To safely tackle the North Fork, you must know how to correctly read a raging river, which comes only with experience.

Chamberlin Falls Rapid, set in a deep gorge of the same name just .25 miles from the Iowa Bridge put-in, drops 10 feet almost straight down into a tumultuous pool. If the river is running low, large, exposed boulders in the main channel can capsize a raft. If the river is running too high, a raft can be trapped in the torrent at the base of the rapid.

Up next are **Bogus Thunder** and **Staircase Rapid**, two stretches of whitewater that have been known to drown unsuspecting boaters. Rafts sometimes become trapped below the drops. In short, if you or your guide aren't sure of their skills to handle these types of situations, hit the shore and portage around the rapids.

> *A note on flow: Veteran river runners will talk long into the night about "CFS," or cubic feet per second, the standard measurement of a river's flow – and, thus, a gauge of how dangerous the river is on a given day. If the flow is too high, obviously the power of the rapids is stronger. But more importantly, boaters have less time between rapids to position themselves for what's coming up. If the flow is too low, boats are threatened by exposed obstacles, including trees and boulders. On the North Fork, optimum flow runs between 1,500 CFS and 3,000 CFS.*

If you plan on camping along the North Fork, you'll need to obtain a special permit and use only specified areas.

The land around the North and Middle Forks is managed by various specific government agencies. In this case, the land is overseen primarily by the California Department of Parks and Recreation, under contract with the US Bureau of Reclamation. US Forest Service stations in Foresthill (Tahoe National Forest) and Georgetown (El Dorado National Forest) manage the area above Ruck-A-Chucky.

Middle Fork

Class II and Class III rapids populate a fantastic and very challenging run from Oxbow put-in to Greenwood take-out that stretches 15 miles. Set aside at least 10 hours of float time, but you won't be bored because you'll also find a few Class IV and V stretches. Take your time and portage if necessary. In fact, the Middle Fork is well-suited for excursions lasting one to three days. Tunnel Chute, Kanaka Gulch and Ruck-A-Chucky are stretches of rapids whose names you won't forget. Boaters who float downstream past Greenwood should take out at Mammoth Bar, before hitting the absolutely unmanageable Murderer's Bar Rapid. Even veterans have never come back from attempts to tame aptly named Murderer's Gorge.

Campers have their choice of many riverside locations and sandbars (there are no developed sites), but you must have a special permit and be on public land of course. If there aren't already folks holed up at the popular Ford's Bar and Cherokee Bar, check out the partially hidden locales between Cache Bar and Ford's Bar.

Miners and their dynamite created what is now **Tunnel Chute** in the 1800s, blasting a deep cleft in the bedrock. This rapid should be approached with extreme caution and the smart money will portage around it altogether, rather than become one of the many injury statistics this whitewater has claimed.

It is necessary to portage around **Ruck-A-Chucky** as well, which is considered unrunnable even by expert boaters, unless you enjoy being dashed against boulders at the bottom of vertical drops. Land managers are so serious about safety here that they've constructed a new portage trail.

Downstream from Ruck-A-Chucky are a few Class III+ rapids that demand careful attention and an expert hand in the boat. Their profiles change dramatically as river flow fluctuates. The take out at Greenwood is about one mile below the last of these rapids at the remains of Greenwood Bridge.

South Fork

The most popular whitewater run in the state is the stretch of the South Fork between **Chili Bar** put-in and **Folsom Lake**. What brings hundreds of thousands to the river each year? A float down the South Fork is more than just a rafting trip past stands of white alder, cottonwood and big-leaf maple. It's also more than the fun of riding the rough water of The Gorge and Triple Threat. A float westward on the American is like a journey through a history book. The bends in the river reveal pages from every chapter of the West's past.

You'll raft past the former homes of the Nisenan nation who lived in the villages of Chapa, now Coloma. James Marshall discovered gold here in a tailrace at Sutter's Mill in 1848, setting off a Gold Rush that quickly brought on the close of the American frontier. In 1860 the Pony Express rode the South Fork along a trail used by native peoples for hundreds of years. Japanese first settled in California near Gold Hill in the 1870s, founding the Wakamatsu tea and silk plantation. Tailings mounds, left over by a 1930s-era gold dredge, can be seen between Coloma and Lotus. In fact, men and women have worked this river since the 1840s, including the people of present-day Northern California, who count on the dams on the Upper American River for power and water. The dams also enable boaters to ride the river all year.

It's rather ironic, however, that because of the flood control measures, flow levels can change rapidly when water is released from behind the dams. On average, summer flow from the Chili Bar Dam runs between 1,000 and 1,775 CFS. That allows roughly four hours of boating every day, although that can vary according to yearly water supplies. Boatable flows are released usually until the first weekend of October. They sometimes resume later in the fall depending on water supply. In the spring, flow levels are closely linked to storms and Sierra snowpack.

> *Beware of dangerously high flow levels after storms or heavy winters.*

This Bureau of Land Management manages some lands adjacent to South Fork, which are indicated by signs. You are asked to let the agency know in advance if you are rafting with a group of more than 24 people.

California State Parks oversees **Marshall Gold Discovery State Park**, where where John Marshall discovered gold in 1848, and it provides interpretive programs. You can put-in near the state park at North Beach, but you can't take out there. There is no camping, but boaters are allowed in the park as day users for a fee. There are two South Fork access sites at Folsom Lake State Recreation Area off Salmon Falls Road. These take-out areas charge for parking.

El Dorado County runs **Henningsen-Lotus Park**, which offers a parking lot, restrooms and a boat launch. Boaters in the Coloma area are asked to use this park to put in.

Following is a mile-by-mile guide to the South Fork's most popular run, 20.5 miles from Chili Bar put-in to tbe Salmon Falls Bridge take-out.

- 0 miles - Chili Bar River Access. Fees charged.
- 0.5 miles - BLM public land to mile 3.4.

- 0.6 miles - Meatgrinder Rapid. Class III+.
- 1.3 miles - Racehorse Bend Rapid. Class III+.
- 1.5 miles - Maya Rapid. Class II-III.
- 1.8 miles - Rock Garden Rapid. Class II.
- 2.0 miles - African Queen Rapid. Class II.
- 3.1 miles - Triple Threat Rapid. Class III. Miner's Creek rest stop.
- 4.4 miles - Indian Creek. Beginning of quiet zone.
- 5.2 miles - Troublemaker Rapid. Class III+.
- 5.2 miles - American River Resort. River Access and Campground. Fees charged.
- 5.5 miles - Coloma Resort River Access and Campground. Fees charged.
- 5.7 miles - Sutter's Mill site.
- 6.0 miles - Marshall Gold Discovery State Historic Park. North Beach River Access Area. Fees charged. Picnic tables and restroom. No take-outs.
- 7.1 miles - Old Scary Rapid. Class II.
- 7.4 miles - Highway 49 Bridge River Access. No parking under bridge.
- 8.0 miles - Henningsen-Lotus County Park River Access. Fees charged.
- 8.5 miles - Lotus Ledge surfing hole.
- 9.0 miles - Camp Lotus River Access and Campground. Fees charged. Barking Dog rapid. Class II.
- 9.7 miles - Beginning of Dave Moore Nature Area (to 9.9 miles).
- 10.6 miles - Current Divider Rapid. Class II+.
- 11.2 miles - Highway Rapid. Class II.
- 11.5 miles - Greenwood Creek. End of quiet zone.
- 12.0 miles - Cable Crossing Rapid. Class II.
- 12.2 miles - BLM land is a good lunch/camping area with restroom facilities.
- 12.8 miles - More lunch/camping sites.
- 13.8 miles - Fowler's Ruck Rapid. Beginning of the Gorge. Class III-.
- 13.9 miles - Gorilla Rock and Convict Rock on river left.
- 15.0 miles - Indian grinding holes on large boulder on right.
- 16.9 miles - Satan's Cesspool Rapid. Class III+.
- 17.0 miles - Son of Satan's Rapid. Class II+.
- 17.6 miles - Lower Haystack Canyon Rapid. Class II+.

- 18.2 miles - Bouncing Rock Rapid. Class II+.
- 18.6 miles - Hospital Bar Rapid Class III.
- 18.7 miles - Recovery Room Rapid. Class II+.
- 19.4 miles - Surprise Rapid. Class II+. Class II rapids continue for 1.6 miles.
- 20.5 miles - Salmon Falls Bridge take-out. Parking fees charged.

Rules & Regulations

As one of California's most popular recreation areas, the South Fork can become quite a crowded river on summer weekends. It's important to follow local rules and regulations to ensure a safe and enjoyable trip and help preserve and protect the natural environment that brings so many visitors to the area.

- **Fishing:** If you're 16 or older you'll need a California fishing license to wet a line. The license must be worn so that it is clearly visible. Rainbow trout are released May through September upstream of the CA 49 Bridge.
- **Boat Registration:** In El Dorado County private boaters need an annual registration tag. The free tags must be displayed on the boat. They can be obtained at river access points, campgrounds and stores. The tag certifies that you are a non-commercial boater and that you will abide by the regulations on the tag.
- **Quiet Zone:** Portions of the bank of the South Fork are private property and abut the homes of residents, so locals and land managers have designated a "quiet zone." In the zone, boaters are asked to reduce noise, especially when within sight of homes. The quiet zone begins at Indian Creek upstream from Troublemaker Rapid and extends downstream to Greenwood Creek.
- **Sanitation:** River rats must clean up their act. The river is not a public outhouse, so always use the public restroom shown on river maps. Campers on public lands with no facilities must have a portable toilet. When bathing or washing dishes, wash at least 200 feet from any stream. Use small amounts of biodegradable, non-phosphate soap. Dig a cathole for dishwater and food drainings, then cover it.

Safety

Both the upper river (Chili Bar to Coloma) and the lower river (Coloma to Salmon Falls) are rated Class III at flows below 6,000 CFS. If the river is running higher than 6,000 CFS, some rapids are Class IV. Use extreme caution under these conditions and portage unless you possess advanced river-running skills. If you lack whitewater experience, choose a professional outfitter. The stretch between Marshall Gold Discovery State Historic Park and Camp Lotus, generally rated Class II, is one of the best spots in California for novice kayakers and canoeists.

Adventures on Snow

Located 30 miles west of Truckee and one mile south of I-80, **Eagle Mountain Nordic** offers 25 cross-country trails and skating lanes totalling more than 75 kilometers around Eagle Mountain. Ski to the top of the area's namesake peak (elevation 6,140 feet) for inspiring views of the surrounding Sierra, then head back to the impressive lodge for a stop in the café. Snowshoers are welcome, and telemark skis are available for rent. ☎ 800-391-2254.

Due east of Auburn, the area north of Foresthill is becoming a popular location for snow trails. Located about 15 minutes north of Foresthills, the area called **China Wall** offers trails groomed by the US Forest Service. When the snow is piled high enough on Foresthill Road, it is closed at China Wall and you can cross-country ski or snowmobile up Foresthill Road and its side roads for miles. For more information, contact **Eldorado National Forest** headquarters in Placerville, ☎ 530-622-5061.

Gold Country North Outfitters

General Outfitters

■ Auburn
Sierra Mountain Sports, 13470 Lincoln Way, ☎ 530-887-8636.

■ Grass Valley
Sports Fever, 682 Freeman Lane, ☎ 530-477-8006.

■ Jackson
Jackson Family Sports, 225 East Highway 88, ☎ 209-223-3890.
Mokelumne Adventure Company, 42 Main Street, ☎ 209-223-2250.

■ Placerville
Kyburz Ski Hut & Sports, 87 Fair Lane, ☎ 209-530-626-1514.

■ Rancho Cordova
Granite Arch Climbing, 11335 Folsom Boulevard, ☎ 916-638-4605.
Wilderness Sports, 12401 Folsom Boulevard, ☎ 916-985-3555.

■ Sacramento
Recreational Equipment Incorporated, 1790 Expo Parkway, ☎ 916-924-8900.

Sierra Outfitters, 2100 Arden Way, ☎ 916-922-7500.

Sports Rack USA, 2401 Arden Way, ☎ 916-487-2222.

On Horseback

■ Arnold
Big Tree Stable & Stage Line, Calaveras Big Trees State Park, ☎ 209-795-7671.

■ Placerville
Crystal Basin Pack Station, 6115 Windle Straw, ☎ 530-626-5349.

■ Columbia
Columbia Stageline & Stable, Wells Fargo Building, Main Street, ☎ 209-965-0663.

■ Jamestown
Aspen Meadow Pack Station, PO Box 154, ☎ 209-984-5427.

On Wheels

■ Auburn
Auburn Bike Works, 227 Palm Avenue, ☎ 530-885-3861.

Bicycle Emporium, 483 Grass Valley Highway, ☎ 530-823-2900.

Kostrikin Cycles, 15371 Pear Valley Lane, ☎ 530-878-9446.

Sacramento Bicycle Show, 12290 Torrey Pines Drive, ☎ 530-268-0144.

■ Folsom
Bicycles Plus, 6606 Folsom-Auburn Road, ☎ 916-989-9670.

Bike Doctor, 146 Market Street, ☎ 916-983-4511.

Folsom Bicycle Works, 312 Natoma Street, ☎ 916-985-3244.

■ Grass Valley
Pat's Bicycle Circus, 20245 Casa Loma Drive, ☎ 530-274-9037.

Sports Fever, 682 Freeman Lane, ☎ 530-477-8006.

Samaurai Mountain Bikes, 10028 Joerschke Drive, ☎ 530-477-0858.

■ Lotus
Velo Coloma Gold Country Cycle, 835 Lotus Road, ☎ 530-622-2453.

■ Rancho Cordova
Precision Bicycles, 12401 Folsom Boulevard, ☎ 916-351-9066.

■ Sacramento
City Bicycle Works, 2419 K Street, ☎ 447-2453.
Dritz Cyclery, 2209 Del Paso Road, ☎ 916-925-4960.
Pacific Bicycle, 2409 J Street, ☎ 916-447-9118.
Rex Cycles, 1930 Capitol Avenue, ☎ 916-46-5706
Sacramento Cyclery, 9655 Folsom Boulevard, ☎ 916-366-6500.

On Water
■ Angels Camp
OARS, PO Box 67, ☎ 800-346-6277.

■ Auburn
Canyon Raft Rentals, 13480 Lincon Way, ☎ 530-823-0931.
Sierra Outdoor Center, 440 Lincoln Way, ☎ 530-885-1844.
Whitewater Excitement, PO Box 5992, ☎ 800-750-2386.

■ Coloma
CBOC Whitewater Rafting, PO Box 554, ☎ 530-621-1236.
Whitewater Connection, 7170 Highway 49, ☎ 530-622-6446.
Whitewater Voyages, 7320 Highway 49, ☎ 530-622-7215.

■ Columbia
Zephyr Whitewater, PO Box 510, ☎ 209-532-6249.

■ Fair Oaks
River Rat Raft Rentals, 9840 Fair Oaks Boulevard, ☎ 916-966-6777.

■ Grass Valley
Free Flight Sports, 153 South Auburn Street, ☎ 530-272-7790.
Tight Lines Guide Service, 15341 Lorie Drive, ☎ 530-273-1986.
Tributary Whitewater Tours, 20480 Woodbury Drive, ☎ 530-346-6812.

■ Lotus
California Canoe & Kayak School, 835 Lotus Road, ☎ 530-295-0452.
River Store, 1032 Lotus Road, ☎ 530-626-3435.

■ Placerville
Adventure Diving Pro Scuba, PO Box 765, ☎ 530-626-6785.
Chili Bar Put-In, 1669 Chili Bar Court, ☎ 530-642-1669.

South Fork Custom Canoe, 907 Hillcrest Street, ☎ 530-621-2058.

■ **Point Richmond**

Mariah Wilderness Expeditions, PO Box 70248, ☎ 800-462-7424; www.mariahwe.com.

■ **Rancho Cordova**

American River Raft Rentals, 11257 South Bridge Street, ☎ 916-635-6400.

California Canoe & Kayak, 12401 Folsom Boulevard, ☎ 916-631-1400.

South Fork Custom Canoe, 2933 Gold Pan Court, ☎ 916-853-8565.

Wilderness Sports, 12401 Folsom Boulevard, ☎ 916-985-3335.

■ **Riverbank**

Beyond Limits Adventures, 5729 Terminal Avenue, ☎ 209-869-6060.

Stanislaus Kayak, 5729 Terminal Avenue, ☎ 209-869-6085.

■ **Sacramento**

Inland Sailing, 2355 Sutterville Bypass, ☎ 916-454-3966.

Where to Stay in Sacramento

Amber House Bed and Breakfast Inn is a historic place. To reach it, take the business exit of Highway 80 to State Route 160 or 16th Street, and drive almost a mile north to N Street, then a half-mile east to 1315 22nd Street, 95816. $$-$$$$. No pets. ☎ 916-444-8085. **Best Western's Harbor Inn and Suites** is four miles west of the exit for Business Loop 80 via Harbor Boulevard, at 1250 Halyard Drive, 95691. Pets are permitted for a $10 charge. $$-$$$. ☎ 916-371-2100. **Best Western's Ponderosa Motor Inn** is downtown and three blocks from the capitol, between 11th and 12th Streets. The address is 11 H Street, 95814. No pets. $-$$. It's on the Sacramento River next to bike trails. ☎ 916-443-6515.

Fountain Suites Hotel is 2.3 miles northwest of Business Loop 80, off I-5 on the Richards Boulevard exit, at 321 Bercut Drive, 95814. $$-$$$. No pets. ☎ 916-441-1444. **Governors Inn** is nearby, 2.3 miles northwest of Business Loop 80, by taking I-5's Richards Boulevard off-ramp to 210 Richards Boulevard, 95814. Rates range $60-70. No pets. ☎ 916-448-7224. **Holiday Inn North East** ($$-$$$) is nine miles east of town. Take the I-80 exit at Madison Avenue, then drive a third of a mile east to 5321 Date Avenue, 95841. No pets. It has a dining room and coffee shop open from 6 AM to 10 PM. Meals cost $9-19. ☎ 916-338-5800. The **Radisson Hotel** is 3½ miles east via 16th Street on State Route 160. Take the Canterbury Road exit to 500 Leisure Lane, 95815. $$. Their restaurant is open from

6 AM to 11 PM, with meals costing $14-18. Pets are permitted, but there's a $50 deposit. ☎ 916-922-2020. The **Red Lion Hotel** is one block off Business Loop 80, via the Arden Way exit, to 2001 Point West Way, 95915. $$-$$$$. There's a dining room and coffee shop open from 6 AM to 11 PM. Meals are $9-22. ☎ 916-929-8855. The **Red Lion's Sacramento Inn** is reached by taking the exit of Business Loop 80 via Arden Way to the Arden Fair Shopping Plaza at 1401 Arden Way, 95815. Pets are allowed for $25 extra. $$-$$$. There's a dining room and coffee shop open from 6 AM to 11 PM, with meals $7-19. ☎ 916-447-5400.

Where to Dine in Sacramento

Aldo's Restaurant is located in the Town and Country Village at Fulton Avenue and Marconi Street at 2914 Pasatiempo Lane. They serve northern Italian dishes priced $21-30. They are open from 11:30 AM to 10:30 PM. ☎ 916-483-5031. For **Bradshaw's Restaurant**, take US 50 get off at Bradshaw Road, and drive to 9647 Nucrib Avenue. It is open from 8:30 AM to 10 PM, and until 11 PM on Friday and Saturday nights. The American-style dinners are priced $11-20. ☎ 916-483-5031. **Chanterell** is in the Sterling Hotel, 1300 H Street, 95814. Open from 7-10 AM, 11:30-2 and 5:30-8:30 PM, its continental meals are priced at $11-20. ☎ 916-442-0451. **Delta King Pilothouse Restaurant** is on the Delta King, Old Sacramento Waterfront, 1000 Front St. ☎ 916-441-4440. **Fat City Bar and Grill** is in the Old Sacramento historic area at 1001 Front Street. It is open from 11:30-2:30 and 4-10, but later on Friday and Saturday nights, serving American food priced from $11 to $20. ☎ 916-446-6788. The **Firehouse** is also in Old Sacramento's historic area at 1112 2nd Street. It is open from 11:30-2:15 and 5:30-10 PM and serves continental meals priced from $21 to $30. ☎ 916-442-4772.

Gold Country South

If you must end your trip at Sacramento for any reason, the fastest route to points south and Los Angeles is on I-15. The distance to Los Angeles is 386 miles. Hopefully, this will not be necessary because the grandest part of your trip lies ahead. Yosemite, Kings Canyon and Sequoia National Parks should not be missed. To reach them you have two possible routes. You can take Highway 99 south and pick up the east-west routes to the parks, or backtrack on Highway 50 to Placerville and pick up Highway 49, a 321-mile heritage corridor that stretches from Vinton in the north to Oakhurst in the south. Highway 99 goes through every community large and small and is maddeningly slow. Unless you have a particular reason for going this way, we recommend returning east from Sacramento to Placerville.

The Golden Chain

The southern Mother Lode countryside south of Placerville is rural, although a busy county seats is located at each end. This is rolling hill country, forested with oaks, pines and heavy brush. It is hot and dry in summer, but mild the rest of the year. In spring, colorful wildflowers carpet the landscape. Elevations range from 870 feet at the bottom of the Merced River Gorge to approximately 2,200 feet near Mt. Bullion.

Highway 49, linking nine counties, serves as a "golden chain" with what's left of mining long after the Gold Rush of the 19th century. The area is littered with debris of mines long-since closed. For most of its length through the southern Mother Lode State Route 49 is a high-speed, two-lane highway with gentle curves and a smooth, wide surface. But there are sharp curves and a steep gradient in and out of the Merced River Canyon. Slow down here and use extra caution. This section of the Mother Lode is joined at several points by major state highways.

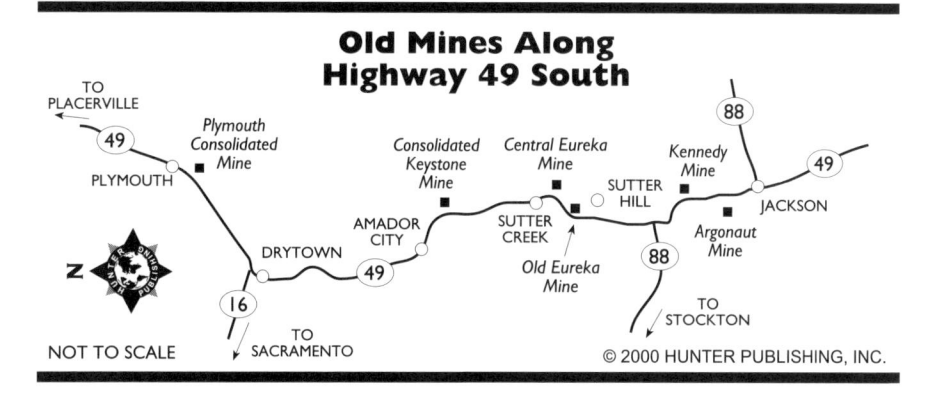

Amador

In their heyday, Amador's mines were part of the Mother Lode belt of gold that stretched 318 miles from Mariposa in the south to the Malakoff diggings in the north. Amador's mines were the richest in the region, producing more than $160 million in gold from the early 1850s to 1950.

The most famous of these mines are the **Kennedy and Argonaut mines**, north of Jackson on Highway 49. Stop at the overlook on the right side near the top of the grade. From here you can look into the bottom of the valley with the Sierra Mountains in the distance. You'll notice the headframe over the deepest, east shaft of the Kennedy. The owners added to their holdings and, in 1870, 2,600 ground surface feet were being worked from vertical shafts. During its productive years, the Kennedy grossed $34 million, based on 1948 prices.

World War II forced closure of the mine in 1942 after it had reached a depth of 5,912 feet – the deepest mine in North America.

Across the highway from the first viewing point is the framework of the **Argonaut Mine**. The hoisting building is just east of the highway. In 1922, this was the scene of the worst gold mining disaster in California's history. Deadly gas, ignited by a mine fire, killed 47 miners. The tragedy made headlines throughout the world as efforts were made to save them.

The Argonaut, from a vertical depth of 5,570 feet, produced more than $25 million in gold.

Where to Stay & Dine in Amador

The **Imperial Hotel**, 14202 Highway 49, ☎ 800-242-5594, $$-$$$, has six rooms in a Victorian home dating back to 1879. All have private baths and two come with their own balconies. The restaurant, which serves American and continental fare in a casual setting, is open for dinner seven nights a week and for brunch and dinner on Sunday. It also provides room service for the hotel.

Central Eureka Mine

If you continue south on Highway 49 you'll run into Sutter's Hill. This is a four-way stop, and by taking a turn to the right past the shopping center, and an immediate left past the Highway Patrol office, you'll spot the framework of the Central Eureka Mine. It was one of the few mines that continued to operate after President Roosevelt ordered closure of the other mines on behalf of the war effort. It produced $36 million during its operation.

The county of Amador is known for its hearty, robust wines – some of which have been award-winners – produced by 16 major wineries.

The county is in the heart of the gold country where the first discovery of gold opened up the West. There's a sense of living history here, with a spectacular scenic background that provides an ever-changing panorama. Highway 88 is called "the most beautiful highway in America." Its views of the Sierra Nevada are spectacular. In spring, **Daffodil Hill** and the surrounding trees and meadows put on a glorious display of multihued blooms and miles of wildflowers. This 400-acre ranch has more than 400,000 bulbs and 100 varieties of daffodils.

Summer days are ideal for lakeside recreation and walking through small towns where history mingles with modern commerce.

Autumn cloaks the trees with scarlet, bronze and gold from the foothills to the mountains.

Winter brings snowy beauty to the Sierra Nevada and crisp air.

> *For information about this region call or write* **Amador County's Chamber of Commerce**, *125 Peek Street, PO Box 596, Jackson, CA 95642.* ☎ *800-649-4988.*

Angels Camp

What to See & Do

Angels Camp dates back to 1848, when merchant Henry Angel set up a trading post here. The area was once filled with gold-hungry miners and the population swelled to 4,000. Today, about 2,400 residents live in Angels Camp. The town is home to the **Calaveras County Visitor Center**, 1211 South Main Street, ☎ 800-225-3764. The centers offers a self-guided tour map for 25¢. If you haven't had your fill of Gold Rush trivia, make a stop at the **Angels Camp Museum**, 753 South Main Street, ☎ 209-736-2963. The small campus is filled with era mining equipment, artifacts and horse-drawn vehicles.

Where to Stay in Angels Camp

Angels Inn Motel, on State Route 49, is in the north end of town at 600 North Main Street. On Friday and Saturday the rate ranges $65-80 and Sunday through Thursday it is $55-70. Pets are permitted. There's a coffee shop nearby. ☎ 209-736-4242. **Gold Country Inn** is one mile north of State Route 49, at 720 S. Main Street. Rooms rent for $49-54. Pets are not permitted. ☎ 209-736-4611.

Jumping Frog Jubilee

Calaveras County lies at the center of the San Francisco/Yosemite/Lake Tahoe triangle. Its relationship with the Gold Rush Museum has long made it a mecca for tourists.

Writer Mark Twain heard a story in at bar at Angel's Camp that he turned into *The Celebrated Jumping Frog of Calaveras County*. It was his first nationally published work and the story lives on each year during the third week of May at the **County Fair and Jumping Frog Jubilee**.

Other Things to Do in Calaveras County

There is an all-season resort with first-class downhill skiing at **Bear Valley Ski Area**. Snowmobiling is a popular sport in a winter wonderland of indescribable beauty. Elevations in Calaveras County run from sea level in western regions to 8,000 feet in the Sierra Nevada. Therefore, most of the county offers year-round activities. "Sun time" adventures in Calaveras involve the whole family. There's river rafting and caverns hundreds of feet below the surface to explore that can be enjoyed by everyone. The area has some of the best bass and trout fishing in California. You can take a four-wheeler across mountainous terrain or backpack it. Eight public access lakes are waiting for you.

Mokelumne Hill

Mokelumne Hill was founded in 1848 and became one of the richest of the "digs." The veins brought thousands to the area and "Moke Hill" became a violent, bawdy town. Today it's a quiet village next to Highway 49 between Jackson and San Andreas. Many of its original buildings are still in place.

West Point

West Point was started in the 1850s by a group of adventurers looking for gold. It remains as isolated today as it was back then, via Route 26 on the road to nowhere. Hunting and fishing are good, and it's a great place to wander back roads.

San Andreas

San Andreas has no relationship to the famous San Andreas Fault. It was started by a small group of miners who worked claims in the winter of 1848 and named the place after their patron saint. In its wild days, the infamous Black Bart and Joaquin Murieta roamed the area. Joaquin Murieta robbed the rich and gave money to the poor. Black Bart was a gentleman bandit who never harmed drivers and passengers and, more often than not, left bits of original limerick verse behind. During one of his robberies at San Andreas, Bart dropped a handkerchief and investigators traced the laundry mark to San Francisco. One of the city's so-called leading citizens, Charles E. Bolton, Esquire, was arrested. This was not Bart's real name. He was a shipping clerk by the name of Charles E. Boles, originally from Illinois.

Bart had acquired a well-developed appreciation for the good life and financed it by robbing stagecoaches. Bart was arrested and held in San Andreas jail, which is now part of the complex that houses the County Historical Archives, the County Museum and the Calaveras Art Council Gallery.

Black Bart.

Murphys

The picturesque village of Murphys, on Route 4 to the east, is known today for its many natural attractions, including the caverns for public viewing. There are wineries, art galleries, gold panning and world-class golf. **Mercer Caverns** are open from Memorial Day through September from 9-5 for guided tours. Saturday, Sunday and school holidays they are open from 11-4, October through May. In the caverns you'll see an enormous variety of beautiful and unusual natural crystalline formations of all sizes, textures and shapes. Nature's artistry has seldom been more beautiful.

Bandit Murieta. NY Public Library.

Where to Stay in Murphys

Dunbar House, 271 Jones Street, ☎ 800-692-6006, $$$-$$$$, built in 1880, is one of the classiest establishments in Gold Country. It has three rooms and a suite, all decorated with antiques and fine furnishings, down comforters and wood-burning stoves. The suite has a private deck and whirlpool tub. A full breakfast is included in the rate.

Bear Valley

Skiing magazine called Bear Valley Ski Area "the best adult-lift ticket value in America." It is an attractive combination of the slope and breathtaking beauty of the Mokelumne Canyon wilderness. You can reach the area throughout the year by car, along with other winter spots on Highway 4 to the east. It is just 2½ hours along scenic Highway 4 East through Angels Camp. The Grizzly Bowl, a dual slalom race course, permits you to race the clock or challenge your friends. There are 1,280 acres of skiing, 1,900 vertical feet and more than 60 runs. Eleven lifts transport more than 12,000 skiers each hour. There are also 35 miles of cross-country ski trails for the Nordic mavens. Adult lift rates are $35 for a full day, $13 for children 7-12, and those under that age go for free.

Where to Stay in Bear Valley

Bear Valley Lodge, ☎ 209-753-2327, $-$$$$, just three miles from the slopes, has 51 rooms, a full restaurant and bar, massage, cable TV and VCRs. Ask about midweek ski-free packages.

The Tamarack Pines Inn, 18326 Highway 4, ☎ 209-753-2080, $-$$$, is 2½ miles from the hill and has five units with private bathrooms, coffee makers and VCRs, and two units with kitchen facilities. A common room features satellite TV, VCR, fireplace, microwave, telephone and children's play area. Ski packages are available, and there's a two-night minimum during the high season. Innkeepers Vicky and Tim Johnson are top-notch.

The **Dorrington Inn**, 3450 Highway 4, ☎ 888-874-2164, $$-$$$, has six cottages and two suites. All feature a fireplace, wet bar/refrigerator, cable TV, VCR, down comforters and private baths. A Gold Country breakfast is included.

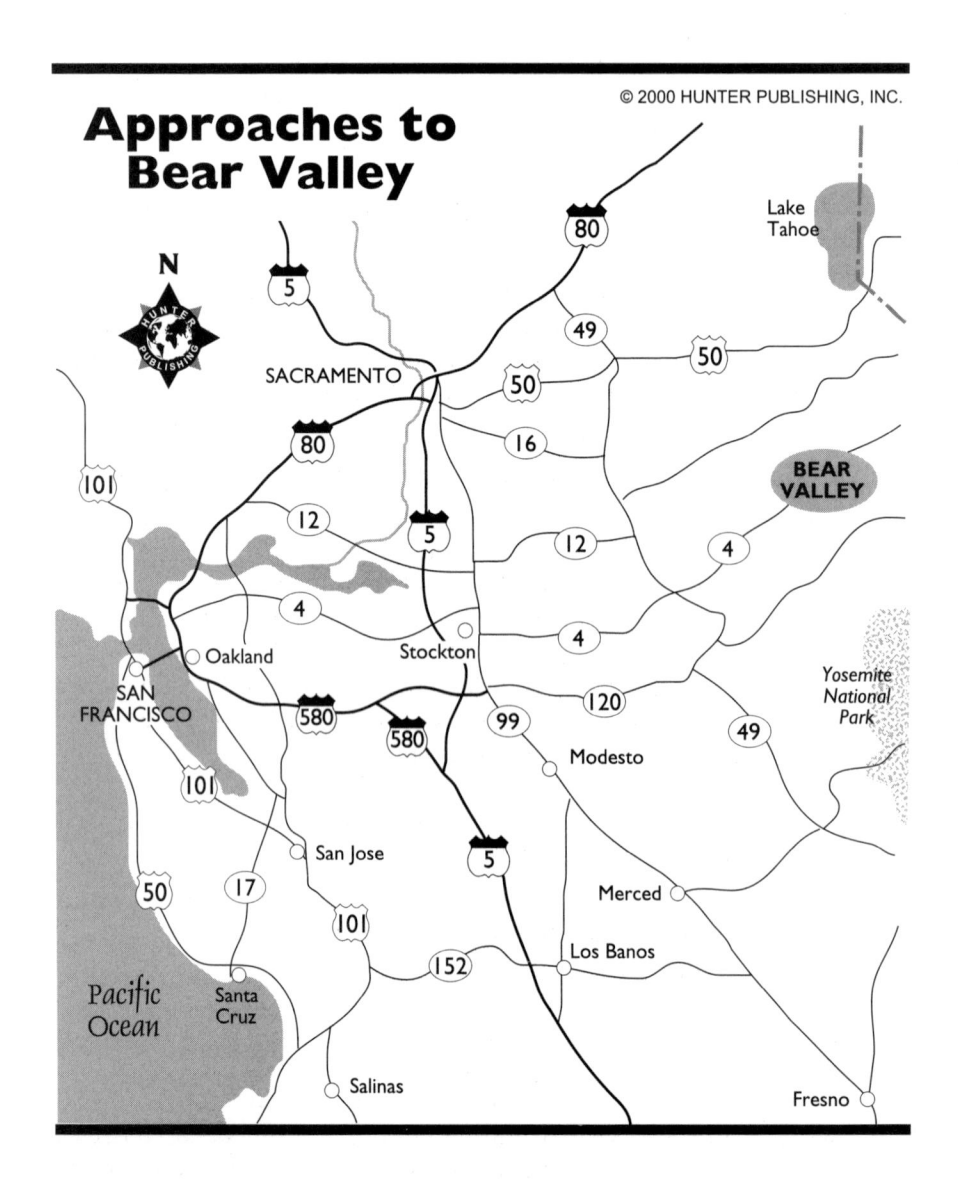

Approaches to Bear Valley

© 2000 HUNTER PUBLISHING, INC.

Gold Country South Adventures

Adventures on Foot
Hiking

As US 50 descends from the High Sierra at South Lake Tahoe toward Placerville, it passes through the heart of **Eldorado National Forest**. The forest contains almost 800,000 acres of public land that is exceptionally varied. The terrain rises from elevations near 1,000 feet in the foothills to higher than 10,000 feet on the Sierra crest. This mountains and hills are sliced by steep drainages of the Mokelumne, Cosumnes, American and Rubicon rivers. Between the steep canyons are relatively flat plateaus that support an abundance of flora and fauna.

For more information on Eldorado National Forest, call the headquarters in Placerville, ☎ 916-622-5061.

There are more than 350 miles of trails in the Eldorado, allowing for every level of adventure, from brisk nature walks to rugged, high-altitude journeys that last as long as your legs and food hold out. It's easiest to divide the hiking between the foothills and the mountains.

Let's start with the foothills. Many of these trails are blisteringly hot in summer months, so consider hiking near a water course to keep your cool.

The **Mar Det Trail**, open to hikers and horses, runs 4.2 miles one way and gains just 600 feet along the way. To reach the trailhead, take CA 193 to Georgetown, continue two miles to Meadowbrook Road and head east. The footpath meanders through a forest of mixed conifers and ends at the Grey Eagle Trail. In the same neighborhood is **One Eye Creek Trail**, a 2.6-mile hike that loses 1,000 feet as it descends from the trailhead into the Rock Creek drainage and affords a great view of Castle Rocks. To reach the trailhead, drive two miles south of Georgetown to Spanish Flat Road and turn east. Continue eight miles to Bear Creek Picnic Area and turn right on a spur road. At a four-way junction, continue straight and take the next road on the right to the trailhead.

There are a number of excellent hikes along **Wentworth Springs Road** east of Georgetown. Reach the **Hunter Trail** by taking Wentworth Springs Road 15 miles east of Georgetown to Eleven Pines Road and turning north. Proceed five miles to the Rubicon River. The trail runs alongside the river for 10 miles, with a 1,500-foot elevation change, and dead ends at Hell Hole Reservoir. On the way you can take your pick of swimming holes, fishing spots and scenic overlooks. **Bald Mountain Canyon Trail**, hidden away off a forest service road, has everything: an aerobic workout, cool waters and great views. To reach the trailhead, take Wentworth Springs

Road 3.5 miles east of Georgetown and turn south on Balderston Road. Continue south on Darling Ridge Road two miles to road 12N89. Turn east and proceed one mile to the end of the road. The trail is only 1.6 miles one way but loses and gains significant altitude as it first descends to Rock Creek, crosses the creek and climbs to Sugarloaf. **Kelliher Trail** follows a 19th-century mining path to Volcanoville. The trail descends to Otter Creek, cruises through the site of a gold-rush-era Chinese settlement and garden and continues up Paymaster Mine Road. And you cover all this in just two miles. To reach the trailhead, follow Wentworth Springs Road three miles east of Georgetown to Breedlove Road and turn north. Drive two miles to Bottle Hill Road and turn left.

There is also months' worth of hiking in the High Sierra, including a backcountry trailhead off US 50 between Tahoe and Placerville. To reach the **Sayles Canyon/Bryan Meadows trailhead**, take Sierra Ski Ranch Road (about 48 miles east of Placerville) for two miles to Bryan Road (17E13) and turn right. Continue 2.5 miles to the parking lot. Hike the Sayles Canyon Trail a mile up the canyon to the Bryan Meadows Trail, which runs three miles east through a forest of lodgepole pine and mountain hemlock. You'll pass the edge of Bryan Meadow just before reaching the **Pacific Crest Trail**, which offers access to multiday backpacking. If you stay on Sayles Canyon Trail, you'll climb back and forth across the creek for 3.5 miles to the wonderful grassland of Round Meadows. The trail continues through the meadows and climbs for a mile to meet the Pacific Crest Trail at the top of a ridge.

You can also reach **Mt. Ralston** from a trailhead along US 50, across from Camp Sacramento on the north side of the highway. The road on the east side of the parking lot leads 200 yards to the trailhead. The strenuous trail climbs about three miles, from 6,500 feet to the peak of Mt. Ralston, 9,235 feet above sea level in the Desolation Wilderness. The .5-mile spur to the summit is just inside the wilderness boundary.

For another hike along US 50, drive to the 42 Mile picnic area (a quarter-mile west of Strawberry) and turn right on the bridge just past Packsaddle Pass Road. Head south for one mile to Strawberry Canyon Road, which you follow .5 mile to the **Lovers Leap Trail**. The trail climbs 2.5 miles to the top of Lovers Leap, a renowned rock climbing destination, and provides stunning vistas of the South Fork American River. You can continue another mile to Camp Sacramento.

Near the town of Kyburz, you can head into the backcountry on the **Caples Creek Trail**. To reach the trailhead, take Silver Fork Road for 10 miles and turn left just before Fitch Rantz Bridge. This rough, four-wheel-drive road leads .25 mile to the trailhead. Caples Creek Trail winds up the north side of the creek, passes the Silver Fork Trail junction and heads across Jake Schneider's Meadow. Here you can pick up **Old Silver Lake Trail**, or continue downhill one mile to the end of Caples Creek Trail at the Government Meadows Trail junction, four miles from the trailhead.

If you opt for the **Silver Fork Trail**, you set out on a moderate climb, then drop alongside Silver Creek before the trail levels and follows the creek past quiet pools. Finally, you'll ascend to the junction of Old Silver Lake Trail, three miles from the Caples Creek Trail junction, for great views of the Caples Creek and Silver Fork drainages.

Old Silver Lake Trail fords Caples Creek (there's no bridge here) and runs through mixed stands of virgin pine and fir. You'll switchback up to a ridgeline and intersect the Silver Fork Trail coming in from the southwest, 1.5 miles from the Caples Creek Trail.

The John Muir Trail

Native Americans have lived in and around the Sierra Nevada for at least 5,000 years. Some of their routes are still hiked today. Joseph Walker crossed the range in 1833, and may have been one of the first white men to see Yosemite Valley. Later in the century much of Sierra Crest was explored and tentatively mapped. Josiah Whitney led the first Geological Survey party through the range in the early years of the American Civil War. He reported that most peaks could be easily climbed and that almost the entire range could be traversed without the need of ropes or other artificial aids. His party found many passes between the isolated ranges (the Crest, Kings-Kern Divide, Great Western Divide, Le Conte Divide, etc.), but they decided not to try some mountains because they believed they were too difficult for their skills. It was Theodore Solomons who first proposed that a trail be built along the crest from Yosemite to Mt. Whitney. Members of the newly formed Sierra Club scouted the range from 1882-1897 for a route. After most problems were identified, in 1915 California funded the initial work on what we now know as the John Muir Trail. (The famed mountaineer had died the year before, after losing the battle to save Hetch Hetchy.) The goal was to have a solid trail, suitable for people and stock, that would traverse the range from north to south and run along as much of the main crest as possible. The Sierra increases in elevation gradually from the west to the east, reaching its main crest in about 40-70 miles. On the east side, however, the mountains drop to 10,000 feet in less than 12 miles in one of the most awesome escarpments in the world. This wall is nearly 100 miles long. The lower ranges, perpendicular to the main crest, tend to collide with it in many areas. The Muir Trail crosses over these ranges in 10 high passes, but actually goes over the main crest only once in the north, just south of Donahue Pass. The southern terminus of the trail is at Mt. Whitney, but it's the Whitney Trail that actually crosses the main crest, at Trail Crest, at an elevation of 13,000 feet.

Except for two links, the route was finished in 1931. The crossing of Kings-Kern Divide was a major problem, but finally a precipitous route was blasted out of the cliff's wall west of Junction Peak. This is Forester Pass, and it remains a most serious problem for all hikers, especially in early season. There's a long, narrow section with at least a 2,000-foot drop-off. The second link is the "Golden Staircase," the notorious climb out of Deer Meadow to the Palisade basin. This was not finished until 1983, and it is also a major problem for some hikers.

Today the Sierra Club is more involved with conservation issues on a worldwide basis, but in those early days its members fought to open up the range to the world. In 1916, the club and the newly organized National Park Service encouraged public travel to these regions. Now they are trying to limit travel to preserve the area for future generations. Many of those who fought for access to the Sierra Nevada have had peaks named for them. Norman Clyde for over 50 years hiked and climbed the range, achieving before his death more than 148 first ascents, and more than 1,000 other climbs.

Sierra names are unique and often amusing, such as Secret Lake, Jackass Meadow, Disappointment Peak (because it never seemed to be on the map where it was supposed to be) and Hell-for Sure-Pass. The mountains exact a stiff toll of dead or injured among those who try routes for which they have had no experience. The needless deaths of hikers from lightning strikes on Half Dome and Whitney could be avoided if they sought shelter or didn't hike during periods of violent thunderstorm activity.

The grizzly bear is gone and the wolf never did inhabit the area. Native Indians are also gone, victims of diseases acquired from white settlers for which they had no immunity. Although the carefree days of the early 1900s are gone forever, it is a miracle so much has been preserved. To explore a real wilderness today you have to go far afield. Eventually even these areas will become overcrowded and constrained by regulations.

The John Muir Trail is often called the finest high mountain hike in the world. It and Ansel Adams Wilderness straddle the Sierra's eastern border and the Sierra Crest. Allow at least 21-25 days for the whole trip. You must be in excellent condition. The trail is 218 miles long, and for 162 miles there is no road across it, nor lodge to spend the night, and few bridges across more than 100 streams or rivers. Plan such a trip, or just a small portion of it, as early as possible. Reserve your permits before May 30 and study topographic maps before you depart. And bring them with you. Please note that National Park Service brochures and maps should never be used for any major high country trip. They are not designed for such a trip. The peak listings for climbers are not representative of true conditions. Class one means a serious, steep walk up; class two indicates handholds are needed because severe drop-offs are common; class three is a warning that the ascent is more dangerous than usual, involving extreme exertion; class four warns that a rope may be needed to climb. Never make a climb unless you're familiar with the route and you have the skill to accomplish it.

Where's the best place to start your trip on the John Muir Trail? If you begin in the north at Happy Isles in Yosemite Valley, you'll be at an altitude of 4,035 feet. In early summer it will be hot and crowded, but most of the higher elevations will be clear of snow. As you head south, climbing steadily, the snow on the higher passes will have melted. There's a decided advantage to starting in the north because elevations are low at first, and you won't have the challenge of Mt. Whitney's 14,494 feet until you have adjusted to this vigorous exercise. If you begin in the south, at Whitney Portal, you will start at that altitude and hike the most difficult sections of the John Muir Trail almost at the start. You need to be acclimated to the rigorous demands of mountain hiking, so this is a disadvantage. By starting in the south, however, by the time you reach the north the days will be noticeably shorter and some of the earlier crowds will be gone. Late in the season poor weather is a strong possibility. Many of your sources of water will have dried up, which may create additional problems. Thunderstorm activity, which in these mountains can be highly dangerous, will have lessened, but there may be prolonged rain. Even experienced hikers take 26 days to walk the entire trail, so such a trip should not be considered lightly.

> If you plan any cross-country travel, such as along Steve Roper's "High Trail," you'll need the seven and a half series of maps. Steve's book, *Timberline Country: The High Sierra Route* (Sierra Club Books, 1982) made famous the hiking paths above 9,000 feet on the Sierra Crest.

This area is time consuming and calls for extra mountaineering skills. Some people get lost in these upper regions, but only because they did not follow the trail's guidelines. Even experts are fooled. What appears to be a pass up ahead may be a frightening cliff wall. Streams that look irrelevant on the map can become an impassable flood in the early part of the season. The rewards of cross-country travel are worth the unknowns, though. The entire Palisade basin is always busy in August, as is the Mt. Lyell area in Yosemite, and the Humphreys basin farther south. Hikers often have problems following the Muir Trail because so many other trails cross it, and not all are marked. Always try to spot landmarks, and make sure they are where they ought to be in reference to your own location. There are backcountry ranger stations throughout the range, and rangers will be happy to assist you, but respect their privacy. Rangers are not always home, sometimes for several days, because their district is so large.

The Pacific Crest Trail

The Pacific Crest Trail through the Sierra often coincides with the John Muir Trail. It crosses or touches on 33 federally designated wildernesses,

24 national forests, seven national parks and five California state parks. It is a wildland route, 2,638 miles long, connecting Mexico with Canada along the crest of the mountain ranges. The route provides solitude, adventure and challenge. You'll share the region's beauty with its teeming animal life. Private landholders have made routes available through their properties by agreements with the federal government.

The trail begins 50 miles east of San Diego, near Campo. An arm of the Mojave Desert is crossed briefly before the trail begins its ascent into the southern Sierra. Just north of Mt. Whitney, where it is coincident with the John Muir Trail, the Pacific Crest Trail crosses its highest divide, at Forester Pass, with an elevation of 13,186 feet.

Northward through the national parks and wildernesses of the Sierra Nevada, the route maintains high elevations. After crossing west of Lake Tahoe, the trail undulates northward and passes through Lassen Volcanic Park and then on to Oregon and Washington.

> *Not many hikers and riders have followed the trail from end to end. Those who have done so are enthused by the sheer adventure of it. Be self-sufficient on the trail. But let me emphasize again: Do not go alone!*

The advocacy group for the Pacific Crest Trail is the Pacific Crest Trail Association headquartered in Walnut Creek, California. A public membership association, it works with the US Forest Service on trail-related matters. Members report trail conditions, which are relayed to appropriate officials. Volunteer trail maintenance crews from the public and the association's membership are fielded by the organization to work on maintaining the trail and its feeder trails in partnership with the Forest Service.

When to Go

Although some hikers have made the trip in winter, the best season is from mid-June to October 15. You will encounter a number of high passes, including Cathedral at 9,700 feet, Donahue at 11,056 feet, Island at 10,250 feet, Silver at 10,900 feet, Selden at 10,972 feet, Muir at 11,000 feet, Mather at 12,080 feet, Pinchot at 12,100 feet, Glen, at 11,989 feet, Forester at 13,186 feet and Trail Crest at 13,600 feet. The elevation at Yosemite Village is 4,035 feet, 10,900 at Evolution, 10,590 at Rae Lakes and 14,494 feet at Mt. Whitney. Such a trip involves much preplanning and should not be undertaken on the spur of the moment. For most people it will be the trip of a lifetime. It is important to make your reservations early. Know in advance what distance you want to make each day and select your camping sites before you leave. Weather conditions are unpredictable in all mountainous regions, so be prepared for all eventualities. The appropriate agency or ranger station will gladly keep you abreast of changing conditions. Be sure you know the depth of the snow and the streams you'll have to cross.

> Two guidebooks cover the complete trail with descriptions, photographs and gray-scale topographic maps. The *Pacific Crest Trail Volume 1* covers the California sections, while *Volume 2* reports on Oregon and Washington. Each volume is $24.95 and may be ordered from Wilderness Press, 2440 Bancroft Way, Berkeley, CA 94704. ☎ 510-843-8080 or 800-443-7227. Another useful reference is *The Pacific Crest Trail Hiker's Handbook* by Ray Jardine (Wilderness Press, 1996).

Rules & Regulations

Conservation groups have been instrumental in establishing rules and regulations, and most of their demands have been met. Trail quotas are now in effect, and they apply to everyone. It is no longer possible to take off and hike for a few days wherever and whenever you wish. The entire Sierra is overused, and efforts must be continued to preserve what is left. Please maintain a reverence for this magnificent region, and leave only your footprints.

Trail Restrictions

There are areas in the high country that are either closed to camping or restricted to one night. In the Baxter Pass area this has been done to preserve the tenuous hold bighorn sheep have there. In other areas, such as the Hall Wilderness, Evolution and Taie Lakes, limits have been imposed due to heavy over-camping in previous years. All access to Mt. Whitney from the east or west is now on a permit reservation basis. All-day hikers from every direction are now subject to a quota system. For overnight backpackers, a wilderness permit from the National Park Service or the Forest Service will not guarantee you access to the summit of Whitney even if you're hiking the entire trail. All permits require a separate stamp for access to Whitney, and the permits are few in number.

Can you bring your pets to the Sierra? There are restrictions throughout the Sierra Nevada and no pets are allowed on any backcountry trail or in the national parks.

Wilderness Permits

File for your wilderness permit during the winter months for the following summer. They cost only a few dollars each and are issued on a first-come, first-served basis. Many areas do not accept reservations. Yosemite National Park uses the reservation system for all but one of its campgrounds. The Tuolumne Meadows campground in the eastern section of Yosemite is one-half reserved and the other half is on a first-come, first-served basis. To make a reservation, call 120 days in advance of the day you plan to arrive. Call at 7 AM, because thousands of people call from all over the United States. During summer months, space in the parks is at a premium. Lines often form at 6 AM.

In Yosemite backpackers who have reserved their permits in advance may pick them up on arrival and camp without a fee the first night.

Permits must be acquired from the National Park Service at the Yosemite Valley District, or at Tuolumne. ☎ 209-372-0308. You'll need a permit to travel through the backcountry in Sequoia, Kings Canyon, Yosemite and Lassen National Parks. In California a campfire permit is required for use of stoves and wood campfires outside of developed campgrounds.

Hikers can also get a permit for the whole trail from the National Forest Service or National Park organization where they begin their journey. The permit will be valid for travel through all wilderness areas between the starting and ending points of the trail.

If you're hiking just a portion of the trail, you'll still need a permit if your plans involve passage through any of the wilderness areas. For permits, contact the Forest Service of the National Parks through which you'll be entering the wilderness.

Forest Service offices for the Pacific Southwest Region are located at 5630 Sansone Street, San Francisco, CA 95825, ☎ 916-978-4754.

Campsite Restrictions

Backcountry camping sites are numerous, but you must not camp within 100 feet of a river or lake. Do not build new fire rings. Fires are forbidden in many areas, so it is wise to use a camp stove. For safety, try to camp below the timberline but, if weather permits, stay up there. It rarely rises above freezing at night at 11,000 feet or higher.

Restrictions have been imposed upon camping in Yosemite. Half Dome is closed to all camping: Mono Pass/Parker Pass, Park Creek Drainage, the entire Gaylor Lakes Basin, the entire High Sierra Loop Trip camps and the Mono Hall Wilderness above Saddlebag Lake are closed to all camping. The Tenaya Lake Campground is closed permanently, and Sequoia has a large number of campgrounds closed to all camping. Before you make final plans for any Sierra Nevada location, check its true conditions. They fluctuate year to year, and sometimes month by month.

Trail Mishaps

For the uninitiated to mountain hiking, a trip can be disastrous. Many hikers have been killed in these mountains through a variety of mishaps. The trail is safe, but you must never take foolish risks. Maps can guide you, but they do not tell the whole story. The trail is steep, extremely exposed throughout its length by drop-offs that are sandy and slippery. Some places are covered by loose granite. There are some permanent snowfields. If you, or any member of your party, is having difficulties, abandon the trip. Sierra weather is unpredictable. In summer the range can receive a major tropical storm with humid, windy weather developing out of the south. Such conditions can last for days. If you are at 11,000 feet or more you could well be snowed in.

A trip should be planned to the smallest detail, and undertaken by people in good physical condition. Be aware of weather conditions that could make your trip hazardous, and rearrange your schedule for a more suitable time. During the planning stage, be aware of all possible contingencies before you depart. If this seems beyond your capabilities, acknowledge that fact and cancel the trip. Although you need a wilderness permit, it does not guarantee that you can be assured of a search and rescue team getting to you in time to save your life. In some areas you can inform an agency where you are going and when you expect to return. They will look for you if you fail to show up on that designated day. It is important to remember that you must return on that date.

Other Precautions

Veteran climbers well know the feeling of Acute Mountain Sickness, which can incapacitate some people as low as 8,000 feet. You may find it difficult to breathe normally, or you may feel nauseated and generally out of sorts. Your body is telling you it needs more oxygen. The low humidity at high altitudes can also be a factor. Symptoms of AMS also include loss of appetite, insomnia, lethargy, a temporary weight gain, and swelling of the face, hands and feet. If the condition becomes serious, you should stop climbing to higher altitudes. An immediate return to lower altitudes will solve the problem.

Those in excellent physical condition should feel only uncomfortable. If you smoke, or have heart or lung ailments, get a doctor's opinion before you start out. Alcohol and certain drugs will increase the problem of adjusting to altitude, so avoid them.

Start ascents gradually to get your body acclimated to the rarefied conditions at high altitudes. During your climb, eat light but nutritious meals and drink plenty of water to keep your body from becoming dehydrated. Unlike at home, a high-carbohydrate diet will keep you in top condition.

Many climbers carry a walking stick as kind of a third leg. It's useful when you stop for a quick breather, and it can be helpful in crossing streams.

Dress in layers to counter wide fluctuations in temperatures. Sunburn can be a problem as well as hypothermia. The ultraviolet rays of the sun are intense, and doubly so when reflected off white granite. Use an unscented sunscreen with a high SPF factor. Scented lotions attract bears! Wear clothes that cover your body to protect yourself from sunburn and to keep the mosquitoes from tormenting you. In summer, mosquitoes in the High Sierra can drive you to distraction.

The Muir Pass region and the entire Forester Pass-Whitney area are above timberline for many miles. Plan your hikes in these areas so you'll be below timberline for your night's camp.

> *Thunderstorms can be deadly, and they take several lives each year. Don't ever seek shelter beneath trees!*

There's an emergency shelter, built years ago by the Sierra Club, on top of 11,955-foot Muir Pass. It is not for general use, but only for emergencies.

Most trails below 8,600 feet are usually clear of snow by mid-June and free to 11,000 feet by mid-July. By mid-August, they are usually completely clear.

Your food will attract animals to your camp, so string it 15 feet off the ground, 10 feet from trees, and five feet from a cross rope. Bear-proof food canisters are helpful, and they can be rented in most parks. They take up valuable space in your backpack, though, and they are unwieldy to load. It is wise to purchase a carrying case for these canisters so you can tie them to your pack.

Carry iodine tablets. "Potable Aqua" is best, and they come with a second tablet to clear the water of its iodine taste. Otherwise, buy a good filter. Don't drink the water in any stream or lake in the High Sierra. You can be assured the water is contaminated. Parasites are a problem in mountain water, so boil it for at least 10 minutes. Do not smoke along hiking trails. It is not only forbidden but could start a disastrous fire. Campsites are the only authorized places where you can smoke.

Stick to your trail. Shortcuts can cause soil erosion and damage to often fragile plant life.

If you're camping outside of a developed recreation area, you'll need a California Campfire Permit. The Forest Service has them for free. You can also contact the Bureau of Land Management or California's Department of Forestry and Fire Protection Office.

The Forest Service has several publications dealing with fire regulations, camping selection, usage, safety and use of horsepacking. Matters such as drinking water, sanitation, firewood and weather are covered in pamphlets. Familiarize yourself with them. They are available at no charge at ranger stations, district ranger stations and national forest headquarters. For information on maps and guides contact the Forest Service. They are priced from $3 to $8 and there are no tax, shipping or handling fees. Send a check or money order to US Forest Service, Attn.: Map Orders, 630 Sansome Street, San Francisco, CA 94111.

The average trail hiker covers 10-15 miles a day, usually with a heavy pack. Take what you absolutely need on the trip, and not an ounce more. Most people overestimate their needs and pack nonessentials. Most gear is expensive and can be functionally inadequate, so shop carefully. The demands on your body will be great, not only due to the strenuous physical activity but because of radically altered diet and the lack of adequate night shelters. Hikers who climb Mt. Whitney in one day are rare. It is advisable to hike 10 miles, set up a base camp, and explore a small area of the high country. Few people ever hike the entire John Muir Trail in one summer.

Necessary Maps

For all of these areas you should acquire US Geological maps of Yosemite and Sequoia/Kings Canyon Parks. From Yosemite to Tuolumne Meadows is a distance of 24 miles. You'll need maps covering Cattle Mountain, Half Dome, Mariposa Grove, Merced Park, Mt. Lyell, Mt. Ritter, Sing Park and Tenaya. Other useful maps are Forest Service maps for the Sierra National Forest and Stanislaus National Forest. The US Geological Survey has a big map of Yosemite National Park. Don't forget to reserve your permit early from Yosemite National Park. It's free.

Rock Climbing

There's a granite wonderland to be found on the western slopes of the Sierra Nevada. Not far from Placerville, the **Cosumnes River Gorge** is a great spot for bouldering and crag climbing by experienced rock jocks. From Placerville, drive south on CA 49 to Diamond Springs and turn east. Drive through Somerset to Bucks Bar and cross the Cosumnes River. Two climbing areas, the **Traditional Area** and the **Main Slabs**, are located on the North Fork of the river. They are both known for first-class granite climbing with superior holds.

You might also try **Hammer Dome**, a 400-foot-high mound of granite. From the town of Pioneer, drive 26 miles east to the west shore of Salt Springs Reservoir. Hammer Dome is off to the left just before the reservoir and **Calaveras Dome** is on the south side of the road. Hammer Dome sports at least 12 multipitch routes, including **Gemini Cracks** (rated 8) and **Red Eye Express** (10a). Calaveras Dome boasts routes up to eight pitches long, including **Wall of the Worlds IV** (10c).

Spelunking

California Caverns

Exploring California Caverns has got to be one of the most unusual adventures in the Golden State. East of the town of San Andreas in the hamlet of Mountain Ranch, California Caverns are the most extensive public caverns in the state. There are numerous large rooms, miles of winding passages, several lakes over 200 feet deep and formations found nowhere else. Opened to the public in 1850, the tubes and passageways are still not entirely explored. In fact, you can recreate the journey of John Muir, who wrote extensively about the caverns in his book *Mountains of California*, on a wild spelunking trip, led by professional guides deep into the underground wilderness.

Rather than a passive walk along well-lighted platforms between a pair of guard rails, the introductory spelunking tour allows visitors outfitted with hard hats, coveralls and headlamps to wiggle and shimmy through narrow passageways and crawl spaces into 13 different cave rooms.

The trip last two to three hours and comes with important caveats:
- Participants should not wear clothes they care about, as everyone will get muddy down to the skin. One layer of loose-fitting warm clothes is best.
- Knee pads are highly recommended.
- Boots or shoes that tie securely around the ankle and cannot be pulled off are a must.
- Showers are available. A complete change of clothing and all shower items should be ready in a plastic bag (there is no changing room).
- The cavern has no bathrooms.

If you're looking for something even more challenging and are in good physical condition, ask about the **downstream circuit trip**. This three- to four-hour excursion covers approximately 80% of the known cave system from the east entrance to the westernmost exit, a distance of about one mile. The first hour involves walking, crawling and squeezing through the historic **Mammoth Cave** area. The second hour explores **Middle Earth**, discovered in 1980, through sticky, knee-deep cave clay. In the final hour, pass through horizontal fissures in the **Cave of the Quills**, raft across **Tom's Lake**, then continue through crystalline rooms. This trip is offered in the summer and fall, with winter tours dependent on the weather.

Reservations are required for wild cave tours and can be made by calling ☎ 209-736-2708.

Mercer Caverns

You can also explore the inner workings of the Sierra, in much tamer fashion, at Mercer Caverns. Located east of the town of Angels Camp, take CA 4 northeast to the Gold Rush-era village of Murphys, turn left and proceed one mile to Mercer Caverns, off Sheep Ranch Road. Guides take visitors down the equivalent of 16 stories into the limestone caverns featuring one of the world's most impressive displays of the rare frost-like formations of the crystal aragonite flos ferri. Cave rooms measuring 200 feet long and 60 feet wide also boast impressive stalactites and stalagmites. For more information, ☎ 209-728-2101 or visit www.mercercaverns.com.

Adventures on Horseback

With 400 miles of riding trails and several group camping sites, the **Stanislaus National Forest** beckons equestrians who are seeking solitude amid the pines and cool, clear streams of the western Sierra. Unless you plan on pulling your own horse trailer, consider riding with a professional packer. See below under *Outfitters on Horseback* for contact information.

Excellent foothill trails abound in the **Mi-Wok Ranger District** around CA 108. Paths lead to such memorable spots as Bourland Meadow, Thompson Meadow, Deer Creek, Reynolds Creek and Camp Clavey. The Groveland Ranger District near CA 120 also has plenty to offer the modern-day buckaroo. The riding and camping are sublime in Anderson Valley, Kibbie Ridge (inside the Emigrant Wilderness) and south of Cherry Dam along the creek.

In the **Summit Ranger District**, one favorite spot is **Clark Fork horse camp**. The camp has 12 sites you can use for free. You can also take day rides into the high country of the **Carson-Iceberg Wilderness**. Keep in mind that a permit is required for overnight camping in the wilderness, and special livestock rules will be attached to your permit. Permits are issued free at any US Forest Service office.

Fence Creek, Eagle Meadow, Herring Creek and portions of the **Emigrant Wilderness** (permit required) are also great for riding and camping with livestock. Groups of 20 or more people should pick up a special-use permit for non-wilderness large group use from the nearest ranger station.

In the vicinity of CA 4, the **Calaveras Ranger District** offers plenty of high-elevation riding and camping. A few of the many fantastic rides include: Pine Marten campground to Duck and Rock Lakes; the loop ride from Wheeler Lake to Sandy Meadow; Stanislaus Meadow to Bull Run, Heiser and Mosquito Lakes; Highland Lakes to Arnot Creek; and from

Frog Lake in the Mokelumne Wilderness (permit required) to Mount Reba.

Adventures on Wheels
Mountain Biking
Eldorado National Forest

In the foothills of the western Sierra, **Martin Trail** on Eldorado National Forest land near Georgetown is open to motorcycles and mountain bikes. The trailhead is located at the end of Road 12N31. Begin at Georgetown and drive 3.5 miles to Wentworth Springs Road. Head south on Balderson Road to Mill Race Road and proceed two miles to 12N31, where you turn left. The 1.1-mile trail drops quickly to the Rock Creek drainage, the climbs even more steeply up the opposite canyon wall on the way to Rock Creek Road.

The nearby **Nevada Point Trail** is open to mountain bikes (closed to all motorized vehicles) and offers a strenuous, 4.6-mile ride in and out of the Pilot Creek drainage. Follow Wentworth Springs Road 11 miles east of Georgetown and turn north on Volcanoville Road. Drive 1.5 miles to Rubicon Road, turn right and continue two miles to a spur road on the right that leads to the trailhead. From 4,000 feet above sea level the path drops to 1,800 feet and Pilot Creek, where a footbridge spans the water. The trial continues to another footbridge over the Rubicon River, then ascends Nevada Point Ridge Road.

Stanislaus National Forest

Stanislaus National Forest is laced with great mountain biking routes.

> The Forest Service even publishes a *Forest Biking Recreation Guide* detailing locations and difficulty ratings. To obtain the guide or more information, contact the Stanislaus National Forest Supervisor's Office in Sonora, ☎ 209-532-3671.

Some of the more popular routes are on the north end of the national forest along CA 4, near the border with Eldorado National Forest. One of the best for advanced riders is the 22-mile **Slick Rock Trail** that utilizes hiking trails, Jeep roads, gravel roads and paved roads in the vicinity of Bear Valley. Begin on a hiking trail that is part of the Old Emigrant Road, then continue on a long segment of rough Jeep road past Slick Rock and onto gravel and paved portions of forest roads. The ride then heads up CA 4 through Bear Valley. Elevations range from 6,400 feet near the Stanislaus River all the way up 7,800 feet on Osborn Hill. The Slick Rock area is filled with swimming holes and offers sublime views of Utica Reservoir.

The **Jelmini Basin Loop** ride covers 17 miles on hiking trails, Jeep roads and dirt paths. Motorcycles and ATVs are allowed on this route, so ride with care. Most of the ride traverses ridgelines that provide incredible vistas and refreshingly long downhill runs through groves of aspen. The route begins at road 7N09 and CA 4 near the Cabbage Patch Maintenance Station.

The **Bear Trap Basin Loop** runs eight miles on Jeep roads and hiking trails. You'll begin and end at Corral Hollow Road west of Bear Valley at CA 4. The ride starts by making a strenuous climb to a ridge crest that affords wonderful views of the Mokelumne Wilderness. Delightful meadows and stands of quaking aspen are found in Bear Trap Basin, along with a seasonal burst of wildflowers. From the loop you also access a 3.5-mile trail around the Bear Valley ski slopes that leads back to Bear Valley.

In the Mi-Wok ranger district along the lower portion of CA 108, **Sugar Pine Railroad Grade** provides a relatively easy six-mile round-trip. Following the **Strawberry Branch**, you will ride alongside the South Fork of the Stanislaus River on the former route of the historic Sugar Pine Railroad System. Begin at Old Strawberry Road or the bridge near Fraser Flat campground. One option is to set out from Fraser Flat and ride uphill to Strawberry, have lunch at a local restaurant, then coast downhill back to your vehicle.

The **Summit Ranger District**, which covers the upper portion of CA 108, is home to the ride on **Gooseberry-Crabtree Trail**. This difficult 15-miler on gravel and dirt roads gains 2,000 feet in about seven miles. The route can be explored as a 15-mile loop from Crabtree to Gooseberry (or vice-versa) or as a one-way trip of any length. The many spur trails offer almost unlimited options for extending your ride. Begin at either of two trailheads on Dodge Ridge Road.

Four-Wheel Driving

Rock Creek Off-Highway Vehicle Area, managed by the US Forest Service, is known far and wide as one of the top off-road areas in the state. Located east of the towns of Cool and Georgetown via CA 193, Rock Creek boasts logging roads, trails and narrow paths to challenge Jeep drivers and ATV and dirt bike riders of all abilities. The area is open all year and receives more than enough snowfall for snowmobiling. The **Five Corners Staging Area** is recommended for beginning and novice riders, while the **Mace Mill Staging Area** is suited for more advanced riders. For more information, ☎ 916-333-4312.

East of Auburn, a drive down **Deadwood Road** combines the fun of four-wheeling with a living history lesson as you drive to a Gold-Rush-era cemetery. From Auburn cruise up Foresthill Road 24 miles to the Deadwood

Road turnoff on the right. The unmaintained dirt road is suited for four-wheel-drive or high-clearance vehicles and should not be attempted when wet. The road hugs the side of Deadwood Ridge for 15 miles, offering spectacular views when the canyon narrows. Watch for the sign to Deadwood Cemetery, park and walk uphill for 100 yards to the graveyard. Deadwood was once a bustling community of miners, but now all that remains are a few grave markers. Return the way you came.

Adventures on Water

While we seldom recommend specific outfitters, **All-Outdoors Whitewater Rafting** should probably be on your short list of river guides. Based in Walnut Creek, just across San Francisco Bay from the Golden Gate, All-Outdoors has set its roots deep in the riverbanks of the western Sierra. George Armstrong and his brother first put a raft in the water in 1961 and were soon taking family and friends on journeys through California's most exciting whitewater. Armstrong, then a high school teacher, also guided rafting trips with a group of challenged teens. Some of them literally turned their lives around on the river, later becoming guides for Armstrong's outfit.

All-Outdoors is still owned and operated by the Armstrong family, but the operation has grown since that spring day in '61. Today more than 150 professional guides lead 12,000 guests a year down 12 of California's most scenic and wild rivers. *Sunset Magazine*, the well-respected travel publication, anointed All-Outdoors one of its "Best of the West" for 1999. Excursions range from half-day trips for $79 to three-day interpretive trips for $459. River rats can also design their own custom trips with help from the All-Outdoors staff. The company prides itself on educating its clients about the environment and the ecosystems through which they float.

If you're planning on venturing into the western Sierra to tackle the American, Merced, Tuolomne, Stanislaus or Kaweah rivers, or Class V+ Cherry Creek, a call to All-Outdoors, 1250 Pine Street, Suite 103, Walnut Creek, ☎ 800-24-RAFTS, might be in order.

The North Fork of the Stanislaus River provides some of the most intense Class IV whitewater in California. The river courses through Calaveras Big Trees State Park near the small town of Murphys northeast of Angels Camp. The adventure will take you tumbling over narrow, granite boulder gardens bordered by a canopy of pines and firs. Running the Stanislaus requires the utmost skill. Even guests riding with professional guides (see below under *Outfitters*) should have rough water paddling experience.

Merced River

The Merced River, flowing out of Yosemite in spring and summer, becomes wild and scenic whitewater. After the Sierra snowpack melts, it's a sight to behold as the river leaps over Yosemite's Vernal and Nevada Falls and plunges to the valley's floor. Whitewater boaters begin their trips after the river leaves Yosemite and rushes through the lower canyon. In spring and early summer the Merced's high waters thrill adventurous rafters with long, unhindered stretches of whitewater with bouncy waves and holes through the rapids. The surrounding hillsides are ablaze with golden poppies, purple lupines, wild iris and redbud.

Along the way, canyons are filled with the sounds of wrens and merganser ducks sweeping overhead as the Merced follows the highway. When it veers off, the river enters the old bed of the Yosemite Valley Railroad.

The flow of water lessens by the end of summer, but the undammed Merced's steep gradient keeps the water flowing briskly. Rapids like "Ned's Gull," "Cornerpocket" and the "Quarter Mile Rapids" await the stalwart. This is the perfect time for first-time rafters to join river veterans and take the Merced's plunge. For the more independent minded, try navigating the river in a self-guided inflatable kayak.

Overnight or day trips start at Cranberry and end about 16 miles downriver at Railroad Flag river camp. If the water level permits, the second day begins at Redbud, two miles above Cranberry, so you can raft to Briceburg, 14 miles downstream. The Redbud section offers some of the best whitewater on the river. At lower flows the run from Cranberry to camp is made on the first day, and continues into the remote lower canyon on the second day, ending at Bagby about 10 miles farther on. This section has a 20-foot waterfall that must be portaged.

For information about the popular Bagby whitewater section, write Box 1161, Columbia, CA 95310, or ☎ 800-359-9790. Seek advice on what to bring for the trip. Most motels in the area are in the $50-100 range.

The Merced trip lasts two days, with the cost to adults of $435 and for youths 17 and under, $235. There's a minimum age of 12 and maximum of 25 guests.

Other Rivers for Whitewater Rafting

There are four other rivers on the western slopes of the Sierra Nevada. They all offer superb rafting. The **Tuolumne** is $435 regardless of age. **Cherry Creek** operates every day with an adult fare of $215 and $185 for children. The **Upper Carson** is only a half-day trip, with a $225 adult fare and $185 for children. The **Stanislaus** is a day-long trip at $90 for adults and $75 for children 17 and under. For further details, ☎ 800-358-9790.

Outdoor Adventure River Specialists operate 1.75 miles south on State Route 49. They offer one to three day whitewater rafting trips on the American, Tuolumne, Merced, Carson, Stanislaus, Kern and California Salmon rivers.

Trips are made daily and meals are provided. One-day trips range $68-115. Children under seven years of age are not permitted. During the high-water season from mid-May to mid-June, children under 12 are not permitted. Reservations are required and cancellation fees are imposed. Write O.A.R.S. Box 67, Angels Camp, CA 95221, ☎ 209-736-4677.

Adventures on Snow

Eldorado National Forest boasts two snow parks. **Bear River Snowmobile Park**, featuring groomed trails and machine rentals, and **Iron Mountain Sno-Park** are both in the forest's Amador Ranger District. For more information, ☎ 209-295-4251.

Dodge Ridge Ski Area, near Pinecrest, is one of the fastest-growing resorts in the Sierra. The mountain offers 60 runs, the longest stretching two miles, for skiers and snowboarders of all abilities. Twenty percent of the runs are rated beginner, 40% intermediate and 40% advanced. Snow cat skiing is also available. Maximum elevation is 8,200 feet, with a base at 6,600 feet, and the full lift capacity is over 15,000 people per hour. The season usually runs from November to April. For snowboarders, the newly redesigned Santa Cruz Snow Park is filled with some of the most extreme terrain in the state. Full dining and rental facilities and a ski school are located at the resort. Dodge Ridge also offers 11 kilometers of groomed cross-country skiing trails. From Oakdale head east on CA 108 to Sonora and continue another 30 miles to Pincrest, where you follow the signs to the mountain. For more information, ☎ 209-965-3474.

Adjacent to the Dodge Ridge Nordic skiing area, the **Stanislaus National Forest's Crabtree Area**, one mile east of Pinecrest off CA 108, offers trails for skiers of all levels. Trails are not groomed and snowmobiles are prohibited.

The Stanislaus National Forest's **Calaveras Ranger District** in the northern portion of the forest has a week's worth of frosty trails. You'll find 20 miles of groomed snowmobile trail from Alpine Sno-Park to Ebbett's Pass or Highland Lakes on snow-covered CA 4. The segment near the lake is suited for beginners. More advanced skiers will want to continue a steady climb east past Lake Alpine to Cape Horn Vista or Mosquito Lakes. Snowmobiles are prohibited at Big Meadow, located one mile east of Liberty Vista and three miles west of Tamarack on CA 4. Skiers of all abilities will appreciate the solitude of this region, where trails are marked but not groomed. Easier trails traverse Big Meadow campground, while the more challenging trails follow the edge of Stanislaus River Canyon. For more information and a copy of the *Nordic Skiing Recreation Guide*, ☎ 209-533-1890.

Routes Home or to the Parks

The lovely and action-packed county of Mariposa ("butterfly" in Spanish) was founded in 1850. The county seat is the Old West town of Mariposa, a major gateway via State Route 120 to nearby Yosemite National Park. The **Lake McClure/Lake McSwain Recreational Areas** offer boating, fishing, camping and house boating. ☎ 800-468-8889. The **Merced River** has campgrounds and trails for hiking and horseback riding. Mountain bike trails follow a historic railroad. ☎ 916-985-4474.

Once you have completed your journey through the Golden Chain region you should take Highway 190 from Springville until you reach Highway 65. There you can either travel south to Bakersfield and head back to Los Angeles or San Bernardino, or visit Yosemite, Sequoia and Kings Canyon Parks. If that's what you want to do, take Highway 65 to Lindsay and pick up Highway 137 to Tulare and then head north on Highway 99 to entrances of the major parks, or continue on to Sacramento.

Mariposa

In this region, plan to stay in hotels or motels at Mariposa or Sonora, because facilities elsewhere are limited. There are campgrounds, however, several miles off the main highway.

After gold was discovered here in 1849, Mariposa grew within two years from a small cluster of miners' tents to 30,000 people. Colonel John C. Fremont lived here after he purchased a Mexican land grant of 45,000 acres for $3,000 prior to the discovery of gold.

The gold mines eventually closed and Mariposa declined rapidly after most of the business district was destroyed by fire in the late 1860s.

Where to Stay in Mariposa

Best Western's Yosemite Way Station is on State Route 140 where it intersects with State Route 496. $$. There's a nearby restaurant. Write PO Box 1989, 95338, ☎ 559-966-7545. **Comfort Inn-Mariposa** is just east of the junction of State Routes 140 and 49 South. $$. No pets. ☎ 559-906-4344. **E.C. Yosemite Motel** is at the junction of State Route 49 and 140 North, at 5180 Jones Street, 95338. $$. ☎ 559-742-6800. **Mariposa Lodge** is on

State Route 140. Write PO Box 733, 95338. $$. ☎ 559-966-3607. Pets are permitted, but there's a $6 charge.

> *For additional information on this region contact the Yosemite-Mariposa County Chamber of Commerce, 5158 Highway 140, PO Box 425, Mariposa, CA 95338.* ☎ *800-208-2434.*

Oakhurst

The southernmost county of the Mother Lode is Madera, whose territory ranges from the San Joaquin Valley to the Sierra Nevada Mountains.

Oakhurst, the county seat and last major town along the Golden Chain Highway, is also a southern gateway to Yosemite National Park.

Gold Country South Outfitters

General Outfitters

■ Angels Camp

Hi-Tec Boots Outlet Store, 155 South Main Street, ☎ 209-736-4188.

■ Arnold

Ebbetts Pass Sporting Goods, 925 Highway 4, ☎ 209-795-1686.

Mountain Sports Chalet, 1771 Highway 4, ☎ 209-795-3885.

Sierra Nevada Adventure, 2293 Highway 4, ☎ 209-795-9310.

■ Bear Valley

Bear Valley Adventure Company, 1 Bear Valley Road, ☎ 209-753-2834.

■ Mi-Wuk Village

S&S Gear, 24191 Highway 108, ☎ 209-586-6500.

■ Pinecrest

Sonora Pass Mountaineering, PO Box 1294, ☎ 209-965-3938.

■ Sonora

Big 5 Sporting Goods, 1051 Sanguinetti Road, ☎ 209-536-9257.

Sierra Nevada Adventure, 173 South Washington Street, ☎ 209-532-5621.

Sports Connection, 13775 Mono Way, ☎ 209-533-4949.

On Horseback

■ Groveland
Cherry Valley Pack Station, ☎ 209-962-5671.
Pine Mountain Lake Equestrian, ☎ 209-962-8666.

■ Oakdale
Western Ridge, 10761 Eaton Road, ☎ 209-847-1172.
Right Here Ranch, 12706 Sierra View Drive, ☎ 209-848-2715.
Bar C Ranch, 4626 Heather Hills Lane, ☎ 209-848-1962.

■ Pinecrest
Aspen Meadow Pack Station, PO Box 1435, ☎ 209-965-3402.

■ Sonora
Flying R Equestrian Center, 10401 Horseshoe Bend Road, ☎ 209-532-
Kennedy Meadows Resort, PO Box 4010, ☎ 209-965-3900 or 209-532-9663.
Prosser Stables, 22245 Conklin Trail, ☎ 209-533-3340.

On Wheels

■ Altaville
Mountain Pedaler, 352 South Main Street, ☎ 209-736-0771.

■ Angels Camp
Glory Hole Sports, 2892 Highway 49, Angels Camp, ☎ 209-736-4333

■ Arnold
Ebbetts Pass Sporting Goods, 925 Highway 4, ☎ 209-795-1686.
Mountain Sports Chalet, 1771 Highway 4, ☎ 209-795-3885.
Sierra Nevada Adventure, 2293 Highway 4, ☎ 209-795-9310.

■ Bear Valley
Bear Valley Mountain Bikes, 1 Bear Valley Road, ☎ 209-753-2834.

■ Sonora
JT Bicycles, 55 South Washington Street, ☎ 209-536-9882.
Sierra Nevada Adventure, 173 South Washington Street, ☎ 209-532-5621.
Sports Connection, 13775 Mono Way, ☎ 209-533-4949.

On Water

■ **Oakdale**

Adventure For All, 14842 Orange Blossom Road, ☎ 209-847-4671.

Sunshine Rafting Adventures, 9616 Jackson Road, ☎ 209-848-4800.

Yosemite National Park

Western Routes to the Park

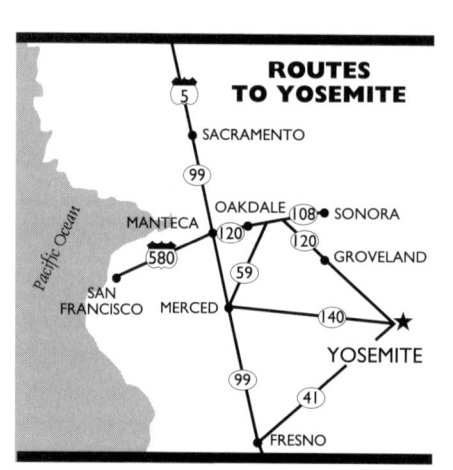

There are two all-weather routes to Yosemite. Those departing from San Francisco to Yosemite should leave the city by the Golden Gate on I-80 across the Bay Bridge. Then take I-580 through Alameda County and travel east into the Livermore Valley. After entering Central Valley on this route, take State Route 132 and turn east at Modesto where the road intersects State Route 99. This route will take you south toward Yosemite. After crossing the Tuolumne River, it is about eight miles to Mariposa on a winding road. This is one of the major towns on the Golden Chain. The California State Mining and Mineral Museum is two miles south of Mariposa, at the county fairgrounds. There you will find one of the world's largest gem and mineral collections. Leave Mariposa on State Route 140 through the Stanislaus National Forest to El Portal and the Arch Rock Entrance Station to Yosemite National Park.

Sacramento to Yosemite

If you have gone to Sacramento, there's an easy 63-mile drive on State Route 99 to Manteca, where you pick up State Route 120. From there it's 114 miles to Yosemite. This is about a four-hour drive.

Los Angeles to Yosemite

If you're interested in visiting only Yosemite, Kings Canyon and Sequoia National Parks, you can make a one-day trip from Los Angeles. Take I-5 north to Wheeler Ridge, where the interstate turns west, and pick up State Route 99 to Bakersfield. This farm and cattle country is of little interest to most people. Nine miles north of Tulare, at Goshen, take State Route 198 East. Turn east on 219 at Salida and drive to Oakdale on 120. Follow it to Yosemite Valley.

The Tioga Road - The Eastern Approach to Yosemite

The Tioga Road is the highest in the Sierra Nevada, and the only road to cross the crest into Yosemite National Park.

History

Tioga is an Iroquois name meaning "where it forks." The route first appeared on Lieutenant McClure's map of 1895. Indians had used it more than 4,000 years ago as they traveled from Yosemite Valley to trade with residents of Owens Valley. Traces of it can still be seen along the old route of the Tioga Road from Crane Flat to Tamarack Flat via Tenaya Lake to Tuolumne Meadows. At the Meadows the route heads south up Parker Creek Canyon and then turns east over Mono Pass through Bloody Canyon. When Josiah Whitney and the California Geological Survey first explored this region in the early 1860s, he noted that north of Tuolumne was an easier route to Owens Valley, one that was 600 feet lower. This new pass was later used by thousands of emigrants who came to California.

After gold was discovered in the Sierras in 1848, large areas were explored beyond the initial diggings. A "Doc" Chase, while camping at Lake Jessie (now Tioga Lake), below the summit of Tioga Hill (part of which is Gaylor Peak today), believed silver could be found in mountains to the west. Chase located a massive outcropping of rock, now known as Shepherd Lode, where he thought silver might be found in quantity. He promptly staked a claim by scratching his name on a tin can. His party went to Monoville to have the ore assayed, but there he heard news of a major silver strike at Aurora, Nevada. This new strike seemed more promising, so his party went there. They never returned to Tioga Hill.

The Great Sierra Wagon Road

A young sheepherder named William Brusky found the rusty can in 1847. He quickly claimed the area. Unfortunately for the new prospector, the silver petered out, so he sold his assets to the Great Sierra Consolidated Silver Company in 1881 for a pittance. He later committed suicide. The company at first believed they had found a major strike and they developed plans for a town of 50,000 people. It constructed the Great Sierra

Wagon Road from Crocker's Station in the west to the new town of Bennettville, just north of the summit of Tioga Pass, right below the mine itself. Hundreds lost their lives during the region's brutal winters before the company abandoned the mine in 1883 and went bankrupt. The properties of the company ended up in the hands of a Mr. R. Swift by 1885, and he held them for another 20 years.

The road only went as far as Bennettville and was not completed to the east for another 26 years, when it was finally built through Lee Vining Canyon. A bunkhouse and the assay office are all that remain at Bennettville. Today's road completely bypasses these areas, but both are accessible by trail. The US Forest Service has restored two of the three cabins at Bennettville, and some of the old mine's machinery is back in place.

After the Great Sierra Wagon Road was extended to Lee Vining, a route across the Sierra was available, but it was treacherous. The east side was considered too dangerous for man or beast.

Stephen Mather, appointed Assistant Secretary of the Interior in 1915, became interested in improving the nation's parks. San Francisco was scheduled to hold a world exposition to attract people from all over the world. Now that the automobile was becoming a more reliable means of transportation, Mather envisioned extensive travel to Yosemite and the Sierra Nevada. He approved plans to upgrade the Tioga Road.

Upgrading of the Tioga Road

Unfortunately, the government didn't own the road. A wealthy man in his own right, Mather decided to buy the region and donate it to the government. There was resistance in the Senate at first, but he finally received permission to go ahead. The Modesto Chamber of Commerce and the Sierra Club collected $8,000. Mather donated $7,500, and William Colby of the Sierra Club made the purchase from the Swift estate. Mather could not make the donation personally because he was a government employee. Congress approved the authorization March 3, 1915, and title was transferred on April 10, for a token $10. Three months later Mather, with Horace Albright and others, while "mute with terror," drove up the "grisly precipice" from Lee Vining and arrived in Tuolumne Meadows on July 28. Only 190 others made the trip that year. The dynamic Mather later helped to establish the National Park Service in 1916, and served as its director.

America's National Parks receive millions of visitors from around the world each year thanks to Mather and others whose vision anticipated the future. Traffic increased on the Tioga Road, but it remained unpaved, narrow and winding for many years. It was almost buried in a forest of trees for 21 miles. On the east side it was terrifying to drive because the road was narrow with steep grades and a drop-off of 3,000 feet. The road from Lee Vining to Tioga Pass was paved between 1935 and 1937 and straightened out. The bad 21 miles west of Tuolumne was realigned and paved 20 years later. Rerouting of the east side was completed in 1968.

The Tioga Road Today

Today the road offers a spectacular route through Yosemite's high country. It crosses open country and the old 21-mile bad section has been eliminated. There are signs at vista points to explain the region's historical, cultural and geological events. There are several campgrounds and a number of hiking trails that cross the road. The summit, at 9,946 feet, is the highest mountain pass in California. It is also the eastern entrance to Yosemite Park.

This road can be used only in summer. Winters are severe and snow sometimes prevents the road from operating until after May 30. The east side is still very steep, but it's an excellent mountain road.

History of the Park

Twenty-five million years ago Yosemite Valley was a lush lowland bordered by gentle hills. Half Dome's ancestor was only 1,500 feet tall. The river, now called the Merced, was sluggish as it flowed through the valley. The land was subtropical and rain frequently drenched the valley. The river eventually carved a 20,000-foot, V-shaped canyon as it rushed toward the sea.

Yosemite's Formative Years

Twelve million years later a huge uplift of the region occurred and snow capped the highest peaks. Erosion removed the soil above the granite base and a cool climate changed the environment as hardwood and evergreen trees began to grow, and possibly the first sequoias. The region began to look like what we see today. About 1½ million years ago, the climate became colder and ice began to form thousands of feet thick in the high country. Glaciers formed and a river of ice moved down from the eastern mountains, filling Yosemite Valley. The erosive effect of glaciers gouged the valley, carving it deeper and wider until the familiar U-shaped valley appeared. Hanging valleys were formed when the river dug its way even deeper into the earth and widened the valley still more.

Near what is now called El Capitan, a ridge of rock debris, a terminal moraine was formed, impounding the waters of the river and forming a lake that covered the valley's floor for hundreds of years. In time the lake silted up and the river broke through the moraine, draining the valley, giving it the unusual flat appearance it has today. The hanging valleys, created during the glacial period, formed channels for the valley's spectacular waterfalls.

Valley Saved for Posterity

An English adventurer, James Mason Hutchings, visited the valley in 1855. He published several articles about the valley's beauty, and visitors began to arrive in growing numbers. He devised some developmental schemes that would have destroyed the valley, but a group of influential people intervened and the valley was saved for posterity.

A Common Danger

John Muir once experienced a common danger in the Sierra Nevada – an avalanche. He was waist-deep in snow, climbing to the top of a peak in Yosemite Valley when the snow crumbled and he started to slide. The bearded mountaineer listened anxiously as a dull, terrifying roar warned him of imminent danger. Soon he was hurtling toward the valley "like a leaf" in a gale. In danger of being buried alive, he spread-eagled himself to remain on top of the snow slide. A minute later he and the mass of snow landed "in the valley on top of the crumpled piles without a bruise." He rejoiced at his miraculous deliverance, saying, "Elijah's flight in a chariot of fire could hardly have been more gloriously exciting." He later recalled the snow ride as "a milky way of snow-stars." Muir made the American wilderness his life's work, fighting anyone who would destroy or pillage nature's magnificent heritage. It wasn't easy, but he was a fighter of courage and determination. He succeeded in his quest far more than any other human being because his knowledge came from nature and not from books.

Muir Follows the Dictates of His Heart

Muir ignored creature comforts and lived on "essences and crumbs." He followed the dictates of his heart and generations who have followed him have been forever grateful. He was a loner, constantly exposing himself to avalanches, bears, isolation and fierce storms. He believed in these opportunities to explore the natural world that he viewed as a temple. He lived in an era when most people believed wilderness lands were to be exploited for their economic rewards.

Muir urged doubters, "Climb the mountains and get their good tidings. The winds will blow their own freshness into you, and the storms their energy, while cares will drop off like autumn leaves."

Many people living in today's world of hustle and bustle are finding a special relevance in Muir's teachings. This is especially true now that the Sierra Nevada is facing ever-increasing encroachment by people seeking a more peaceful existence.

Fortunately, today much of Muir's world still exists, wild and free as ever, despite concern about the earth's growing fragility. Disbelievers need only walk through a virgin forest and feel, as Muir did, "Nature's peace flow into you as sunshine flows into trees." In gazing at the tall spires of the giant sequoias you will feel, as Muir did, "that the clearest way into the Universe is through a forest wilderness."

Muir hated wars, such as the Civil War that he refused to fight, saying, "If a war of races should occur between the wild beasts and Lord Man, I'm tempted to sympathize with the bears." His love for wild creatures was all encompassing, admiring their freedom and closeness to nature. He called the grasshopper "the mountain's merriest child," and it was one of his favorites.

John Muir.

In the fall of 1869, Muir returned to Yosemite for the second time after having first seen it in the spring. He called the valley "a tree-lovers' paradise," with "noblest walls – sculpted into an endless variety of domes and gables, spires and battlements and plain mural precipices – all a-trembling with the thunder tones of the falling water." He said the unforgettable skyline of Half Dome, Glacier Point and El Capitan sent his heart soaring. At dawn today, young people take off from Glacier Point in hang gliders, riding the updrafts for 3,000 feet and landing in the valley 20 minutes later. Muir would have loved to do that.

First Visit

During Muir's first visit to Yosemite he worked for a sheepherder to permit him to remain in the valley throughout the summer. "No pain here," he later wrote. "No dull empty hours, no fear of the past, no fear for the future. These blessed mountains are so completely filled with God's beauty, no petty personal hope or experience has room to be." He called the sheep, which he helped to tend, "hoofed locusts" because they ate the shrubbery down to the bare earth.

Muir spent five years in Yosemite, making it the base for his travels throughout the region. He carefully observed the flowers, such as the spectacular milkweed, making sketches of it and many others. His love for Yosemite was expressed eloquently when he said, "Into this one mountain mansion, nature has gathered her choicest treasures."

Muir loved this area of bare, granite peaks carved by glaciers into domes, and arching layers of rock. Near here is the source of the Merced and Tuolumne Rivers, which he called "the brightest of all Sierra landscapes." His theory that the land was carved by glacial flows was ridiculed at the time, but after he found a living glacier – the first discovered in the Sierra – much of the criticism evaporated. Tenaya Lake was created by a river that once flowed through here. The Indians called it *Py-we-ak*, or "Lake of the Shining Rocks." Muir believed the shine was caused by glacial polishing through the millenniums, and he was right. For centuries icy rivers crushed and eroded the granite, giving it its present smooth finish.

The surrounding mountain peaks survived, but their once jagged spires have also been worn down.

Yosemite Today

The park occupies 1,169 square miles. The valley, which is all most people see, is about seven miles long and three-quarters of a mile wide, or 1% of the park. There are 196 miles of primary roads and 800 miles of trails in the park; much of it is accessible to motorists as well as hikers. The park is open all year but during the summer months automobile traffic is restricted in parts of the valley.

The admission price is $20 per vehicle for seven days. Be advised that chains may be required for your car any time during the year.

Each summer, 4.2 million people crowd into Yosemite Valley, straining the park's resources to the limit. If possible, go in the off-season for a more relaxed visit.

Temperatures may reach 100°, but nights are usually cool. The high country has warm summer days and crisp, cool nights. Yosemite Valley seldom experiences severe weather in winter and temperatures range from the mid-20s to mid-50s. Some nights the temperature drops to 15. Snow arrives in the high country in mid-November and remains until April at levels above 6,000 feet.

Pets are not permitted on the trails or in public buildings. They must be leashed at all times. Cats and dogs are permitted in Upper Pines in Yosemite Valley, the west end of the Tuolumne Meadows Campground, and at White Wolfe's Section C, Section A at Bridalveil, Section A at Crane Flat, Wawona and Bogdon Meadows at Yosemite Valley from late May to mid-October.

What to See & Do in Yosemite Valley

The main entrance to Yosemite Valley is made from the west through the dark Wawona Tunnel.

After the road breaks into bright sunshine, **El Capitan** rears to 3,000 feet above the pine and fir-clad slopes above the valley on your left side.

As you continue through the valley, **Bridalveil Falls** seems to emerge from the side of a mountain on your right, its mistlike water pouring down 620 feet. It reaches its peak flow in May when warm temperatures dissolve the snows of winter.

Glacier Point

Glacier Point, at an elevation of 7,314 feet, is 3,214 feet above the valley's floor. It has a breathtaking panoramic view of the region's domes, pinnacles, waterfalls and the sheer face of Half Dome. It is 30 miles from Yosemite Valley by way of Wawona Road to Chinquapin, and then Glacier Point Road.

Half Dome

Rock climbers each year come from all over the world to challenge the face of the 3,600-foot giant monolith at the eastern end of the valley. Half Dome is the largest single granite rock pile on earth. Even veteran mountain climbers are challenged by Yosemite's famous landmark. It's an eight-mile hike from Happy Isles at the bottom to the point where the mountain further tests the mettle and strength of climbers. This point, 8,350 feet from the valley's floor, can be climbed only by using hand cables over the sharpest pitch of the granite wall. After that the grade is not as steep, and you're soon walking on an 11-acre stone desert like an "island in the sky," and the summit looks like cabbage leaves made of stone, or granite shingles on a house.

From the top of Half Dome, the Merced River is just a silver stream. You can study the detail of the crest of the Sierra and the ranges around it from the stone lookout.

Although there may be thousands of people in Yosemite Valley, they are all but invisible at this height, and even their cars seem small. To the east, the view is magnificent with domes, ridges, forests and snowy peaks as the Sierra Nevada rises tier after tier in a display of scenic splendor seldom seen anywhere on earth.

Mirror Lake

From the top of Half Dome, Mirror Lake reflects the light from its surface much like quicksilver on the back of a mirror. It is normally dry in late summer, and someday it will silt up and disappear.

Sunnyside Ranch

Sunnyside Ranch was one of Muir's favorite observatories for Yosemite Falls, and it remains so for climbers today. You can still smell the fragrance of California laurel – known as bay leaf. The air is also filled with the perfume of manzanita in bloom. This is a tough plant with the necessary hardiness to withstand the harsh winters, even though it has no bark.

Mount Watkins

Mount Watkins rises to 8,500 feet above Tenaya Canyon in the northeast corner of Yosemite Valley. From its summit you can see the **Grand Canyon of the Tuolumne**, a huge granite gash through the high country of Tuolumne Meadows. Here the Tioga Road cuts the park. Sierra Club members seek out this spectacular canyon in the heart of the wilderness and climb the high meadows from Yosemite Valley, with their club's canvas cabins placed a day's walk apart. This is a land of unspoiled beauty. Granite surfaces, with mirrorlike finishes, were polished by ancient ice many years ago. They still glisten as they have for millions of years. Glaciers, which had pushed in from the east, made the valley a frozen sea of ice. These ancient ice flows, gathering huge rocks as they moved slowly over the land, created the Merced River's sharp bends, widened the valley's floor, and formed hanging glens. Today, a half-dozen falls make Yosemite Valley a fairyland.

East of Tenaya Lake you'll see **Tuolumne Meadows**, the largest glacial meadow in all the Sierra. Both the Pacific Crest Trail and the John Muir Trail pass through here. They cross the flowery meadows and lead south about 200 miles to Mt. Whitney.

Thousands of backpackers, rock climbers and horsemen each year use the Tuolumne Meadows campground as their headquarters. Yosemite's backcountry is pure wilderness, and you'll rarely encounter another human being during a trip of several weeks.

Thousands of blossoms carpet the meadows in season along the Tuolumne River. Heather, tiny shooting stars and yellow buttercups seem to dance in the wind.

The surrounding mountain peaks survived, but their once jagged spires have been worn down. Below them, the blueness of Tenaya Lake is a startling contrast. The water is so clear you can see the bottom while California gulls swoop down to pluck food from it.

> **Information Sources**
>
> You can receive prerecorded information about camping, roads and weather conditions and recreation, ☎ 559-372-0200.
>
> Yosemite's Visitor Center is open all year. It has exhibits and audiovisual programs, while the nearby Indian Cultural Museum depicts the history of the Miwok and Paiute. Centers at Big Oak Flat and Tuolumne have park naturalists during summer months.

Shuttle Buses & Park Services

The valley is only 1% of the park and the rest of it remains uncrowded – particularly the Merced River region (River of Mercy) that flows through the valley and usually is remarkably free of visitors.

Shuttle buses operate at frequent intervals. During the summer months it is wise to leave your car at your hotel, campground or the **Curry Village day-use lot** where "Shuttle Bus One" stops. Then you can avoid the hassle of heavy traffic, assuming there are no restrictions on automobiles, and take a two-hour tour of the valley. A tour guide will narrate for you and answer your questions. There are occasional trips after Labor Day. You need reservations; they are available at Ahwahnee Hotel, Camp Curry and Yosemite Lodge. In summer, tours depart daily to Glacier Point and Mariposa Grove. There are horseback tours of Yosemite Valley, Wawona, Wolf and Tuolumne Meadows.

Naturalists will take you on year-round **nature walks** lasting from half an hour to all day. **Evening programs** are presented all year at the Valley Visitor Center and Yosemite Lodge, and in summer at Lower River, Camp Curry, Lower Pines, Wawona, White Wolf and Bridalveil Creek Campgrounds. Happy Isles has exhibits and a slide program daily from 10-4 in summer.

Maps and information are available at the Yosemite Valley Visitor Center, and park entrances have schedules of events in the valley. A free shuttle bus operates in the east end of the valley from 9-9 from early April to late October and from 10-9 the rest of the year.

Air tours over the valley, Tuolumne Meadows and the Cathedral and Ritter Mountains, are conducted by **Golden Eagle Air Tours**. They last about 1½ hours and a narrator describes the area for passengers.

Yosemite National Park

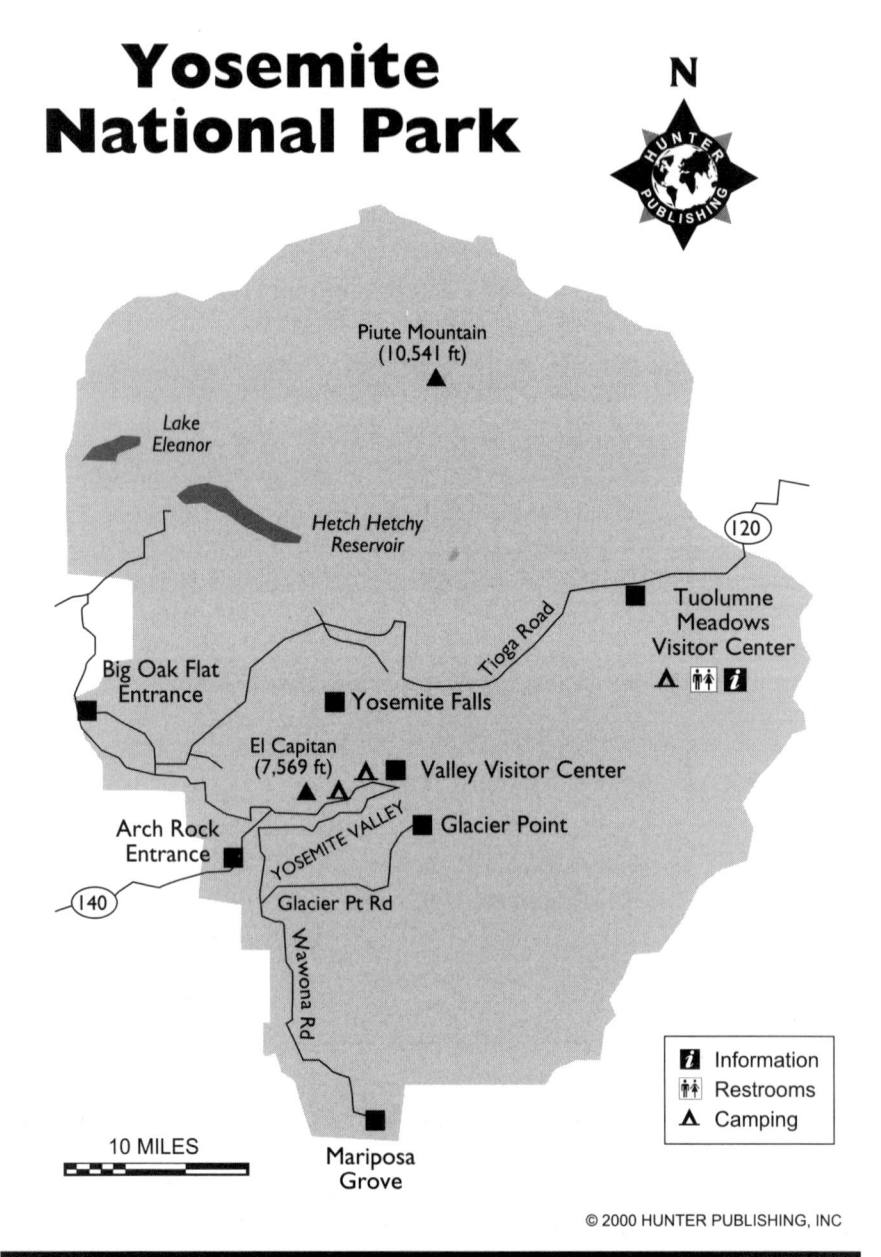

In winter, there's excellent **skiing and skating**. Camp Curry has an outdoor skating rink, Badger Pass Ski Area has downhill and cross-country skiing. Ski trails leave from Badger Pass.

Valley Bus Tours

Bus tours are available in summer on paved roads, through forests of pine and fir, to Glacier Point, with ranger-naturalists to describe what you're seeing. There's a one-mile walk from the parking area to Sentinel Dome's 8,122-foot peak. This road is open from June through October.

Hunting

Hunting is prohibited and firearms must not be brought into the park unless they are declared, unloaded, cased or broken down. Hunters are permitted to use park campgrounds as base camps for hunting outside of park boundaries.

Fishing

Fishing is permitted in the park's 200 lakes and 550 miles of streams. The best fishing is away from crowded areas. Stream fishing is best in late June or early July when the water clears after the spring runoff. Lake fishing is best during the first few weeks after the snow melts and in the fall when cooler weather and water bring trout to the surface (see *Appendix A* for license information).

Activities for Children

The **Ski Tots Playhouse** at Badger provides child care for a fee in the winter. In the summer, the Junior Ranger Program of nature walks and classes is open for students in grades three through six. For grades seven and up a special program of hiking activities is available. ☎ 559-372-0200.

Park Animals

When soldiers of California's Mariposa Battalion entered Yosemite Valley in 1851, they named it for the Indian tribe they were sent to overcome – *uzamati*, or grizzly bear. With a different spelling, it became the valley's designation. There are no grizzly bears anymore, but black bears are everywhere. Three hundred kinds of birds and mammals inhabit the park. Mule deer are in the high country, moving up through the valleys in spring when the bucks' antlers are clothed in velvet.

A Helping Hand For Yosemite

As big, bold and beautiful as Yosemite National Park might seem, underneath the surface are fragile Sierra ecosystems that are constantly reeling from an onslaught of tourists, tour buses and campers, especially in and around Yosemite Valley and Toulumne Meadows. A number of non-profit groups are dedicated to keeping Yosemite as wild as possible, and even restoring parts of the park to their natural state. If your visit to Yosemite National Park inspires you to action, consider lending your support to the following organizations.

- **Yosemite Restoration Trust** is the public advocate for the protection and restoration of the park and its ecosystem. As the public voice for the park, YRT builds consensus in the gateway communities, advocates for a regional transportation system, seeks to establish a greater park community and educates park constituencies and the media. ☎ 510-763-1403.
- The **Yosemite Fund** raises money for the park to be used for restoration projects. Among their projects are the restoration of Glacier Point and Mirror Lake. ☎ 415-434-1782.
- The **Yosemite Assocation** publishes the *Yosemite Guide*, the newsletter given to park visitors. The association also publishes and sells maps and books, sponsors field seminars, the park's Art Activity Center, the Wilderness Center and Ostrander Lake Ski Hut. ☎ 559-379-2646.
- The **Yosemite Institute** runs environmental education programs in the park for children, teachers and seniors. ☎ 559-379-9511.
- The **Yosemite Guardian** is a project of Earth Island Institute concerned with the protection of the park's natural resources. ☎ 415-788-3666.

Adventures In Yosemite

Adventures on Foot
Hiking

The glacier-scoured valleys, peaks, walls and lakes of Yosemite National Park are a hiker's and climber's paradise. Sure the park bulges under the boots and sneakers of more than four million visitors a year (despite the recent 300% increase in the entrance fee to $20), but the vast majority of them descend on Yosemite Valley. At only seven square miles, Yosemite Valley is but a tiny fraction of the 1,169-square-mile park, leaving more than a lifetime's worth of human-powered adventures waiting to be discovered by those courageous enough to leave behind the tour buses and sport utility vehicles.

That's not to suggest that Yosemite Valley is Times Square with ponderosa pines. Surely the writers and artists who have immortalized this area as one of the most spectacular natural wonders in North American knew what they were talking about. If you don't have the time or wherewithal to leave the vicinity of the valley, there are still many enticing trails that will get you in touch with the park's wilder side.

Glacier Point

Ninety-five percent of Yosemite visitors stick exclusively to Yosemite Valley, so when the crowds become unbearable, you can head for the hills, or at least the heights of the valley's south rim at Glacier Point. If you enter Yosemite from the south on CA 41 through the village of Wawona, you can turn right at Chinquapin onto Glacier Point Road and drive almost the entire way – about 16 miles – to the rim of the valley. Below are a few hiking options from the Glacier Point area.

From the floor of Yosemite Valley, the **Four Mile Trail** climbs 4.8 miles and gains a head-throbbing 3,200 feet in elevation to Glacier Point. It's an easier walk from the top. From the parking lot at Glacier Point, the Four Mile Trail drops down the southern face of Yosemite Valley five miles to the valley floor. The route begins at the 7,500-foot level and loses 3,200 feet in elevation, so you must be in shape to make the trip back up unless you've left a car shuttle at the bottom. The path winds below Sentinel Dome, offering views across the valley of Eagle Peak, Upper Yosemite Falls and North Dome. The trail ends near a picnic area on Southside Drive.

From the Glacier Point parking area, you can head south on the **Buena Vista Trail** toward Illilouette Falls and the Panorama Cliffs viewpoint, an eight-mile round-trip. The trail descends into the Illilouette Creek drainage for 1.5 miles, losing about 700 vertical feet along the way, to a fork; a left turn leads toward the falls. Keep an eye to the east for incredible views of Half Dome's profile (it looks more like a finger from here) and Vernal and Nevada Falls below Little Yosemite Valley. It's another mile to the falls viewpoint, where you'll enjoy a look at the cascade from above. Just upstream from the falls a metal bridge crosses Illilouette Creek. The trail continues by switchbacking up through the pines and offering stunning views of Yosemite Valley for another 1.9 miles before reaching a junction with the **Mono Meadow Trail** near the Panorama Cliffs. If you are out for a day hike, this is a good spot to eat lunch and turn around. If you wish to lengthen the hike, try heading east and descending 1.1 miles to the top of Nevada Falls on the **John Muir Trail**.

For an excellent overnight backpacking adventure, try continuing south on the **Buena Vista Trail** instead of turning left toward Illilouette Falls. The path runs right alongside Illilouette Creek and under the shadows of the pines for 2.1 miles to a four-way trail junction. Continue south, sticking to the Buena Vista Trail, and check out the views of Mount Starr King to the east. About two miles from the junction, you'll be in an area that was badly burned in a fire in the early '90s. The trail bends around a granite promontory, then heads west and south again. The trail crosses a stream leading toward **Edison Lake**. Use the USGS topo for Half Dome to scout out a cross-country route to the little lake. Just south of Edison Lake, the three **Hart Lakes** are also a short cross-country jaunt away, at the base of Horse Ridge.

Valley Floor Trails

Once in Yosemite Valley proper, the first chance for a good day hike presents itself at the parking lot for Bridalveil Falls, just south of the valley off Wawona Road. From the parking area the **South Valley Floor Trail** heads east through the center of the valley eight miles to Happy Isles, a regular tour bus stop. You can hop a shuttle bus for the ride back to Bridalveil Falls if your legs poop out. Leaving the parking lot, the trail crosses a stream and proceeds on an abandoned road to the bottom of Middle Cathedral Rock. Continue east as the trail joins a road and skirts a picnic area, then turn left to proceed to El Capitan Meadow. Beyond Leidig Meadow, the path crosses the road again, passes Sunnyside Campground and Yosemite Village, then meanders near the Ahwahnee Hotel before crossing the Merced River. The trail finally reaches Happy Isles, where you can return the way you came or take the North Valley Floor Trail.

The **North Valley Floor Trail** leaves Happy Isles and runs through Curry Camp, then alongside LeConte Lodge. Look for wispy Sentinel Falls just before crossing Sentinel Creek and continuing west toward the picnic area you encountered on your hike along the South Valley Floor Trail. From the picnic grounds retrace your steps along the roadway to the foot of Middle Cathedral Rock, then along the abandoned road to the parking area at Bridalveil Falls.

Yosemite Falls

Although not much of an adventure, a **walk to the base of Yosemite Falls**, the tallest waterfall in North America and the third-highest in the world, is a must for the first-time visitor. The paved path winds a little more than half a mile to the wet, slippery foot of Lower Yosemite Falls. Hit this spot first thing in the morning to avoid huge crowds, and keep in mind that you won't be able to see to the top of the 2,425-foot cascade from here because the water drops down a series of huge steps cut back into the towering granite.

If the spray from the lower falls whets your appetite for more water of the vertical variety, try the less-crowded **trail to the top of Yosemite Falls**. After a few strenuous steps, you'll know why this trail is left to only the hale and hearty. The 6.6-mile round-trip trek leaves the northwest edge of Sunnyside Campground and climbs a thigh-busting 2,700 feet. Each switchback offers another jaw-dropping view of the falls and the surrounding Yosemite Valley. Stop at Columbia Rock after about one mile for a breather. On the rest of the climb, you'll be cooled off and inspired by the spray from the plummeting stream of water.

Mirror Lake

For a more leisurely half-day trek, you might want to head for Mirror Lake and the banks of Tenaya Creek, about 3.2 miles round-trip to and from a valley floor trailhead located across from Clarks Bridge. The paved path welcomes bicycles and wheelchairs, so hike with caution. Mirror Lake, under the very nose of Half Dome, is slowly being reclaimed by meadow grass and sediment and certainly won't be around for your children's children to see. In the past the lake was dredged, but now nature is being allowed to run its course. You can continue past Mirror Lake, following Tenaya Creek on its west bank for about three miles until the trail turns around. Retrace your steps to Clarks Bridge, or cross over to the east bank to join the trail back to Happy Isles. For a shorter hike, ride the Yosemite shuttle to stop 17 and jump off for the one-mile round-trip walk.

Vernal & Nevada Falls

The **Mist Trail** begins at Happy Isles in the southeast corner of Yosemite Valley (hop off the free shuttle at stop 16) and ascends an easy, paved .7 mile to a bridge affording a view of Vernal Falls. If you've put up with the hordes of people on one of the most popular trails in America, might as well continue another .5 mile up the steepening asphalt path to the top of the falls. Just past the bridge, the Mist Trail forks. The Mist Trail continues on the left and the John Muir Trail goes right, so stay left and take note of the dozens of tourists slumped on the 500 granite steps of the trail who bit off more than their sneakers could chew. The John Muir Trail heads 211 miles across the High Sierra to Mount Whitney, the highest point in the Lower 48.

After almost 1.5 miles of some moderate aerobic exercise, you'll reach the top of Vernal Falls and bask in their refreshing spray. To extend this trek into an all-day affair and leave at least some of the crowd behind, continue huffing up the trail for a little less than two miles to the top of Nevada Falls. Return the way you came, unless you've come prepared – with equipment and permits – to continue into Yosemite's backyard.

Half Dome

Backcountry buffs knock Yosemite Valley as little more than a tourist trap and scoff at the "paved" trails and guided tours. But at least one valley-based trail offers the kind of wild, hair-raising adventure that will leave you panting. Many trekkers tackle the hike to the top of Half Dome in one very long day. If you plan on spending the night, you'll need a wilderness permit and must be prepared for all types of Sierra weather. The hike to the summit is an unforgettable 16.5-mile round-trip from the valley floor and gains 4,900 feet in elevation. From the Mist Trail at Happy Isles, climb the **John Muir Trail** branch past Vernal Falls and Nevada Falls.

The trail skirts the base of Liberty Cap (7,076 feet) and climbs north-northeast into Little Yosemite Valley. This is the overnight spot for backpackers. Once on the **Half Dome Trail**, locate a spring just off the trail atop a short spur path and fill up, as this is the last water on the trek. The trail continues its ascent, heading north and west, until finally reaching the backside of the granite behemoth. This is where things get dicey. The walk up the back of Half Dome is so steep that a set of cables has been installed over the final 200 feet to give hikers at least some form of handhold. Don't look down; before you know it you'll be on the flat summit at 8,842 feet above sea level. Watch the weather closely and don't even think of tackling the top if thunderstorms are in the area.

South of the Valley

When Yosemite Valley is packed with visitors, there just might be a little more elbow room south of the valley near the village of Wawona. There are plenty of trails that don't take the pounding of the more popular footpaths.

Chilnualna Falls: This eight-mile round-trip leads to one of the higher cascades outside of the valley. To reach the trailhead from CA 41, turn east on Chilnualna Falls Road just north of the Wawona Hotel and drive about 1.5 miles to a dead end. The hike climbs through manzanita and clover toward Chilnualna Creek and the falls, gaining a strenuous 2,500 feet of elevation in only four switchbacking miles. If that doesn't take your breath away, the view of hulking Wawona Dome to the east just might. The cascade drops through a series of chutes that can make quite a splash after a heavy winter. From just beyond the top of the falls, trails branch toward the north for Bridalveil Campground near Glacier Point Road and to the northeast for Chilnualna Lakes.

The trek to **Bridalveil Campground**, nine miles one way, climbs 1,000 feet in the first three miles to a fork. Turn due north and head six miles to Bridalveil Campground. First you'll cross through heavenly Turner Meadow. Take a right at the next fork, climb gradually toward an open plateau, hang a left at the next two forks, and continue about 2.2 miles to the campground, just beyond Bridalveil Creek.

Chilnualna Lakes, almost six miles distant, make a good overnight backpacking spot. From the head of the falls, hike east for about half a mile and ford Chilnualna Creek with caution. The water can be dangerously swift here. The trail climbs gradually, gaining another 700 feet in elevation over the next 1.5 miles to another creek crossing. Shortly thereafter, bear north at a fork in the trail and descend through a lodgepole pine forest for half a mile to another fork. Turn east and proceed another 3.2 miles, gaining another 1,000 feet in elevation, to the first of the eight lakes. The trail heads north and winds around another 1.5 miles to a second lake. You can reach the rest of the lakes via cross-country routes. Use the USGS topo for Mariposa Grove.

Mariposa Grove: Beginning near the Wawona Hotel, this 13-mile round-trip heads to the Mariposa Grove of giant sequoias. With an elevation gain of 3,000 feet along the way, this hike is more strenuous than it appears on the USGS topo map of Wawona. Less conditioned hikers can opt to ride the summer shuttle bus that runs to the Mariposa Grove parking area and walk back to the hotel. The trail first goes east, climbing gently for a mile before reaching a junction. Bear right on this sometimes hot and dusty equestrian path and continue another 1.2 miles to the intersection with the Mariposa Grove Trail. Turn left and begin climbing in earnest for nearly three miles toward the grove, switchbacking steadily for the last half-mile to another fork. Turn left and continue uphill for three-quarters of a mile to a junction. From here a left leads one mile to Tunnel Tree and the branch of the path to Wawona Point. A right will lead you south for about 1.5 miles to the base of the Grizzly Giant tree. Retrace your steps back to the hotel.

North of Yosemite Valley

High Sierra Camps: If your idea of roughing it does not include snoozing on the ground or eating and bathing out of the same aluminum pot, Yosemite's High Sierra Camps are the alternative you're after. Located in the geographic center of the park north and south of Tioga Road, the six camps are little jewels in an oblong tiara that makes a perfect backcountry loop trip for hikers unwilling or unable to carry a 50-pound pack for a week. The camps are about seven to nine miles apart and feature tents that sleep four to six (be prepared to make friends quickly), running water and hot breakfast and dinner. Bag lunches are also available. Each camp holds about 50 people, so if you've come for solitude, forget it.

Most High Sierra hikers begin and end the loop at **Tuolumne Lodge** just off Tioga Pass Road near Tuolumne Meadows. The other five camps, moving clockwise along the foot trail, are **Vogelsang, Merced Lake, Sunrise, May Lake** and **Glen Aulin**. Demand far exceeds supply in the camps, so reservations are awarded in an annual lottery. Applications are accepted between October 15 and November 30 and the drawing is held in mid-December.

Backpackers carrying their homes on their shoulders are also welcome to eat at the camps, with reservations made well in advance. For more information, ☎ 559-253-5674.

Along **Tioga Pass Road** (CA 120), which runs through the geographic center of the park, there are enough hiking trails to last a lifetime. While this area is popular during summer months, it's nowhere near as crowded as Yosemite Valley. Assuming you are approaching Yosemite from the west along 120, you want to head north to Mather just before entering the park. Hetch Hetchy Reservoir lies just east of Mather. From the parking area at the O'Shaugnessy Dam, you can access **Rancheria Falls Trail**, which leads deep into the backcountry. The trail heads 5.5 miles along the reservoir past Hetch Hetchy Dome to the **Rancheria Mountain Trail**. Check out the falls from the bridge at this junction. Turn right and proceed up a steep incline through several areas that show signs of a past forest fire. You'll walk through dreamy, wildflower-filled meadows before dropping to the **Pleasant Valley Trail** about 15 miles from the trailhead. You can turn right and hike two miles to Pleasant Valley, 10 miles to Pate Valley or 30 miles all the way to Toulumne Meadows.

Farther east along Tioga Pass Road (CA 120), you can hike 16-miles round-trip to the top of Upper Yosemite Falls along the **Yosemite Creek Trail**. Find the trailhead by driving 20 miles east of Crane Flat to the turnoff for White Wolf campground and trailhead. Continue east for another two miles to the trailhead. A trail on the north side of the road goes to Lukens Lake. Yosemite Creek Trail is on the south side of the road. The trail leads due south for .8 miles and crosses Old Tioga Road, then continues along a stream, descending moderately for 3.5 miles to a junction and stream crossing. Bear right, cross the stream on a log and continue south, this time along Yosemite Creek to another intersection 7.8 miles from the start. A right will take you to **Eagle Peak** (2.3 miles) and **El Capitan** (4.1 miles). Proceed straight ahead another .8 miles to an intersection. A left turn will take you .2 miles to the top of **Upper Yosemite Falls**, while walking straight will eventually lead you to the bottom of Yosemite Valley, 10.7 miles from the trailhead at Tioga Pass Road.

Two miles east of Yosemite Creek, check out the north side of Tioga Pass Road for the **Ten Lakes Trail**, which leads 6.4 miles north to the lakes. The first hour of hiking is a relatively flat walk through a forest peppered with granite boulders. At 2.3 miles, turn right and ascend through the woods to **Half Moon Meadow** (4.4 miles) and another junction (5.3 miles). Turn left and walk another 1.5 miles to the **Ten Lakes Basin**. The fishing here is excellent. Backpackers can continue east beyond the basin on a strenuous up-and-down stretch of trail all the way to **Tenaya Lake**,

21 miles from the start, where you can access paved Tioga Pass Road and take your prearranged car shuttle back to the trailhead.

A trip into Yosemite's heartland is not complete without bagging the strenuous hike to **Cloud's Rest**, a hunk of granite 9,926 feet above sea level that offers views you'll never forget. From the trailhead on Tioga Pass Road at the southwestern tip of Tenaya Lake, hike south 2.5 miles (climbing steeply the last .7 miles) to a trail junction. Turn left to visit **Sunset Lakes**, 2.5 miles distant. Turn right to continue 4.7 miles to Cloud's Rest. The trail passes through semi-open forest that becomes more sparse as you make the short, relatively easy climb toward the summit.

Tuolomne Meadows, farther east along Tioga Pass Road, is like a backpacker's roosting spot. The **John Muir Trail** and **Pacific Crest Trail** run through the area and long-range hikers can usually be found stocking up at the store here. The PCT heads northwest, dropping gently into a meadow and crosses the Tuolomne River a few times before dropping again. Beautiful waterfalls are visible from this section of the trail as it descends toward a junction at **Glen Aulin High Sierra Camp**, 5.1 miles from the start. From here you can springboard deep into the backcountry. Head north to visit **Waterwheel Falls** (3.5 miles away), **Matterhorn Canyon** (14 miles) or **Benson Lake** (25 miles). Walk south to check out **McGee Lake** (.8 miles), **Tenaya Lake** (6.8 miles) or **Ten Lakes** (15.2 miles).

If you hike south from Tuolomne Meadows, you can opt for an easy, flat two-mile stroll to dazzling **Elizabeth Lake**. Or you might try something more challenging, like an 11-miler to **Donohue Pass**, which takes you east along the heavily used **John Muir Trail**. The trail skirts the meadows in Lyell Canyon and follows the Lyell Fork of the Tuolomne River, then begins climbing up precipitously above treeline into the aerie of Donohue Pass, at an elevation of just over 11,000 feet. The pass is 14.8 miles from and 3,095 feet above the trailhead. From here the John Muir Trail continues deeper into the backcountry, where your hiking options are practically unlimited.

Rock Climbing

Yosemite is the ultimate for serious rock jocks and probably the only place in California where the sight of people perched high above on a granite wall actually causes traffic snarls. If Yosemite is the climber's heaven, then Yosemite Valley is the golden road. **El Capitan**, rising 3,300 feet above the valley floor, is the largest granite monolith in the country and the stuff of a climber's dreams. Other popular big wall climbs can be found on **Leaning Tower, Sentinel Rock, Glacier Point Apron, Washington's Column, Quarter Dome** and the world-famous **Half Dome**.

North of the valley, the area around **Hetch Hetchy Reservoir** might receive less publicity but is still a stupendous haven for climbers. The **Grand Canyon of the Tuolomne** is one favorite stop. East of Hetch Hetchy, **Tuolumne Meadows** has sparkling granite domes and excellent bouldering. Of course, most of the climbing in Yosemite National Park should be left to the experts. If you are not an advanced climber but want to come face to face with the rock, a visit to the renowned **Yosemite Mountaineering School**, ☎ 559-372-8344, is a must. Classes, taught by some of the best ever to scale a granite boulder, run from a day to a week.

Adventures on Wheels

Mountain bikes are banned from Yosemite's trails, as in all national parks, but that shouldn't stop you from seeing Yosemite Valley the way it was meant to be enjoyed – without the help of the infernal combustion engine. A paved bike route runs through the center of the valley, making for an easy, relaxing five-mile round-trip that is the perfect antidote to sitting in gridlock every time some rube in his Chevy spots a deer in a meadow. Begin early in the day to avoid the dangers of distracted drivers gawking at the scenery.

Park at the picnic area across Southside Drive from the **Four Mile Trailhead**, in the southwest corner of Yosemite Valley. From here the bike path heads north across a bridge over the Merced River and toward Yosemite Lodge. Past the lodge's parking area the path leads to Lower Yosemite Falls, where you'll have to park your bike and stroll 150 feet or so to the base of the falls. Back in the saddle, backtrack to Northside Drive, turn left and after a short ride rejoin the bike path on the left. The route runs through Yosemite Village, past the Visitor Center and rejoins Northside Road. Continue east as the trail again leaves the road, paralleling it through the Village Store parking lot and into the heart of the valley.

At the next fork stay left and cross and recross the Merced River. The bike path now runs through the relatively quiet northeast corner of the valley, with Royal Arch Cascade and the Royal Arches towering above it to the north. Soon the path turns toward Tenaya Creek and reaches a three-way intersection. Follow the sign to Mirror Lake and – if you're not riding a rented bike – continue cranking uphill to the foot of the lake. Rented bikes, which are available year-round at Yosemite Lodge, ☎ 559-372-1200, and during the summer at Curry Village, ☎ 559-372-8319, are not allowed up the hill (because of the potential danger of coming back down).

From the lake return to the three-way junction and turn left to cross Tenaya Creek and the valley floor to Happy Isles. Turn right to return to the start of the bike path via Yosemite Village.

Adventures on Snow

Yosemite comes complete with its very own downhill skiing area. Located 22 miles south of Yosemite Valley on Glacier Point Road, **Badger Pass Ski Area**, ☎ 559-372-1446, has nine runs aimed mainly at beginners and intermediates. The longest trail stretches for a mile and the hill offers a total of about 800 vertical feet of skiing. The season generally runs from Thanksgiving until the first week of April.

But when it comes to skiing in Yosemite, it's not the mogul mavens who are drawn to this region in winter, it's the cross-country crazies. Badger Pass is also the site of **Yosemite Cross Country Ski School**, ☎ 559-372-8444. Since the winter of 1970-71, the school has trained and outfitted thousands of Nordic skiers eager to explore this white-blanketed wonderland when it's devoid of the summertime crowds. Director Vicki McMichael oversees the school and the maze of nearby trails, including more than 40 kilometers of machine-groomed track, 155 kilometers of marked trails and a 17-kilometer skating lane from Badger Pass to Glacier Point. In all, there are more than 350 miles of skiable roads and trails in Yosemite, and the folks at the school know just about every inch of them.

The school offers rental equipment, beginner lessons and more advanced instruction in diagonal striding, speed control, skating, telemark skiing and off-track skiing. Guides lead overnight trips to the Glacier Point Hut and through the Sierra backcountry. Every March, Badger Pass hosts the Nordic Holiday Race.

Where to Stay in Yosemite Valley

The **Ahwahnee Hotel** (☎ 559-252-4848) is a historic landmark in Yosemite Valley three-quarters of a mile east of park headquarters. It is expensive, but worth it. This is an outstanding hotel with spectacular views. From February 3 through November 26, holidays, and November 27 through February 2, the Friday and Saturday rate for one person is $201, and $208-231 for two people. From November 27 to February 2, Sunday through Thursday the one-person rent is $182 and $188-231 for two people. There's a charge of $20 for each extra person, although children 12 and under stay for free. You must check in by 5 PM. There are 132 units and 24 two-bedroom duplex cottages. Units have refrigerators, some shower baths, and air conditioning. There's a pool, tennis courts, rental bicycles and horseback riding for which you must pay a fee. Secretarial services are available and there's valet parking. The dining room is open from 7-11 AM, 11:30-4 and 5:30-9. Dinners range in price from $18-30 and reservations are required. They have a dress code. **Bracebridge Dinners** are held as a special treat each year December 12 through 25 in the old English tradition. Reservations for dinner and a hotel room are by lottery, with applications accepted December 12 through January 1 and February 2 through 15 the year before. The hotel is located in a wooded setting and is open all year. The dining room has long been known for its fine food. It is the only one recommended in Yosemite Valley.

The Bracebridge Dinner

The Bracebridge Dinner is a pageant held every Christmas at Yosemite's Ahwahnee Hotel. It has become one the of most anticipated Christmas events in the US. The Bracebridge Dinner is based on the words of Washington Irving's *Sketch Book* of a Christmas dinner at Squire Bracebridge's Old English Manor in 1718. The Ahwahnee's main dining room plays the part of Squire Bracebridge's manor. Professional singers and actors play the parts of Squire Bracebridge and his family, with entertainment provided by San Francisco's Eugene Fulton Chorale and by jugglers and jesters. A magnificent seven-course meal, served to all 335 guests simultaneously, is the highlight of the evening.

Admission to the dinner is by lottery, which now draws up to 60,000 applicants for the 1,675 spaces available on December 22, Christmas Eve and Christmas Day. Each pageant takes three hours and involves more than 100 players. Applications are accepted from December 1 through January 15 for the following year's dinner. Each dinner seat costs about $215, including tax and gratuity. Applications for the lottery may be obtained by writing to Yosemite Concession Services Corporation, 5410 E. Home Avenue, Fresno, California 93727.

There are other places to stay in Yosemite Valley, although they are not recommended. They include **Curry Village**, two miles east of park headquarters; the housekeeping camp 1½ miles southeast of park headquarters; and **Yosemite Lodge** in Yosemite Valley. The latter is three-quarters-of-a-mile west of park headquarters, near Yosemite Falls. The rates are a lot cheaper, but the accommodations leave much to be desired. If you wish to try one of them, insist on an inspection of the premises before you commit yourself. There are better accommodations at cheaper rates just outside the park at El Portal and Fish Camp, plus many others.

Camping in Yosemite Valley

There are several campgrounds in the Yosemite Valley with a seven-day limit from June 1 to September 15. During the rest of the year, there's a 30-day limit. Reservations can be made by phone, ☎ 559-252-4848 or fax 559-456-0542.

The winter of 1996-97 brought record flooding to Yosemite Valley, sending a wall of water, boulders, trees and other debris slamming down the Merced River. Structures, roads and campgrounds were severely damaged, perplexing park managers, confusing tourists and making guidebooks suddenly outdated. Many of the valley's facilities were cut down to size by the flooding, and in a move that won praise from conservationists everywhere, Yosemite officials decided not to rebuild in many spots. The result is a new Yosemite Valley that is a little less convenient for those used to simply driving into a campsite, whipping out the portable espresso maker and having an "outdoor experience." But it's also a Yosemite Valley that is a bit less crowded, a bit quieter and just a tad closer to the land in which John Muir reveled.

The following information is current as of our press date. Check with the **Yosemite Valley Visitor Center**, ☎ 559-372-0299, for current conditions. Lower River and Upper River campgrounds have been closed permanently, wiping out 209 campsites. All remaining drive-in campgrounds in the valley charge $15 per night, require reservations and offer tap water, flush toilets, tables and fire pits, as well as adjacent showers, laundry facilities and groceries. Campfires are permitted between the hours of 5 PM and 10 PM only, to preserve the air quality in the valley, which in years past took on the kind of brown haze usually seen over the freeway-choked Los Angeles basin.

Lower Pines, northeast of Curry Village, is open all year. There are 60 sites (reduced from 172). **Upper Pines**, on the eastern edge of Yosemite Village, is open March through November. There are 238 sites (up from 226). **North Pines**, northwest of Curry Village, has 85 sites.

There are two walk-in campgrounds in the valley, both with tap water, flush toilets, tables and firepits. **Sunnyside Campground**, a quarter-mile west of Yosemite Lodge, is open all year on a first-come, first-served basis. It charges $3 per person per night, and is frequented by climbers and mountaineers. There is a parking lot, 35 tent sites, piped water, flush toilets, fireplaces and tables. The **Backpackers Campground**, on the Merced River near North Pines Campground, is open May through October on a first-come, first-served basis. The fee is $3 per person per night with a two-night maximum stay. There is no parking available.

Tioga Road Campgrounds

Tuolumne Meadows, along the Tioga Road, is the largest meadow in Yosemite National Park. There's a camp there, and the main trailhead for the Loop Trip starts here. Reservations are required. ☎ 559-454-2002 well in advance of your trip. Other High Sierra camps in this region include **Glen Aulin, May Lake, Sunrise, Merced Lake and Vogelsang**. They offer dormitory housing for about 25 people, with family-style dining. A tiny store carries a few items. Each camp is about seven miles from the next, and the whole trip takes about a week to hike.

Other **trails** starting at Tuolumne are **Lambert Dome, Mono Pass, Parker Pass, Lyell Canyon** via the **John Muir Trail, Vogelsang** via **Rafferty Canyon, Sunrise** via **Cathedral Lakes, Glen Aulin** and **Waterwheel Falls** to **Hetch Hetchy, Young Lakes** and **Gaylor Lakes**.

This is a wilderness, so a permit is required for all overnight travel. Some of the hikes can be completed in a day. Permits may be obtained at the Tuolumne Tanger Station, just below the Tioga Road opposite Lambert Dome. You can reserve your permit in advance by writing the park between March 1 and May 31, at Box 577, Yosemite, CA 95389. Include a check for $3. Ranger station permits are available after May 31 on a first-come, first-served basis 24 hours in advance.

Other facilities at Tuolumne include a mountain shop, grocery store, grill and gas station. There's a large campground that is partly reserved. For reservations, ☎ 800-365-0450.

Tioga Pass Campgrounds

There's a small parking area at the Tioga Pass summit from which you can climb to the **Great Sierra Mine and Gaylor Granite Lakes**. You can also start here to climb White Mountain or Mt. Dana and the Dana Plateau. No camping is permitted in the Gaylor Lake area.

Farther east, at Tioga Lake, there are US Forest Service campgrounds. They include **Junction Campground**, and the **Sawmill and Saddlebag** camps. They are located on the Saddlebag Road, two miles east of Tioga Pass summit, and at Ellery Lake. These campgrounds are popular and available only on a first-come, first-served basis. Fishermen love this area.

There is also a small resort two miles east of the pass's summit, **Tioga Pass Resort**, PO Box 7, Lee Vining, CA 93541, www.tiogapassresort.com.. There's a lodge there, with a few cabins and a restaurant. This is the headquarters for fishermen who backpack through the Hoover Wilderness or other areas of the eastern Sierra Crest.

Other Campsites in the Vicinity of Tioga Road

The following facilities may not always be open. ☎ 559-372-0200 to confirm conditions. The campground at **Crane Flat** has a gas station and a small store. ☎ 800-365-2267. **Tamarack Flat** has a small walk-in campground. **At White Wolf** there's a similar small camp and a lodge with cabins. ☎ 559-262-4848 for reservations. **Porcupine Flat** has a walk-in campground. One of the High Sierra camps is located at **May Lake**, and reservations are required. ☎ 559-454-2002. There's a picnic area at **Tenaya Lake**, but the campground is permanently closed. This is the trailhead for climbing Cloud's Rest. Only skilled rock climbers should try to hike the rough Tenaya Canyon to Yosemite Valley.

Group Camps

The **Bogdon Meadow Group Camp** charges $35 per site. There are four sites for up to 30 people with piped water, flush toilets, fireplaces and tables. The **Tuolumne Meadows Group Camp** has 11 sites for up to 30 people, each costing $35. They have piped water, flush toilets and fire rings.

The **Wawona Group Camp** has the same price for its single-site accommodations for 10-30 people. It, too, has piped water, flush toilets, fireplaces and tables.

Reservations

If you want to stay in or around Yosemite Valley you are strongly advised to make reservations. In summer, they are absolutely essential. Most reservations can be made by phone at ☎ 559-252-4848 or by fax 559-456-8542. You can also write the **Reservations Office, Yosemite Concession Services**, 5410 E. Home Avenue, Fresno, CA 93727. The office is open daily from 8-5. A three-day cancellation fee is usually required.

Pets are not allowed in accommodations, although kennels are available at Yosemite Valley Stables in summer.

What to See & Do Outside Yosemite Valley

You can escape summer's congestion in Yosemite Valley by climbing out of the seven-mile long, three-quarter-mile-wide valley. On either side of the one highway that carries traffic there are miles of roadless wildernesses. Here the Sierra Nevada is as pristine as when Muir saw it more than a hundred years ago. The following places are of special interest, and some can be reached by car.

Grand Canyon of the Tuolumne

The Cathedral of Unicorn Peaks are still snow-tipped in mid-July, framed by a cloudless blue sky. Through the area runs the Tuolumne River, with deer by the hundreds seemingly unconcerned by your presence.

The river's serenity undergoes a sharp change as it leaves the meadowland and descends as foamy waterfalls. As the grade becomes steeper, the river turns into a torrent of raging water as it roars downslope. Standing majestically above the river is the 12,590-foot Mount Conness. Few trees grow on its granite sides.

A **hiking trail** takes you among granite rocks until you reach **Waterwheel Falls**, where sheets of foam thunder through rugged terrain. At the third cascade, fountains of spray leap over an upturn in the rock's surface, spangling the air with foam.

Waterwheel Canyon's walls surround the river, forming the Grand Canyon of the Tuolumne. One section is named **Muir Gorge**. Chipmunks chatter happily in this severe environment. The voices of robins, finches, nuthatches and blue jays help to break the silence. If you stray off the trail, you'll regret it. Manzanita will entrap your feet, slashing at tender skin, until you get wise and return to the path others have made for you.

Take the trail, a few hundred feet above the water. At sunset the view is magnificent, and sunrise can be equally rewarding. The beauty of it all will set your pulse racing. The mountains turn from deep purple to a bright red as the full rays of the sun hit them.

The trail follows the Tuolumne, and you can cross the river on a self-operated ferry. Now the trail ascends in a series of switchbacks until you're 3,000 feet above the river.

Nearing Lake Harden, you will have traveled 28.9 miles, with only another 2.8 miles to the roadhead. Although it may seem like you've traveled a great distance and explored Yosemite Park, actually you've seen only a small fraction of it. As Muir would have said, "You've seen only one portion of the great Sierra loaf."

Tuolumne River Rafting

While hundreds of thousands of river rats head for the American River west of Lake Tahoe to get their whitewater fixes every year, many of them are missing the Sierras' best rafting adventure, located near, of all places, Yosemite National Park.

The Tuolumne (pronounced too-WALL-uh-me) River has been used as a liquid backyard by humans for hundreds of years. The exact origin of the English spelling of Tuolumne is nowhere near as clear as its pristine waters, however. It might come from the Yokuts Indians who once lived on its rocky shores and were known as the Tahualamne. Or it might come from the Miwok word "talmalmne," the meaning of which has been lost to the ages. The river was the traditional southern border of Central Sierra Miwok territory.

Whatever the name means, today it represents an outstanding place to recreate, in the truest sense of the word. In 1984, the Tuolumne River was added to the California Wild and Scenic River program, which designates waterways of extraordinary scenic, recreational, fishery or wildlife value to be preserved in a free-flowing state. This came too late, of course, to stop the damming of the river in Yosemite. The Tuolumne begins on the eastern edge of Yosemite near Mount Lyell, flows westward through Tuolumne Meadows and the Grand Canyon of the Tuolomne, and into Hetch Hetchy reservoir behind O'Shaughnessy Dam. At the turn of the 19th century, San Francisco's city fathers wanted a reliable water supply for their growing metropolis and pushed the dam project through the federal bureaucrarcy despite intense opposition from the Sierra Club and its founder, John Muir. The Hetch Hetchy area, Muir argued, rivaled Yosemite Valley in beauty as an unspoiled paradise filled with glacier-carved domes and thundering waterfalls plunging hundreds of feet down granite palisades. Alas, the dam project was approved by the US Congress in 1913, a full 23 years after the area had been "protected" as a national park. Muir died in 1914, and many say it was the exhausting loss of Hetch Hetchy that killed him.

O'Shaughnessy Dam was completed across the Tuolumne in 1923. Just downstream from the dam, rafters and kayakers can put in. The 18-mile run on the Tuolumne is a nearly nonstop ride through 25 identified rapids, holes, chutes and generally unbridled water that should be attempted only by those ready for Class IV and Class V conditions. Unless your whitewater skills are world class, it's best to ride with an experienced guide.

To reach the put-in near Lumsden Bridge in Stanislaus National Forest, take CA 120 east out of the town of Groveland 7.5 miles and turn left. Proceed one mile and turn right onto a dirt road that leads six miles to the first of three camping areas. Lumsden Bridge campground is another half-mile up the road.

A half-mile from the put-in, the river thunders through Nemesis; then comes whitewater like Sunderland Chute (one mile from the put-in), Ram's Head (1.6 miles), Evangelist (4.8 miles), Gray Grindstone (9.5 miles), Thread-The-Needle (11 miles), Hell's Kitchen (13.1 miles) and Pinball (17.6) before the take-out at Wards Ferry Bridge, about 8.5 miles northwest of Groveland via CA 120 and Wards Ferry Road.

There are more than a dozen undeveloped campsites downstream from Lumsden Bridge, including **Tin Can Cabin** (3.5 miles), **Powerhouse**

(7.6 miles), **Wheelbarrow** (8.8 miles), **Driftwood Paradise** (11.4 miles), **Mohican** (14.1 miles) and **North Fork** (15 miles).

Camping in Stanislaus National Forest

Rafters who want to try the Tuolumne River in Stanislaus National Forest can choose from three small, primitive campgrounds near the put-in at Lumsden Bridge. Camping is free, and available on a first-come, first-served basis from roughly April through October. Set at an elevation of 1,500 feet, this area gets mighty warm during the height of summer. There is no piped water, so bring all you'll need or use proper purification techniques.

From the town of Groveland, take CA 120 east 7.5 miles and turn left. Proceed one mile and turn right onto a dirt road that leads six miles to the first of the three camping areas, **Lumsden**, which has 11 tent sites with picnic tables, fire rings and vault toilets. **South Fork Campground** is another half-mile up the road. It has eight tent sites, picnic tables, fire rings and vault toilets. **Lumsden Bridge Campground**, another half-mile up the road, has nine tent sites, picnic tables, fire rings and vault toilets.

If you'd like more amenities, **The Pines Campground**, just off CA 120 eight miles east of Groveland, has 12 sites for tents or motor homes, piped water May through October, and a market nearby. The fee is $8 per night. **Lost Claim Campground**, 11 miles east of Groveland just off CA 120, has 10 sites for tents or motor homes, well water and a nearby market. The fee is $7 per night. For information on camping in Stanislaus National Forest, call ☎ 530-962-7825.

Merced River Hiking

The old Yosemite Valley Railroad right-of way on the north bank of the Merced River offers trekkers a level, though mostly unshaded, river trail from near El Portal to Bagby (28 miles). Because the old railroad bridges have fallen, the swift side streams (particularly on the North Fork of the Merced) may not be crossable during wet weather and snow runoff periods. Plans are under way to improve its condition.

An alternative is the 8.5-mile trail between the Jerseydale Road trailhead and the confluence of the Merced River, which is called the South Fork.

Some lands along the river, hiking trails, and the adjacent hills are privately owned. Respect this private property where it is posted.

Yosemite Valley Route North to Tuolumne River Region

Few people explore north of the Tuolumne River, despite the beauty of the lakes and valleys. You have to hike part of it, but there are many trails that are well marked. For those of you seeking a true wilderness experience, this is the place.

Hetch Hetchy Reservoir

Big Oak Flat Road will take you to Hetch Hetchy Reservoir from Yosemite Valley. It's a 38-mile drive through forests of sugar pine and white fir, easily driven in two hours. A paved road 9½ miles long takes you from Mather to the 132-foot dam. It was built in 1913 to provide water for San Francisco over the intense opposition of environmentalists. The valley, equal in beauty to Yosemite Valley before the dam was built, is now covered by 300 feet of water.

Yosemite's Big Trees

Yosemite's big trees were discovered by Joseph R. Walker's expedition to California in 1833. *Sequoiadendron giganteum*'s bark grows to a thickness of up to 24 inches. The trees have survived despite huge forest fires because the bark is like asbestos and resists fire. The trees are nurtured by the inner bark and the outer rings, or sapwood. They carry water and food through the trunk while the inside of the tree dies.

Mariposa Grove

Mariposa Grove is at the extreme southern end of Yosemite, over a 30-mile paved road. You can drive there on Wawona Road (State Route 41). It's a trip well worth taking because it has the finest sequoia grove in the Sierra. The grove's oldest tree is Grizzly Giant, with a base diameter of 30.7 feet, a girth of 96½ feet and a height of 210 feet. The 232-foot California Tree and the 40-foot stump Dead Giant in Tuolumne Grove have tunnels through their bases.

Wawona Tree

Wawona Tree's living tunnel in Mariposa Grove was cut in 1881 for stagecoach traffic. It is still used today.

Yosemite to Mariposa Bus Tours

Bus tours run from Yosemite to Mariposa Grove, with a stop at Wawona. There's an overlook en route at the east portal of the 4,323-foot Wawona tunnel that offers a view of the entire Yosemite Valley. You may not park in the grove. It is open daily from 9-6 from May to October. Trams leave from the parking area every 10-15 minutes. Admission is $5.25. Those over 64 pay $4.50 and ages four-12 $2.50. There's a 2½ mile foot trail that leads to the upper grove.

Mariposa Grove Museum

The Mariposa Grove Museum has exhibits on the sequoias. It is open to coincide with the tram schedule. Near the museum is the remains of the 200-foot Massachusetts Tree. It had a diameter of 28 feet before it toppled over. It lies in sections on the ground, where you can inspect its structure.

Tuolumne Grove

Tuolumne Grove, 17 miles from Yosemite Valley, has 20 sequoia trees, including the Dead Giant. Big Oak Flat Road starts in the south at Crane Flat. No trailers or motorhomes are permitted on it.

Tuolumne Meadows

Tuolumne Meadows is surrounded by lofty peaks that rise above its 8,600-foot altitude. This is the real High Sierra. You can reach it by taking Big Oak Flat and Tioga Roads from Yosemite Valley for a distance of about 56 miles. This is a good camping place and the starting point for fishing, hiking and mountain climbing trips. You can drive here from late May through October. A wise motorist carries chains because of the possibility of sudden snowstorms even during summer months. A number of other interesting places, including Waterwheel Falls, Mount Lyell, Lyell Glacier, Lambart Dome, Glen Aulin, Muir Gorge, Soda Springs and Tenaya Lake are accessible only on foot or horseback. Tuolumne Meadows, Tioga Pass and Mono Lake, however, are served in summer by daily busses. Each of these places provide nature walks, and hikes and evening campfire programs during the summer months. They have saddle horses to rent and gas stations, stores and post offices.

Where to Stay Outside Yosemite Valley

Outside the valley and within easy driving distance, you might try any one of the following: **Cedar Lodge**, five miles west at 9966 Highway 40, 95318. It has a wide variety of rooms from singles to doubles to suites. Tour groups are welcome and there's a fine dining room, and a gift shop specializing in bears of all kinds. There are family units for up to 10 people. $$-$$$. Pets are not allowed. Write Box C, El Portal, CA 95318. ☎ 800-321-5261. Just west of the gate to Yosemite at El Portal is **Yosemite View Lodge**, at 11136 Highway 140, 95318. $$-$$$. There are 158 rooms along the Merced River, with a restaurant nearby. There's a charge of $5.45 for pets. At Fish Camp, the **Apple Tree Inn Bed and Breakfast** lodging is open all year. It is two miles from the south entrance to the park, at 1110 Highway 41, 93623.

There are only six rooms, some with fireplaces and private porches. It is nestled in seven wooded acres. $$-$$$. There's a $10 charge for each extra person. ☎ 559-683-5111. The **Narrow Gauge Inn** is also located at Fish Camp, but it is open only from May 1 to October 15. It is located four miles south of Yosemite on State Route 41, at 48571 Highway 41, 93623. There are 26 rooms in a picturesque mountain setting with a balcony or deck for each room to give you a forest view. $$-$$$. The **Tenaya Lodge** is two miles south of Yosemite on State Route 41, at 48571 Highway 41, 93623. Write to them at PO Box 159. ☎ 559-683-6555. This is an outstanding resort hotel and the rates are correspondingly high, but at different levels throughout the year. $$$$. The facility has 242 rooms in a landscaped setting with up to four stories. Pets are charged $50 a day. There's a full line of services and the coffee shop is open from 7 AM to 11 PM, with prices ranging from $14-25.

The **Wawona Hotel** (☎ 559-252-4848) is on State Route 41, four miles from the south entrance to the park. $$. It's a historic lodge in a charming setting. Dinners at the restaurant run $12-24.

Campgrounds Outside Yosemite Valley

Nine miles west of Crane Flat, off Tioga Road, is **Tamarack Flat**, at an elevation of 6,315 feet. There are 52 tent sites with stream water, pit toilets, fireplaces and tables.

At **Tuolumne Meadows**, at an elevation of 8,600 feet, the rate is $12. It has 314 tent or RV sites with piped water, flush toilets, showers (for a fee), fireplaces and tables. For reservations ☎ 559-252-4848 or fax 559-456-0542. If you write, contact Yosemite Concession Services, 5410 Home Avenue, Fresno, CA 93727.

White Wolf is north of White Wolf Lodge on the Middle Fork of the Tuolumne River. The elevation is 8,000 feet, and there are 87 tent or RV sites with piped water, pit toilets, fireplaces and tables.

Yosemite Creek is 6½ miles southeast of White Wolf, off Tioga Road, at 7,659 feet. Its 75 tent spaces cost $6 per night. There's a stream for water, pit toilets, fireplaces and tables.

Five areas for tents only have been set aside for the exclusive use of organized groups. Reservations are advised for Hodgon, Tuolumne and Valley. Mail requests should be sent to the Wawona Ranger Station, Box 2027, Yosemite, CA 95389, or ☎ 559-372-0400.

The sites at **Bridalveil Creek** are $35 each. There's piped water, flush toilets, fireplaces and tables. Bridalveil Creek Campground is located eight miles east of Chinquapin on Glacier Point Road, at an altitude of 7,146 feet. There's a 14-day camping limit and a nightly charge of $10 from the middle of June to the beginning of October. There are 110 tent or RV sites with piped water, flush toilets, fireplaces and tables. One site can accommodate 10-30 people.

Hetch Hetchy Backpackers Campground is at the end of a road leading to the reservoir and O'Shaughnessy Dam. It is open all year, with a nightly fee of $3. At an elevation of 3,800 feet, there are 25 walk-in tent sites, piped water, flush toilets, tables and bear boxes. Fires are not permitted, and there's a one-day camping limit. This campground is restricted to people beginning or ending trips into the backcountry. For this region, a wilderness permit is required.

The **Big Oak Flat** and **Tioga Roads Campgrounds** are usually open to September or October, and a 14-day camping limit is in effect from June 1 to September 15. Portions of State Route 120, between the Tioga Pass Entrance Station and Lee Vining, are steep, winding and narrow.

Near the junction of Big Oak Flat and Tioga Roads is **Crane Flat**. Reservations for these $12 spaces are required except in winter. The camp is at an altitude of 6,190 feet. There are 166 tent or RV sites, with piped water, flush toilets, fireplaces and tables.

Hogdon Meadow is five miles west of Grand Flat on Big Oak Flat Road. It is open all year, and the $12 sites must be reserved from May through October. There's no charge in winter. The meadow is 4,927 feet in elevation, and there are 10 tent or RV sites with piped water, flush toilets, fireplaces and tables.

The **Wawona Campground** is a mile west of Wawona Hotel, at an elevation of 4,096 feet. There's a charge of $10 per night. It is open from June 1 to September 15. There's a 14-day camping limit for this period, but a 30-day limit for the rest of the year. There are 100 tent or RV sites with piped water, flush toilets, fireplaces and tables.

More Distant Accommodations & Dining

There are a number of places in Visalia and as far as Mariposa that are within easy driving reach of the park. Many are hotel/motel chains, and I've only listed those places that, in my opinion, are worthwhile for the discriminating traveler.

Where to Stay

Visalia

The **Ben Maddox House** is near downtown. Take the central Visalia exit off State Route 196 to 601 North Encina Street, 93291. This historic bed and breakfast house was built in 1876. No pets. $$. ☎ 559-739-0721. **Best Western's Visalia**

Inn Motel is just north of State Route 198, at 623 W. Main Street, 93291. $$. Small dogs only. ☎ 559-732-4561. **Holiday Inn Plaza** Park is on State Route 198 a half- mile east of the junction to State Route 99, adjacent to Visalia Airport at 9000 West Airport Drive, 93277. $$. It accepts pets. The dining room is open from 6-10 PM, with prices of $7-17. ☎ 559-651-5000. **Lamp Liter Inn** is on State Route 193, a half-mile west of the junction with State Route 63 at 3300 W. Mineral King Avenue, 93291. $$-$$$. No pets. There's a dining room and coffee shop open from 6-10. Meals are priced at $8-21. ☎ 559-732-3411. The **Visalia Radisson Hotel** (☎ 559-636-1111) is just east of State Route 198, by exiting on the Central Visalia ramp to 300 S. Court Street on the corner of Mineral King, 93291. $$. Its restaurant is open from 6 AM to 11 PM, with prices of $7-24.

Oakhurst

Best Western's Yosemite Gateway Inn is about one mile north of State Route 41's junction with State Route 49, at 40530 Highway 41, 93644. $$. Small pets only are permitted. There's a restaurant nearby. ☎ 559-683-2378. The **Chateau Du Bureau** is west of State Route 41, at 48688 Victoria Lane, 93644. This place is expensive, but richly appointed. $$$$. No pets. ☎ 559-683-6860. The **Comfort Inn** is a half-mile north of the junction of 41 and 19, and 15 miles south of the entrance to Yosemite. Its address is 40489 Highway 41, 93644. Small pets only. $$. ☎ 559-683-8282. **Ramada Limited** is on State Route 41, at the junction with Royal Oaks Drive, at 48800 Royal Oaks Drive, 93644. Dogs are acceptable, but no other animals. ☎ 559-658-5500. $$-$$$.

Where to Dine

Visalia

Michael's on Main Street is downtown at 123 West. It is open from 5:30 PM on Friday and Saturday until midnight. It serves continental meals for $11-20. The **Vintage Press** is downtown, just north of Main Street, at 216 N. Willis Street. It is open from 11:30-2 PM and 5:30-10 PM. Featuring an American menu, dinners are priced at $23-30. ☎ 559-733-3033.

Oakhurst

Erna's Elderberry House, west of State Route 41, is at 48688 Victoria Lane. Entrées are priced at over $31, but their French cuisine is excellent. Open for lunch and dinner. ☎ 559-683-6800. **Viewpoint** is on State Route 41, one mile north of the junction with State Route 49, at 4030 Highway 41. It is closed for lunch in winter. ☎ 559-683-5200.

Yosemite Information Sources

Good sources for information for this area include:

Southern Yosemite Visitors Bureau, 49074 Civic Circle, PO Box 1404, Oakhurst, CA 93644, ☎ 559-683-4636.

Springville Chamber of Commerce, 35625 Highway 190, Springville, CA 93264, ☎ 559-539-2312.

Tuolumne County Visitors Bureau, 55 W. Stockton Road, PO Box 4020, Sonora, CA 95370, ☎ 559-533-4420 or 800-446-1333.

Yosemite Concession Services Corporation, 5410 E. Home, Fresno, CA 93727, ☎ 559-252-4848.

South of Yosemite

After leaving Yosemite Village, the junction with State Route 99 and State Route 140 is about 80 miles on a southwest heading. State Route 140 is often narrow, steep and winding, and caution is advised if you're pulling a trailer. You can also leave the park on State Route 41, but this is a slower route. Both 99 and 41 meet at Fresno for the drive east to Kings Canyon and Sequoia or directly to Los Angeles.

Sierra National Forest

When most visitors head south from Yosemite, they make a beeline for Kings Canyon and Sequoia national parks, without realizing that they are passing through some of the most wondrous and least explored parts of the Sierra Nevada. East of CA 41 in Madera County, Sierra National Forest covers 1,300,000 acres of incredibly varied terrain extending from the Merced River south to the Kings River and bordering Yosemite National Park. The terrain is incredibly varied, from rolling, oak-dotted foothills along the San Joaquin Valley to the craggy, soaring, snow-capped peaks of the Sierra crest.

The Sierra has 11 man-made reservoirs, 528,000 acres of designated wilderness, over 60 family campgrounds, two National Wild and Scenic Rivers – the Kings and the Merced – and 1,100 miles of hiking trails. No, that's not a typo: 1,100 miles. For details, see below under *Adventures*.

Five federally designated wilderness areas, where motorized vehicles are prohibited and the loudest sound you are likely to hear is your own gasping as you marvel at the beauty, can be accessed from Sierra National Forest land. These are the famous **Ansel Adams Wilderness, Dinkey Lakes**

Wilderness, Kaiser Wilderness, Monarch Wilderness and **John Muir Wilderness**.

For more information, contact Sierra National Forest headquarters in Clovis, ☎ 209-297-0706.

Nelder Grove

Sierra National Forest even has its own big trees, which are every bit as fantastic as Yosemite's, but much less visited. Nelder Grove, a 1,500-acre parcel containing 101 giant sequoias, is the best place to see them. Unlike the big trees found in nearby national parks, Sierra's giant sequoias have no paved roads and no crowds blocking the view. The forest around them is also thicker, so the mammoths seem to appear suddenly as the adventurer walks through the forest. Head north of Oakhurst, turn right at Sky Ranch Road and follow the signs to Nelder Grove. The **Shadow of The Giants trailhead** is about two miles down the road.

According to archaeologists, the Southern Sierra Miwok camped in the grove for several thousand years while gathering acorns and hunting. The grove is named in honor of original 49er John Nelder, who left New Orleans in 1849 to search for gold in California. But he grew tired of prospecting and by 1875 had constructed a log cabin near the huge trees on land he was homesteading. That same year naturalist John Muir met Nelder and described him as was exploring the sequoia groves south of Wawona to establish the boundaries of Fresno Grove. The famed naturalist came upon Nelder sitting outside his new log cabin. Muir described Nelder as a man who "loves nature truly and realizes that these last shadowy days with scarce a glint of gold in them are the best of all." Nelder died in a cabin fire in 1889.

Walk three miles from Nelder Grove campground and you'll find the **Graveyard of the Giants**, where several large sequoias that were killed by a wildfire can be examined.

Two major highways take you into this forest wonderland. State Route 41 and 168 make these areas accessible. **Huntington** and **Bass Lakes** offer camping facilities and outdoor sports. **Florence Lake, Redinger Lake** and **Pine Flat Reservoir** can be reached by roads branching off from 168.

Trails into the Sierra National Forest

Approximately 1,100 miles of trails lead into backcountry wildernesses like Ansel Adams, John Muir, Dinkey Lakes, Monarch and Kaiser. There are off-highway vehicle trails, reservoirs for sailing, water skiing and swimming. Sixty campgrounds, most of which require reservations, are family campsites that should be reserved well in advance of your trip.

Reserving Campsites in the Sierra National Forest

Campers are now able to reserve family and group campsites up to seven months in advance, with more choices for camping as well as easier access to the reservation system.

Although the Sierra National Forest has no visitor center, you can obtain information about campgrounds and recreational opportunities at the district's ranger stations. Reservations are usually required for June, July and August at Huntington, Kinkey Creek and Bass Lake.

For more information, contact the Forest Service, Sierra National Forest, in Clovis. ☎ 209-297-0706.

California State Parks provide recreational resources for more than a million children through formal school programs. The majority visit the Sierra Nevada. Yosemite National Park receives an average of 4½ million visitors a year, while Kings Canyon and Sequoia receive 1½ million. The **Call Home Corporation**, formerly MISTIX, now makes state park reservations. Write Destinet, 9450 Carroll Park Drive, San Diego, CA 92120, ☎ 800-444-2275.

Kings Canyon & Sequoia

Sequoia and Kings Canyon National Parks, where the High Sierra trail winds through a giant wilderness of silent forest, is a region of savage canyons and granite peaks. It seems almost incredible that this region is within a day's drive of Los Angeles or San Francisco. The backcountry of the parks, totaling 847,000 acres, is accessible only on foot. The parks are only 142 miles from Yosemite, or approximately four hours driving time by taking State Route 99 to Fresno and then turning east on State Route 180. It is 84 miles to Sequoia from Fresno.

The parks' canyons seem skeletal and cut to their geological quicks. Kings Canyon reaches a depth outside the park of about 8,200 feet from the level of the river up to Sanish Mountain's peak. There, downstream from the confluence of the Middle and South Forks of the Kings River, the canyon is without peer in North America. It is deeper than the Snake River's Hells Canyon in Idaho or the Grand Canyon in Arizona.

Kern Canyon in southern Sequoia National Park is 6,000 feet deep; several other canyons exceed 4,000 feet in depth. Sierra canyons show both stream-cut, V-shaped outlines and U-shaped profiles that are characteristic of glacial gouging. Both Generals Highway and King's Canyon Highway thread through these canyons. At roads end on Kings County

Highway, closed from about November 1 to May 1, you can stand on a flat, glacial valley and look at canyon walls rising nearly a mile above you.

Palisade Crest in Kings Canyon and the Mt. Whitney group in Sequoia each have six peaks more than 14,000 feet high. There is no road in this region of high peaks, so you have to hike or ride a horse. From roadside pullouts atop Moro Rock, the view is superb along the Generals Highway. From Panoramic Point near Grant Grove and from pullouts before Kings Canyon the surroundings are incredibly beautiful. Mineral King Valley provides superlative hiking to meadows, alpine lakes and Sierra peaks.

Camping Precautions

Campgrounds have drinking water (except for South Fork), tables, fire grills, garbage cans and either pit or flush toilets. Most camps have bear-proof food storage bins that you must use. Black bears are attracted to human food and they cause severe property damage trying to get it. If they do become aggressive, they must be killed by park rangers. Keep all food and anything with an odor in the metal boxes provided at campsites. Lodge guests should bring all items indoors. Keep your camp clean by depositing all garbage in bear-proof containers. If a bear approaches, scare it away by making loud noises and by throwing stones. Keep a safe distance or you could get mauled. Black bears are the only kind of bears in these parks.

Sequoia can be reached by way of Highway 198. Vehicle access to Kings Canyon is via Highway 180. The Generals Highway connects both, so you can make a big loop through the parks. Between Potwisha and Giant Forest Village in Sequoia, travel is not recommended for trailers more than 22 feet long. Highway 180 provides easier access for longer vehicles. There is no road connecting the parks with 395 on the eastern slope. Public transportation is limited to tour companies outside the parks. Air, bus, Amtrak and rental cars are available in the nearby cities of Fresno and Merced. Lodgepole, Atwell Mill and Grant Grove campgrounds are near the sequoias. There's year-round camping in some areas, and sites are on a first-come, first-served basis except for Lodgepole. For summer reservations ☎ 209-561-1314. Group campsites, available only in summer, are reserved by writing to the parks from June 14 through September 14. You can camp for only 14 days or a total of 30 days for the year.

Emergencies

Do not feed park animals for their protection and yours. Small animals should not be touched because they may have fleas or ticks and may carry plague. The parks can be dangerous. If you get hurt, seek help from a visitors center where rangers are trained in first aid. In an emergency, call 911 from any park phone. No coins are needed.

Hiking Trails

Trail hikes are available in all areas. For extended day-hikes and backpacking use trail maps. Motorbikes, mountain bikes and pets are not permitted on park trails. Horses, burros, and llamas are allowed. Wilderness permits are required for all overnight trips. You can reserve them by mail or fax only, postmarked each year no earlier than March 1 and at least 21 days in advance of your trip. Some first-come, first-served permits are available after 1 PM the day before departure. Specific information about regulations for trails and forage areas can be obtained at ☎ 209-565-3708.

Visitor Centers

Generals Highway

Along the Generals Highway, Lodgepole's Visitor Center is an excellent place to begin your visit. Exhibits and audio-visual programs describe Sierra Nevada and sequoia history. Rangers are on duty to answer questions, and books and maps are available for purchase. It is located 4½ miles north of Giant Forest Village.

- The *Sequoia Bark*, a free newspaper, gives current park information, schedules of naturalist programs, and a list of facilities.
- Information is available in German, Spanish, French and Japanese at visitor centers.
- For park information, ☎ 209-565-3134.
- For 24-hour recorded road and weather information, updated at 1 AM daily, ☎ 209-565-3351, and for backcountry information, ☎ 209-565-3708.
- Lodging, food and gasoline are available from concessionaires in several park areas.
- For lodging reservations, ☎ 209-561-3314.
- Only Lodgepole Campground in Sequoia accepts reservations, and then only from mid-May to mid-October. Reservations are available through Destinet, ☎ 800-444-2275.

- There's a $10 entrance fee for vehicles, or $3 per person on a bus, on foot, bicycle or motorcycle, that is good for seven days. As noted before, there are reduced rates at all parks for senior citizens and those permanently disabled.

Grant Grove

Grant Grove, in Kings National Park, has an easily accessible group of giant sequoias, plus small waterfalls, miles of quiet trails and glorious vistas. Originally it was called General Grant National Park. It was created in 1890 to protect these sequoias from the lumbermen's axes. Loggers were already at work in nearby Big Stump Basin.

The Grant Grove Visitor Center is the place to begin your visit. Exhibits explain the natural and human history of the region. A 10-minute slide program is shown every 30 minutes. Rangers are on duty to answer questions, and maps and books can be purchased.

The General Grant Tree

The General Grant Tree is the third-largest living tree in the world and the nation's Christmas tree. It is a national shrine and the only living memorial to Americans who gave their lives for freedom. The trail to the tree is wheelchair accessible, and about a third of a mile in length. It begins a mile northwest of the visitor center and includes the historic Gamblin Cabin and the Fallen Monarch.

Converse Basin

Early in this century, virtually every mature sequoia was cut down in Converse Basin, once the largest grove of giant sequoias. The Boole Tree was spared, along with a few others that lumbermen found too difficult to reach. The oldest known sequoia is the Muir Snag, which is located here. It was well over 3,000 years old when it died. John Muir was the first to discover it. You can reach the basin by graded dirt road off Highway 180, six miles north of Grant Grove. The visitor's center there has a map of the area.

Getting Here & Getting Around
Airlines, Bus & Rail Service

Major airlines, bus lines and car rental agencies serve Fresno and Visalia. Amtrak serves Hanford, with bus connections to Visalia and Fresno. Shuttle buses serve Giant Forest, Lodgepole, Moro Rock and Crescent Meadow.

Sequoia & Kings Canyon National Parks

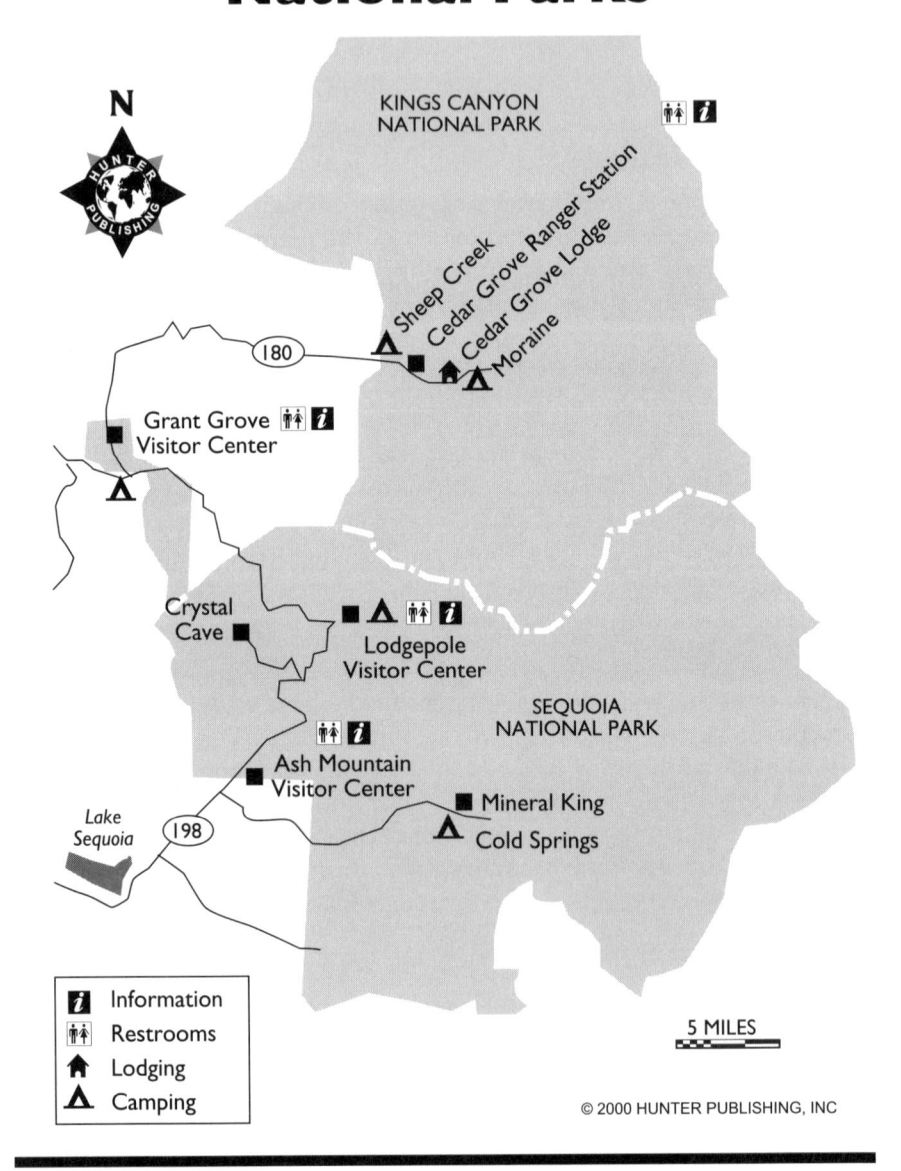

Driving Conditions

Park roads are steep, narrow and winding. Downshifting helps to prevent a burned out transmission when going uphill and burned out brakes going downhill. When you stop to look at scenery, use one of the safe turnouts. Slow-moving vehicles must pull over to let others pass. Motorcyclists should avoid the oil buildup in the center of uphill lanes. By all means, use seat belts. That's the law in California.

Trailers

Trailers are permitted at most campgrounds, although many sites are not suitable for them as recreational vehicles. A limited number of campsites can accommodate vehicles or trailers over 30 feet long. No hookups are available at any park campgrounds. There are sanitary disposal stations year-round in Potwisha and Grant Grove, but they are available only in summer at Dorst, Lodgepole and Cedar Grove.

Vehicle Lengths

On the Generals Highway between Potwisha Campground and Giant Forest Village, a limit of 22 feet of vehicle length is advised. The absolute length is 40 feet for single vehicles, 35 feet for trailers. Combination vehicles may not exceed 50 feet. The width limit for all vehicles is eight feet. The Generals Highway from Potwisha to Giant Forest is extremely narrow, winding and steep. Vehicles over 22 feet long should use Highway 180 from Fresno, or camp in the foothills and use a smaller car to reach the Giant Forest.

Steep Grades

On steep grades of 5-8%, in hot weather and heavy traffic, your brakes may overheat. Use a low gear for downhill travel. While driving uphill, turn off your air conditioner so as not to overheat your engine.

Winter Driving

In winter, chains may be required at any time. Entry roads are kept open to Grant Grove and to Giant Forest-Lodgepole, but they may be closed temporarily for plowing. The Central Highway between Lodgepole and Grant Grove is kept open as conditions permit. It is usually closed during and after a heavy storm. The Foothill, Lodgepole and Grant Grove Visitor Centers are always open. For further information, write the Superintendent, Sequoia and Kings Canyon National Parks, Three Rivers, CA 93271-9700, or ☎ 209-565-3134.

Other Hazards

There are rattlesnakes in the parks. Watch where you're stepping or reaching. Rivers, streams and waterfalls are treacherous at all times, but especially when water levels are high in spring and early summer. Be alert for undermined banks and slippery rocks. Fast currents and cold water are a deadly combination. Do not swim above waterfalls or in swift water. Never let your children out of your sight.

If you drink surface water in the parks, boil it for at least three minutes. The water contains *Giardia lamblia*, a protozoan that is a parasite often harmful to man and beast.

Ticks

If you camp or hike in the foothills, check your clothes frequently for ticks. They can carry Lyme disease. Talk to the ranger or the nearest visitor center to see how to remove them if you've been bitten. Once you're infected, Lyme disease can be cured only by antibiotics.

Cougars

Although sightings are very rare, if you encounter a cougar, do not run or crouch down. Stand your ground or back away slowly. Wave, shout and throw stones.

Weather

When a thunderstorm threatens, get inside a vehicle or large building. Do not stand under a natural lightning rod such as a tree by itself. Avoid open meadows and high places such as Moro Rock. Stay away from bodies of water. If you feel your hair stand on end during a thunderstorm, drop to your knees and bend forward, putting your hands on your knees. Do not lie flat on the ground.

The Earth's Largest Living Thing

In volume of total wood, the giant sequoia stands alone as the earth's largest living thing. Its nearly conical trunk – like a club, not a walking stick – has a majestic look. Only one other tree species lives longer, and only one other has a greater diameter. Three others grow taller, but none is larger. Sequoias grow naturally on the west slope of the Sierra Nevada, usually at altitudes of 5,000 to 7,000 feet. There are 75 groves in all.

The world's largest remaining sequoia groves are at Redwood Mountain in Kings Canyon and at Giant Forest in Sequoia National Park. Redwood Mountain's grove covers 3,100 acres and has 15,800 sequoia trees more than a foot in diameter at the base. Giant Forest covers 1,800 acres and has 8,400 such trees. About 36,500 acres of sequoia groves remain in the Sierra Nevada, mostly under federal or state protection.

John Muir was one of the first white travelers to see the big trees. He said, "Most of the Sierra trees die of disease, fungi, etc., but nothing hurts the Big Tree." That's only partially correct.

Chemicals in the wood and bark provide resistance to insects and fungi, but the sequoia does topple over because it has a shallow root system and no tap root. Soil moisture, root damage and strong winds contribute to the trees' demise. When early lumber barons proposed cutting the trees, Muir objected. "As well sell the rain clouds and the snow and the rivers to be cut up and carried away, if that were possible."

The **General Sherman Tree** stands 275 feet high, weighs 1,385 tons and is 103 feet in circumference. Two miles north of Grant Grove Village, it is at least 3,500 years old. It began as a tiny, winged seed no larger than a flake of oatmeal, and grew into a seedling about the time of the Exodus of the Jews from Egypt in 1240 BC. Each year the General Sherman adds enough wood growth to make a 60-foot-tall tree of conventional proportions.

Giant sequoias do not die of old age. They are resistant to fire and insect damage. These trees sprout only from seeds produced by chicken egg-sized cones; a tree produces an average of 2,000 cones. Cones hang on the tree green and closed for 20 years. Once they open, about 500,000 seeds are dispersed. Douglas squirrels or the larvae of a tiny cone-bearing beetle may cause the cones to open, but fire is the key agent in dispersting the seeds. It causes the cones to dry, open and drop the seeds. Fires also consume logs and branches that have accumulated on the forest floor. Their ashes fertilize the seeds and help them survive in the earth.

Moro Rock - Crescent Meadow Road

The Moro Rock-Crescent Meadow Road begins at the village and explores the southwest portions of the Giant Forest. Three miles long, it completes its route at a dead end. It is not recommended for trailers or RVs. The road is closed in winter to vehicular traffic, but can be used as a ski trail.

For the following sights allow one to two hours. You can drive your car to the top of **Auto Log**, a fallen giant sequoia about .9 mile from the village.

Adventures on Foot

In general, park roads do not go above 7,800 feet. Those who would like to experience the alpine countryside – and you should do so if at all possible – must hike or go by horseback. Above 9,000 feet the harsh climate cannot support tall trees or dense forests. There are no trees above 11,000 feet, only boulders and gravel around small alpine lakes. Low-growing shrubs are scattered here and there in the meadows. Sparkling mountain lakes are numerous, some in small bowls, called cirques, carved by glaciers.

For years the streams and lakes have been stocked with fish that are not native to the region. They include brown, golden and cutthroat trout and "Little Kern" golden trout. The latter are native to the Sierra's west slope.

The **Congress Trail** is a two-mile walk on a loop trail through the heart of the sequoia forest, starting at the Sherman Tree. If you have only limited time, be sure to include the trail. You should allow one to two hours.

The trail for "**All People/Round Meadow**" is accessible to the handicapped. It forms a two-thirds of a mile circle around this meadow that is surrounded by sequoia trees. This is a good place for wildflowers during summer. Forest and meadow life are described on trail signs along the way. It is adjacent to Giant Forest Lodge, about a quarter of a mile from the village.

Hazelwood Nature Trail is a one-mile loop that features information about the sequoias and man's impact upon them. It begins across the highway from the Giant Forest Lodge's Registration Office.

Moro Rock is a granite dome with a steep quarter-mile staircase to the summit. There are spectacular views of the Great Western Divide and the western half of Sequoia National Park. It is two miles from the village. The Parker Group is a well-known group of sequoias 2.6 miles from the village. It is particularly photogenic for camera buffs. The Tunnel Log is a fallen sequoia that has a tunnel through it for automobile passage. Larger vehicles have a bypass. It is 2.7 miles from the village. Crescent Meadow is 100 yards from the end of Crescent Meadow Road and three miles from the village. John Muir was especially enamored of the area because of the wildflower show in midsummer. These are fragile areas, so stay on designated trails. Walk only on fallen logs for access into the meadows. This is a popular hiking and picnicking area. Many trails start here, including the one-mile Tharp's Log. This area was the summer home of the first settler in Giant Forest. The **High Sierra Trail** begins here and travels 71 miles to the summit of Mt. Whitney.

It will be worth your while to take time to explore the Giant Forest on foot. There are more than 40 miles of foot trails that lead to every part of the grove. For information, ask any park ranger or purchase the $1 map of the Giant Forest.

The **Tokopah Falls Trail** is 1.7 miles in length, running along the Marble Fork of the Kaweah River. It dead ends below the impressive granite cliffs and waterfall at Tokopah Canyon. The trail starts in Lodgpole Campground, 4½ miles north of the village. It will take you 2½ to four hours to complete.

The **Big Stump Trail** is a one-mile loop through a regenerating sequoia forest with the huge sequoia stumps remaining from Smith Comstock's lumbering operation. Now a shrubland and meadow, it is filled with joyous birds and lovely wildflowers. There's an alternate trail that leads across the highway and past the Sawed Tree. This sequoia was cut most of the way through a century ago but stubbornly clings to life. It is located 2½ miles southeast of Highway 180.

You'll appreciate the High Sierra if you stop at **Panorama Point**. You'll see from Mt. Goddard in northern Kings Canyon to Eagle Scout Peak in Sequoia Park. Mt. Whitney is not visible from here because of the height of the Great Western Divide. To reach the point, follow the road east through the visitor center's parking lot, curve to the left around the meadow, then bear right at the intersection where a sign directs you to Panorama Point – 2.3 miles. Trailers and RVs are not recommended because the road is steep and narrow. The viewpoint is a quarter-mile walk from the parking lot. The four-mile Park Ridge Trail begins here.

The **North Grove Loop** is a lightly traveled 1½-mile stretch that gives a closer look at the big trees. You can enjoy a quiet walk past meadows and creeks, through mixed conifer and sequoia forest. The trailhead is at the Grant Tree parking lot, one mile northwest of the visitor center.

The **Sequoia Lake Overlook/Dead Giant Loop** provides a picturesque view of a historic mill pond. The 1½-mile round trip begins at the lower end of the Grant Tree parking area. Follow the old road about a mile until it branches off.

To reach the **Buena Vista Peak**, you start just south of the Kings Canyon Overlook on the Generals Highway, six miles southeast of Grant Grove. Your view from this granite peak is a full 360°, showing the sequoias in Redwood Canyon, and as far as the eye can see across the High Sierra. The round-trip takes two hours.

Redwood Canyon

Miles of trails wind through Redwood Canyon, the world's largest grove of sequoias. Short walks, day hikes and overnight backpacking trips will take you through a sequoia-mixed conifer forest, meadow and shrubland. There are cascades and pools along Redwood Creek. Acres of new sequoia growth are visible due to fires purposely set during the last 25 years to reduce the undergrowth. It has long been known that fire is a critical factor for the health and vigor of sequoia forests. The trailhead is at Redwood Saddle, eight miles north and east of Grant Grove. Be forewarned that two miles of this drive is on a bumpy dirt road.

Crystal Cave

During the summer months, approximately June through October, guided tours of Crystal Cave are offered by the Sequoia Natural History Association. The tours operate from mid-May through late September, depending upon the weather. Tickets must be purchased at least 1½ hours in advance at the Lodgepole or Foothill Visitor Centers. Please note that tickets are not sold at the cave. The charge for adults is $4, children and Golden Age Passport holders get in for half-price. Tours are scheduled from 10-3 from mid-May to early June. They take place Friday through Monday on the hour. From early June to Labor Day, they are held daily on the half hour. From Labor Day to late September, tours on Friday through Monday are on the hour. No buses, trailers or vehicles over 20 feet long are allowed on Crystal Cave Road.

Adventures on Water
Hume Lake

Hume Lake, built as a mill pond, supplied water for a flume that floated rough-cut sequoias to the planing mill at Sanger, 54 miles below. The lake is in Sequoia National Forest and offers fishing, swimming, boat rentals at Hume Lake Christian Camps and a Forest Service Campground during the summer. Gasoline, groceries and a small laundry are available. It is located eight miles north of Grant Grove on Highway 180 and then another three miles south on Hume Lake Road.

Campgrounds in Sequoia & Kings Canyon

In the parks there are more than 1,000 sites at 14 campgrounds, ranging in elevation from 2,100 to 7,500 feet. From June 14 to September 14 your stay at a camp is limited to 14 days, or a total of 30 days for the year. All campgrounds permit a maximum of one vehicle and six people. Parking is available nearby for extra vehicles.

Trailers and RVs are permitted at Potwisha, Dorst, Grant Grove, Cedar Grove and parts of Lodgepole Campgrounds. Each campground has a sanitary disposal station, but there are no trailer hookups.

For reservations at **Stony Creek, Grant Grove** and **Cedar Grove**, write or call Guest Services, PO Box 789, Three Rivers, CA 93271. ☎ 209-561-3314.

Lodgepole, Stony Creek, Grant Grove and **Cedar Grove** concessionaires provide meals, groceries, camping gear, fishing tackle/licenses, ice and other necessities.

There are service stations in some areas. The one at **Lodgepole** can supply you with gasoline, diesel, propane and limited mechanical service. **Grant Grove** has gasoline, propane and limited mechanical service. **Cedar Grove** has only gasoline available.

There are pay showers and laundromats at Lodgepole, Stoney Creek and Cedar Grove. Grant Grove has only showers, and it is open only for limited hours. Drought conditions may effect their availability.

Horse stables are available at **Cedar Grove Peak Station**, PO Box 295, Three Rivers, CA 93271, ☎ 209-565-3464; **Mineral King Pack Station**, PO Box 61, Three Rivers, CA 93271, ☎ 209-561-3404; **Wolverton Pack Station**, PO Box 641, Wood Lake, CA 93286, ☎ 209-565-3445; and **Grant Grove Stables**, PO Box 295, Three Rivers, CA 93271, ☎ 209-565-3464.

There are **post offices** at Lodgepole and Grant Grove. They provide daily service except on Sunday. Visitors' mail should be addressed: c/o General Delivery, Sequoia National Park, CA 93262 at Lodgepole; or General Delivery, Kings Canyon National Park, CA 93633 at Grant Grove.

Campground Regulations

There are strict regulations governing campgrounds. Do not cut limbs from trees. Use only dead and downed wood. You might consider bringing wood from home or purchasing it at a market to assure yourself of an adequate supply. Before you leave your campsite make certain your fires are completely out.

In deference to others and to comply with regulations, observe the quiet hours from 10 PM to 6 AM. Use generators from 9 AM to 9 PM only. Music should be audible only in your campsite.

You may not reserve campsites in campgrounds that have a policy of first-come, first-served. You also may not hold a site for someone who has not yet arrived. Sites not occupied for 24 hours are considered abandoned and your property is impounded.

All food must be stored in metal, bear-proof boxes. Most boxes are 2 x 2 x 4 feet. Do not bring coolers that won't fit in the boxes. Be neat and deposit all garbage in bear-proof containers.

You must never use soap in rivers, and digging, trenching or leveling ground is not permitted.

Sequoia Campgrounds

Lodgepole has 250 sites, four miles north of Giant Forest Village, at an elevation of 6,700 feet. During the reservation season the cost is $14 a night; it's $2 dollars less at other times. There's no fee in winter. Facilities are limited. Flush toilets, a telephone, laundromat and service station are available. From mid-May through September there are pay showers, a market, a delicatessen, a gift shop, an amphitheater, a nature center and a sanitary disposal station. You are limited to one vehicle with six people and a single vehicle of 35 feet. Reservations at Lodgepole are available only eight weeks in advance for mid-May through mid-October.

There are 218 sites at **Dorst**, located 12 miles north of Grant Forest Village at an elevation of 6,800 feet. The charge is $12 per night from Memorial Day to Labor Day, when the campground closes. There are flush toilets, a phone, amphitheater and a sanitary disposal station. Only one vehicle and six people can occupy a site.

In Foothills area, **Potwisha** has 44 sites on Generals Highway, four miles from Ash Mountain's entrance at Highway 198, at an elevation of 2,800 feet. It is open from mid-April until mid-September. You are limited to one vehicle and six people per site. No trailers or recreational vehicles are permitted.

South Fork, 13 miles from Highway 198 on South Fork Drive, has 13 sites at 3,600 feet. Part of this road is unpaved. Open from mid-May through October, the site's fee is $6, but there is no fee in winter. There is no drinking water and only pit toilets are provided. South Fork is limited to one vehicle and six people per site. It is not recommended for trailers or RVs.

Atwill Mill in the Mineral King area has 21 sites and another 40 at Cold Springs. They are located 20-25 miles up Mineral King Road from Highway 198. This is a very steep, winding road and RVs are not recommended. Trailers are not permitted in these campgrounds. The campgrounds are at elevations of 6,650 and 7,500 feet and open from Memorial Day through September, weather permitting, for $6 a night. After that the water is turned off and no fee is charged. The campgrounds and the road are closed from mid-November to spring, but even then they are governed by the weather. There are pit toilets, phones, and an amphitheater at the ranger station. The camps are limited to one vehicle and six people per site.

The **Kings Canyon National Park campsites** are located in two areas. At **Grant Grove**, there are three campgrounds. They include **Azalea**, with 114 sites; **Sunset**, with 119 sites; and **Crystal Springs**, with 66 sites. They are located three miles from the big Stump entrance on Highway 180, at an elevation of 6,500 feet. Each site costs $12 per night and limits are one vehicle and six people. Azalea is open year-round, Sunset from Memorial Day to mid-September, and Crystal Springs from mid-May to late September. They provide flush toilets, phones, a market, a service station, cabins, a restaurant, pay showers, an amphitheater at Sunset and a sanitary disposal station at Azalea.

In the **Cedar Grove** area there are four sites 32 miles east of **Grant Grove** on Highway 180, at an elevation of 3,500 feet. **Sentinel** has 83 sites, **Moraine** 120, **Sheep Creek** 111 sites and **Canyon View** 37 sites. The fee is $12 per night. The campgrounds and the road are closed from late October to early May. They open at varying times, with Moraine and Sentinel opened as they are needed. You are limited to one vehicle and six people per site. There are flush toilets, a phone and a sanitary disposal station. From mid-May through September there is a market, a motel, a fast-food restaurant, pay showers, laundromat, a service station and an amphitheater at the ranger's station.

Park Information Sources

For additional information about Sequoia and Kings Canyon, write the park's **Guest Services**, Box 789, Sequoia National Park, Three Rivers, CA 93271. ☎ 209-561-3314. The **Sequoia Regional Visitor Council** is also helpful. They are at 4125 W. Mineral King, Suite 104, Visalia, CA 93277. ☎ 209-733-6284.

Fresno

Upon completion of your tour of the parks, take 180 to Fresno, where you can drive to Sacramento on Highway 99 north or take 120 from Manteca until it joins Interstate 205, which becomes 580. This is the fastest route to San Francisco. If you're traveling south to Los Angeles, take 198 to Visalia and pick up 99 and, a few miles west of there, Interstate 5. From Bakersfield it is 235 miles to Los Angeles.

What to See & Do in Fresno

Sure you're in a hurry to get into the mountains, so to you Fresno might be little more than a place to gas up the truck and grab a sandwich. But it has more to offer the weary traveler than just fuel and food. For instance, more turkeys are raised in the Fresno area than any other place in the US.

Kearney Mansion Museum, 7160 West Kearney Boulevard, ☎ 559-233-8007, boasts original furnishings and wallcoverings from the early days of California. The **Fresno Art Museum**, 2233 North First Street, ☎ 559-441-4221, offers changing exhibits of national and international artists in eight galleries. The **Fresno Museum of Art, History and Science**, 1555 Van Ness Avenue, ☎ 559-441-1444, features the Salzer collection of European and American still-life paintings, a collection of Asian art and regional and hands-on exhibits.

Roeding Park, off US 99 at the Olive Avenue or Belmont Avenue exits, features recreational facilities, a kids playland, the historic Fort Miller blockhouse and the Japanese-American War Memorial. Nearby is **Chaffee Zoological Gardens**, ☎ 559-498-2671, which houses reptiles and South American plants and animals in a rain forest setting. **Wild Wa-**

ter **Adventures,** 11413 East Shaw Avenue, ☎ 559-299-9452, is the perfect spot for those hot summer days. This water park features 20 rides, including slides and a wave pool.

Adventures on Foot

Trails lead into **Kaiser Wilderness** and its spectacular backcountry from Huntington Lake. Trailheads are located along the north shore of the lake. Take CA 168 north from Fresno past Shaver Lake and continue north to the reservoir.

There are six campgrounds and the **D&F Pack Station** on the northeastern end of the lake. Trails lead in all directions from the pack station. **Kaiser Loop Trail** heads north toward Kaiser Peak. The first 4.5-mile section gains more than 3,100 feet on the way up to the summit at 10,200 feet. The views of the Silver Divide are spectacular and below the ridge it's a short walk to **Bobby, Bonnie** and **Line Creek lakes**. Hike west from the summit along the ridgeline 3.4 miles to a trail junction. Turn left, cross a stream and descend steeply to another intersection at Mary's Meadow and follow a creek two miles to another junction. Turn left and walk back to D&F Pack Station to complete the 15-mile loop.

Back at the junction where you left the ridge and turned left, you can opt to turn right and continue north, dropping quickly toward a dirt road four miles away.

By heading east from D&F Pack Station 1.8 miles, you'll come to a fork on Potter Creek. Take the right fork and climb away from Potter Creek 1.7 miles to a junction with the **California Riding & Hiking Trail**. Turn left and head over Potter Pass to **Round Meadow**, five miles from the trailhead, where you'll find paths going west to **Lower** and **Upper Twin lakes** and **George Lake**. Continue north across a road at Sample Meadow and on to Portuguese Flat, 12 miles from the trailhead. From here you can hike west to **Crater Lake Meadow** and a dirt road that leads to **Hoffman Meadow**; hike north into **Tule Meadow** and a maze of trails and paths leading all the way to **Rock Creek Lake, Margaret Lake** and beyond; or hike east along **Rattlesnake Creek Trail** back to Portal Forebay campground on paved Kaiser Pass Road.

Just west of the Kings Canyon National Park boundary, trails lead into the western portion of the John Muir Wilderness. **Woodchuck Lakes Trail** begins at Wishon Reservoir, near the end of Dinkey Creek Road east of CA 168 at Shaver Lake. The footpath undulates six miles to the first junction. Head north one mile to another intersection. Turn right and climb toward Crown Pass and **Halfmoon Lake**, 16 miles from the trailhead. You can also turn left and make a short loop around **Woodchuck Lake** and end up on the main trail.

In the Sierra foothills northeast of Fresno, the **San Joaquin River Trail** system is a combination of old trails, such as the French and Mammoth Trails, and new trails to be constructed on Sierra National Forest land. The trail system will run from **Millerton Lake**, near sea level, to join the Pacific Crest Trail in the High Sierra near Devil's Postpile National Monument. Covering a distance of 73 miles, the trail climbs Granite Stairway at more than 9,000 feet above sea level. The San Joaquin River Trail is being built for hikers and equestrians by volunteers with the cooperation of the Sierra National Forest, Bureau of Land Management, California Department of Parks and Recreation, Nature Conservancy and private land owners.

Adventures on Wheels

Bass Lake, just east of the town of Oakhurst, is the trailhead for a number of exhilarating mountain bike rides. **Goat Mountain Trail** offers a 10-mile loop ride that begins at Forks campground on the west shore of Bass Lake. Although the trail is well-kept, there are the occasional rock steps and blown-down trees that will require you to dismount. Start off by switchbacking up Goat Mountain on a moderately steep and rocky trail. At the three-mile mark you hit an intersection with a dirt path that descends to another Bass Lake campground. Proceed up Goat Mountain Trail for another mile to a dirt road and turn left. Follow the road for about 1.5 miles to the top of Goat Mountain. Retrace your tire tracks to the Goat Mountain Trail and descend until reaching the above mentioned dirt path. Turn right here and drop three miles to the campground, where you turn left and pedal one mile back to Forks campground to complete the loop.

At **Millerton Lake** just east of Fresno, try a moderate ride on the **Millerton Madera Trail**. The ride begins near the park entrance on the west side of the lake and winds four miles one way adjacent to the paved lake access road before dead-ending. On the east side of the lake. Just east of Shaver Lake off CA 168, try the **Tour de Granite**, an 8.5-mile figure-eight loop ride. The ride begins on the north side of Dinkey Creek Road and utilizes a four-wheel drive road for part of the trip.

A more difficult 13-mile loop covers **007 Trail**, which begins near Bass Lake Dam. Take Malum Ridge Road to signed Central Camp Road. The trail starts on the left side of the road. For more information on cycling in the area, contact **Oakhurst Cycling Center**, ☎ 209-642-4606.

Sequoia National Forest is also a haven for mountain bikers. Singletrack and fire roads wind through the forests, getting riders up close and personal with giant sequoias. There are plenty of old logging roads waiting to be explored near **Hume Lake**, just off Hume Road northeast of Kings Canyon National Park's Grant Grove area. From the eastern end of Hume Lake, you can head out from Sandy Cove and pedal on pavement for .25 mile to a dirt road on the right near the dam. This is road 13S06, which you follow for about half a mile across Tornado Creek to a junction. Stay left and continue as far as possible (the trail becomes narrow and overgrown). Back at the Tornado Creek intersection, you can turn south into a labyrinth of doubletrack dirt roads that seem to run in all directions, enabling an entire day of exploring.

Off CA 180 north of The Wye entrance to **Kings Canyon National Park**, you can ride to what is probably California's most famous tree stump. Take CA 180 to Cherry Gap and park your vehicle. Follow the dirt road on the west side of the highway, noting the signs pointing to the **Chicago Tree**. The tree is actually a stump, what's left of a giant sequoia that was cut and sent to the Chicago World's Fair. Just past the stump, turn right on to road 13S65 and drop into a forest of redwoods toward Converse Creek and continue straight at each junction. Climb out of the Converse Creek drainage and continue east and then south to return to CA 180, about one mile north of where you started. On this loop you'll pass a spur trail leading to the **Boole Tree**. This route is closed to bikes. If you don't want to ride back on CA 180, you can turn south on road 13S99 just before reaching the highway. You'll pass a cabin and make a difficult ascent on the way back to Cherry Gap.

On the east side of CA 180 you can embark on another moderate loop ride following the **Cherry Gap cross-country skiing route**. Take road 13S77 east for a mile to the top of a ridge and continue east across a clearing, pedal through a series of climbs and dips, then drop steeply down the ridgeline. At a large clearing, you'll reach a four-way junction. Continue straight ahead on a dirt road and begin ascending the ridge. This doubletrack will turn north and then west and hit paved Hume Road (13S09). Turn left and ride until you spot a dirt road, 13S48, on the left. This climbs back to Cherry Gap.

Adventures on Water
Kings River

Beginning near Kings Canyon and Sequoia national parks, the Kings River is the longest water course in the area, and one of the few rivers in the western Sierra that remains undammed and untamed. Rafters are attracted to the Kings for its unique mixture of whitewater that doesn't present the tremendous technical skills of the Tuolumne or Merced rivers. The Kings is fit for both the novice river rat and the expert rafter. During heavy spring runoff, the Kings is perhaps the most powerful, and dangerous, river in the state. Waves can reach 10 feet and up and wetsuits are not an option but a requirement.

Late in the season – which usually lasts from mid-April through mid-July – when the water level drops, the Kings is well-suited for families.

The 10-mile run on the Upper Kings River through Garnet Dike to Kirch Flat campground is probably the most popular run. The put-in is about 63 miles east of Fresno via Belmont Avenue eastbound toward Pine Flat Reservoir.

Mammoth Pool Reservoir

Mammoth Pool Reservoir, pooling five miles long and half a mile wide behind a dam on the San Joaquin River, is 90 miles northeast of Fresno. You can enjoy fishing for rainbow, eastern brook and German brown trout. Boating, swimming and hiking along the **French Trail** are also popular pursuits. The trail was first surveyed and built in 1880 by John French, a mining promoter from San Francisco who was developing mines in the Mammoth area. His trail, starting at Ross's Ranch and ending due south of Devil's Postpile, is being incorporated into the San Joaquin River Trail.

Mammoth Pool is closed to the public from May 1 until June 16 to allow migrating deer to swim across the reservoir. Yes, you read that right: migrating deer. Fishing is prohibited in the lake and 300 feet above the high water mark in all tributaries. Roads accessing Mammoth Pool are closed at Mammoth Pool Campground and the Chiquito Creek bridge. The access roads are also closed in winter.

Tule River

Outdoor recreation is plentiful in the Tule River country in this little-traveled region of the Sierra Nevada. You can stick to main roads or travel on almost deserted back roads.

From there you can backpack into the Sierra Nevada. Pack animals are available to rent from three stations in the mountains. For information on horse packing and horseback riding, contact Sequoia National Forest, 900 West Grand Avenue, Porterville CA 93257, ☎ 559-784-1500.

The north and middle forks of the Tule River converge in Springville, south of Sequoia, on State Route 190. The closest campground is only five miles east of Coffee Camp. This is a popular spot for swimming, fishing and picnicking.

Tule River Region

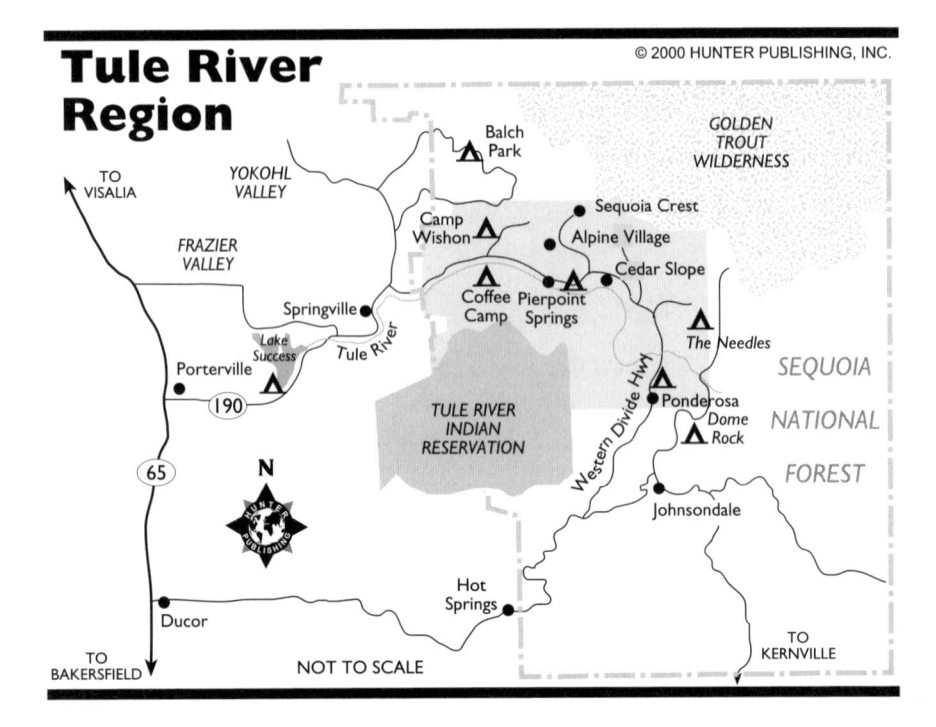

Only a few miles to the west lies Lake Success, a large man-made reservoir where all kinds of water sports are enjoyed. Over 100 developed campsites are available, along with boat rentals and other activities.

Local campsites provide an easy way for families to enjoy the region. Some campsites are only partially completed, but most are fully improved.

Almost 100 campsites in seven campgrounds are available for free use in **Mountain Home Demonstration State Forest**, and there are another 80 campsites in **Balch Park** for a small fee. At an elevation of 5,400-6,400 feet, this area is open from May to November, as snow conditions permit.

Several streams and ponds offer fishing for native rainbow, brown and brook trout. Hunters can find whitetail deer, black bear, squirrels, quail and grouse. Hikers can enjoy moderately easy to difficult nature trails among the giant sequoias and marvel at the wondrous tub-shaped rock formations that collect rainwater following storms.

A pack station is located here, and several trails lead to wilderness areas. The **Upper Tule Recreation Area** is high in the Southern Sierra mountains with dozens of streams that are unsurpassed for brown and golden trout fishing. Most are easily accessible by car. Trails are well marked and there are many of them. Hikers often start here and walk to Lake Tahoe or Mt. Whitney. Pack horses can be rented by the hour, day or week.

There are squirrel, raccoon, deer and bear in abundance, and successful hunters return year after year.

Those who prefer to hunt with a camera will find the flora, fauna, the majestic peaks, waterfalls, streams, lakes and general geography a wonderful opportunity.

Highway 190, and most paved roads, have a good snow removal program, so you need not confine your trips to summer.

This area is ideal for snowmobiling, cross-country skiing and snowshoeing. The trails are well marked, flat and wide, and make even the novice comfortable.

There are more than 1,000 parcels of private property here if you wish to buy your own vacation retreat or full-time home. Many older people have chosen the area for retirement.

> *Visitor permits are easily acquired from the US Forest Service's Tule River District Headquarters at Springville.*

Adventures on Snow

Sierra Summit Mountain Resort, 65 miles northeast of Fresno on CA 168, offers all types of skiers and snowboarders a fine mid-sized mountain experience. The resort boasts 400 acres of skiable terrain with runs up to 2.25 miles long. There are three double chairs, two triple chairs, a T-bar and two beginner tows. New skiers can obtain lift tickets, lessons and rentals at substantial discounts. Sierra Summit also features a full-service ski school and rental shop. The entire mountain is open to snowboarders, with a terrain garden, special lessons and rentals available. For flatlanders, there are plenty of marked cross-country skiing and snowmobiling trails nearby. For more information, call ☎ 209-233-2500.

The US Forest Service also maintains cross-country skiing trails along CA 168 that range from one-mile jaunts to six-mile gut-busters. For details, call the **Sierra National Forest Pineridge Station**, ☎ 209-855-5355.

Where to Stay in Fresno

There are four Best Western motels in Fresno. The three best are the **Tradewinds Motor Inn**, 3½ miles northwest of State Route 99 via the Clinton Avenue exit, at 2141 North Parkway Drive, 93705. Pets are acceptable for a $5 charge. $$. ☎ 209-237-1881. To reach the **Best Western Village Inn** ($$), drive north on State Route 99 and exit at State Route 41. The motel is almost three miles north via the Shields Avenue exit. Southbound traffic should take the Clinton Avenue exit. The hotel is at 3110 North Blackstone Avenue, 93703. ☎ 209-226-2110. The **Water Tree Inn** ($$) is about six miles north of town on State Route 41. Take the State Route 99 freeway exit to the Ashlan Avenue exit and go to 4141 North Blackstone Avenue, 93726. Pets are not allowed. ☎ 209-222-4445. The **Piccadilly Inn Airport** ($$) is five miles northwest of town. Take State Route 99's exit via McKinley, then go six miles east to 5115 McKinley, 93727. There's a dining room and coffee shop open from 6 AM to 10 PM, with meals at $7-15. ☎ 209-251-6000.

The **Piccadilly Inn-Shaw** ($$-$$$) is 5½ miles northwest of town, and three miles east of State Route 99. Take the Shaw Avenue exit to 2305 W. Shaw Avenue, 93711. No pets. Their restaurant is open from 6-2 and 5-10, with meals costing $10-20. It is rated very highly. The **Piccadilly Inn-University** ($$-$$$) is equally highly rated. It is 7½ miles northeast of Fresno, and east of State Route 41. Take the Shaw Avenue exit to 4961 North Cedar Avenue, 93726. No pets. There's a dining room, and coffee shop that is open from 6:30 AM to 10 PM, with meals priced $11-15. ☎ 209-224-4200. The **Ramada Inn** ($$) is located about five miles north on State Route 168. Take the Shaw Avenue freeway exit to 324 East Shaw Avenue, 93710. The dining room and coffee shop are open from 6:30 AM to 10:30 PM. ☎ 209-224-4040.

The **San Joaquin** is a suites motel 3½ miles east of State Route 99. Take the Shaw Avenue exit to 1309 W. Shaw Avenue, 93711. $$-$$$$. No pets. ☎ 209-225-1309. The **Sheraton Smuggler's Inn** is outstanding. $$-$$$. It is located about three miles north of Fresno on State Route 41. Go southbound on State Route 99 and take the Shaw Avenue exit. If northbound, take the Clinton Avenue exit to 3737 North Blackstone Avenue, 93726. No pets. The restaurant is open from 6:30-10:30 AM and 3-11 PM, with meals at $10-18. ☎ 209-226-2200. To reach the **Fresno Hilton Inn** ($$-$$$), take the southbound exit of Ventura Street on State Route 99, drive about one mile south to Van Ness Avenue, then four blocks north to 1055 Van Ness Avenue, 93721. If you're northbound on 99, take State Route 41 exit and drive to Van Ness Avenue. It will accept only small pets. There's a dining room and a coffee shop open from 6:30 AM to 10 PM, with meals for $10-18. ☎ 209-485-9000.

The **Holiday Inn Airport** ($$-$$$) is six miles east of State Route 99. Take the Clinton Avenue exit to 5090 E. Clinton Avenue, 93727. Pets are not permitted. Their restaurant is open from 6 AM to 10:30 PM, with meals priced at $8-18. ☎ 209-252-3611.

The **Holiday Inn-Center Plaza** is east of State Route 99 near the convention center. Northbound cars should take the exit marked State Route 41 and Van Ness Avenue. Southbound cars should take the Ventura Street exit to 2233 Ventura Street, 93709. Small pets only. $$-$$$. There's a restaurant and coffee shop, with meals priced at $8-19. They are open from 6 AM to 10 PM. ☎ 209-268-1000.

The **La Quinta Inn** is east of State Route 99. Southbound traffic should exit at Fresno Street, and northbound should use the State Route 41 exit. Drive north to 2926 Tulare Street, 93721. Small pets only. There's a nearby restaurant. $$. ☎ 209-442-1110.

The **Courtyard by Marriott** is a motor inn 4½ miles north on State Route 168. From State Route 99, take the Shaw Avenue-East exit to 140 E. Shaw Avenue, 93710. Pets are not allowed. The dining room is open from 5-10 AM and 6:30-10 PM weekdays; Saturday, 7-10 AM and 5-10 PM; Sunday, 7 AM-1 PM. $$-$$$. ☎ 559-221-6000.

Where to Dine in Fresno

Nicole's is four blocks west of State Route 41, off the Shields Avenue exit, located at 3075 N. Maroa Avenue. It is open from 11:30-4 and 5:30-10 week nights, but until 11:30 PM on weekends. Reservations are suggested. Dinners cost $11-20. ☎ 209-224-1660.

Don't miss **Veni, Vidi, Vici**, easily the most exciting restaurant in town from a gourmet's perspective. Located at 1116 North Fulton, the restaurant's menu is best described as Northern Californian. Sample dishes include roasted pork loin with Chinese black bean and citrus glaze or vegetarian moussaka. The ice cream is made on premises. Open for dinner Wednesday through Sunday. Entrées run $16-$20. ☎ 559-266-5510.

Bakersfield

What to See & Do

The old saw "Bakersfield isn't the end of the Earth, but you can see it from there" no longer applies. The city of more than 175,000 offers all the amenities and attractions of a modern burg and is second only to Fresno as a shipping, industrial and agricultural center in the San Joaquin Valley. The **California Living Museum**, about 3½ miles northwest of town at 14000 Alfred Harrell Highway, ☎ 805-872-2256, is a must-see for natural history buffs. There's a full spectrum of California flora and fauna, along with displays of fossils and minerals. The museum is open Tuesday through Sunday, 9 AM to 5 PM. Admission is $3.50 for adults. The **Kern County Museum**, 3801 Chester Avenue, ☎ 805-861-2132, is a huge complex that spans 56 different buildings, exhibiting everything from plants and animals to 19th century housewares. There is also a hands-on children's museum. The museum is open 8 AM to 5 PM, Monday through Saturday, 10 AM to 5 PM, Sunday, excepting Thanksgiving, December 24-25 and January 1. Admission is $5 for adults.

Where to Stay in Bakersfield

Bakersfield South-Travelodge is a good value. $-$$. It is adjacent to State Route 99, a half-mile northwest of the White Lane exit, at 3620 White Lane Road, 93309. Pets are not permitted. There's a coffee shop nearby. ☎ 800-367-2250.

There are three Best Westerns. **Hill House** offers the best value. $$. It is two miles east of State Route 99, using the California Avenue exit to Chester Avenue, then north to 700 Truxton Avenue at S Street, 93301. Pets are permitted, but there's a $3 charge. There's a dining room and a coffee shop, with meals priced at $9-17. ☎ 800-327-9651.

Days Inn is adjacent to the west side of State Route 99 and State Route 58 from the Rosedale Highway exit, at 3601 Mariot Drive, 93308. $$. No pets. The coffee shop is open from 6 AM-11 PM. ☎ 805-326-1111.

Sheraton's Four Points Hotel ($$) is 1.3 miles west of State Route 99, near the California exit, at 5101 California Avenue, 93309. It does not permit pets. Dining room service is available 24 hours. ☎ 805-325-9700.

The **Holiday Inn** is on Truxton Avenue, near the Convention Center. $$.

La Quinta ($$) is adjacent to the east side of State Route 99 from the Rosedale Highway's southbound exit or at Pierce Road exit northbound, at 3232 Riverside Drive, 93308. ☎ 805-325-7400.

There are two **Quality Inns** ($$). The best value is at the one adjacent to State Route 99, near the California exit, at 1011 Oak Street, 93304. There's a coffee shop nearby. ☎ 805-325-0772. **Radisson Suites** ($$-$$$) is adjacent to State Route 99, a third of a mile southwest of the California exit, at 828 Real Road, 93309. ☎ 805-322-9988.

The **Red Lion Hotel** is adjacent to the west side of State Route 99, off the Rosedale Highway exit, at 3100 Camino Del Rio Circle, 93308. Pets are allowed. There's dining and entertainment for guests. $$-$$$$.

Where to Dine in Bakersfield

Benji's French Basque Restaurant is west of State Route 99, at 4001 Rosedale Highway. It is open from 11:30-2 and 6-10. It is closed on major holidays and on Tuesday. Benji's serves a complete Basque meal in traditional style, priced at $11-20. ☎ 805-328-0400. The Bistro is 1.3 miles west of State

Route 99, off the California exit. Reservations are suggested. ☎ 805-323-3905. Semiformal attire is expected. The **Hungry Hunter** is on the west side of State Route 99, just north of Brundage Lane, at 200 Oak Street. It is open from 11:30-2:30 and 5-10 PM. On Sunday, it is open from 4-9:30 PM. Dinners are $11-20. **Misty's** serves continental food at the Red Lion Hotel, 3100 Camino Del Rio Court, 93308, from 11:30-1:30 and 5:30-10 PM, and an hour later on Saturday nights. Misty's is open on Sunday from 9-2, and

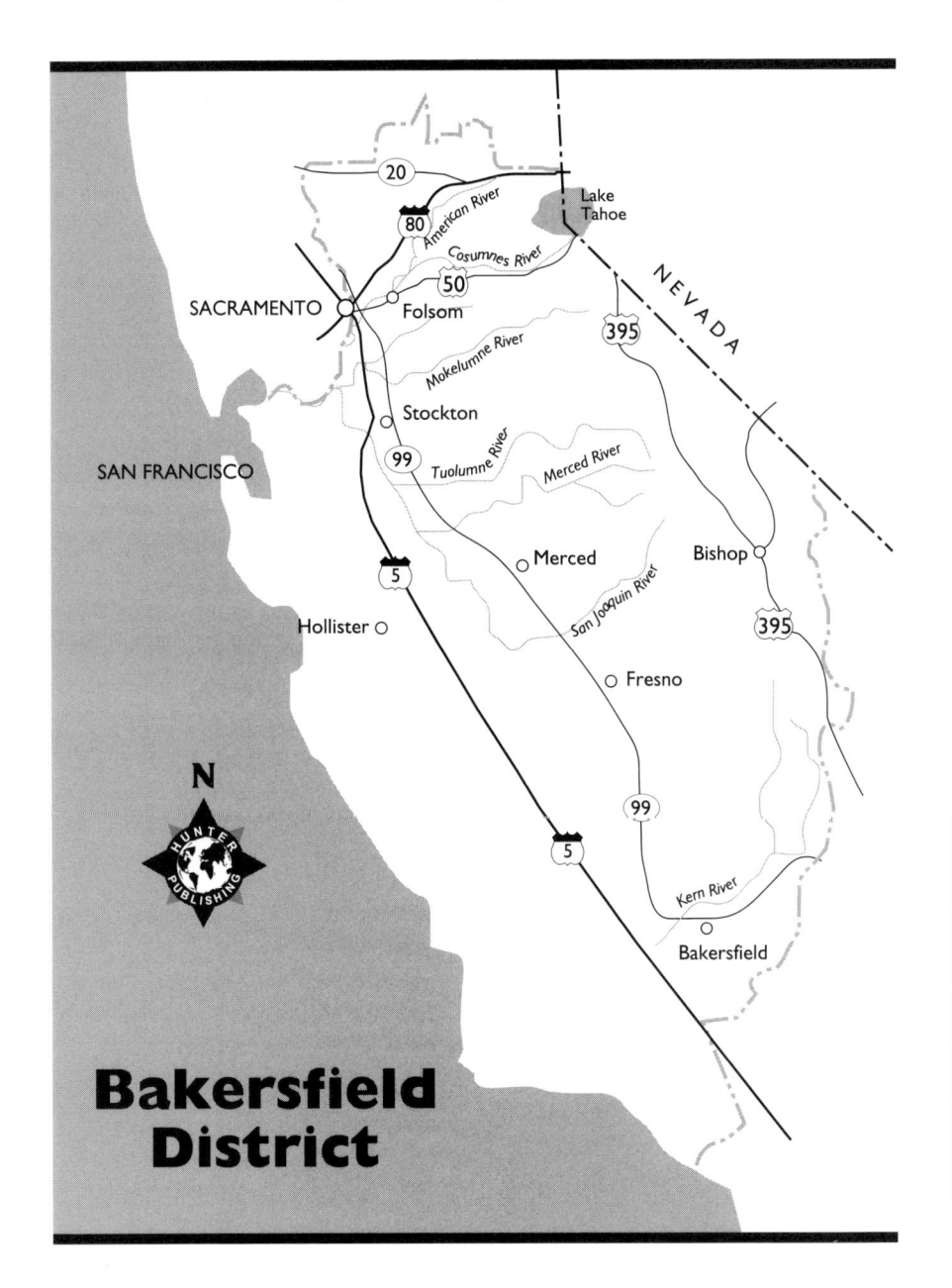

Bakersfield District

for dinner from 5:30-10 PM. It is suggested that reservations be made and that you wear semiformal attire. ☎ 805-323-7111. Dinner costs $11-20.

Sequoia National Forest

Northeast of Bakersfield, Sequoia National Forest public lands range from the Kings River in the north to the Kern River in the south. The eastern border is the Sierra Nevada crest where it joins the Inyo National Forest. The western boundary reaches to the foothill woodlands of the San Joaquin Valley.

The standout feature of the forest is, of course, the royalty of the forest, the giant sequoia (*Sequoiadendron giganteum*). The sequoias rise higher than 27 stories and have diameters of over 30 feet. The largest tree in the US national forest system is the **Boole Tree**, located just north of Converse Mountain on Hume Lake Road. This giant sequoia is 269 feet high and has a base circumference of 112 feet.

Other highlights include deep canyons and mountain creeks that form dazzling waterfalls such as **South Creek Falls** near Johnsondale and **Grizzly Falls** near Hume Lake. The **Western Divide Highway** is a photographer's dream road. **Dome Rock**, a huge granite monolith, forms a vista point overlooking the North Fork of the **Kern Wild and Scenic River**.

Adventurers will find opportunities for camping (at more than 50 campgrounds), picnicking, horseback riding, hiking, biking, fishing, soaking in hot springs, winter sports and nature studies. Guided rafting trips on the Kern River are another option. For more information, contact forest headquarters in Porterville, ☎ 209-784-1500.

Recreation opportunities spread along the Western Divide Highway as it heads south. From here you can reach the Kern and Little Kern Rivers, Pine Flat, California Hot Springs and Kernville. The pristine **Golden Trout Wilderness** can be entered by good hiking trails from either the Mt. Home-Balch Park areas, or the Upper Tule Recreation Area.

Over 360,000 acres have been set aside to regenerate and preserve the native habitat of the golden trout, the California State Fish. If you really want to get away from it all, this is the place to go. This area is accessible by trail from six different points, and runs in elevation from 4,800 feet at the forks of the Kern to 12,432 feet on Mt. Florence.

Fishing in one of the nine natural lakes, or hunting in the **Golden Trout Wilderness**, is permitted under California State Fish and Game regulations (see Appendices A and B). The Wilderness Area, with 147 miles of trails, has lush meadows, vast contour forests and rugged granite peaks.

South of Yosemite Outfitters
General Outfitters
■ Clovis
Big 5, 480 Shaw Avenue, ☎ 559-297-8285.

Copeland's Sports, 1050 Shaw Avenue, ☎ 559-323-0161.

Sierra Sportsman Supply, 2727 San Jose Avenue, ☎ 559-298-1312.

Valley Rod & Gun, 840 Herndon Avenue, ☎ 559-322-9999.

■ Fresno
Alcorn's Sporting Goods, 4169 East Ashlan Avenue, ☎ 559-225-1838.

Big 5, 5488 North Blackstone Avenue, ☎ 559-439-3351; 4902 East Kings Canyon Road, ☎ 559-255-1821; and 3022 West Shaw Avenue, ☎ 559-277-8135.

California Outfitters, 6650 North Blackstone Avenue, ☎ 559-435-2626.

Copeland's Sports, 5577 North Blackstone Avenue, ☎ 559-435-3250.

Herb Bauer Sporting Goods, 6264 North Blackstone Avenue, ☎ 559-435-8600.

Mel Cotton's Sporting Goods, 6511 North Blackstone Avenue, ☎ 559-432-4649.

Out 'n About Sports, 868 East Decatur Avenue, ☎ 559-435-8079.

Sports Authority, 7527 North Blackstone Avenue, ☎ 559-432-6850.

Tri-Sport Unlimited, 132 West Nees Avenue, ☎ 559-432-0800.

■ Porterville
Big 5, 1287 West Henderson Avenue, ☎ 559-784-3701.

■ Prather
Mid-Mountain Sporting Goods, 29533 Auberry Road, ☎ 559-855-3600.

■ Shaver Lake
Four Seasons Ski & Bike, 41781 Tollhouse Road, ☎ 559-841-2224.

Shaver Lake Sports & Fishing, 41698 Tollhouse Road, ☎ 559-841-2740.

■ Visalia
Big 5, 1430 South Mooney Boulevard, ☎ 559-625-5934.

Copeland's Sports, 1100 South Mooney Boulevard, ☎ 559-627-3660.

Sports West, 400 North Johnson Street, ☎ 559-734-7515.

Turtle Mountain Sports, 110 West Main Street, ☎ 559-741-9888.

On Water

■ Clovis
Golden Trout Anglers, 425 Pollasky Avenue, ☎ 559-322-9378.

■ Three Rivers
Kaweah Whitewater Adventures, 41881 Sierra Drive, ☎ 559-561-1000.

■ Visalia
Buz Buszek Fly Shop, 400 North Johnson Street, ☎ 559-734-1151.

On Wheels

■ Clovis
Bike World, 601 West Shaw Avenue, ☎ 559-299-2286.

■ Dinuba
City Street Bicycles, 125 East Tulare Street, ☎ 559-591-4449.

■ Fresno
Bike Dr., 5091 North Fresno Street, ☎ 559-222-1231.

Reg Bauer's Bike Shop, 6248 North Blackstone Avenue, ☎ 559-435-4844.

Cycle West, 1093 East Champlain Drive, ☎ 559-433-9202.

Steven's Bike Shop, 3132 North Palm Avenue, ☎ 559-229-8163.

Sumner's Schwinn Bicycle Shop, 4676 North Blackstone Avenue, ☎ 559-222-4823.

■ Porterville
Mike's Bikes, 1563 Olive Avenue, ☎ 559-781-9429.

Schortman's Cyclery, 152 North Hockett Street, ☎ 559-784-3238.

■ Reedly
Bike Trax, 1048 G Street, ☎ 559-638-2398.

■ Visalia
College Cyclery, 1911 West Meadow Avenue, ☎ 559-733-2453.

Tri-Sport, 400 North Johnson Street, ☎ 559-741-0700.

Visalia Cyclery, 1829 West Caldwell Avenue, ☎ 559-732-2453.

Wilson's Cyclery, 115 North West Street, ☎ 559-734-6175.

Appendices
Appendix A

Fishing Regulations

Every person engaged in fishing or amphibian or reptile gathering (except rattlesnakes) must display a valid sports fishing license on their outer clothing, at or above the waistline so it is plainly visible. The penalty for not doing so can result in a fine of at least $250.

Anyone 16 years or older must have a fishing license in California to take any kind of mollusk, invertebrate, amphibian or crustacean. None of these products may be sold.

Resident licenses are specified only for those who have resided continuously in the state for six months or more, or persons on active military duty with the armed forces of the United States or an auxiliary branch or Job Corps enrollees.

Anyone 16 years or older fishing anywhere in Lake Tahoe or Topaz Lake must possess either a California fishing license or a Nevada fishing license. Nevada also requires a trout stamp.

The fee for a California resident license is $25.70, $69.95 for a nonresident. Fees are nonrefundable.

The California Department of Fish and Game offers free and reduced-fee fishing licenses for eligible persons. Certain low-income senior citizens who are 65 years of age or more, and honorably retired veterans with a service-connected disability of at least 70% qualify for reduced-fee licenses. Free licenses are available for the blind, low-income American Indians, wards of the state who reside in a state hospital, developmentally disabled persons who receive services from a state regional center, and residents who are so physically disabled that they are permanently unable to move from place to place without a wheelchair, walker, forearm crutches or comparable mobility devices. For further information contact the nearest Department of Fish and Game office.

There are also lifetime licenses with fees determined by age groups. ☎ 916-227-2290 for details.

For detailed information about fishing regulations write or call the License and Revenue Branch, 3211 S. Street, Sacramento, CA 95816. ☎ 916-227-2244.

Appendix B

Special Passes

California's Bureau of Land Management has a number of special passes for senior citizens and those with disabilities. The Golden Age Passport is a lifetime pass for individuals 62 and older for a $10 one-time fee. You can obtain it at any bureau office or by mail. Enclose a copy of your driver's license or other identification that contains your birthdate and signature. Ask for a pass and enclose the fee. The Golden Access Pass is a free lifetime pass for those individuals who have been classified blind or permanently disabled. There is no charge, but you must visit a bureau office in person or mailing the pertinent information. You'll need a physician's statement as to your disability. The Golden Eagle Pass is issued annually to individuals 16 to 61 years of age for $25. Either visit a bureau office or mail in your request with the fee.

Index

Accommodations: Amador, 163; Angels Camp, 165; Auburn, 138-139; Bakersfield, 248; Bear Valley, 167; Big Pine, 35; Bishop, 44; Bridgeport, 74; Carson City, 81; Coloma, 140; Fresno, 239-240; Grass Valley, 137-138; Independence, 33; June Lake/Mammoth, 64; Lone Pine, 32; Mammoth Lakes, 52; Mono Lake, 66; Murphys, 167; Oakhurst, 223; Placerville, 142; Reno, 132-133; Sacramento, 161-162; Tahoe, 121-122; Virginia City, 87; Visalia, 222; Yosemite, 211-215, 220-221

Acute mountain sickness (AMS), 177

Adventures, 2-3

Alabama Hills, 25

Alpine Meadows Ski Area, 114

Alpine skiing, *see* Skiing (downhill)

Altitude, acclimatizing to, 26

Altitude sickness, 27, 177

Amador, 163-164

American River, 152-158

AMS (acute mountain sickness), 177

Ancient Bristlecone Pine Forest, 41-42

Angels Camp, 165

Animals and plants, 7-10; bear-proofing, 227; Yosemite, 201

Apple Hill, 141-142

Auburn, 138-139

Backpacking: to Mt. Whitney, 29-30; safety, 175-179

Badger Pass Ski Area, 201, 211

Bakersfield, 247-249

Ballooning, Tahoe, 94, 128

Barney Lake, 43

Beaches, Tahoe, 111

Bear-proofing, 227

Bear Valley, map, 168

Bear Valley Ski Area, 166, 167-169

Belcher Mine, 86

Big McGee Lake, 43

Big Pine, 33-37

Biking: Bishop, 41; Death Valley to Mt. Whitney, 25; Gold Country North, 150-151; June Lake/Mammoth, 56-62; Yosemite, 210; *see also* Mountain biking

Bishop, 37-49; accommodations, 44; camping, 44-49; fishing, 43-44; hiking, 38-40; mountain guides, 42; outfitters, 50-51; rock climbing, 40; sightseeing, 37-38; on wheels, 41-42; where to dine, 49

Bishop Creek Canyon, 37-38

Black Lake, 35

Blue Lake, 43

Boating, Lake Tahoe, 112

Bodie, 69-72

Bodie State Park, 69-72

Boreal Ski Area, 114

Bracebridge Dinner, Yosemite, 212

Brewery Arts Center, 80

Bridgeport, 72-74

Buena Vista Peak, 235

Bungee jumping, 119

Calaveras County, Jumping Frog Jubilee, 165

California: agricultural inspections, 19-20; history, 10-16; information, 20-21; marriage licenses, 97; today, 16-18

California Caverns, 180

Camino, 141-142

Camping, 3, 4; Bishop to Mammoth, 44-49; Kings Canyon/Sequoia, 236-239; Lone Pine to Bishop, 35-37; Mono Lake, 66-68; permits required for, 175-176; restrictions on, 175-176, 237-238; Sierra National Forest, 226; Stanislaus, 218; Tahoe Basin, 122-123; Yosemite, 213-215; Yosemite area, 221-222

256 Index

Camp Richardson, 114-115
Carry it in, carry it out, 3-5
Carson City, Nevada, 79-82
Carson River, rafting, 113
Casinos, Tahoe, 95-97
Caves, spelunking, 180-181
Central Eureka Mine, 164
Chilnualna Falls, Yosemite, 206
Clair Tappan Lodge, 115
Coloma, 139-140
Comstock Mine, 86
Convict Lake, 43, 54
Cottonwood Lakes, 31-32, 35
Cross-country skiing, see Skiing
Crowley Lake, 43, 49
Crystal Cave, 235

Daffodil Hill, 164
Davis Lake, 43
Death Valley to Mt. Whitney, biking, 25
Desolation Wilderness, 101, 141
Devil's Postpile National Monument, 45-46, 52-53
Diamond Peak Ski Resort, 115
Diaz Lake, 35
Dingleberry Lake, 43
Diving, Tahoe, 112-113
D. L. Bliss State Park, 101, 106
Dodge Ridge Ski Area, 186
Dogsledding: June Lake/Mammoth, 63; Tahoe, 119-120
Dome Lands Wilderness, 23-24
Donner Ski Ranch, 115
Dorothy Lake, 54
Downhill skiing, see Skiing (downhill)
Driving, 19, 231

Eagle Falls, 101
Eastern Sierra, 22-77; Big Pine, 33-37; Bishop, 37-49; Bodie, 69-72; Bridgeport, 72-74; Devil's Postpile, 52-53; Independence, 33; June Lake/Mammoth, 53-64; Lone Pine, 25-32; Mammoth Lakes, 49-52; map, 22; Mono Lake, 65-68; outfitters, 75-77; Owens Valley, 23-25
Eldorado National Forest, 182
Elizabeth Lake, 209
Emerald Bay, Lake Tahoe, 98-99
Emerald Bay State Park, 101
Emigrant Wilderness, 181

Fallen Leaf Lake, 114-115
Film festival, Lone Pine, 25
Fires, 5
Fishing: Bishop to Mammoth Lakes, 43-44; Lone Pine to Big Pine, 35; Mono Lake, 65-66; regulations, 254; Tahoe, 113; Yosemite, 201
Fish Slough Pine, 43
Flora and fauna, 7-10
Flower Lake, 35
Folsom, 143; biking, 150-151
On foot, 2; Big Pine, 33-35; Bishop to Mammoth, 38-40; choosing a mountain guide, 42; Cottonwood Lakes, 31; Fresno, 240; Gold Country North, 149-150; Gold Country South, 169-181; June Lake/Mammoth, 53-56; Kings Canyon/Sequoia, 234-235; Lake Tahoe, 100-107; Lone Pine, 26-31; Mono Lake to Bridgeport, 72-74; Mt. Whitney, 26-30, 180; Owens Valley, 23-25; safety on the trail, 176-177; trail tips, 4; USGS maps, 179; Yosemite, 203-210
Foresthill, 149-150, 151
Fourth Recess Lake, 43
Four-wheel driving, see Off-road driving
French Canyon, 43
Fresno, 239-247

Garnet Lake, 43
Genevieve, Lake, 43, 54
Genoa, Nevada, 100
Genoa Peak, 111
George Lake, 43

Ghost town, Bodie, 69-72
Gilbert Lake, 35
Glacier Point, Yosemite, 197, 203
Gold Country North, 135-163; adventures, 149-158; outfitters, 158-161
Gold Country South, 162-190; adventures, 169-187; outfitters, 188-190
Golden Access Pass, 254
Golden Age Passport, 254
Golden Chain, 163, 187
Golden Eagle Pass, 254
Golden Trout Lakes, 34, 35
Golden Trout Wilderness, 24, 250
Gold Rush, 15-16, 139-140; Amador, 163-164; Coloma, 139; Grass Valley, 136; Virginia City, 86
Golf, Tahoe, 107
Grand Canyon of Tuolumne, 216
Granite Chief Wilderness, 102
Granlibakken ski area, 115
Grasslands, 8-9
Grass Valley, 136-138
Green Lake, 43
Gulf Lake, 66

Half Dome, Yosemite, 197, 206
Heart Lake, 35
Heavenly Ski Resort, 115-116
Hetch Hetchy Reservoir, 219
High Sierra Trail, 234
Hiking: Bishop to Mammoth, 38-40; Fresno, 240; Gold Country North, 149-150; Gold Country South, 169-178; June Lake/Mammoth, 53-56; Lake Tahoe, 100-104; Mammoth Lakes, 51; Merced River, 218-219; Mono Lake to Bridgeport, 72-74; rules and regulations, 175; safety, 176-179; USGS maps, 179; Yosemite, 203-209
Hilton Creek Lakes, 43
History: California, 10-16; Tahoe, 88-89; Virginia City, 82-85; Yosemite, 193-196

Hope Valley Cross-Country Center, 116
On horseback, 2; Gold Country South, 181-182; June Lake/Mammoth, 56; Tahoe, 108
Horseshoe Lake, 43, 54
Hot Creek Fish Hatchery, 60
Hot springs, East Carson, 113
Hot Springs Geologic Site, 60
Hume Lake, 235
Humphreys Basin, 43

Ice climbing, June Lake/Mammoth, 63-64
Independence, 33
Information, 20-21; Kings Canyon/Sequoia, 238; Lake Tahoe, 94; Yosemite area, 224
Inyo Craters, 59
Inyo National Forest, 26, 28, 37, 49, 52

Jet skiing, Tahoe, 112
John Muir Trail, 171-175, 178-179; Big Pine, 34; Bishop, 38; June Lake/Mammoth, 55; Yosemite, 204, 205-206, 209
Jumping Frog Jubilee, 165
June Lake/Mammoth, 53-64; accommodations, 64; fishing, 66; on foot, 53-56; on horseback, 56; ice climbing, 63-64; on snow, 62-64; on wheels, 56-62; where to dine, 64
June Mountain, 53

Kaiser Wilderness, 240
Kearsage Lakes, 35
Kennedy Meadows, 24-25
Kings Canyon/Sequoia National Parks, 226-239; adventures, 233-235; camping, 236-239; getting here and getting around, 229-232; information, 239; map, 230; mountain biking, 241-242; USGS maps, 179; visitor centers, 228-229
Kings River, 242-243
Kirkwood ski area, 116

258   Index

Lake Tahoe, 88-129; accommodations, 121-122; ballooning, 94, 128; camping, 122-123; casinos, 95-97; environmental activism, 92; facts, 92; family activities, 94-95; on foot, 100-107; getting here and getting around, 93; history, 88-89; on horseback, 108; information, 94; maps, 78, 90; outfitters, 125-129; sightseeing, 94, 98-100; on snow, 114-121; today, 89, 91; visitor center, 98; on water, 111-114; water quality, 91-92; weddings, 97-98; on wheels, 108-111; where to dine, 124-125

Lakeview Cross-Country Ski Area, 116

Lamarck Lakes, 38, 43

Land, Sierra Nevada, 5-7

Leave no trace, 3-5

Little Lakes Valley, 40, 43

Loch Leven Lakes, 149

Lone Pine, 25-32; camping, 35-37

Lone Pine Lake, 35

Long Lake, 35

Lower Twin Lake, 66

Lyme disease, 232

Mamie, Lake, 43

Mammoth Lakes, 49-52; *see also* June Lake/Mammoth

Mammoth Mountain, 49-50; Bike Park, 57, 60-61

Mammoth Pool Reservoir, 243

Maps: Bakersfield, 249; Bear Valley approaches, 168; Eastern Sierra, 22; Highway 49 routes, 163; Kings Canyon/Sequoia, 230; Lake Tahoe, 90; mileages to Yosemite, 190; Pacific Crest Trail, 39; Placerville routes, 143; Reno-Tahoe, 78; Sacramento, 147; Tule River, 244; USGS Maps, 179; Western Sierra, 135; Yosemite, 200

Marathon, Lone Pine, 25

Maria Wilderness, 152-153

Marie Louise Lakes, 43

Mariposa, 187

Mariposa Grove, Yosemite, 207, 219-220

Marriage licenses, 97-98

Mary, Lake, 43

Merced River: hiking, 218-219; rafting, 185

Mercer Caverns, 181

Meysan Lake, 28-29

Mirror Lake, 205

Mokelumne Hill, 166

Mokelumne Wilderness, 102-103

Mono County Museum, 72

Mono Craters, 65

Mono Lake, 65-68

Moro Rock, 233

Mother Lode, 15, 188

Mountain biking: Fresno, 241; Gold Country South, 182-183; June Lake/Mammoth, 56-62; Kings Canyon/Sequoia, 241-242; Tahoe, 108-110

Mountain guides, choosing, 42

Mt. Ralston, 170

Mount Rose, skiing, 117

Mount Rose Wilderness, 103

Mount Watkins, 198

Mt. Whitney, 25; backpacking, 29-30; biking from Death Valley to, 25; on foot, 26-30, 179

Murphys, 167

National Forest Service, 178-179

Native Americans, 10-11, 88, 99, 172

Nelder Grove, 225

Nevada, 78-135; Carson City, 79-82; marriage licenses, 97-98; mountain biking, 109-110; Reno, 129-134; Virginia City, 82-87

Nevada Falls, Yosemite, 205-206

Nordic skiing, *see* Skiing (cross-country)

North Lake, 44

North Lake Tahoe Cruises, 112

Northstar-at-Tahoe ski resort, 117

Oakhurst, 188, 223, 224

Index

Off-road driving: Bishop, 41-42; Gold Country North, 151; Gold Country South, 183-184; Tahoe, 110-111

Onion Valley, 33-34

Outfitters, 3; Bishop and Mammoth, 50-51; Eastern Sierra, 75-77; Gold Country North, 157-160; Gold Country South, 188-190; South of Yosemite, 251-252; Tahoe, 125-129

Owens River Gorge, rock climbing, 40

Owens Valley, 23-25

Pacific Crest Trail, 174; Barker Pass, 102; Bishop, 38; Echo Lakes, 104; Fresno, 240; guidebooks, 180; June Lake/Mammoth, 55; map, 39; Sayles Canyon, 170; Yosemite, 209

Pack it in, pack it out, 3-5

Pack train, 25

Palisade Glacier, 34-35

Parasailing, Tahoe, 113

Passes, special, 254

Pets: rabies certificates for, 20; restrictions on, 175

Pine Lake, 44

Placerville, 141-142; map, 143

Planning, 4, 172-173

Plants and animals, 7-10

Pleasant Valley Reservoir, 44

Plumas Eureka Ski Bowl, 117

Ponderosa Ranch, 99-100

Purple Lake, 44

Rabies certificates, 20

Rafting: Gold Country South, 184-186; Tahoe, 113-14; Tuolumne River, 217-218

Rainbow Falls, 53

Rattlesnakes, 231

Redwood Canyon, 235

Reno, 129-134; accommodations, 132-133; getting here and getting around, 130-131; map, 78; sightseeing, 131-132; where to dine, 133-134

Robinson Lake, 34

Rock climbing: Gold Country South, 179-180; Owens River Gorge, 40; Tahoe, 105-7; Yosemite, 210; Yosemite Decimal System, 105

Rock Creek Lake, 44

Rodeo, Bridgeport, 72

Royal Gorge Cross-Country Resort, 117

Sabrina, Lake, 43

Sacramento, 144-149; accommodations, 161-162; map, 147; where to dine, 162; see also Gold Country North

Saddlebag Lake, 66

Safety, 3; acclimatization to high altitude, 26; altitude sickness, 27, 178; drinking water, 179, 232; driving cautions, 231; ticks, 232; on the trail, 176-179; water adventures, 157-158; weather, 232

Sam Mack Lake, 35

San Andreas, 166-167

Scuba diving, Tahoe, 112-113

Scurfing, Tahoe, 112

Senior citizens, passes for, 254

Sequoia National Forest, 250

Sequoia National Park, see Kings Canyon/Sequoia National Parks

Sequoias, 225, 232, 233

Sierra at Tahoe Ski Resort, 118

Sierra Club, 171, 172, 178

Sierra National Forest, 224-226, 245

Sierra Nevada: crest, 18, 19; foothills, 8-10; forest, 10; getting here and getting around, 18-20; history, 10-16; information, 20-21; land of, 5-7; today, 17-18

Sierra Summit Mountain Resort, 245

Silver Lake, 66

Ski Homewood, 118

Skiing (cross-country): Gold Country North, 158; Gold Country South, 186-187; June Lake/Mammoth, 63; Mammoth Lakes, 50; Tahoe, 114-119

Skiing (downhill): Bear Valley, 166, 167-169; Gold Country South, 186-187;

260 Index

Mammoth Mountain, 49-50; Tahoe, 114-119

On snow, 3; Fresno, 245; Gold Country North, 158; Gold Country South, 187-188; June Lake/Mammoth, 62-64; Mammoth Lakes, 49-50; Tahoe, 114-121; Yosemite, 211

Snowmobiling, Tahoe, 120-121

Soda Springs, skiing, 118

Sotcher Lake, 44

South Lake, 44

Special passes, 254

Spelunking: California Caverns, 180-181; Mercer Caverns, 181

Spooner Lake, skiing, 118

Squaw Valley: Bike Park, 109; skiing, 118-119

Stanislaus National Forest, 182-183, 186-187, 218

Sugar Bowl, skiing, 118

Summit Lake, 66

Tahoe Donner, skiing, 119

Tallac Historic Site, 99

Tamarack Lakes, 44

Tennis, Tahoe, 107

Ticks, 232

Tioga Lake, 66

Trail tips, 4

Treasure Lakes, 35

Truckee River, rafting, 113

Trumbull Lake, 66

Tule River, 243-245

Tuolumne River, 216-218

Twain, Mark, 87

Twin Lakes, 44

Upper Twin Lake, 66

US Geological Survey Maps, 179

Valentine, Lake, 43, 54

Vernal Falls, Yosemite, 205-206

Vikingsholm, 98-99

Virginia, Lake, 43, 66

Virginia City, Nevada, 82-87

Visalia, 223

On water, 2; Big Pine, 35; Bishop to Mammoth Lakes, 43-44; Cottonwood Lakes, 31-32; Fresno, 242-245; Gold Country North, 152-158; Gold Country South, 184-186; Hume Lake, 236; Mono Lake, 65-66; rules and regulations, 157-158; Tahoe, 111-114; *see also* Fishing

Water, drinking, 178, 232

Water skiing, Tahoe, 112

Weather, 232

Weddings, Tahoe, 97-98

Western Sierra, 135-252; Gold Country North, 135-163; Gold Country South, 163-190; map, 135

West Point, California, 166

On wheels, 2; Bishop, 41-42; Bridgeport, 74; Fresno, 241; Gold Country North, 150-151; Gold Country South, 182-184; June Lake/Mammoth, 56-62; Tahoe, 108-111; Yosemite, 210-211

Where to dine: Amador, 164; Auburn, 139; Bakersfield, 248; Big Pine, 37; Bishop, 49; Carson City, 81-82; Fresno, 249; Grass Valley, 138; June Lake/Mammoth, 64; Lone Pine, 32; Mammoth Lakes, 52; Oakhurst, 224; Placerville, 142; Reno, 133-134; Sacramento, 162; Tahoe, 124-125; Virginia City, 87; Visalia, 223

Where to stay, *see* Accommodations

Wilderness: leave no trace in, 3-5; permits required for, 175-176

Willow Lake, 35

Windsurfing, Tahoe, 112

Yosemite Decimal System, 105

Yosemite Falls, 205

Yosemite National Park, 190-224; accommodations, 211-213, 220-221; adventures, 203-213; animals in, 201-202; Bracebridge Dinner, 212;

buses and services, 200-201, 202; camping, 213-215, 221-222; environmental concerns for, 202; fishing, 201; getting to, 190-191; history, 193-196; hunting prohibited in, 201; information, 224; map, 200; map of mileages to, 190; permits, 175-176; sightseeing, 197-202, 216-224; Tioga Road, 191-193; today, 196-197; USGS maps, 179